The Presidency of
WILLIAM
McKINLEY

AMERICAN PRESIDENCY SERIES

Donald R. McCoy,

Clifford S. Griffin,

Homer E. Socolofsky,

General Editors

The Presidency of George Washington
by Forrest McDonald

The Presidency of John Adams
by Ralph Adams Brown

The Presidency of Thomas Jefferson
by Forrest McDonald

The Presidency of James Buchanan
by Elbert B. Smith

The Presidency of Andrew Johnson
By Albert Castel

The Presidency of William McKinley
by Lewis L. Gould

The Presidency of William Howard Taft
by Paolo E. Coletta

The Presidency of Warren G. Harding
by Eugene P. Trani and David L. Wilson

The Presidency of Dwight D. Eisenhower
by Elmo Richardson

The Presidency of
WILLIAM
McKINLEY

by

Lewis L. Gould

THE REGENTS PRESS OF KANSAS
Lawrence

© 1980 by The Regents Press of Kansas
Printed in the United States of America

Library of Congress Cataloging in Publication Data
Gould, Lewis L
The Presidency of William McKinley.
(American Presidency series)
Bibliography: p.
Includes index.
1. United States—Politics and government—1897-1901.
2. McKinley, William, Pres. U.S., 1843-1901.
3. Presidents—United States—Biography.
I. Title. II. Series.
E711.G68   973.8′8′0924   80-16022
ISBN 0-7006-0206-2

Editors' Preface

The aim of the American Presidency Series is to present historians and the general reading public with interesting, scholarly assessments of the various presidential administrations. These interpretive surveys are intended to cover the broad ground between biographies, specialized monographs, and journalistic accounts. As such, each will be a comprehensive, synthetic work which will draw upon the best in pertinent secondary literature, yet leave room for the author's own analysis and interpretation.

Each volume in the series will deal with a separate presidential administration and will present the data essential to understanding the administration under consideration. Particularly, each book will treat the then current problems facing the United States and its people and how the president and his associates felt about, thought about, and worked to cope with these problems. Attention will be given to how the office developed and operated during the president's tenure. Equally important will be consideration of the vital relationships between the president, his staff, the executive officers, Congress, foreign representatives, the judiciary, state officials, the public, political parties, the press, and influential private citizens. The series will also be concerned with how this unique American institution—the presidency—was viewed by the presidents, and with what results.

All this will be set, insofar as possible, in the context not only of contemporary politics but also of economics, international relations, law, morals, public administration, religion, and thought. Such a broad approach is necessary to understanding, for a presidential administration is more than the elected and appointed officers composing it, since its work so often reflects the major problems, anxieties, and glories of the nation. In short, the authors in the series will strive to recount and evaluate the record of each administration and to identify its distinctiveness and relationships to the past, its own time, and the future.

Donald R. McCoy
Clifford S. Griffin
Homer E. Socolofsky

Preface

William McKinley was the first modern president. During his four and a half years in the White House the executive office began to resemble the institution as the twentieth century would know it. These statements do not accord with the customary view of the twenty-fifth president as the spokesman for untamed business in the Gilded Age, the compliant agent of Marcus A. Hanna, and the irresolute executive in the Cuban crisis that led to war with Spain. Such erroneous stereotypes have long obscured McKinley's historical significance. Even the work of talented biographers and historians has not shaken the picture of this president as a hidebound Republican conservative whose ideas were obsolete before his death and whose career was only a prelude to the excitement of the Theodore Roosevelt years.

The study of McKinley's presidency that follows endeavors to show his important contributions to the strengthening and broadening of the power of the chief executive. His impact on the institution and the policies of the nation was large. Under McKinley, relations between the press and the White House took on a formal character from which a regular role for journalists would evolve. The demands of war and overseas expansion led to the development of a telegraphic and telephonic capacity that brought fresh information to the president and allowed him to make policy and to disseminate news on a systematic basis. Through the use of commissions, McKinley brought experts and academics into the governing process. He traveled so much that Theodore Roosevelt, William Howard Taft, and Woodrow Wilson had a strong precedent on which to rest their highly mobile presidencies. McKinley also enjoyed good relations with Congress because he accepted the legislative branch as an equal partner in the government and actively consulted with both parties in framing programs. Nonetheless he employed such devices as threats to veto, prospects of special sessions, and statements in annual messages to have his way in a manner that succeeding presidents emulated.

Foreign-policy issues dominated McKinley's presidency, and he engaged them in a way that made his office far more powerful by 1901. The Spanish-American War was not the result of presidential weakness or cowardice in the face of public hysteria. McKinley sought to persuade Spain to relinquish Cuba peacefully and then turned to war when it became apparent that Madrid would never acquiesce. His diplomacy in 1897/1898 was tenacious, coherent, and courageous. He took the nation into war with the presidential prerogatives in foreign affairs strong and undamaged.

During the war, McKinley directed the American military effort and the diplomacy that brought territorial acquisitions and peace. His guiding role as a war leader facilitated the accretion of power in the executive and in the federal government generally. An unprepared nation did not perform with efficiency in every aspect, as the record of the War Department showed. Yet the striking result of the brief conflict with Spain was how broadly and creatively McKinley used his power as commander in chief.

The process of making peace with Spain—involving, as it did, American annexation of the Philippines—and of securing the ratification of the resulting treaty in the Senate underscored McKinley's expansive view of presidential power. From the sending of senators on the peace commission to the personal supervision of the terms of the negotiations, he functioned as chief diplomat. At home he made tours of the West and South in 1898 to lead popular opinion to his position in a way that no president had done before him. For the Senate he evidenced a readiness to dispense patronage, woo votes with personal persuasion, and marshal the resources of the political system behind his treaty.

Later episodes in his administration built upon these examples. In administering Puerto Rico and Cuba and in suppressing an insurrection in the Philippines, McKinley relied further on the war power and shaped affairs from the White House. He sent troops to China during the Boxer Rebellion in 1900 without congressional authorization, governed the new possessions through presidential commissions, and allowed Capitol Hill only a subsidiary role in the process. By 1901 the nation had an empire and a president whose manner and bearing anticipated the imperial executives of six decades later.

Because of the overriding importance of foreign affairs in his presidency, McKinley broke little new ground in domestic policy. He did not enact the New Deal in 1900. He believed instead in moderate tariff protection and reciprocity, government promotion of business enterprise, and a diffusion of economic benefits to labor through employment and prosperity. Still, even on such issues as currency and banking, the civil service, and the trusts, there were manifestations of presidential activism that fitted with the assertiveness that McKinley displayed in foreign policy. When he was shot, for example, he was beginning another round of speeches to rally public opinion behind favorable Senate action on the tariff-reciprocity treaties he had pushed as a central theme of his economic diplomacy.

This analysis of McKinley's presidency is based on an examination of the relevant primary source materials relating to the administration. When they published their biographies of McKinley in 1959 and 1963 respectively, Margaret Leech and H. Wayne Morgan drew on the rich resources of the McKinley Papers at the Library of Congress and other manuscript collections. Leech, in particular, was given access to the diary of the president's secretary, George B. Cortelyou, with its ample fund of insights into McKinley's decisions. Neither scholar, however, could look at Cortelyou's papers on the McKinley era. This collection did not become generally available to researchers until the late 1960s. The twenty or so boxes on McKinley and on the Spanish-American War contain substantial portions of what once were the president's own office files. The Cortelyou Papers fill the gaps in the McKinley Papers and provide new light on numerous episodes of the presidential years.

With the evidence that also exists in such collections as the John Bassett Moore Papers and the William R. Day Papers, both at the Library of Congress, as well as the collections of other Republican and Democratic legislators, government officials, and journalists, a reconstruction of decision-making in the McKinley years becomes readily possible. Documents in the British and French diplomatic archives fill out the picture for colonial policy and economic relations. The general thesis that McKinley was a strong president owes much, of course, to the work of Margaret Leech, H. Wayne

Morgan, Paul Holbo, J. A. S. Grenville and George Berkeley Young, and Robert L. Beisner, among others, but in this book I try to assert the case for McKinley's claims as the first modern president in a systematic and detailed way.

Because of limitations of space and the format of this series, the notes do not attempt to do more than indicate the source of quotations and occasionally to comment on the evidence presented. Scholars who wish to examine a fully annotated copy of the manuscript may do so at the University of Texas at Austin archives, where the text and footnotes will be available for inspection.

It is not possible to thank all the librarians and archivists who helped me, but I owe special acknowledgment to the staff of the Manuscript Division, Library of Congress, and to the staff of the Perry-Castaneda Library, University of Texas at Austin. Richard Holland was particularly cooperative in securing microfilm materials for my work in Austin.

For permission to quote from documents and letters, I am happy to express my gratitude to Ambassador Henry Cabot Lodge and the Marquess of Salisbury. Unpublished Crown Copyright material in the India Office Records and the Public Record Office appears in this book by permission of the controller of Her Majesty's Stationery Office. The editor of the *Historian*, Gerald D. Nash, kindly granted permission for me to use material in chapter 3 that originally appeared in his journal; the editor of *Ohio History*, Nelson Lichtenstein, was equally kind about the use of passages in chapter 10 from an article that was published in his journal.

Grants from the Dora Bonham Fund, History Department, University of Texas at Austin; the University Research Institute, University of Texas at Austin; and the National Endowment for the Humanities made possible the research for this study and assisted in the final preparation of the manuscript.

For information, criticism, and other help, I owe thanks to Richard Bradford, Gene Gressley, Richard McCulley, Arthur N. Newberry III, Gordon Phillips, and Phil Lyman Snyder. Many of my ideas and views about William McKinley were formed and tested in talks with H. Wayne Morgan over the past dozen years.

As scholars of this period know, he is always generous with his time and encouragement. Three friends—Paul Holbo, Herbert F. Margulies, and R. Hal Williams—read the manuscript in draft form and gave me invaluable guidance and patient corrections. They are not responsible for the weaknesses in the final product; its strengths derive in large measure from their thoughtfulness. Though he has seen little of William McKinley, Bud Lasby has provided indispensable support and unfailing kindness in the past decade. Mrs. R. C. Stephenson typed the manuscript with skill and an editor's precision. My mother-in-law, Helen K. Keel, is as good at proofreading as she is at anything she undertakes. Without the patience, good humor, and scholarly example of Karen Gould, this book would not have been written.

Lewis L. Gould

Austin, Texas
September 1979

Contents

1

★★★★★

FROM CANTON
TO THE WHITE HOUSE

On November 3, 1896, after a long and tumultuous campaign, American voters elected William McKinley of Ohio as the twenty-fifth president of the United States. When he took the oath of office four months later, McKinley entered upon the responsibilities of a position that differed dramatically from the powerful, cohesive, well-staffed, and often imperial presidency of the last quarter of the twentieth century. Strong and effective presidents had been the exception in the nation's past, and the experience of the post–Civil War generation offered scant suggestion that a new departure was imminent.

The striking features of the presidency at the end of the Gilded Age were its modest size and the even more modest aspirations that citizens in and out of government held for it. The Executive Mansion was old, cramped, and crumbling. "The perfect inadequacy of the executive offices to the present demands is apparent at a glance," concluded a newsman in March 1897; "nor is the lack of room less obvious at the social functions which custom as well as reasons of state impose upon the President." In the same month a White House aide wrote privately that every important government bureau had better furnishings than the presidential quarters.[1]

Within this dilapidated building, a tiny staff did the president's business. Servants and gardeners easily outnumbered the single private secretary and the half-dozen clerks who dealt with the two hundred to a thousand letters that arrived each day. "The clerical force is very limited in numbers," McKinley's secretary, John Addison Porter, told a senator, "and the utmost dispatch is required to keep up with each day's work."[2] The flow of visitors was equally persistent. The White House stood open to the public, who crowded in for the regular receptions that every president was expected to hold. There were no cadre of bright young assistants, no corps of speech writers, and no trappings of pomp. Though there was a growing popular interest in presidential activities, the office retained an understandable, human dimension.

The president might be "Our Fellow-Citizen of the White House," but he did not dominate the landscape of American politics. Since Lincoln's death, the presidency had stood in the shadow of legislative ascendancy. There had been some erosion of congressional supremacy since Reconstruction, but most lawmakers would have agreed with Senator John Sherman of Ohio that "the executive department of a republic like ours should be subordinate to the legislative department."[3] The Whiggish heritage of the Republicans made them suspicious of a strong executive; a powerful Congress was the appropriate vehicle for their nationalism. Among the Democrats a president could be forceful, as Thomas Jefferson or Andrew Jackson had been, but he had to use a negative strength to prevent the achievement of the activist programs of the Republicans.

Despite the relative weakness of the presidency in this period, a substantial body of thought agreed that the executive already had too much power. Speaking of Grover Cleveland's reputation as a strong president, the *Richmond* (Va.) *Times* remarked: "The truth is, all this idea of prerogative in the President is wholly out of place in our Constitution." Lawyers and jurists criticized the rise of executive power. The journalist Henry Loomis Nelson advanced a distinctly minority opinion when he contended in January 1899 that there should be a "readjustment of the relations between the executive and legislative branches of the government" away from Congress.[4]

The unfortunate second term of Grover Cleveland confirmed the views of those who found that the president was too dominant. It also plunged the prestige of the office to a very low point. Coming into the White House in March 1893 after a solid victory over Benjamin Harrison in 1892, Cleveland encountered innumerable problems. The Panic of 1893 and the ensuing depression placed intense strains upon the government. The Democratic president responded with force and independence in compelling Congress to repeal the Sherman Silver Purchase Act in 1893, in standing firm for

2

the gold standard thereafter, and in dealing with domestic unrest from 1894 onward. As Cleveland prepared to leave office, his admirers applauded a record of rectitude and determination from which historians later drew a picture of a president who was the embodiment of political courage.

A more accurate assessment would note that the president had become only a caretaker chief executive by late 1894 and would ask why, when Cleveland left office, only shreds of the presidency's prestige remained intact. The courage for which the outgoing president was so admired also included ample doses of maladroitness. In handling such issues as free silver, tariff revision, and patronage, Cleveland committed blunder after blunder that drove the majority of Democrats away from him. He missed reasonable chances to mollify those who disagreed with him on the currency, alienated Congress over the Wilson-Gorman Tariff in 1894, and used the patronage to compel adherence to his policies. "As President he could not dominate," said journalist Henry L. Stoddard, "and he did not know how to persuade."[5]

Beset with opposition and naturally aloof, Cleveland retreated inside the White House as his second term proceeded. He made few speeches or public appearances in his last two years and became "constantly more hedged in and mysterious" behind a network of guards and regulations. The president's secretary, Henry T. Thurber, was very unpopular and unsuccessful in his encounters with the public. "After the President had rubbed the skin off a visiting statesman Thurber came in the nature of strong fish brine to make his wounds smart." Disliking and distrusting newsmen, Cleveland sought to frustrate their efforts. Relations with the press deteriorated, and the gathering of information about the administration, David S. Barry remembered, was done "much after the fashion in which highwaymen rob a stage-coach." Repudiated by his party and closeted in the White House, the president seemed to be a cold, insensitive figure as his term concluded.[6]

The economic and social forces that overwhelmed the Cleveland administration also changed the shape of American politics in the 1890s. For two decades after the presidential election of 1872, the political system had been in equilibrium. The Republicans, following Ulysses S. Grant's victory over Horace Greeley, did not win a popular majority in a presidential contest again until 1896. In the GOP's three victories between 1876 and 1892, only James A. Garfield in 1880 managed a thin plurality. The Republicans held both houses of Congress for only four years between 1872 and 1895;

the Democrats did so for only two years during this period. Outside the Solid South, where the Democrats dominated, and to a lesser extent in New England, where the GOP held a solid but not unchallenged edge, the struggle was intense and sustained, with victory never certain for either party.

In this age of electoral stalemate, American politics bore scant resemblance to the usual picture of a dull, tawdry, and issueless combat between torpid and leaderless Republicans and Democrats. Between 1884 and 1894 the Democracy under Cleveland appealed to voters by means of a potent mixture of state rights, racism, and opposition to attempts to use the power of the national government to promote economic growth. The Republicans asserted doctrines of nationalism and of active governmental intervention to accelerate the expansion of the economy. These divergent positions affected such national issues as the protective tariff in addition to the local, ethnocultural questions of Sunday closing laws, temperance, and religious education in state-supported schools. Drawn to the political arena for enlightenment, entertainment, and the resolution of important problems, the eligible electorate of predominantly white, male Americans turned out to participate at rates that made the United States one of the most politically active nations in the world.

The balance between the parties broke down as the 1880s ended. Controlling the White House and Congress after Benjamin Harrison defeated Cleveland in 1888, the Republicans pursued policies of tariff protection, costly government, and religious activism in local politics in the Middle West. The party was proud of such measures as the McKinley Tariff and the Sherman Antitrust Act, but the voters, unhappy with activism and the threat of higher prices, responded with a crushing defeat for the GOP in the congressional elections of 1890. Two years later, Cleveland won a commanding 400,000 vote majority over Harrison. In March 1893 it seemed as if the Democrats might be on the verge of majority status.

Economic distress and social protest soon swept aside the Democratic dreams. The Panic of 1893 opened four grinding years of a depression that linked the Democracy with hard times for a quarter of a century. Out of the South and the Great Plains the Populist party arose from the agricultural misery that had sent prices for wheat and cotton downward and had made farm debts ever more burdensome. With a force that shook and then split the Democrats after 1892, the People's party advanced the free and unlimited coinage of silver as an inflationary remedy for the nation's difficulties. Meanwhile, Cleveland's stubborn adherence to the gold

4

standard, his ineptness with the Wilson-Gorman Tariff, and his errors of political leadership crippled the party.

The congressional elections of 1894 dealt a devastating setback to the Democrats and repudiated Cleveland's administration in emphatic terms. In the largest turnover of House seats from one party to another in American history, the Democrats lost 113 seats. The Republicans, who gained 117 members, controlled the House for the next sixteen years. Asked to choose among the policies of the Cleveland administration and the Democrats, the agrarian alternatives of populism, and Republican proposals that linked tariff protection and cultural pluralism to prosperity, the electorate turned to the GOP. The election of 1894 remade national politics. It terminated the years of even balance, opened a generation of Republican dominance, and condemned the Democrats to a minority status, with the exception of the accident of Woodrow Wilson's presidency, until the Great Depression and the New Deal.

The upheavals of the 1890s brought several new figures to national prominence. William Jennings Bryan experienced the most spectacular rise from obscurity, but the decade also furthered the careers of Theodore Roosevelt, Albert J. Beveridge, Robert M. La Follette, Henry Cabot Lodge, Champ Clark, and Marcus A. Hanna. More than any other single individual, however, William McKinley stood preeminent during these years. The record of his achievement and fortunes reveals the changes that came to the nation. McKinley was not elected president in 1896 because of the guiding genius of his associate Mark Hanna, because of coerced voters and Republican cash, or simply because of Democratic errors. He stood at the top of American politics as the result of his own masterful skill and because he was as much the dominant political personality of his time as Franklin Roosevelt would become in the 1930s.

By the time the Republican party nominated William McKinley at its national convention in June 1896, the basic facts of the candidate's life, political career, and stance on public questions were familiar. Born on January 29, 1843, in Niles, Ohio, McKinley had been educated in local schools and had attended Allegheny College for one term in 1860. At eighteen he joined the Twenty-third Ohio Volunteer Infantry as a private, fought bravely during four years of the Civil War, and left the army with the brevet rank of major and a title that accompanied him to the White House. After the war he studied law, settled in Canton, Ohio, and married Ida Saxton in 1871. Friendship with Rutherford B. Hayes helped

5

McKinley's early rise in Ohio politics. In 1876 he ran successfully for Congress, where he served, with a brief interruption, until 1891. Defeated for reelection in 1890, he won the Ohio governorship in 1891 and again in 1893, retiring from that office as the front runner for the GOP nomination in 1896. He received 661½ votes on the first ballot at the St. Louis convention, easily defeating a divided and dispirited opposition.

McKinley has never come into clear historical focus. Gray and dull beside the pinwheel ebullience of Theodore Roosevelt, he has remained a catchword for Republican conservatism or an inviting target for scholars who find his Victorian values either cloying or hypocritical. The wife of a political associate once wrote of "the masks he wore!"[7] McKinley built a public personality with great shrewdness; he admitted few men to the reality behind the façade. So deftly did the various aspects of his character blend together to form a politician of wide national appeal that critics and enemies who sought an explanation for McKinley's emergence looked at any force or circumstance but the candidate himself.

McKinley is responsible for a good part of the mystery. Never a discursive letter writer before he became president, he apparently made a conscious decision to restrict his personal correspondence while in office. From 1898 on, the pressure of work reconfirmed his course on this point; therefore the student of his administration lacks the rambling, dictated effusions that Theodore Roosevelt provided to his biographers. Reconstructing McKinley's thought processes is very difficult; it requires the accumulation of small clues, some inference, and a close knowledge of his working habits.

The public McKinley in 1896 could be summed up in a few ready phrases. He was the champion of the protective tariff, a cause he had advanced since entering Congress. In the debates over the Mills bill in 1888 or the McKinley Tariff Act of 1890, he had asserted that "the protective system meets our wants, our conditions, promotes the National design, and will work out our destiny better than any other." Defeated in the 1890 election, when the Democrats exploited popular apprehension about higher prices from the Republican tariff measure, McKinley said in a friend's newspaper: "Protection was never stronger than it is at this hour." The panic of 1893 made his linkage of the tariff with economic well-being both plausible and popular.[8]

McKinley's protectionism embraced more than simple economic calculations. He wove together themes of nationalism and an appeal to American labor. "Vote the Republican ticket, stand by the protective policy," he told a Virginia audience in 1886, "stand by American industries, stand by that policy which believes in American work for American workmen, that believes in American wages for American laborers, that believes in American homes for American citizens." Ten years after saying that he was a high protectionist, McKinley had added an important variation to his tariff philosophy.[9] While he was working on the McKinley Tariff Act, the Ohio congressman had become a convert to James G. Blaine's concept of reciprocity. Envisioning the controlled reductions of tariff rates through treaties with the nation's trading partners, reciprocity promised both to forestall more drastic revision of protected schedules and to expand American markets overseas.

His popular standing as the spokesman for the Republicans' central economic doctrine was the core of McKinley's appeal, but other elements enhanced his position within the GOP. As congressman and governor he had mastered the demanding political environment of Ohio in a way that made him the embodiment of Republicanism in its midwestern heartland. Though he saw the future of the nation as being linked with the health of business, he found no necessary disharmony between labor and management. From an early case in which he defended striking miners to the labor disputes of his governorship, he was even-handed in dealing with strikes, sympathetic to unions, and able to demonstrate to industrial laborers how the tariff worked to their benefit. On the touchy ethnic and religious questions that animated local politics, he was tolerant and inclusive. His going through personal bankruptcy in 1893 did nothing to injure his popularity. If anything, his national reputation grew when Americans learned how a friend's business failure had involved notes that McKinley had endorsed. Even the private funding that relieved him of his debts did not destroy the public's perception of him as being an unwitting victim of the general economic distress.

The country became familiar with McKinley in the 1880s and 1890s as he crossed the nation, speaking on behalf of Republican candidates and causes. He enjoyed traveling, and he came naturally to the journeying that marked his presidency. In front of an audience, McKinley was an effective orator in an age that venerated that now vanished art. During his presidential race he still displayed his capacity even to make statistics about the tariff more than the stuff of an arid recitation. Once in the White House, his speeches, all of which he wrote, tended to be shorter, more abstract, and, to the modern ear, often less specific. His listeners supplied the context and grasped the message in ways that gave his utterances great influence.

When people spoke of McKinley in his prime, they used such words as "dignity," "kindness," and "understanding." The tragedies of his personal life—two daughters had died in infancy, and his wife was virtually an invalid—closed off his private life from the public, who saw him as an example of marital devotion and appropriate reserve. McKinley once said to Charles W. Fairbanks, "Never keep books in politics,"[10] and he avoided making unnecessary enemies through recriminations or vengeance. He possessed charm, tact, and an ability to put himself in the place of others. After his death the theme of his small acts of thoughtfulness ran through the memorials to him.

Because he had so many friends, McKinley faced the charge that he had no firm convictions and that he gained affection and popularity by being weak and compliant. Opponents pointed to his pragmatic course on the money issue, where he responded to inflationary pressures in Ohio and was never a staunch advocate of a rigid gold standard. In the spring of 1896 Senator Thomas Collier Platt of New York said that he was "simply a clever gentleman, much too amiable and much too impressionable to be safely intrusted with great executive office."[11] Joseph G. Cannon, in a notorious gibe, said that the Major's ear was so close to the ground it was full of grasshoppers.

Buttressing the apparent impression of McKinley as the instrument of the will of others was his friendship with the Cleveland industrialist Marcus A. Hanna. The two men met first in the 1870s, but did not become a political team until the period 1888 to 1892. Hanna, who was fifty-nine in 1896, had been a force in Ohio politics for more than a decade. The relationship was easily caricatured in contemporary cartoons, and the notion lingers that Hanna made McKinley president when, in fact, the politician used the businessman to reach the White House. Hanna was not the swollen plutocrat that his enemies depicted; he was a capitalist who dreamed about harmony between employers and workers, and his position with McKinley was always that of a subordinate. McKinley needed the organizational skills and fund-raising ability that Hanna brought to politics. Their intimacy was always a political rather than a personal one, however; there were lines of behavior that Hanna knew he must never cross. Their friendship, which was at its height in 1896, would undergo important alterations once the new president had been inaugurated.

McKinley's ascendancy in his dealings with Hanna was characteristic of his management of people generally. "He had a way of handling men," said Elihu Root, "so that they thought his ideas were their own." Listening more than he talked, patient with those who bored him, McKinley moved toward his objectives steadily and unobtrusively. "He was a man of great power," Root continued, "because he was absolutely indifferent to credit. His great desire was 'to get it done.' He cared nothing about the credit, but McKinley *always had his way*."[12] From such men as Elihu Root, William Howard Taft, and John Hay, the president secured exemplary service and enduring respect.

Whether they were his critics who assailed him or his friends who idolized him, most men who knew McKinley recognized that he kept the core of his personality away from public view. The private McKinley had a strain of stoicism and reserve that made him a cold and, on occasion, a ruthless figure. He had ambition and a sense of his own destiny, traits that he usually kept well hidden. "I don't think that McKinley ever let anything stand in the way of his own advancement," said Senator Charles Dick in 1906. "McKinley was not altogether to blame for this trait in his character. He had been petted and flattered until he felt that all the fruit on the tree was his."[13] Dick knew that McKinley always gave a little less than he received from friends. The Major could use and discard people when it suited his purposes.

As a political leader, McKinley had the defects of his qualities. Charisma was not a concept that McKinley would have understood. If he pleased Americans, whose goodness he affirmed, he infrequently inspired them. He surrounded the presidency with a dignity that became almost imperial by 1900, but there was never the drama that Theodore Roosevelt or Woodrow Wilson supplied. The party, the Congress, and the nation moved toward the president's goals in small, cumulative steps without a sense of passing from one great event to another. When McKinley died, his political approach disappeared, leaving large results but few traces of their architect.

It was easy to find weaknesses in McKinley's style of governance. The president's adversaries usually lost, but after innumerable minor wounds rather than one decisive stroke. While the process of attrition continued, patience seemed to be evasion, maneuvering to be irresolution, and compromise to be defeat. Sometimes these harsh judgments were true; usually they were not. The central part of the indictment of McKinley as president and politician rests on

9

his diplomacy with Spain in 1897/1898, and on his management of the empire that the United States thereby acquired. A detailed review of these problems shows that he was an important contributor to the emergence of the modern presidency.

McKinley was fifty-three when the Republicans nominated him. Conducting his campaign from his front porch in Canton, he attracted newspapermen, who came in vain to interview him. The British reporter George W. Steevens, who visited the candidate on October 1, 1896, found a "strong, clean-shaven face" with "clear eyes, wide nose, full lips—all his features suggest dominant will and energy rather than subtlety of mind or emotion." Only five feet six and sensitive about his height, McKinley, in well-tailored clothes and stern bearing, sought to seem taller than he actually was. He was addicted to cigars, though never photographed with one, and Steevens saw that he was also "not unmindful of the spitoon."[14] Despite Steevens's pleas, McKinley would not be interviewed, and the journalist had to content himself with the nominee's set speech to his visitors.

By the time that Steevens came to Canton the Republican presidential campaign had survived the scare of William Jennings Bryan's nomination and was on its way to a decisive result in November. The Democrats' selection of the "Boy Orator of the Platte" in early July had disrupted the careful strategy that McKinley and Hanna had followed in gaining the GOP nomination. The Ohioan had campaigned as "The Advance Agent of Prosperity," whose tariff views would restore good times after four years of Democratic error. Within the party he depicted himself as the midwestern champion, challenging the party leaders of the East. So his candidacy also became "The People against the Bosses." Solid on tariff protection and moderate on the controversial currency question, McKinley expected to wage a positive campaign against either a legatee of the Cleveland administration or an ineffectual advocate of the inflationary wing of the Democracy.

Two events transformed the race into the "Battle of the Standards"—of free silver against gold. At the Republican Convention, McKinley and Hanna accepted a platform that reaffirmed "unreservedly" the party's commitment to sound money. "We are therefore opposed," the plank continued, "to the free coinage of silver, except by international agreement with the leading commercial nations of the earth, which agreement we pledge ourselves to promote."[15] The references to an international agreement reflected the Republican sentiment for a resolution of the currency problem

10

through diplomatic negotiations. It was also designed to appeal to the Far West and to those who were suspicious of eastern rigidity on gold. The platform fight over this plank, the bolt of the western silver Republicans, and the pleasure of the gold men at the wording combined to leave the strong impression that the party was now the unswerving champion of the gold standard.

The Democrats' nomination of William Jennings Bryan on a free-silver platform at Chicago on July 10 surprised the Republicans and confronted them with a formidable challenge. The Democracy's nominee was young, dynamic, and atop an apparent wave of enthusiasm for free silver. The Populists also nominated Bryan; so, with the South securely Democratic and the Far West for silver, he seemed, in the summer of 1896, as he said before his nomination, to represent "the logic of the situation."

Eastern Republicans, who regarded the selection of Bryan with shocked horror, talked of the imminence of social revolution. While respecting his rival's abilities, McKinley remained faithful to his plan of campaign organization and resisted efforts to tie the GOP canvass to sound money and the gold standard. The 1896 campaign is famous for the amounts of money that Hanna raised from the business community, between $3.5 and 4 million by the most careful estimates. McKinley's victory did not, however, depend on bought voters and coerced workers, but on the abundant campaign literature, an attractive candidate, and the potent political themes that he struck to which the electorate responded. Under Hanna's efficient supervision, the Republican organization, with headquarters in New York and Chicago, carried out the strategy that McKinley had developed. The men around him used and recognized the state leaders within the GOP, but Charles G. Dawes of Illinois, Hanna, and the other Ohio lieutenants gave the effort a strong midwestern flavor.

"This is a year for press and pen," McKinley said; so the GOP apparatus poured out two hundred million pamphlets to targeted segments of the populace.[16] Newspapers carried specially prepared inserts about McKinley, his family, and his positions. McKinley was the first presidential aspirant to be filmed, and the Republicans used the crude movie in the campaign. Meanwhile, the candidate delivered more than three hundred speeches to three-quarters of a million guests from his front porch in Canton. His remarks were carefully prepared and coordinated in order to avoid blunders. They sounded the keynotes of his canvass felicitously and garnered a newspaper coverage that was fully equal to what Bryan achieved in his travels. McKinley also seemed to be more stable and states-manlike in his home setting.

In his comments, McKinley joined free silver and free trade as connected and disastrous Democratic answers to the depression. He did not adopt the easterners' views that there should be an assault on the free-silver idea alone; instead, he maintained a bal-ance between monetary and protectionist arguments, saying, "Thou-sands of men who are somewhat tinctured with Free Silver ideas keep within the Republican party and will support the Republican nominee because of the fact that they are protectionists." McKinley also appealed in a pluralistic, inclusive way to ethnic groups that once had normally been Democratic. German-Americans were, he said on August 29, "conservative, industrious, steady, sensible, fond of home and family"; furthermore, they were "not deluded by false theories of finance, nor by catch phrases of the campaign."[17]

By October 1896 it was evident that the Republicans would win. After his initial surge, Bryan encountered monetary problems, a divided party when the Gold Democrats bolted, and difficulty in moving the appeal of the free-silver issue beyond its natural agrar-ian base. His tours drew large, friendly crowds to which he made stirring, moralistic appeals. His evangelistic rhetoric not only at-tracted Americans who wanted society reformed and purified but also produced defections among previously Republican pietists. Whatever the Democrat gained with crusading zeal, however, he lost elsewhere. In the East, which he loosely styled "the enemy's country," and among the working men and small businessmen of the Midwest, Bryan did poorly. The inflationary appeal of free silver did not command support in the cities, and Democrats made no effective counter to McKinley's tariff arguments. On October 28 Hanna told a potential campaign contributor: "It is all over. Re-ports are satisfactory just where we wanted them most."[18]

The election results bore out Hanna's confidence. McKinley received 7,035,638 popular votes to Bryan's 6,467,945 and had a margin of 271 to 176 in the electoral college. Not since Grant's victory in 1872 had the difference between the popular votes cast for the major candidates been as large. The turnout reached record levels in a contest that American voters had followed closely and cared about intensely. More than 78 percent of the eligible voters went to the polls in the North. The election of 1896, which con-firmed the outcome of 1894, opened a long period of Republican electoral ascendancy. McKinley had constructed a winning coali-tion of urban residents in the North, prosperous farmers, industrial workers, and most ethnic groups except the Irish. Electoral trends now favored the GOP as they had appeared to help the Democrats four years earlier. The unhappy example of the Cleveland administration indicated, however, that changing circumstances and poor leadership could produce sudden realignments. It became the political task of the new president to bring the prosperity that he had promised and to see that the Republican victory was not transitory.

The two related initiatives of the first year—tariff legislation and international bimetallism—were in motion by the end of 1896. Wishing to avoid the errors of Harrison and Cleveland, McKinley decided, in consultation with Nelson Dingley of Maine, chairman of the House Ways and Means Committee, to call a special session of Congress in March 1897 for the purpose of writing a tariff bill. By December 10, 1896, the committee was at work, and formal hearings began on December 28. At the same time, senatorial advocates of an international bimetallic agreement explored with the new president his views on their cause. The leader of the bimetallists, Senator Edward O. Wolcott of Colorado, who met with McKinley on December 27, obtained approval to undertake a private mission to Europe to consult about international action. Wolcott was on his way to England by January 1, 1897. In the Congress, legislation was prepared that would authorize the incoming president to send bimetallist commissioners abroad.

While foreign-policy questions also pressed in on McKinley, with the troubled situation in Cuba being his most prominent worry, the main task in the preinaugural period, of course, was the selection of a cabinet. That complex and exacting chore occupied most of McKinley's time after the election. In an era of intense partisan loyalty, the composition of the cabinet represented one expression of a new administration's sensitivity to factional, sectional, and philosophical nuances. How large a recognition should New York Republicans obtain from a midwestern president who knew that his region distrusted Empire State politicos? What should be the balance between gold-standard advocates of the East and more inflationary party members in the West? Should the southern Republicans be encouraged by being given a slot in the cabinet? In view of the GOP's tenuous hold on the Senate, what hopefuls might be found there without doing damage to the legislative program? Related to all these was the question of how Mark Hanna should be rewarded for his friendship and his management of the campaign.

The course of McKinley's administration, and especially the Spanish-American War, proved that two of his selections, John

Sherman to head the State Department and Russell A. Alger for War, were mistakes. The process by which Sherman was selected, moreover, though it was intended to end criticism about Hanna's relationship to McKinley, intensified the problem and further solidified the popular impression that there was influence and outside pressure on the president-elect. McKinley's cabinet, chosen in the customary way, was better than it appeared in retrospect, and his talent for finding strong subordinates would improve dramatically during his term. There is no question, however, that crucial weak spots flawed the original cabinet.

Two of the cabinet slots were easily filled. For the Department of Agriculture the choice was James ("Tama Jim") Wilson of Iowa. Supported by Senator William Boyd Allison and the rest of the otherwise divided state party in Iowa, Wilson had served in Congress, had been active in agricultural education, and was a close student of midwestern politics. Wilson remained in office until 1913 under Roosevelt and Taft; for McKinley he provided reliable intelligence while on numerous trips in the West. Equally simple was the placing of John Davis Long of Massachusetts in the Navy Department. He and McKinley had been colleagues in the House in the 1880s, and he was popular in New England, an area that was responsive to the flow of naval appropriations. Once Nelson Dingley had declined to be secretary of the treasury, Long emerged as the favorite of New England, and McKinley offered him the post on January 30.

For postmaster general, McKinley at first wanted Hanna. Because of his senatorial ambitions, however, Hanna was not interested, and the office slipped back into a secondary category while other slots were being filled. The regular Republicans of Wisconsin put forward Henry Clay Payne, the vice-chairman of the Republican campaign, whom Hanna favored. Members of the faction that was aligned with Robert M. La Follette had their own choice for secretary of agriculture from their state; so they reminded the president-elect about Payne's railroad connections, his antilabor reputation, and his corporate lobbying on Capitol Hill. Poor health also crippled Payne's chances. In the end McKinley decided on James A. Gary of Maryland. Since he was a long-time party contributor and a wheelhorse, Gary's selection represented a recognition of southern Republicanism in a very mild way.

Because of the money issue, the secretary of the treasury would be a central figure in the new administration. Dingley's expertise on the Ways and Means Committee had impressed McKinley. "You

14

are the man for the place," he told Dingley on December 3. "Will you take it?"[19] Illness and a desire to stay in the House caused Dingley to refuse three weeks later. Now the problem of the treasury became more intricate. Talk of a Gold Democrat was speculative, and the naming of an eastern Republican was unlikely. Since Illinois had been a decisive state in the Middle West, it should have a cabinet seat, but whom to pick? Senator Shelby M. Cullom wanted the treasury place, despite his opposition to McKinley's nomination; but it is unlikely that the incoming president gave Cullom even passing consideration. To another Illinoisan, the young Charles G. Dawes, who had worked so hard and so well in the campaign, McKinley was more solicitous, but his youth and lack of experience made Dawes more suitable to be comptroller of the currency.

Through Dawes, however, with help from Hanna and others, McKinley did find a strong candidate. During a conversation in Canton on January 20, McKinley brought up with Dawes the name of Lyman J. Gage, president of the First National Bank of Chicago. Since Gage was the candidate whom Dawes had planned to suggest, Dawes readily agreed to sound Gage out about the treasury. The banker was a Republican with a difference. He had supported Cleveland over James G. Blaine in 1884, and he had declined an offer to become secretary of the treasury in 1893. The defense of sound money in 1896 renewed his ties with the GOP. After the Haymarket Riot of 1886, Gage favored pardoning the accused participants and became an advocate of "more friendly consultation and less inconsiderate action on the part of capital and labor." Within two days of Dawes's overture, Gage indicated a willingness to accept the treasury post, and he and McKinley agreed on their views about the gold standard at an interview on January 27. "I never met a man in my life with whom I was so favorably impressed by a day's acquaintance," McKinley told a friend. While the regular Illinois party was unhappy at the elevation of a persistent enemy, the appointment drew applause in the press.[20]

The places of attorney general and secretary of the interior became intertwined in a shifting alignment of sectional recognition and the continuing problem of how to deal with New York State. There the new president confronted factional rivalries of a marked complexity. Senator Platt had led an organization that opposed McKinley's nomination; but if the senator's wishes went unheeded, his vote could endanger the administration's legislative aims. Insurgents against Platt, of whom the publisher of the *New York*

Tribune, Whitelaw Reid, was the most celebrated, had helped McKinley in 1896 and now sought presidential favor. New Yorkers pressed forward for a cabinet slot and competed with equal intensity for the coveted ambassadorship to the Court of St. James's in London. Seeking a middle ground, McKinley first offered a portfolio, perhaps secretary of the navy, to Cornelius N. Bliss in early January. Acceptable to both extremes but close to neither, Bliss, a veteran fund raiser for the party, was an adroit choice, but his wife's health and his own business commitments led him to decline. He did not rule out serving under any circumstances, but his refusal left the fate of New York dependent on other forces.

To recognize the West, McKinley thought of an old friend from the House, federal judge Joseph McKenna of California, for the Interior Department. At the same time, he offered the attorney generalship to Nathan B. Goff of West Virginia. Goff said no in late January. It then became evident that McKenna, a Roman Catholic, would be attacked by Protestant churchmen, since the Interior Department ran the Indian schools, which, in turn, Catholics administered for the most part. McKinley switched McKenna to the Justice Department and then began to try to find a New Yorker for the Interior Department. The place was offered to John J. McCook, a friend of McKinley's who was a Manhattan corporation lawyer and a busy backstage presence in the GOP. He said no, and on March 3, under the urging of McKinley and friends such as Elihu Root, Bliss reconsidered and came in as secretary of the interior.

The secretary of war was not a job that in 1896 evoked images of guns firing and armies marching. The peacetime army, with twenty-five thousand officers and men, had only a modest military role. Politicians looked upon it as an agency whose civilian responsibilities—exploration, flood relief, and construction of rivers and harbors—required business experience in order to be properly managed. Given such assumptions, the candidacy of Russell A. Alger of Michigan made sense to McKinley. At sixty-one, Alger looked back on his military service in the Civil War, which brought him the rank of general, his success in the lumber industry in Michigan, and a career in politics as governor and favorite-son presidential candidate in 1888.

Before naming Alger in late January, McKinley checked into the substance of the aspirant's war record to refute charges that he had resigned from the army in 1864 under a cloud. Having established Alger's fitness to serve in the last war, the president-elect did not take up the issue of how his choice might handle a future conflict. Alger's business and governmental record was less impressive than it appeared. Neither as an industrial executive nor as governor of Michigan had he displayed the capacity to meet the larger responsibilities of war. Alger was not an utter disaster as secretary of war, but he was over his head when the Spanish-American War came. At the time of his designation, the *Brooklyn Eagle* noted: "We certainly tremble to contemplate the outcome of a war conducted under his direction."[21] McKinley erred in not giving careful thought to that eventuality, and his administration suffered as a result.

The choice of John Sherman as secretary of state became the most controversial of McKinley's cabinet appointments because of Sherman's failures in the post and because Mark Hanna succeeded him in the United States Senate. Did McKinley pick Sherman, heedless of his waning mental powers, in order to provide Hanna with a place in Congress? It is clear that Hanna wanted to be a senator and that he saw the opportunity, if Sherman were to go into the new administration, to achieve a goal that he had quietly desired for some years. McKinley would have preferred to have Hanna in the cabinet as a clearly defined subordinate, and he offered his friend the postmaster generalship in mid November. Hanna refused, proposing instead to sound out Sherman about becoming secretary of state. McKinley agreed to let the subject be explored, and news of Hanna's ideas was public by the last week in November.

John Sherman, at seventy-three, was approaching the end of the Senate term that he had won in 1892. He now faced the prospect of concluding his political career in 1899 through retirement, waging a hard race for reelection to the Senate, or finishing his public life with a cabinet post. Having been secretary of the treasury under Rutherford B. Hayes, he could only gain further fame in the State Department. Hanna and Sherman had once been political allies, and on November 13, 1896, the senator wrote to his former associate: "If you wish to enter political life, I would like to be one of your backers." When word of Hanna's scheme circulated, Sherman dismissed the reports. In early December, however, the two men met and discussed the subject. On December 15 Sherman told Hanna that he had made up his mind to say yes if McKinley offered him the State Department portfolio.[22]

If McKinley were part of a Hanna plot to elevate Sherman so as to create a senatorial opening, his next actions were hardly designed to complete the transaction. With Sherman's agreement in hand, the president-elect authorized his emissaries in Iowa to approach Senator William Boyd Allison about the State Department post. In the week before Christmas, Allison indicated that he was not interested and would not accept the position if it were offered to him. Informed of these facts shortly after the holiday, McKinley now saw Sherman as an attractive option. On January 4, 1897, he wrote the senator: "I would very much like to have you in my administration as Sec'y of State." The letter was delivered on January 6, and McKinley's agent reported: "I could see that he was delighted to receive it."[23]

After leaving the cabinet in 1898, Sherman wrote that McKinley and Hanna had "deprived me of the high office of Senator by the temporary appointment as Secretary of State."[24] Sherman had forgotten that he had taken the cabinet appointment voluntarily, indeed with some eagerness. Anxious about his reelection, Sherman was quite willing to occupy the place for his own advantage. As to whether it was to be a "temporary" term of office, McKinley expected the future secretary to serve for at least two years. Sherman's tenure was shorter because of his own incapacity, not as a result of any prearrangement by McKinley.

Would Sherman have been a candidate if Hanna had not had any ambitions for the Senate? Among Republican elders, Sherman stood on the same level of popular reputation as Allison, and he ranked higher than Nelson Aldrich of Rhode Island or Orville H. Platt of Connecticut. Sherman could hardly have been ignored in the cabinet-making process. The central question is whether McKinley knew that Sherman lacked the physical and mental resources that the job required. That Sherman's intelligence had faded somewhat was well known in Washington. McKinley was aware of some of this talk, but he had heard from a close friend in December that Sherman's mind was very clear. After the appointment had been announced, when talk of the prospective secretary's deficiencies was widespread, the new president wrote angrily: "When I saw him last I was convinced both of his perfect health, physically and mentally, and that his prospects of life were remarkably good."[25]

Despite these claims, McKinley had not checked thoroughly enough into Sherman's condition, nor had Sherman's family hastened to enlighten the president-elect about the senator's health. Expecting to be his own secretary of state and intending to have his friend William R. Day as Sherman's first assistant in due course, McKinley had made an expedient choice. The extent of the misjudgment emerged quickly. Sherman was one of the few advisors who was invited to offer suggestions for the inaugural address. He responded with a draft on the Cuban problem that threatened American intervention in the island. The memorandum silently disappeared, but the Sherman problem lingered on.[26]

Achieving for Hanna his goal of the Senate added to the cloud around Sherman and the State Department. The outgoing senator was glad to have Hanna succeed him. The difficulty lay with the governor, Asa S. Bushnell, and with Senator Joseph B. Foraker. Their faction had several aspirants for Sherman's seat in 1899, including Bushnell, and they were little disposed to give their rival a running start toward a full term. For a month after Sherman's appointment was known, Bushnell and Foraker stalled. They offered the seat to Congressman Theodore E. Burton, who declined it, and they canvassed the Ohio party for other hopefuls.

The delay vexed Hanna. "They do not intend to let me into the Senate," he told McKinley. In order to win he exerted public pressure on his enemies. Hanna addressed a legislative dinner at the end of January, he prodded Bushnell in interviews, and his friends spoke out on his behalf. After making a final appeal to Hanna to enter the cabinet, McKinley sent William R. Day to the governor in late February with a request that Hanna be selected for the Senate. Bushnell and Foraker now had no credible option in the face of strong Republican opinion behind McKinley's friend. On February 21 Bushnell announced that he would make the appointment. McKinley called it an action that "will receive the hearty approval of not only the people of Ohio, but of the whole country. Personally I am highly gratified."[27]

When the composition of the new cabinet was revealed, comment was generally friendly but restrained. It was, observed the *Washington Post*, "a body of active, experienced and successful men of affairs." The age of the incoming ministers drew attention, since only Secretaries McKenna and Long were under sixty, and Sherman, of course, was over seventy. "I think, myself, the cabinet unusually weak," said a writer for the *New York Tribune* in private, and he predicted that "it cannot last a twelfthmonth."[28] Balancing the weak choices of Sherman and Alger were the solid qualities of Long and Gage, and the placing of Day in the State Department offset, to a degree, problems at the top. It was an average, competent group that could easily have handled the anticipated domestic policies of the new government. When war came, McKinley strengthened his official family and grew much more discerning in his choice of subordinates.

Some indications of McKinley's capacity to attract governmental talent were revealed in several of his subcabinet and diplomatic selections. Dawes went in as comptroller of the currency, and future Supreme Court justice Willis Van Devanter served as an assistant attorney general assigned to the Interior Department. In the Post Office Department the Kansas editor Joseph L. Bristow became the fourth assistant in charge of patronage, beginning an administrative career that led him to the Senate in 1908. As ambassador to Great Britain the president named John Hay, after disposing of the ambitions of Whitelaw Reid in a graceful, if disingenuous letter. Although he had reservations about Theodore Roosevelt's temperament, McKinley accepted the urgings of Henry Cabot Lodge, John Hay, Speaker Thomas B. Reed, and others. Assured that the candidate had "no preconceived plans which he would wish to drive through the moment he got in," the president named Roosevelt as assistant secretary of the navy in April 1897.[29]

The McKinleys reached Washington on March 3, 1897. Dawes noted in his diary: "The streets are crowded—the hotel is full to overflowing and an air of expectancy is abroad. The army of office-seekers has its advance guard here." That evening McKinley dined with President Cleveland. They talked about Cuba and the danger of war with Spain, and the outgoing president told friends that McKinley said: "Mr. President, if I can only go out of office, at the end of my term, with the knowledge that I have done what lay in my power to avert this terrible calamity, with the success that has crowned your patience and persistence, I shall be the happiest man in the world."[30]

As the Republican revelers prepared for the gala activities of March 4, editorial writers ruminated on the change of administrations. On the Pacific Coast the San Francisco Examiner proclaimed that, despite the nation's troubles, "on this auspicious day the sky is blue, the birds sing and joy is unconfined. It is the last day of the Cleveland administration." Across the continent, looking back on the economic unrest of the decade and possible foreign turmoil, the Washington Post decided on March 5 that "no President, since the time of Lincoln thirty-six years ago, has come into power under circumstances more important and in the face of possibilities more tremendous than those under which Mr. McKinley now assumes the reins of government."[31]

2

★★★★★

McKINLEY TAKES OFFICE

Inauguration Day, March 4, 1897, was clear and crisp when McKinley took the oath of office on the Senate steps of the Capitol. As he read his inaugural address, "his voice was under perfect control, and his clear and well-modulated tones could be distinctly heard by thousands of people."[1] The speeches that new presidents deliver on such occasions rarely attain the oratorical or intellectual distinction that those of Abraham Lincoln or Franklin D. Roosevelt achieved. McKinley's remarks were not memorable, but in the problems that he discussed and in the solutions that he advanced, the incoming president provided a review of the nation's situation as he assumed power.

Since McKinley's presidency occurred at the end of the 1890s, estimates of the nation's population lacked the precision of the 1900 census. In 1890 the population of the United States was 62,979,766; seven years later, according to a Bureau of the Census estimate, the figure had risen to 72,189,000. The 1890 census reported 32,237,000 males in the population as compared with 30,711,000 women. Ten years later the margin had widened slightly, with 38,816,000 men and 37,178,000 females. The 1900 census also recorded 66,901,000 whites, 9,193,000 blacks, 238,196 Indians, 24,326 Japanese, and 89,863 Chinese in the nation.[2]

The majority of Americans, 39,817,386 in 1890 and 47,379,699 in 1900, lived in the northeastern and north-central areas of the country. The South's population rose from 20,028,059 to 24,523,527 during these ten years, and the West was much less densely populated, with 3,102,269 people in the 1890 tally and 4,091,349 a decade

21

later. The most populous states were, in order, New York, Pennsylvania, Illinois, and Ohio. Texas and Georgia led the South, and California dominated the West.

During the 1890s the nation experienced a growing urbanization. There were 22,106,265 Americans who lived in the towns of 2,500 or more that the census called urban areas in 1890; whereas 40,841,449 resided in rural settings. When the century ended, the urban population had swelled to 30,160,000, and the rural population had increased to 45,834,654. In these ten years the number of individuals living in cities of one million or more rose from 3,662,115 to 6,429,474. New York City encompassed more than 3,400,000 people in 1900; Chicago and Philadelphia totaled 1,699,000 and 1,294,000 respectively. The two presidential candidates in 1896 came from more modest cities, ones which were more typical of the urban experience. Canton, in northeastern Ohio, had fewer than 30,000 people; they depended on railroads, coal mining, and farming for their living. Lincoln, Nebraska, which claimed more than 50,000 inhabitants, was a hub for western railroads and the shipping of agricultural goods.

Americans in 1898 moved across the United States on a railroad system that had grown to 245,334 miles of track and that carried 501,067,000 passengers in that year. On 13,380,000 passenger miles, the railroads earned $266,970,000 of their total operating income of $1,247,326,000. Travelers could expect a large degree of personal service if they were willing to pay a slightly higher fare. The mail moved efficiently as well, and politicians around the country exchanged letters at a speed that would seem improbable eight decades later. Proponents of the railroads contended, with some plausibility, that the United States led the world in rail service.

The depression of the 1890s was changing the American railroad system from the profusion of financially weak and overbuilt companies of the late nineteenth century to the banker-supervised, consolidated, and more stable communities of interest that characterized the early years of the new century. Freight rates were steady or actually declining, and the railroads were improving their physical plants. To critics of the rail lines or to the shippers who desired lower rates, the railroad problem remained one of obtaining greater regulation from the state or national government so that prices would be lowered and rate discrimination would be prevented. Strengthening the power of the Interstate Commerce Commission (ICC) became a rallying point for railroad reformers, especially after the Supreme Court decided in 1897 that Congress had not given

22

the ICC the authority to establish rates. That situation did not change during the McKinley administration, though by 1901 the public pressure that produced regulatory legislation under Theodore Roosevelt would show itself.

After an initial paragraph "invoking the guidance of Almighty God," McKinley said that the new administration would confront the difficulties of "the prevailing business conditions, entailing idleness upon willing labor and loss to useful enterprises." It had been nearly four years since the Panic of 1893 had signaled the start of a severe depression, and the economy was still stagnant. Following the initial sharp downturn between May 1893 and June 1894, the outlook improved through the end of 1895. It was, however, far from a complete recovery. The nation then experienced a second harsh contraction, which commenced in December 1895 and endured into 1897. "The country is suffering from industrial disturbances from which speedy relief must be had," the new president concluded.[3]

One measure of the impact of the depression was the gross national product. Expressed in 1929 prices, it had averaged $27.3 billion between 1889 and 1893. The yearly average for the period 1892 to 1896 was only $29.6 billion, as compared with a yearly figure of $37.1 billion between 1897 and 1901. Farm products contributed an average of $6.8 billion annually to the total from 1892 to 1896, an increase over the $6.6 billion of the years 1889 to 1893. Nonfarm products stood annually at $19.7 billion in the four predepression years, rose to $21.7 billion for the years 1892 to 1896, and moved ahead to $27.4 billion during the years of McKinley's presidency.

The work force that suffered through the slump of the 1890s reflected the industrializing character of the economy. The number of employed Americans rose from 23,740,000 in 1890 to 29,070,000 in 1900. Agriculture accounted for 9,990,000 of this total in 1890 and for 10,710,000 a decade later. In the nonfarm pursuits, manufacturing comprised 6,340,000 people in 1900, up from 4,750,000 ten years before. Manufacturing had become, at the end of the 1890s, a dominant part of the nation's economy. Construction in 1900 employed 1,660,000 people, 1,530,000 were in transportation, and 1,990,000 in trades, financial, and real-estate positions. There were 3,860,000 who worked in service employment, and another 300,000 had government jobs.

Working conditions and wages, which were those of an era before social-welfare programs, mirrored the troubled state of the economy. The average work week was around fifty-nine hours in these years, and the average annual income for all professions in 1897 was $411. With farm labor omitted, the total rose to $462. As to the cost of living, students of the problem agreed that an income below $500 a year placed an urban family of five people in the Northeast at or below the subsistence level and was no more than a minimum income in other northern urban centers. One and three-quarters million children were listed as being employed in some form of work in 1900.

Labor-union members made up only a small percentage of the total working population. The 447,000 union members in 1897 were centered in the railroad, building, metal, printing, and food industries. In manufacturing, union men worked almost six fewer hours per week and received about thirteen cents more per hour than their nonunion counterparts. Work stoppages rose slightly—from 1,066 in 1896 to 1,110 in 1897; they involved 416,000 employees, and 680 of the strikes dealt with wages and hours.

After the improvement in business conditions in 1895, the economy slid backward over the next year. Farm income and prices struck their low points for the decade, and the unemployment rate moved upward toward 20 percent. Only a modest improvement, to 15 percent, marked 1897; unemployment persisted in 1898 and was still at around 8 percent two years after McKinley's term began. At the time of the inauguration, a rise in orders for steel, a stronger woolen industry, and prospects of larger farm exports led the correspondent of the *London Economist* to write: "The general business situation continues to move slowly in the direction of improvement." Within a week, however, caution returned: "While the movement of general trade, then, is unquestionably in the direction of improvement, it is seen to be halting, irregular, and thus far not up to expectations."[4]

The new president first addressed the issue that had agitated the electorate so profoundly in 1896. "Our financial system needs some revision; our money is all good now, but its value must not further be threatened." The outgoing administration had incurred substantial budget deficits, totaling $137,800,000 between 1894 and 1896; and McKinley believed that an "adequate revenue" had to precede changes in the financial system. He proposed to name, with congressional agreement, a commission to consider revision of the banking and currency laws. Since the Republicans lacked a dependable majority in the Senate, where silver advocates held the balance of power, any more ambitious initiative was probably doomed. The president did stress his commitment to government supervision of the currency, and he was critical of "the several forms of our paper money," which were, he thought, "a constant embarrassment to the government and to a safe balance in the Treasury." The currency that was in circulation in 1897 consisted of gold coin ($517,590,000), gold certificates ($37,285,000), silver dollars ($51,940,000), silver certificates ($357,849,000), treasury notes of 1890 ($83,470,000) subsidiary silver ($59,616,000), in addition to $306,915,000 in United States notes and $226,318,000 in national bank notes. On November 1, 1896, the amount of money in circulation per capita was $22.63, only a slight rise from the $22.55 of 1895. Since the last year of Harrison's presidency, the amount of money in circulation per capita had fallen almost $2.00.[5]

The subject of monetary policy had been a political issue of varying intensity since the Civil War. During the 1890s, advocates of inflation through the free and unlimited coinage of silver at a ratio of 16 to 1 with gold had pressed their proposal as an answer to economic distress. The "silver men" contended that free coinage would raise the depressed price level and also would provide funds for agrarian America to escape the weight of debt. McKinley's victory had slowed but not stopped the silver proponents. "Those who fought in the battle," Bryan announced, "will continue in the ranks until bimetallism is restored."[6]

Supporters of the gold standard, who were centered in the Northeast, regarded the 1896 result as a temporary escape from financial chaos. The size of the vote for Bryan, however, served notice that the issue remained alive, and the unsettled state of the economy during the first half of 1897 kept the friends of the yellow metal alert against attempts to alter the existing system. While the administration had to wait for a more favorable congressional alignment in order to pursue monetary action, it endeavored to reassure the gold constituency of its intentions. Speaking in Chicago in late May, Secretary of the Treasury Gage said: "If any of you harbor the suspicion that the Administration, but just now installed into the responsibilities of high office, has forgotten or is likely to forget the mandate of the people, whose voice in behalf of honest money and sound finances rang out loud and clear in November last, put that suspicion aside."[7]

Between the extremes on the silver issue lay the third approach —international bimetallism. Envisioning a multination agreement to promote a wider use of the white metal. McKinley promised his "constant endeavor to secure it by cooperation with the other great commercial powers of the world." When he spoke on March 4, the new president was aware that preliminary negotiations with France on a bimetallic initiative were under way, and the prospects were promising. Senator Wolcott had also found Great Britain more sympathetic than he had anticipated, and Congress had just authorized the United States to send commissioners overseas to arrange an international monetary conference. While these talks proceeded, McKinley pledged that "the credit of the government, the integrity of its currency, and the inviolability of its obligations must be preserved."[8] For that purpose he urged economy in government and an end to the deficits of the depression years. This statement led McKinley naturally to the question of tariffs and protection.

The nation, the president remarked, "is committed by its latest popular utterance to the system of tariff taxation," and he advocated a tariff measure "as will give ample protection and encouragement to the industries and the development of our country." In 1896, customs duties of $160,022,000 were the largest single component to government revenues, which amounted to $338,142,000. Alcohol taxes of $114,454,000, tobacco taxes of $30,712,000, and stamp taxes of $260,000 were the internal-revenue duties in an era that did not have a federal income tax. "It is the settled policy of the government, pursued from the beginning and practiced by all parties and administrations," said McKinley, "to raise the bulk of our revenue from taxes upon foreign productions entering the United States for sale and consumption, and avoiding, for the most part, every form of direct taxation, except in time of war."[9]

That the country had decided to raise much of its governmental revenue from customs duties may have been a "settled policy"; but the precise level of those taxes and the degree of protection that they afforded to American industry constituted a significant point of difference between Republicans and Democrats. To encourage the expansion of domestic industry, the GOP stood for high tariffs on foreign imports. "It enables us," wrote Senator George Frisbie Hoar of Massachusetts, "to maintain a scale of wages which makes of the workingmen intelligent citizens, enables them to live in comfort, to educate their children, to have leisure to be inventors, and makes them fit to take their share in the government of the republic."[10]

Hoar's words suggest the potent political appeal that the Republicans had developed in the tariff issue in the 1890s. Seeing the nation as being composed of interdependent producers, the GOP identified protection with prosperity, broadened the scope of the policy to include labor, and used nationalistic appeals to offset charges that the tariff meant only profit for the rich. In 1896 McKinley endorsed "a good American protective tariff law" that would "provide adequate revenues for the Government and gladden the home of every American workingman." On March 4, 1897, he indicated that Congress would soon convene in special session to enact a Republican substitute for the Wilson-Gorman Tariff of 1894.[11]

Throughout the Gilded Age the Democrats had opposed protectionism. Since an outright endorsement of free trade would have been politically disastrous, the party had lacked an explicit, precise alternative to protectionism. Their broad appeal was to Americans as consumers. Lower duties, a tariff "for revenue only," would mean lower prices in stores and shops, the Democracy contended. In the decade and a half after 1880 the tariff-reform position had been a viable one for the party, and it played a part in Democratic victories in 1890 and 1892. The fiasco of the Wilson-Gorman Tariff, however, had wounded the reformist claims of Cleveland and his party. Controlling both houses of Congress, the Democrats in 1893/1894 had produced a measure that raised many rates, that split the party, and that President Cleveland had allowed to become law without his signature. From 1895 onward, the rise of the silver issue had muted the Democratic use of the tariff question. Still, the party remained substantially unified against Republican plans for a higher tariff.

McKinley asked in his tariff paragraphs that "especial attention" be given, when a bill was written, "to the reenactment and extension of the reciprocity principle" of the McKinley Tariff of 1890. The new president was the most prominent advocate of reciprocity in his party, and he had apparently already advanced a long distance in his evolution away from simple protectionism. As he told a British diplomat in November 1898, he thought "the time had come to reconsider the question of the Tariff" and that fresh circumstances had "rendered freer trade relations with countries outside the States expedient." These private comments would have struck many Republicans as heresy, and McKinley had to move carefully in pursuing reciprocity as a means toward a reduction of tariffs.[12]

After some general remarks about the need for patience in anticipating the return of prosperity, McKinley asked Congress for intelligent action to assist in the restoration of confidence and the revival of business. He then reminded his audience that Americans had met other emergencies with wisdom and courage, and he rested his faith on the nation's precious free institutions. Among the blessings of the society, he went on, were "free speech, a free press, free thought, free schools, the free and unmolested right of religious liberty and worship, and free and fair elections." It followed then that "lynchings must not be tolerated in a great and civilized country like the United States; courts, not mobs, must execute the penalties of the law."[13]

These general observations were the closest that McKinley came to a direct reference to the status of the nation's black citizens. The condition of the more than nine million Negroes at the end of the nineteenth century was desperate and deteriorating. In the South, segregation had gathered strength in the 1880s and was approaching completion as a social policy when McKinley took office. In *Plessy* v. *Ferguson* (1896) the Supreme Court approved a segregation law from Louisiana and, with it, the principle of "separate but equal." Lynchings averaged 188 per year during the 1890s, and nearly 70 percent of them involved black victims. While the South, which had the bulk of the Negro population, led the way in racial injustice, prejudice and bigotry were national phenomena.

When McKinley entered the White House, he had the positive support of black Americans. As governor of Ohio, he had denounced lynchings, and he had said to a Negro correspondent in 1894: "I sympathize with you in your aspirations for your race, and I join with you in the hope that the race problem will soon cease to cause any political or social misunderstanding." As McKinley began his presidential race, the *Washington Bee*, a black newspaper, predicted that he would "make a safe, sound President upon whom black and white may rely for an old time, rock ribbed, dyed in the wool Republican administration."[14]

By the standards of the late nineteenth century, William McKinley did not evince the blatant racism that some of his colleagues displayed. As president he made small private gestures that placed him "in favor of fair and impartial treatment of my colored fellow-citizens." Yet, at best he was paternalistic toward black people, and he used an ample amount of condescension. "Patience, moderation, self-control, knowledge, character," he said to the students at Tuskegee Institute in December 1898, "will surely win you victories and realize the best aspirations of your people."[15]

The president's attitude on the issue of race derived in large part from the higher policy value that he placed on sectional reconciliation between North and South. In his letter of acceptance he noted that "the feeling of distrust and hostility between the sections is everywhere vanishing, let us hope never to return." He returned to this theme in his inaugural: "The North and South no longer divide on the old lines, but on principles and policies; and in this fact surely every lover of the country can find cause for true felicitation." Inevitably black citizens received less attention in the process of promoting sectional harmony, and the McKinley administration did little to offset the worsening of America's race relations before 1901.[16]

After making his allusion to lynching and the preservation of law and order, McKinley contended that "immunity should be granted to none who violate the laws whether individuals, corporations or communities." He pledged to carry out the Republican platform's earlier declarations against "all combinations of capital, organized in trusts," and he assured his listeners that "this purpose will be steadily pursued, both by the enforcement of the laws now in existence and the recommendation and support of such new statutes as may be necessary to carry it into effect." A Democratic newspaper warned that McKinley's words "must be taken with many grains of salt," but the speech had referred to a problem which was, after the monetary issue, "the most absorbing one before the American people to-day."[17]

From 1895 onward, the nation recognized that the rate of corporate consolidation was accelerating. Each year through 1905 an average of three hundred companies merged into larger businesses; in 1899 a record twelve hundred firms were absorbed. Contributing to the proliferation of holding companies and trusts were the examples of successful combinations, a friendly legal environment in states like New Jersey and Delaware that facilitated mergers, the encouragement that judicial interpretation of the Sherman Act offered to horizontal combinations, and the emergence of a market for industrial securities. In 1896 the Democrats said that "the formation of trusts and pools" required "a stricter control by the Federal government," and the Republicans alluded disapprovingly but very briefly to "domestic monopoly."[18]

Just why McKinley included the reference to the trusts is not clear. The subject had not been of large concern to him in his pre-presidential career. "I have no sympathy with combinations, organized for this or any other purpose, to control the supply and thereby control prices," he said in 1888; but he added, "they are, however, in no wise related to the tariff, and the tariff is in no way responsible for them." Two years later he listed the Sherman Antitrust Act among the achievements of the Fifty-first Congress, because it struck at "trusts, or unlawful combinations of capital to raise prices according to their own sweet will, and extort undue profits from the mass of the people." After 1890 McKinley's references to the problem virtually disappeared. In the depression he sought to restore prosperity through business growth and attached less weight to the impact of consolidation. His campaign in 1896 concentrated on silver and the tariff.[19]

Preparing his inaugural address, McKinley considered more detailed language that balanced a pledge to enforce the antitrust law with comments about the economic value to the nation of large corporations. After deciding on the cautious wording that he delivered on March 4, 1897, the president did not devote much additional thought to the issue of monopoly until the latter years of his presidency. When the questions of the tariff and the trusts became linked, he sought to defuse the tariff through reciprocity. Foreign-policy problems from late 1897 onward probably precluded attention to antitrust policy, but the low level of interest in the White House and the Justice Department before early 1899 supported the opposition's judgment that McKinley's remarks were rhetorical.

Two days before the inauguration, Grover Cleveland vetoed a bill that would have used a literacy test as a means of restricting immigration into the United States. Cleveland called the provisions of the bill "unnecessarily harsh and oppressive" and concluded that "its defects in construction would cause vexation and its operation would result in harm to our citizens." McKinley, for his part, asserted on March 4 that "our naturalization and immigration laws should be further improved, to the constant promotion of a safer, a better, and a higher citizenship." Significant changes in the nature of immigration from abroad provided the context for these contrasting presidential statements. In 1896 the amount of what became known as the "new immigration"—newcomers from southern and eastern Europe—had equaled and then exceeded the "old immigration" from Great Britain and northern Europe.[20]

As these developments became apparent in the 1890s, a movement to limit immigration appeared. The Immigration Restriction League, the leading force in the campaign, was founded in Boston in 1894, and Senator Henry Cabot Lodge became its preeminent legislative spokesman. In the session of Congress that began in December 1895, Lodge pushed his bill to keep out adults who could not read forty words of English. The bill passed the House in 1896 by a wide margin but lingered in the Senate until after the presidential contest. It then was passed easily in December 1896, but the conference version, which was more restrictive than the original bill, encountered a growing coolness in the upper house. With nativist sentiment abating, the Senate did act favorably on the conference report in February 1897, but the majority was too small to override Cleveland's veto.

The Republicans were the advocates of immigration legislation. Their 1896 platform pledged that immigration laws would "be thoroughly enforced and so extended as to exclude from entrance to the United States those who can neither read nor write." McKinley's letter of acceptance agreed that immigration restriction was "of peculiar importance at this time, when our own laboring people are in such great distress." He favored legislation "as will secure the United States from invasion by the debased and criminal classes of the Old World," and his inaugural address reiterated that "against all who come here to make war upon" American institutions and laws, "our gates must be promptly and tightly closed." Returning prosperity, the successes of the nation in the Spanish-American War, and a revival of national confidence eased nativist apprehensions during McKinley's presidency. The flow of immigrants went on, and after the turn of the century, pressures for exclusion would resume.[21]

The final domestic question on which McKinley touched was civil-service reform. Urging that it must go on, he quickly added that "the changes should be real and genuine, not perfunctory, or prompted by a zeal in behalf of any party, simply because it happens to be in power." Throughout his political career, the president had spoken on behalf of the civil-service idea as it established itself after the passage of the Pendleton Act in 1883. "The merit system is here, and it is here to stay," he said in Congress in 1890; and his letter of acceptance, six years later, promised that the GOP would "take no backward step upon the question." Before leaving for Washington he assured a German-American spokesman, George Frederick William Holls, that "he believed in Civil Service Reform and would take no backward steps from any position taken by President Cleveland, even though this might be an advantage to Democrats in many instances."[22]

In 1897 the federal government employed about 150,000 people; during McKinley's tenure that number would rise to over 239,000. Included in the classified service were 87,000 positions for which merit and competitive examinations determined who received jobs. Less than a year earlier, on May 6, 1896, President Cleveland had added more than 31,000 positions to the merit system. Professional Republican politicians, for whom patronage was an important tool, hoped to persuade McKinley to reclassify some places so that they could remove Democrats whom Cleveland's order had safeguarded. Cabinet members found that the law's limitation on their ability to choose their subordinates was restrictive, and they also sought amendments in Cleveland's decision.

For advocates of the civil service, however, change had not gone far enough. They were suspicious of McKinley's sincerity; they had supported him in 1896 largely because of Bryan's monetary views and because of Democratic attacks on the merit system. Dorman B. Eaton, William Dudley Foulke, and Carl Schurz, who was president of the National Civil Service Reform League, arranged to have a committee in Washington to oversee the administration's record in this area. Placed between a party that was hungry for the spoils of office and a highly visible and vocal reform lobby, McKinley would not find it an easy matter to enforce the law "in the spirit in which it was enacted."[23]

Foreign policy occupied the next portion of McKinley's speech. From a call for a larger merchant marine he went on to discuss the basic premises of the nation's role in the world. Since his political career had focused on internal politics during an era when foreign policy was only a sporadic issue, McKinley began his presidency without a well-defined record on international questions. When Grover Cleveland's annual message in December 1895 challenged Great Britain on the Monroe Doctrine over Venezuela, McKinley told reporters that what the president had done "enforces with strength and vigor the position of the United States in its relations with European powers for more than seventy years. It is American in letter and spirit, and its calm and dispassionate manner upholds the honor of the Nation and insures its security." He said little on the Cuban problem in 1895 and 1896. A writer on foreign policy in April 1897 said about McKinley: "We know more about him than during the last forty years we have known of any other President up to the hour of his taking office," but politicians interested in diplomatic questions did not display a confidence about where McKinley stood. Henry Cabot Lodge visited him in Canton in December 1896, asked about Hawaii, Cuba, and other matters, and told Theodore Roosevelt, with a trace of surprise, "his whole attitude of mind struck me as serious, broad in view, and just what we all ought to desire."[24]

Given the purposeful record of the McKinley administration in world affairs and the close knowledge that he displayed of international problems, the apparent vagueness of his public utterances before entering the White House does not disclose the full extent of his preparation for conducting foreign policy. By its very nature, the tariff, while seemingly a domestic question, required a grasp of international commerce, and McKinley's wide reading in the statistics of world trade emerges from the speeches of his protectionist phase. As he shifted his emphasis to reciprocity after 1891, his outlook correspondingly broadened still more.

Throughout his presidency, men seemed to be surprised when McKinley showed himself well informed on international bimetallism, Hawaiian annexation, the tariff laws of the nation's trading partners, or the currents of world politics generally. They should not have been. As a congressman he understood the significance of Pearl Harbor to American interests in Hawaii. He argued for an improved and revitalized merchant marine, and he encouraged naval expansion while he was in office. He told Robert M. La Follette that he hoped "to round out his career by gaining for America a supremacy in the markets of the world . . . without weakening the protective system." By the end of his presidency, foreign observers were calling him "a man of will and perseverance" who wished to break down the foreign tariffs that excluded American exports.[25]

Shortly after becoming president, McKinley informed Carl Schurz: "You may be sure there will be no jingo nonsense under my administration."[26] Schurz naturally took this comment as a pledge against expansion, but McKinley probably meant that his foreign policy would pursue expansion in a decorous and methodical way. The Republican platform of 1896, which reflected McKinley's ideas, sought American control of Hawaii, a Nicaraguan canal, and purchase of the Danish West Indies. In office, McKinley moved promptly to achieve the annexation of Hawaii, to secure American rights to an isthmian canal, and to broaden the nation's foreign commerce. As an advocate of penetrating the overseas markets, William McKinley was aware of those in the United States who thought that a surplus of manufactured products would threaten social stability. Overproduction, if not resolved through expanded markets, could, in this view, both perpetuate the economic distress of the depression and threaten drastic change in the political order.

For his part, McKinley conceived of the spread of American trade as a positive, benevolent force. Convinced of the soundness of the nation's institutions and believing that citizens of the United States achieved morally defensible goals when they extended capitalism outside America's borders, he thought that measures to enhance his country's economic influence were in the nation's best interest.

The diffusion of United States commerce did not, in practice, prove as simple and beneficent as it was depicted to be in articles and campaign speeches. Experience in the Caribbean and in Asia revealed to men like McKinley the complexities of such an apparently straightforward goal as "the extension of trade to be followed by wider markets, better fields of employment, and easier conditions for the masses."[27] The record of American imperialism after 1898 would impel later historians to regard the language of McKinley and his generation as fatuous and hypocritical. Who could believe any longer that the pursuit of the national interest of the United States could be a positive good? McKinley did; and the shape of his foreign policy evolved from the premise that greater power and influence for his nation would also promote the betterment of mankind.

In setting forth his foreign-policy goals, McKinley began with a congenial subject. He asked Congress to give prompt attention to the merchant marine, because "few more important subjects so imperatively demand its intelligent consideration."[28] The merchant marine of the United States had been in decline since the Civil War. Before that conflict, of the total merchant tonnage leaving American ports, United States vessels carried more than 50 percent. Thirty-five years later the figure had dropped to 17 percent. Sporadic campaigns for improvement climaxed under Benjamin Harrison with the Merchant Marine Act of 1891, which extended a system of subsidizing the movement of mail on American ships. This measure proved inadequate, however; so sentiment within the GOP looked for a more ambitious approach to subsidies for shipping companies. The subject evoked powerful opposition from farmers in the South and West; therefore, the new administration, even after the difficulties encountered during the Spanish-American War, would not find it feasible to implement these proposals.

The more abstract statement of foreign-policy principles that followed the passage on the merchant marine offered little to those who sought a clear comment on the new president's position regarding Spain and Cuba. When he praised George Washington's policy of "non-interference with the affairs of foreign governments," he added that the United States had been "content to leave undisturbed" with friends and enemies "the settlement of their own domestic concerns." Since Spain believed that the uprising in Cuba was an internal matter, the latter clause was mildly encouraging.

Almost at once, however, the speech promised "a firm and dignified foreign policy" that would insist upon "the enforcement of the lawful rights of American citizens everywhere." What this meant for United States citizens and their property in Cuba was not revealed.[29]

After rejecting Secretary of State Sherman's maladroit paragraphs on Cuba, McKinley had considered a noncommital remark about holding off on a statement of his views. He also drafted a passage that expressed his sympathy for the Cuban people, noted that the nation had recognized the belligerency of earlier revolts against Spanish rule, and then concluded that a policy of nonintervention was best at that time. In the final version, he deleted these phrases. "We want no wars of conquest; we must avoid the temptation of territorial aggression," he said. "War should never be entered upon until every agency of peace has failed; peace is preferable to war in almost every contingency." McKinley's policy with regard to Cuba remained a blank as his administration commenced.[30]

One last subject received McKinley's attention in the foreign-policy realm. As an aftermath of the Venezuelan imbroglio, Secretary of State Richard Olney had concluded a general arbitration treaty with Great Britain in January 1897. McKinley, who had been a proponent of labor arbitration in railroad disputes during the 1880s, cited the precedents and process that had led up to the Olney-Pauncefote pact, and he gave the treaty his support. Despite this presidential push, the treaty, much amended, failed in the Senate on May 5, 1897. By implication McKinley had also sounded one of the important themes of his administration—better relations with Great Britain.

The last three paragraphs of the inaugural address contained only one substantive subject. The president announced that on March 15, 1897, he would call Congress into special session to deal with the tariff. With his grasp of the nuances of the legislative process, McKinley wanted to avoid the mistakes that Harrison and Cleveland had made in delaying consideration of the tariff until the regular session, which was almost ten months in the future. Interestingly, McKinley added language that was conciliatory toward congressional opinion: "I do not sympathize with the sentiment that Congress in session is dangerous to our general business interests." The members were "the agents of the people, and their presence at the seat of government in the execution of the sovereign will should not operate as an injury, but a benefit." It was such recognition of legislative feelings that was to make McKinley a successful manager of the lawmakers throughout his administration.[31]

At the end of the speech, he referred to sectional harmony, and then he repeated the part of the oath of office that called for faithful execution of the presidential office and pledged to "preserve, protect, and defend the Constitution of the United States." Calling on his countrymen to observe the oath in their respective spheres, so far as applicable, McKinley described his words as an "obligation I have reverently taken before the Lord Most High."[32] After one more sentence, which asked for the help of the people, his first inaugural address was over. It was a typical McKinley speech. When he wished to, he could make a direct appeal for action in phrases that left no doubt about his meaning. At other points he invoked vague and elastic language, which left him enough room for making tactical shifts. He would not carry out all parts of his inaugural program, but the address set forth the basic outlines of his policy during the first year.

McKinley reviewed the inaugural parade after the speech, and he attended the ball that evening. Mrs. McKinley managed to attend only part of the ceremonies before retiring to her quarters. On March 5 the president rose at 7:30, signed John Sherman's commission as secretary of state as his first official act, and then talked briefly with his private secretary. The callers soon arrived. The first was Senator Shelby M. Cullom of Illinois, a defeated rival in 1896 but now a lawmaker with patronage on his mind. The ceremonies were over, and now the ceaseless routine of office got under way. William McKinley's presidency had begun.

3

★★★★★

THE FIRST YEAR

By 1897 the concept of the "presidential honeymoon," in a simple form, had gained enough currency that reporters evaluated McKinley's early weeks in those terms. The president promoted this congenial spirit through a more relaxed and open atmosphere within the Executive Mansion. The sentry boxes and detectives of the Cleveland era disappeared, and visitors were welcomed rather than discouraged. Politicians of both parties received cordial invitations to return again to see their old colleague from the House. After two weeks a Pittsburgh newspaper reported: "Everybody seems to feel that a cloud has been lifted from over the White House. The feeling that the executive mansion was a place, exclusive, reserved, and guarded has disappeared."[1]

To the general public, McKinley also turned an accessible and affable face. He went around openly in Washington "as Grant used to do," and he resumed the regular public receptions that Cleveland had discontinued. McKinley relished these encounters with his fellow citizens. He told Henry L. Stoddard: "Everyone in that line has a smile and a cheery word. They bring no problems with them; only good will. I feel better after that contact." In these initial months the president traveled. He attended the dedication of Grant's Tomb in New York in late April, spoke at the unveiling of a statue of George Washington in Philadelphia on May 15, and returned on June 2 to the same city for the opening of the Philadelphia Museums. This accessibility was an important element in restoring popular interest in the presidency after Cleveland's policy of reclusiveness.[2]

Relations with the press, to which the president devoted quiet attention, also prospered. Three weeks after taking office he greeted the press corps in the East Room, when he proved that his "memory for faces and names" had not "been exaggerated." In contrast to Cleveland's coldness, the administration set up a long table on the second floor. There, newspaper reporters who had been assigned to cover the White House had seats. The president's secretary, John Addison Porter, circulated constantly, and at noon and 4:00 P.M. he spoke formally with the newsmen. Eventually, from these simple initiatives would evolve a White House press room and the presidential press conference.[3]

Public and private recognition of the legitimacy of the press's role further warmed McKinley's relations with the Fourth Estate. In March he attended a dinner at the Gridiron Club, a ritual that Harrison had started but Cleveland had disdained. The early wooing of the press climaxed in June, when, on a presidential junket, efforts were made to bar reporters from Commodore Vanderbilt's mansion. If the newsmen were excluded, the White House announced, the president would not enter the estate. Later in 1897, after the Christmas holidays, an official reception was scheduled for the press, "the first time in the history of the government when the newspaper correspondents have been included in the list to be socially received at the Whitehouse." The president did not give interviews and was not to be quoted directly, but reporters had greater access to him as president than students of his press relations have realized. McKinley's deft handling of the journalists in his first year not only reestablished the White House as a significant source of news, it also was a large step in the enhancing of presidential power.[4]

The chief executive worked in the president's offices, on the second floor of the White House. Using the Cabinet Room as his private office in order to escape those who waited to see him, he sat at the head of a long table in a swivel armchair with ink, stationery, and books at hand. Beneath a portrait of Thomas Jefferson, in front of a crowded bookcase, McKinley, in long coat, high collar, and bow tie, scratched out the handwriting that could, on an Executive Mansion card, obtain an appointment with a cabinet officer or gain a hearing for a job applicant. Though he deliberately wrote few personal letters, McKinley wanted all mail to be acknowledged and letters directed to the appropriate department. Presidential letters did go out to veterans' organizations, labor unions, and charitable or religious bodies for their annual conventions or special occasions. A never-ending pile of clippings, letters, and memoranda passed before a hard-working executive, who labored into the evening in the comfortable surroundings he had created.

Success for McKinley's executive style depended on the quality of his personal secretary. The president specified that the formal title should be secretary to the president, and he hoped that John Addison Porter would be the useful aide on whom he must rely. Porter, who had been an early supporter in Connecticut, was pompous and erratic. Soon he lost real power to George B. Cortelyou, a Cleveland holdover, who exercised impressive good sense and efficiency. Whether it involved arranging the tours that McKinley loved, working with the press, or acting as a presidential confidant, Cortelyou soon emerged as a prototype of the modern White House staff member.

McKinley and his cabinet met every Tuesday and Friday morning at eleven in the run-down and slightly shabby Cabinet Room. In their recollections, cabinet members said that the president usually began with a brief anecdote and then turned to business. "Sometimes he led discussion," said Charles Emory Smith; "quite as often he first elicited the views of his counselors." Whatever their experience with McKinley, the cabinet officers knew who ran the administration. When John Sherman resigned, he wrote that McKinley "evinced a disposition to assume all the functions of the members of his Cabinet and especially of the duties of the State Department." The outgoing secretary of state added that McKinley's "cabinet counsels were not a free exchange of opinions but rather the mandates of a paramount ruler." Publicly, the president had nothing but praise for his cabinet. Nonetheless, Cortelyou, whose opinions followed those of McKinley, wrote at the height of the Cuban crisis: "It is a good working Cabinet but in some respects not a strong one, not strong in the direction of being trustworthy advisors of the President in great emergencies."[5] The addition of John Hay in 1898 and of Elihu Root almost a year later did much to improve the quality of the official family.

The majority of visitors to the White House in these early weeks came to talk about patronage. With a tariff to enact, McKinley did not want to dole out the offices in advance of congressional action on his revenue program. The administration announced in mid March that the only appointments, other than diplomatic posts, that would be "made before the tariff legislation has been completed are domestic ones, which are absolutely necessary for the proper management of business under the new Administration." Two weeks after the inauguration, reports circulated that Republicans were finding the pace of appointments too slow and were complaining about it. McKinley would not, however, be hurried, and the allocation of places went on into 1898, when the administration allowed some Cleveland-era officers to finish their four-year terms.[6]

Far more important on the president's list of objectives was the passage of a new tariff law. During the winter and spring of 1897 a complex relationship emerged between the tariff and the other McKinley initiative, international bimetallism. Both subjects were well advanced by the time of the inauguration. When the lawmakers were summoned into special session on March 15, Chairman Nelson Dingley and the Ways and Means Committee offered a tariff bill that would produce more revenue while protecting American industry. Among its notable features were duties on wool, replacing those that the Wilson-Gorman Tariff of 1894 had repealed; higher rates on silks; the substitution of specific for ad valorem rates; and taxes on luxury items, particularly goods from France. To offset the importation of goods before the bill took effect, the House proposal had a clause making its rates retroactive to April 1, 1897. Reported out on March 18, the bill sailed through easily because of the iron control of Speaker Thomas B. Reed and the heavy Republican majority. The House passed Dingley's bill on March 31 by a vote of 205 to 122.

The tariff's fate in the Senate now became connected with the administration's diplomatic campaign for bimetallism. French officials watched the progress of the House bill with apprehension. It threatened such staples of Franco-American commerce as art works, champagne, china, and gloves; and it placed a limit of one hundred dollars on the amount of goods a traveler might bring in duty-free. The French also deplored the retroactive clause. Faced with higher rates in the Dingley measure, they looked to private lobbying to counter potential damage to their trade.

Republican interest in bimetallism provided France with its opportunity. By March 1897 the prospects for united action with France in order to persuade Great Britain seemed promising. Senator Edward O. Wolcott found in February that the French government would be mildly interested in bimetallism if American tariff concessions could be obtained. In London he discovered a greater receptivity to bimetallism than Britain's public position as the champion of the gold standard would have indicated. By now, the balance of power in the United States Senate and the political situation of the Republicans had created a climate in which French

40

entreaties could gain a positive response from the party's senatorial leadership.

Virtually all segments of the party wished to see prompt action on the tariff in order to restore business confidence, raise revenue for the treasury, and move to a protectionist posture. Yet the Republicans had only forty-two certain votes in the ninety-member Senate. Since there was unlimited debate, the bill could linger for months, vulnerable to amendments and the sorry fate of the Wilson-Gorman measure in 1894. As Dingley's bill was going through the House in March, France, Senator Wolcott, and the Republican leader in the Senate, Nelson Aldrich of Rhode Island, found that they had certain interests in common. The French wanted reductions; Wolcott wanted French cooperation with bimetallism; and Aldrich wanted the votes of Wolcott and his western silverite colleagues for a tariff bill.

The Senate Finance Committee, to whom the House bill was directed, created a subcommittee for the purpose of drafting its own version. During April, Senators Edward O. Wolcott, Nelson Aldrich, William Boyd Allison, and Orville H. Platt of Connecticut worked to produce "a conservative tariff bill which will be accepted by the country and remain on the statute books." With French memoranda in hand, Wolcott, Aldrich, and their associates put works of art back on the free list, removed the one-hundred-dollar limit on tourist imports, and lowered rates on French luxury products. "Our Senate Committee," Wolcott wrote, "has cut down the tariff bill materially on every hand, and the measure is a very different one from the Dingley Bill as it was reported from the House."[7]

In mid April, McKinley appointed Wolcott, a Boston businessman named Charles J. Paine, and former vice-president Adlai E. Stevenson to the bimetallic commission to arrange for an international monetary conference with the European countries. Because of the concessions in the Senate bill, the French were more forthcoming. Their ambassador in Washington believed that Wolcott's "serious pledges of good will" merited a favorable response. A joint Franco-American effort on bimetallism was now possible, though the tariff understanding on which it rested was fragile. The Finance Committee had to guide its bill through the Senate and the inevitable conference committee. Since Wolcott's deal with the French was an oral one and since Wolcott would be out of the country, the reductions that France had gained would be vulnerable.[8]

McKinley was aware of these negotiations; therefore, from late April onward, he urged lawmakers who visited the White House to push forward with the tariff bill. Procedural delays, however, put off the formal introduction of the Senate Finance Committee's bill until the end of May. Meanwhile, critics assailed the sugar schedule as being too generous to the Sugar Trust; westerners attacked the lower rates on wool and woolens; and eastern senators complained about the duty that the committee proposed to place on cattle hides. Dingley argued that concessions to the French would mean a loss of revenues. Republican displeasure emerged openly on May 24, the night before Aldrich presented the committee bill, when party senators caucused. The gathering agreed to broaden the caucus's power to offer individual amendments, and it added members to the Republican contingent on the Finance Committee.[9]

Aldrich offered his version on May 25 with the observation that "in the readjustment of rates suggested the committee have tried in every instance to make them sufficiently protective to domestic interests without being prohibitive."[10] But the combined pressures from the Republicans, who desired more rapid action on the bill, and from local interests, which wanted more protection, pushed against the committee's proposals and in the direction of higher rates. On the question of the sugar schedule, the caucus lowered the rates of June 8, which favored the Sugar Trust, and decided, in the process, to make the decisions of the caucus binding on the participants in it. Two days later, Aldrich fell ill and left the struggle for a month. His replacement was the cautious, irresolute William Boyd Allison. By the middle of the month the caucus was in command, and the Wolcott understanding with the French suffered as a result.

As western wool growers and midwestern woolen manufacturers made their influence felt, rates on wool and woolens moved back toward what the House had proposed. Duties on silks rose because of pressure from northeastern senators. The rates on gloves, olive oil, and works of art went up again, and the one-hundred-dollar limit on tourist purchases reappeared. A French diplomat wrote his superiors on July 2: "Each public meeting of the Senate this week has been a disappointment for me."[11]

To ease this unhappiness, Senate friends of international bimetallism worked on tariff reciprocity, hoping that a mechanism for negotiating future trade concessions would placate France. The Senate reciprocity section, as passed on July 2, authorized the president to make treaties that would specify a reduction of duties up to 20 percent of the Dingley rate. Last-minute efforts to aid the French on specific products proved to be futile, and the Senate bill passed on July 7 by a vote of 38 to 28. Maintenance of the remnants of the Wolcott agreement now depended on the conference committee.

The deliberations of that body did little to help France or international bimetallists. The House, more protectionist than the Senate in this case, insisted on its sugar schedule and kept the high rates on wool, silks, and art works. Dingley secured the retention of the one-hundred-dollar limit for travelers. Concessions to the Senate, as in the case of the duty on cattle hides, raised rates still more. Aside from some minor reductions on wines, gloves, ceramics, and preserves and the ultimate disappearance of the retroactive clause, the French had to be content with a revamped reciprocity section.

To strike an acceptable balance between the House and the Senate, the conferees combined two approaches. Section 3 of the final bill, which set forth the products on which the president might lower duties in return for concessions to the United States, was directed at France. Section 4 made a general grant of authority to the president to conclude tariff treaties in the two years after passage of the bill. He could negotiate reductions up to 20 percent, move products of the other country to the free list, or retain its products on the free list. Since the treaties would be subject to both Senate and House approval, these sections left the French unimpressed. They would, said one Frenchman, lead to nothing.[12]

Dingley's bill came out of conference on July 19 and rapidly cleared both houses. McKinley signed the measure on July 24, 1897. Without a dependable majority in the Senate, the Republicans had enacted a tariff bill with relative speed and a minimum of party friction. Protectionists praised the new law, and when prosperity returned in the second half of 1897, the Dingley Act, in the minds of high-tariff Republicans, became irrevocably associated with the maintenance of economic health. In its final form the law was far from the moderate measure that the Wolcott-Aldrich initiative had envisioned. Pressure from the more protectionist House, especially in the conference committee, and the absence of a reliable Republican coalition in the Senate, which gave significant power to small groups like the western wool men or the eastern advocates of silk, helped to produce this result.

Although the administration did not lobby directly for the tariff, McKinley endeavored to guide the Republicans toward a bill that the party could tolerate. He pushed for prompt action, encouraged Wolcott's proposals, and consulted with the House conferees about French products. If he thought the final bill too extreme in its schedules, as he probably did, he said nothing publicly; but he assured French diplomats that the United States wanted to move ahead with reciprocity. For McKinley the specific rates in the Dingley Act were less important than the possibility for negotiating reductions in the future, which the reciprocity clauses offered.

After Congress adjourned, McKinley escaped the heat of Washington by going to Lake Champlain. While he was gone, the administration and France commenced tentative discussions about reciprocity under Section 3 of the new law. With prolonged negotiations likely, the State Department was heavily pressed by the Cuban problem. To assist in the talks, McKinley asked John A. Kasson, an Iowan who was "an old friend of the system of reciprocity," to be reciprocity commissioner for the department in early October. Announcing the appointment, newspapers observed that "the interest of the President in reciprocity is especially keen."[13] McKinley's willingness to draw on the diplomatic expertise of men like Kasson as a means of supplementing the formal bureaucracy would be one of the characteristic devices of his presidency.

Kasson and the French ambassador pursued their discussions from October 1897 until they reached an agreement on May 31, 1898. There were numerous obstacles. The French Parliament seemed determined to raise tariff rates on American hog and pork products, as well as cottonseed oil, much to the unhappiness of southern and western farmers. The United States in turn wanted France to lift restrictions on the importation of American cattle. Besides these issues, French sympathy for Spain caused Franco-American relations to deteriorate in early 1898, and the need for revenue to finance the approaching war led congressional leaders to question reciprocal reductions in tariffs. Extended bargaining, however, produced an accord in which France allowed the minimum tariff rates to be imposed on American canned meats, fruits, and lumber products, and the United States granted reductions on French wines, brandies, and works of art. According to the French, McKinley, who displayed "much satisfaction" at the favorable outcome, had "personally guided M. Kasson in the course of these negotiations." Reciprocity was now established as an important economic policy of the United States, and broader departures in this area with other nations would mark 1898 and 1899.[14]

The administration encountered failure in the fall of 1897 in its second major diplomatic initiative, international bimetallism. For some months in the summer it appeared that the Wolcott Commission might achieve tangible results. The envoys arrived in France on May 16, and two weeks later they presented to the government their proposals for a wider use of the white metal. By no means unanimous behind bimetallism, the French still hoped to secure American tariff concessions; and they reached an understanding with Wolcott and his associates in mid June. The two countries agreed to open their mints to free coinage of silver at a ratio of 15½ to 1 with gold, once other nations, especially Britain and Germany, had taken favorable actions to help silver. The United States Congress and the French Parliament would also have to approve the program before it would go into effect.[15]

Armed with French support the commissioners for bimetallism arrived in Great Britain in early July. Although the French ambassador was absent, they submitted their proposals to the prime minister, Lord Salisbury, on July 12, 1897. The Americans asked the British to reopen the mints of India, which had been closed since 1893, to the coinage of silver; requested that the Bank of England hold one-fifth of its bullion reserves in silver; and urged Britain to take a variety of other steps to encourage more reliance on silver in the Empire. In return, the United States and France would open their mints to free coinage at the 15½ to 1 ratio. Three days later, this time with the French ambassador present, the envoys repeated their ideas, and Wolcott was asked to submit a formal résumé of the Franco-American arrangement.

The British government at first looked favorably on Wolcott's requests. The world price of silver was falling rapidly during these months, and it would be advantageous to India to reopen its mints at a ratio of 15½ to 1 if the United States and France did the same. There would be a greater stability in the exchange value of the rupee, and the decline in the price of silver would be halted and perhaps reversed. The British also appear to have been impressed with Wolcott's arguments that action on bimetallism was necessary in order to avert a Bryan victory in 1900. The seriousness with which the bimetallic ideas were discussed in the Salisbury government also suggests that the seeds of an Anglo-American rapprochement were already germinating in 1897.

As the British Cabinet prepared to go forward with the reopening of the Indian mints to silver in late July, one of its members offered "the chance suggestion that the Indian Government should be consulted" before the final action was taken. A telegram to India produced an unfavorable response. This opposition in India impelled the cabinet to initiate a formal review of the Franco-American proposal. On August 5, 1897, Wolcott was told that the process "must be somewhat prolonged" and that the Americans could not expect an answer before October.[16]

Wolcott and Hay at first believed that the delay would not be harmful, but that judgment was soon corrected. The possibility that Great Britain would give even a slight encouragement to bimetallism aroused the advocates of gold on both sides of the Atlantic to public outcries. When the Bank of England announced in mid September that it would hold one-fifth of its note values in silver once an agreement had been reached, the Gold Standard Defence Association rushed to protest. In the United States, Secretary of the Treasury Gage and other officials of his department made disparaging public references to bimetallism to the dismay of its senatorial adherents. The world price of silver fell, while the price of wheat rose. Finally, the opponents of bimetallism portrayed McKinley's call for a commission to study the monetary and banking system as a rejection of international bimetallism.

The fatal obstacle remained the opposition of the Indian government. In mid September, British officials in India contended that "practically the whole risk of disaster from failure would fall on India alone" and recommended that the Franco-American ideas be disapproved. Once the report from the Indian government had reached London, it compelled the British government to reject the American proposals. On October 19 the United States received the official British rejection of the bimetallic requests. A disappointed Wolcott made his way home. The failure of his mission marked the end of international bimetallism as a serious policy issue in world financial diplomacy. The discovery of large gold supplies in the Yukon and South Africa would appear to provide monetary inflation within the framework of the gold standard. By 1898 the McKinley administration, persuaded that bimetallism was dead, would endorse legislation to confirm America's adherence to gold.[17]

Contemporary critics suggested at once that the Wolcott mission was a sham. The documents that survive do not support this allegation. In a letter to John Hay, written when bimetallism seemed about to succeed, McKinley described it as one "of the administration's greatest efforts," and he gave close attention to the mission's fortunes. By mid September, however, he recognized that "recent events had been working strongly against" advocates of bimetallism, and he took care not to identify his government too closely with the crippled initiative.[18] What is most striking about the whole episode is the prospect, had the British been favorably disposed on India, that the McKinley administration might have proposed to the Congress that some kind of free-silver policy be adopted in compliance with the Wolcott agreements. All the countries involved had different conceptions of what they had assented to, and it may have been fortunate for McKinley that the Indian government proved recalcitrant. That the administration had gotten to the brink of difficult decisions over the implementation of bimetallism and was disappointed over the mission's collapse confirms the seriousness of this important policy campaign during McKinley's first year. It also underlined the new president's commitment to the exercise of executive authority in the shaping of international economic policy.

On the domestic side of the money issue, the administration made some preliminary moves in 1897 and early 1898, but the strength of the silver supporters in the Senate foreclosed serious legislative action. The proposal for a monetary commission, which McKinley made in his inaugural address, did not reappear until the end of the special session. On July 24, 1897, he urged Congress to create a commission to recommend changes in the nation's banking system. The House passed a bill easily, but the Senate sent the measure to the Finance Committee and then adjourned. There were complaints that the message was only a gesture; nevertheless, the Senate was not able to consider this issue in the brief time left after the end of the tariff struggle.

The circumstances that doomed bimetallism in the second half of 1897 pushed the administration toward a more direct affirmation of the gold standard and toward a public airing of the various ideas on banking reform then current. As the Wolcott commission faltered and the price of silver fell, McKinley announced in late October that "remembering our recent panic and financial experience, we should strengthen the weak places in our financial system and remove it forever from ambiguity and doubt." His annual message in December advocated that notes of the United States, redeemable in gold, should be "only paid out in exchange for gold," and he called for a larger gold reserve in the treasury. Further indications of how far McKinley had moved away from international bimetallism and toward the gold standard appeared when he addressed the banquet of the National Association of Manufacturers on January 27, 1898: "It will not suffice for citizens nowadays to say simply that they are in favor of sound money. The people's purpose must be given the vitality of public law."[19] The difficulties in the way of this goal remained. That same month a majority of the Senate supported a resolution, which Henry M. Teller of Colorado introduced, stating that all United States bonds were payable in gold or silver. Further efforts on behalf of the gold standard would have to await the results of the fall elections.

In foreign policy, during 1897 the administration addressed the substantive issues with Great Britain that blocked better relations between the two countries. Eager to establish an ascendancy in the Caribbean, the United States wanted to remove the obstacle that the Clayton-Bulwer Treaty of 1850 posed for an American canal in Central America. To achieve that purpose required resolution of disputes over such disparate questions as fur seals in the Bering Sea, fisheries in Newfoundland, and, most sensitive of all, the Alaskan boundary with Canada. Fur seals became the first matter of discussion, and talks continued with the British, the Canadians, the Russians, and the Japanese throughout 1897. The Alaskan problem also grew in importance with the discovery of gold in the Yukon and the resulting flow of population into the disputed area. American negotiators proposed a joint high commission of Canadian and United States representatives in early 1898. Several months later, in an interview with the British ambassador, McKinley suggested that the commission be promptly created and that all outstanding issues be left to its deliberations. By August 1898 the work of the commission had begun. Many difficulties remained ahead in Anglo-American relations, but the essential direction of McKinley's policy had been established.

The persistent question of the annexation of Hawaii became a significant component of McKinley's diplomatic activity in the Pacific. Throughout his first year the president pushed hard for United States acquisition of the islands in a manner that foreshadowed future uses of his executive leadership. Republican support for annexation of Hawaii was long-standing. After a revolution in Hawaii in 1893, the lame-duck Harrison administration sent the Senate a treaty of annexation. Grover Cleveland disapproved of American involvement in the revolt, probed its circumstances, and withdrew the pact. In 1896 the Republican platform asserted that the United States should control the islands and prevent foreign interference. The friends of annexation, both on the islands and among American expansionists, looked expectantly to McKinley for positive action. Until he was inaugurated he was characteristically reticent. "Of course I have my ideas about Hawaii," he told representatives from Hawaii in November 1896, "but consider that it is best at the present time not to make known what my policy is."[20]

Once in office, McKinley pursued a course that, as it would so often, revealed his determination to add Hawaii to the territory of the United States. On March 11 he discussed with John W. Foster, Harrison's secretary of state, and Senator William P. Frye of Maine the merits of pursuing annexation either by treaty or by joint congressional resolution. Two weeks later, McKinley informed another visiting Hawaiian delegation that once the tariff problem had been resolved, annexation would receive his early attention. On April 3 Hawaii's minister officially asked the United States to open talks about a treaty. With the tariff in the hands of Congress, office seekers besieging the White House, and Secretary Sherman's liabilities as a cabinet officer becoming apparent, the administration did little about Hawaii for several months.

By June, however, events brought the issue up in a critical way. Because of the influx of laborers from Japan, the Hawaiian government had refused in March to admit the latest contingent of immigrants. The Japanese sent one of their naval vessels in May, and their minister gave out strident interviews that suggested the possibility of more drastic action. The status of the sugar schedule of the tariff bill also influenced the administration's timing. The Republican senatorial caucus seemed ready to discard the reciprocity treaty of 1875 and to bar Hawaiian sugar from the American market. It is not clear whether the treaty was hastily drafted to forestall this legislative action or whether the State Department used a text that John W. Foster had prepared in May. After a cabinet meeting, a presidential message was sent to the Senate on June 16. Annexation, McKinley said, "despite successive denials and postponements, has been merely a question of time," and, he concluded, it was "not a change. It is a consummation."[21]

There was no hope that the Senate would act on the treaty at the special session. Meanwhile, the Japanese protested that "the maintenance of the status quo of Hawaii is essential to the good understanding of the Powers that have interests in the Pacific." The administration took naval precautions against possible Japanese action in the summer of 1897, and officials such as Theodore Roosevelt remarked publicly that the nation did not have to ask other powers about acquiring territory. McKinley told George Frisbie Hoar: "If something be not done, there will be before long another Revolution, and Japan will get control." Once the initial apprehension about Japan had eased, the problem ebbed away in diplomatic correspondence, and the Japanese eventually withdrew their protest in December 1897.[22]

McKinley's problem, when Congress reconvened in December,

was finding a two-thirds majority for the treaty. Three Republicans opposed annexation, but the bulk of the opposition came from the Democrats, especially southerners, who disliked the racial mix of Hawaii's people. Beet-sugar interests, fearful of Hawaiian sugar, also worked against the pact. McKinley wanted the treaty to be acted on promptly. He worked on senators on behalf of approval, and Henry Cabot Lodge decided in early January 1898 that "annexation has been gaining steadily since Congress met, and we are near now the necessary two thirds." Lodge was too optimistic. The annexation forces were two to three votes short of two-thirds as January began, and despite McKinley's exertions, the balance remained stable through February and into March. By the middle of that month, treaty advocates conceded that they could not obtain a two-thirds majority. With the Cuban crisis impending, it was decided to shift to a joint resolution, which required only a simple majority, once pending legislation and troubles with Spain had been resolved.[23]

The Hawaiian campaign disclosed McKinley's willingness to exercise presidential power on behalf of his legislative program. So persistent was he that opposition such as the *Nation* wondered why he was "so busy and earnest" about Hawaii. The president, reported Sanford B. Dole, president of the islands, "seems to have heart and soul in the annexation treaty." McKinley's comment to George B. Cortelyou revealed his priorities in June 1898: "We need Hawaii just as much and a good deal more than we did California. It is manifest destiny." Once the Cuban crisis had been faced, the president would return to the Hawaiian issue and renew a campaign that represented one of his early attempts to woo Congress on behalf of his foreign-policy objectives.[24]

By the end of 1897 McKinley had taken the direction of diplomacy into his own hands. Secretary Sherman showed his growing mental incapacity in several unfortunate interviews on sensitive topics. Deaf and forgetful, the secretary became an embarrassment to the administration, and the running of his department passed to William R. Day. Clearly, Sherman would have to go, but it was not easy to find the right time as war with Spain approached.

Amid the diplomatic beginnings and problems of the first year, patronage and its effect on the Republican party claimed McKinley's continuing attention. Allocating the offices was part of McKinley's pursuit of the more important purpose of confirming the political dominance of the GOP. That campaign achieved only partial results through the off-year state elections of 1897. Before the war in

Cuba thrust new issues into national politics, Republicans looked forward anxiously to the congressional elections in anticipation of the losses that the party in power could expect two years after a victory in the presidential race.

Despite the impact of the civil-service law, the patronage system in 1897 still possessed much of the political significance it had enjoyed since the days of Andrew Jackson. The network of foreign and domestic appointees offered the president an effective means of molding partisan support, but could, if mishandled in the fashion of Grover Cleveland, rapidly erode party morale. McKinley devoted long hours to the spoils, in part because of the number of office seekers who swamped the administration after March 4. Because the long years that he had spent traveling on party affairs had made him aware of the web of reciprocal relationships that held the GOP together, he wanted the tedious task of making appointments to be a positive element in the success of his administration.

Certain broad principles governed McKinley's conduct in the patronage field. Republicans who had held office under earlier Republican presidents received few places. Those who had worked for Benjamin Harrison were especially excluded, thus reflecting the coolness between the former president and McKinley. Silver Republicans who had bolted in 1896 obtained nothing, but a loyal westerner like Senator Wolcott was allowed to dominate patronage in his state, Colorado. Within the practical limits of party regularity, early supporters of McKinley's nomination could look for presidential favor. Most important, of course, was his use of patronage to enhance his power in Congress. Republican senators and congressmen usually gained a favorable verdict on their requests.

The press, the public, and many politicians believed that Senator Hanna was the dominant force in the administration's decisions regarding patronage. In Ohio the senator did determine the majority of the selections. Senator Foraker was not ostracized, but Hanna could prevent the appointment of men whom he found offensive. For other northern and western states, Hanna had to defer, in most cases, to his Republican colleagues. Hanna had much more to say about offices in the South, where the shadow party organizations looked to the senator as a way of influencing the president. He and McKinley formalized the system of "referees," composed of defeated party candidates and the Republican national committee member, to advise on southern patronage. These activities helped to shape the opinion that "more than any other single man, with the exception of the President himself, Mr. Hanna was

51

responsible for the operation of that most vital of party functions, the distribution of patronage."[25]

For all this reputation of being McKinley's Warwick, Hanna's power depended on influence that the president wished for him to have. In the early months of the administration, McKinley's old friend Joseph P. Smith, who had once been state librarian of Ohio and now was director of the Bureau of American Republics, shared with Hanna the burden of making patronage choices. Until Smith died in January 1898, his impact may have equaled that of the senator. In such states as Missouri, Colorado, and Kansas, Hanna never built up, or tried to build up, a personal organization that would be loyal to him; and his support in the South would not long outlast McKinley's death in 1901. Joseph L. Bristow, who was closely involved with patronage as fourth assistant postmaster general, wrote some years later that McKinley "gave Hanna's requests great consideration and had confidence in the clearness of his opinions, but in the end he always followed his own judgment."[26]

McKinley met the waves of applicants with his customary urbane courtesy, and his genial ability to refuse requests without being offensive became a Washington byword. Sometimes, however, his patience would run out, and he would tell Cortelyou about his ire at men who were overly impressed with their own importance. When one spokesman protested too much and asked McKinley why he would not make a certain appointment, the answer came: "Did it ever occur to you that in matters of this kind the President does not have to give his reasons?"[27]

While he gave proper weight to the sensibilities of Republican lawmakers in the patronage process, McKinley took advantage of his power to make numerous appointments of friends and political associates. William McKinley Osborne, a cousin and close confidant, became consul general in London; James K. Gowdy was named to a similar post in Paris; and other allies of the chief executive appeared in choice spots in the government service. "The President seems bent upon looking out for his personal friends first," noted the *New York Tribune* reporter at the White House; "and precious little will be left for the rest, it seems to me." McKinley, like Theodore Roosevelt after him, was careful, however, not to place men in jobs that were beyond their abilities. Significant positions were confined to those, such as John Hay, who not only were friends but also were genuinely talented.[28]

In at least two important states, McKinley followed patronage policies that quietly managed to discipline party leaders who had opposed him in 1896 and simultaneously shifted the balance of power in state politics. Senator Shelby M. Cullom of Illinois, who had been bested for the nomination and was bitter, wrote letters in which he said that McKinley was "hunting for men who are utterly and entirely subservient to him, and a man who has any independence of character has not much show if he knows him to be such." One letter that reached McKinley produced a hot exchange between the two men, but then at least an apparent reconciliation. Within the complicated politics of Illinois, the administration also favored the ambitions of Charles G. Dawes and men who had been linked to McKinley's campaign.[29]

Senator Thomas C. Platt of New York also experienced a series of quiet but telling rebuffs over patronage. After naming Cornelius N. Bliss to the Interior Department portfolio, McKinley then put Horace Porter in as ambassador to France, Andrew D. White of Cornell as ambassador to Germany, Stewart Woodford as minister to Spain, and, in 1898, Joseph Hodges Choate as ambassador in London. Theodore Roosevelt's selection for the Navy Department was another reverse for Platt. The president did not give Whitelaw Reid anything more than temporary diplomatic assignments in 1897 and 1898. Greater honors would have certainly alienated Platt, who detested Reid. Platt did have a decisive voice in choosing the postmaster for New York City, the collector of the port, and other once powerful positions that civil service had weakened. By 1899, however, a journalist close to the New York situation commented: "One by one the prominent Republicans of the Union League Club— formerly Senator Platt's most determined opponents—have been accorded high office either on Mr. Platt's personal recommendations or with his gracious consent."[30]

Civil-service reformers monitored McKinley's patronage actions as part of their plan to keep "a close watch upon all that was done" and to criticize "with impartiality any proved shortcomings of the administration." Cabinet officers were unhappy because the orders of President Cleveland prevented them from selecting their aides without going through the Civil Service Commission. Republican politicians, meanwhile, attacked the system as being restrictive and unfair. "The people of my State," said Senator Cullom, "are for wiping out the civil service law"; and action to modify the law seemed likely at the regular session of Congress.[31]

The president agreed with many of the complaints of his cabinet, but he did not share the vituperative assessments of Cullom, Senator Hanna, and Congressman Charles Grosvenor. Drastic changes that aroused the opposition of Carl Schurz and his vocal colleagues would have been suicidal during the first year. Instead, on July 24, 1897, McKinley ordered that the removal process be made more open, with written notice and just cause required. "President McKinley has strengthened the civil service law instead of weakening it," said a Republican editor, who predicted that doubts about his "fidelity to civil service reform must vanish now." Reformers were not so easily satisfied. In October 1897 Schurz asked McKinley to say "a strong word in favor of the merit system" in his annual message, which the president did. Later in December, Schurz once again complained of violations of the July 1897 removal order and renewed his recommendations that cabinet officials make a public affirmation of their loyalty to the civil service. The running war between partisans and reformers finished its first phase in 1897; but future battles lay ahead.[32]

As the president returned from his summer vacation, the onset of the 1897 elections found some Republicans in an optimistic mood. Municipal elections in the spring revealed Democratic gains, but the return of prosperity renewed the confidence of the GOP. In New York and Ohio the situation was less promising. Running for a full term, Hanna confronted determined Democratic opposition and covert Republican disaffection. The main contest in the Empire State involved the New York mayoralty race, in which the reformer Seth Low and the choice of the regulars and Platt, Benjamin F. Tracy, opposed the hand-picked candidate of Tammany Hall, the Democratic machine.

Both anti-Tammany factions looked to McKinley for assistance. In mid September the president wrote privately: "I am not interfering in the local politics of New York City. I have enough burdens of my own." When Secretary Bliss came out for Tracy in October, Low's supporters were reassured that McKinley "was taking no stand one way or the other in the New York contest." A *Tribune* reporter close to the White House wrote Whitelaw Reid, saying that "each side in the contest, therefore, may claim him as its devoted adherent, without fear of contradiction at first hand." In November the divided Republican-reform vote gave the election to the Democrats, and Low's supporters grumbled that McKinley had not done enough for their candidate.[33]

The 1897 elections were a setback for the Republicans generally. Party candidates lost in Nebraska, New Jersey, New York, and Kansas; and the GOP vote fell off in Ohio and Pennsylvania. The defeat for reelection of Democratic senator Arthur Pue Gorman in Maryland was only partial consolation for the downturn in Republican fortunes since November 1896. McKinley told a reporter that he was well pleased with the outcome, but the *New York Tribune* noted that "Republican majorities of a year ago have been reduced or extinguished in most of the States voting." How the party would fare in 1898 continued to be an open question.[34]

The voting in November did not resolve Senator Hanna's difficulties in Ohio. To counter the vigorous Democratic campaign, the Republican organization and the administration sent in national figures such as Theodore Roosevelt on Hanna's behalf. McKinley even asked Carl Schurz, without success, to make a speech for "the cause of sound money" and to help elect "an honest and capable man." Initial returns indicated a Republican victory, and the president wrote to his friend: "How the election illustrates the need of every vote. I do hope there will be nothing happen to change the result."[35]

Anti-Hanna Republicans wanted to overturn the result, and within a week, reports indicated that "Hanna is going to have a rocky road to travel to get back to the Senate." For the next two months, McKinley, "very much concerned" about Hanna's fate, watched events in Ohio carefully. When the vote of one legislator seemed likely to be decisive, the president prepared a letter to the lawmaker, warning that a vote against Hanna "will inflict upon the Republican Party of Ohio an injury which it will require long years to heal." McKinley wrote to Hanna: "I have prepared the letter because I want no failure on my part to result in your defeat, which I would regard as a great calamity." Hanna decided not to deliver the letter, which did not prove necessary in order to secure the narrow victory that came on January 11, 1898.[36]

On March 3, 1898, the Republican Club of the 28th Assembly District in New York gave a "Grand Ball . . . in commemoration of the first year of Republican National supremacy." At the end of McKinley's first twelve months, other evaluations, from less friendly sources, appeared. "With every desire to be fair," said the *New York World*, "it must be admitted that his Administration this far has been mediocre and unsatisfying."[37] Between these partisan assessments lay a measured record of accomplishments and failures. The Dingley Tariff had been passed without the disasters that had wounded Harrison and Cleveland; reciprocity was under way; and the administration had given bimetallism an honest chance to succeed before turning to affirm the gold standard. Among Republicans there had been reasonable amity in the allocation of patronage, and the losses of the 1897 elections were bearable. In foreign policy, negotiations with the British and Hawaiian annexation were stalled, but the president had in hand procedures that could restore the impetus of these expansionist programs.

The outlines of McKinley's presidential style had also emerged during this year of executive apprenticeship. Improved relations with the press demonstrated that he understood how modern methods of communication could serve as a weapon of governmental leadership. Extensive travel had personalized the presidency and familiarized the electorate with the man in the White House. Six months into his term, McKinley had attained a level of personal popularity that gave him a powerful lever in public controversies. Wooing Congress on one level, McKinley had set in motion forces that would give him an ascendancy over the legislative branch as his term progressed. Within the executive branch he had tested subordinates. Some, such as Secretary of State Sherman, were quietly superseded, and others were marked for lesser jobs or eventual replacement. Though he lacked the bureaucratizing impulse of Theodore Roosevelt and a younger generation, McKinley emphasized formal procedures in the conduct of domestic and foreign policy that enhanced the role and power of the federal government. Imperceptibly but inexorably, the power of the presidency expanded under McKinley's deft direction. He left no overt statement that he intended to restore the prestige and authority of his office, but his actions during his first year reveal a president with an instinct for power and a clear purpose of augmenting it.

McKinley would need all the assets that he had painstakingly amassed in 1897. Behind the varied diplomatic activity of the new administration lay the recurrent issue of Cuba and its effect on the nation's relations with Spain. The problem did not erupt into a crisis during these months of writing a tariff act, negotiating over bimetallism, and making decisions with regard to patronage; so the public was unaware of the downward spiral of Spanish-American relations. Inside the government the Cuban question continued to be a source of worry. "There can be no doubt that the Administration feels extremely anxious on this point," wrote George Frederick William Holls after a visit with the president in September 1897, "and in fact sees hardly any escape from a war within a comparatively short time."[38] As the McKinley administration entered its second year in March 1898, the prospects for a war with Spain were increasing daily. Despite elaborate diplomatic maneuvers from the inauguration onward, the gap between the two nations was unbridgeable. McKinley stood on the edge of a conflict that would give his presidency its special character and would fix his historical reputation.

4

★★★★★

"THE WAR IN CUBA MUST STOP"

Because of its expansionist consequences, the Spanish-American War has become one of the most studied and criticized conflicts in the history of the United States. At the center of the controversy stands William McKinley. His actions and policies toward Spain and Cuba from March 1897 to April 1898 have received close attention and, since the First World War, almost uniform censure. That McKinley gave in to jingoist pressure from a hysterical press and an overheated public and therefore accepted war with a nation that had capitulated to American demands has become a staple of textbook accounts of his presidency.

During the 1960s an alternative hypothesis evolved. Departing from the usual picture of a feckless leader, some scholars have depicted a Machiavellian and cunning executive, bent on expansion and heedless of the interests of Cubans and Filipinos, whom Americans believed they were assisting. Sensitive to every wish of the business community, McKinley went to war when conditions were right for an economic imperialism that relied on overseas markets.

Neither of these portrayals does justice to the complexity of the diplomatic problems that Spain and the United States encountered over Cuba between 1895 and 1898, and neither captures how McKinley sought, in the end unsuccessfully, to discover a way out of the impasse in which both nations found themselves. What is significant is not that war came. The divergent perceptions of Spanish and American national interests made conflict likely, once revolution began in Cuba in 1895. McKinley's ability to postpone war for as long as he did and to control the terms on which the United States commenced hostilities indicates that his presidential leadership during the coming of war was more courageous and principled than his critics have realized.

General agreement exists about the conditions in Spain, Cuba, and the United States that created a context for conflict. On February 24, 1895, Cuban insurgents started a revolt against Spanish rule. The roots of the uprising went back to the unsuccessful rebellion of 1868 to 1878, a war that had stopped but whose underlying causes persisted. To long-term unhappiness with the arbitrary, inept, and corrupt supremacy of Spain was added economic distress in 1894. Duties imposed on Cuban sugar by the Wilson-Gorman Tariff crippled the island's principal industry. Leaders of the independence movement, which had been active since the early 1890s, decided in late 1894: "We must force the situation—precipitate the events." Though not all the elements of their plans were in place, fighting broke out in late February 1895.[1]

To win the war the Cubans followed a strategy that made the most of their limited military resources. Avoiding battles with the numerically superior Spanish, they directed their energy against the Cuban economy. By destroying crops, disrupting transportation, and engaging in incessant hit-and-run assaults, the rebels pinned down Spanish soldiers and ate away at the island's economy. The war aim of the revolutionaries remained clear and explicit throughout the two years before McKinley became president. In June 1896 Antonio Maceo said that when Cuba became free, it could "laugh at the negotiations which do not favor its independence." A year later a rebel leader in the United States, Tomas Estrada Palma, wrote: "The Cubans are more determined today than ever to accept nothing short of independence." To offers of autonomy under some form of Spanish rule and to all peace feelers from Madrid, the Cubans were equally opposed. If the rebels participated in the diplomatic process, they would insist on nothing less than independence.[2]

While thirty thousand soldiers fought for the rebellion inside Cuba, a junta in the United States raised money, sought to send weapons to the insurgents, and waged an effective propaganda war to win over American public opinion. The filibustering expeditions that the junta mounted required a naval response in order to maintain the provisions of American neutrality. The junta's access to the press and its ready supply of atrocity stories and eyewitness accounts of Spanish brutalities did much to sustain popular interest in Cuban affairs. The presence of the junta convinced the Spanish that the Americans were not doing all that they could to remain neutral, but the Cuban spokesmen had achieved such strong ties with labor, politicians, and Americans generally that their position was secure.

For Spain the outbreak of fighting in the "Ever Faithful Isle" admitted of only one possible response in 1895. The rebellion must be suppressed, and Spanish sovereignty must be preserved. In pursuit of that end the Madrid government committed several hundred thousand soldiers, who endured staggering casualties. Spanish deaths reached fifty thousand, and an equal number of men were wounded or became sick. Two successive commanders sought to defeat the rebellion. General Arsenio Martinez de Campos attempted, during the first year of the war, to repeat the success that he had achieved in 1878. By confining the revolt to the eastern part of Cuba, he hoped to use his superior numbers to destroy the guerillas. When this strategy failed to overcome the rebels, Spain replaced Campos with General Valeriano Weyler y Nicolau in January 1896. Appointed as a commander who would use repressive measures and proceed "with the greatest energy, without hesitations of any sort," Weyler adopted a "reconcentration" policy that was designed to destroy the popular base of the uprising. The Cuban people were moved out of the countryside and into fortified areas. Unsanitary conditions, overcrowding, and disease caused thousands of deaths, confirming the accuracy of Weyler's nickname, "Butcher," and still the rebellion went on.[3]

The war in Cuba placed great strain upon the fragile political structure of the Spanish nation. The human and economic cost aroused bitterness and discontent across the Iberian peninsula. One Spanish politician recalled a popular song of the day: "Today you are going to Cuba / You are going to Cuba / And you will never return." For the two major political parties, the Liberals and the Conservatives; for the shaky monarchy of the queen regent, Maria Cristina; and for the powerful armed forces, disputes over the way in which the war should be prosecuted did not shake a pervasive consensus about Cuba. The island was part of Spain, and Spanish sovereignty was not negotiable. "It is not possible," said the Spanish minister in Washington, Enrique Dupuy de Lôme, "to think that the Island of Cuba can be benefited except through the agency of Spain." Even war with the United States would be preferable to a negotiated humiliation.[4]

To a large extent, Spanish diplomacy toward the United States rested on the view that the passage of time would make the situation better. Perhaps the Cubans would yield; perhaps the Americans might become more sympathetic and restrain the rebels; perhaps other European powers would curb the United States. Meanwhile, the internal condition of Spanish society was too delicate and the sentiment for retaining Cuba was too strong to allow for more than token concessions over the issue. The Spanish held a weak hand, and procrastination and dissimulation accorded with what policy makers deemed to be the national interest. Diplomats and politicians never concealed their belief that a negotiated Cuban independence was intolerable, but they did not, understandably, point out that Americans erred when they believed that Spain would ultimately recognize that Cuba must be free. If Washington stated that Spain must relinquish Cuba, the two nations would hold mutually contradictory positions. Short of surrender, then, war would become inescapable.

Numerous forces, interwoven and reinforcing, animated American interest in the course of the Cuban revolt. Many citizens believed that Cubans should not suffer from the rule of Spain, a vestigial survivor of Europe in the New World. Periodic revolts tried the patience of the United States and strengthened the conviction that Spain had forfeited both its hold on Cuba and its place in the Western Hemisphere. Problems connected with preventing filibusterers from operating from American waters and with the fate of citizens who were caught up in the fighting were specific diplomatic irritants that arose out of this climactic rebellion.

Humanitarian and economic motives fused with historical experience over Cuba to shape popular attitudes. Accounts of atrocities resulting from the Spanish treatment of individuals were occasionally fabricated; more often they were verifiable. The horrors of the reconcentration policy were abundantly documented. Americans responded with funds for relief of the suffering, sympathy for the rebel cause, and pressure on the government to stop the fighting. Just because they were interested in the Cuban conflict did not mean that Americans had a well-defined perception of what should exist there after Spain had departed. In varying proportions, opinions favored the annexation of Cuba, diplomatic recognition of the rebels, or American military intervention. But the conviction grew, as the months of fighting passed, that something must be done.

The role of sensational journalism in creating an anti-Spanish mood in the United States has been one of the most scrutinized aspects of this subject. Did reporters furnish the ammunition, and did yellow-press publishers such as William Randolph Hearst of the *New York Journal* and Joseph Pulitzer of the *New York World* furnish a war? To newspapers that thrived on large headlines and lurid reporting, Cuba was a natural running story, but it is too simple to assign primary blame for the conflict to Hearst and Pulitzer. They printed colorful, exciting bulletins, some of which were true, and they did not cool popular emotions. They served the propagandistic purposes of the junta well, but they did not create the real differences between the United States and Spain. They spoke for only a small part of the journalistic community, and they reflected what the public wanted, rather than shaping it.

The impact that the fighting had on the economic intimacy of the United States and Cuba added tangible, realistic causes to the former's concern over the island's future. Cuban-American trade, which had already weakened during the depression, sagged; and the destruction affected the $50 million that Americans had invested in Cuba. More important in the minds of many businessmen, the persistence of uncertainty in relations with Spain—the possibility of war—threatened to thwart recovery from the depression. Some in the business community who had interests in Cuba favored intervention; the rest, including many investors in the island and a substantial body of opinion on Wall Street, wanted war to be avoided and the economic suspense to be relieved. The extent of business influence on McKinley's foreign policy has been overrated, but no administration could ignore what the continuation of property depredations, violence, and chaos in Cuba could mean to the American economy.

Beyond the emotions that events in Cuba stirred lay the immeasurable effect of general expansionist sentiment within the United States in the 1890s. Historians still debate how the elements of imperialism interacted to make the nation a world power, but they agree on some causes that a plausible explanation must include. A search for overseas markets to counter alleged industrial overproduction moved some low-tariff publicists and businessmen to advocate not only the expansion of trade but also a direct American presence in foreign countries. Spokesmen for a stronger navy and merchant marine, such as Theodore Roosevelt and Alfred T. Mahan, saw Cuba both as evidence for their position and as an opportunity to be exploited. A swelling sense of national pride, a rekindled faith in Manifest Destiny, and a belief that the United States should take its place among the shapers of world affairs combined to give the Cuban crisis an immediacy that would have been improbable ten years before.

Partisan politics made the Cuban question inescapable. For the Democrats, split by free silver and the agonies of the Cleveland administration, sympathy for the rebels might provide the means of regaining power from the GOP. Before the Philippine issue emerged, the Democracy was interventionist. Recognition of Cuban belligerency, said Ohio Democrats in 1897, was "an act of justice to an American nation struggling for liberty against foreign oppression."[5] The Republicans had long been more expansionist-minded than their rivals, and substantial elements within the party favored taking strong action against Spain. A number of conservative, influential Republican senators, however, worried over the effect that a war would have on the economy; so they counseled restraint. But neither major party could afford to let the other have the credit for chastising Spain and freeing Cuba. In Spain, no government could continue if it publicly accepted the loss of Cuba; in the United States, no administration could succeed politically if it was perceived as being pro-Spanish. Within those irreconcilable assumptions, Grover Cleveland and William McKinley operated from 1895 to 1898.

Grover Cleveland dealt with the Cuban issue for more than two years, and his policy and McKinley's are usually depicted as being continuous and similar. In fact, their approaches differed fundamentally on one essential point: Cleveland and his secretary of state, Richard Olney, pursued a course that was pro-Spanish; McKinley tilted toward the rebels. The Cleveland administration believed that the maintaining of Spanish sovereignty over Cuba was preferable to having an independent island whose consequent internal turmoil might lead to European intervention. The continuation of Spanish rule was also better than having America annex Cuba. Cleveland sought to obtain reforms from Spain for the Cubans, but always within the framework of the hegemony of Madrid.

In pursuit of these goals, President Cleveland opposed in 1896 repeated congressional efforts to accord belligerent rights to the Cubans or to recognize their independence. He did his best to enforce neutrality laws against filibustering to Cuba. For a time in 1895 Secretary Olney edged away from an anti-Cuban posture, but his tolerance for the insurgent cause ebbed in early 1896. He came to believe that the junta was merely a propaganda agency, that the rebellion was resulting in the destruction of property, and that Cuban independence would lead to a racial war. After Congress adjourned in April 1896, Cleveland and Olney proposed to the Spanish that their two countries cooperate "in the immediate pacification of the island on such a plan as, leaving Spain her rights of sovereignty, shall yet secure to the people of the island all such rights and powers of local self-government as they can reasonably ask."[6] That this idea would have had little support in Congress and no hope of acceptance in Cuba seemed not to have entered Cleveland's thinking.

The Spanish declined Cleveland's proposals. They pointed out that the rebels would not countenance mediation, and they concluded that "there is no effectual way to pacify Cuba unless it begins with the actual submission of the armed rebels to the mother country."[7] In the summer of 1896 Madrid sought to offset any kind of American action on Cuba by forming a coalition of European powers that would restrain the United States. This strategy, to which Spain would return, came to little when the American minister obtained a copy of the memorandum on which the effort relied. To the informal overtures that Spain made after the United States had protested, most of the nations that were approached made polite, noncommital responses.

Despite these rebuffs, the Cleveland administration persisted in its attempt to work out a negotiated settlement that would perpetuate Spanish control. For Spain a prolonged diplomatic interchange was in line with its policy of procrastination. Among the ideas discussed were a commercial treaty, which would set out reforms, or some form of Cuban autonomy. A presidential emissary went to the island in 1896/1897 to determine whether the rebels would accept autonomy. They would not.

It is in light of these ongoing activities that Cleveland's annual message of December 7, 1896, must be evaluated. During his discussion of Cuba, the president noted: "It can not be reasonably assumed that the hitherto expectant attitude of the United States will be indefinitely maintained. While we are anxious to accord all due respect to the sovereignty of Spain, we can not view the pending conflict in all its features, and properly apprehend our inevitably close relations to it, and its possible results, without considering that by the course of events we may be drawn into such an unusual and unprecedented condition, as will fix a limit to our patient waiting for Spain to end the contest, either alone and in her own way, or with our friendly cooperation."

These comments, in addition to Cleveland's remark that "the United States is not a nation to which peace is a necessity," have been taken as a warning to Spain that America would intervene if reforms did not occur.[8] More plausibly, the administration wanted to have the Spanish immediately grant reforms that would form the basis for the rebels to accept autonomy. To make that possible, the

65

message had to preempt any congressional action on Cuban independence that might cause the rebels to reject autonomy. Cleveland's words did not foreshadow a lessening of his pro-Spanish stance. They constituted a diplomatic maneuver designed to safeguard his domestic flank while negotiations on autonomy continued.

When Cleveland left office, the nation had no viable Cuban policy. The president and Olney had repelled the most recent congressional attempt to recognize Cuban belligerency in December 1896. They had tried to find a solution within the framework of Spanish sovereignty, a course that allowed Madrid ample time to try a military solution on the island. The Cleveland administration prevented war for two years, but it did so through policies of endorsing Spanish dominance and of opposing the rebels, which fewer and fewer Americans accepted. There was little in Cleveland's actions to persuade Spain that time was running out in Cuba. The belief in Madrid that Spain might procrastinate with some hope of success would be an important obstacle to McKinley's new program of escalating pressure on the Spanish to give up their most important remaining possession in the western hemisphere.

The comparative calm in Spanish-American relations in the spring of 1897 gave the new president a period in which to shape his Cuban policy. Between March and May the administration had only to deal with such long-standing but comparatively minor issues as the status of Cuban prisoners in Spanish jails, filibustering, and losses of American property. During its special session on the tariff, Congress also turned to Cuba. In mid May the Senate passed a resolution to recognize the belligerent rights of the rebels; but it died in the House, where Speaker Thomas B. Reed bottled it up. The question of suffering among American citizens in Cuba arose in the Senate debate, and the ensuing inquiry led to a presidential message in which he sought $50,000 for relief of these individuals. Congress responded affirmatively later in May. "The policy of the Administration in reference to Cuba," said the *New York Tribune*, "is not likely to be criticised, as was that of its predecessor, on the score of vacillation or indifference to the rights of American citizens."[9]

McKinley's policy on the larger questions concerning Cuba emerged slowly. He made some overtures to Spain about selling the island, but received a negative response. With that option temporarily closed, the administration sought hard, reliable information about Cuba. The consul in Havana, Fitzhugh Lee, was a Cleveland appointee who favored intervention and was prorebel in his reports and public statements. Cleveland and Olney had distrusted him, and suspicions about his reliability persisted. To remove Lee, however, might suggest a repudiation of his views. Instead, the president decided to send to Cuba a personal representative on whose judgment he could rely.

McKinley first looked to his old friend William R. Day. As Secretary Sherman's mental weaknesses became apparent, however, Day was named assistant secretary of state in late April. The Canton attorney was just forty-eight years old when he came to Washington. Though he liked to style himself as just a country lawyer, his firm of Lynch and Day was one of Canton's most prosperous. Day had known McKinley since the early 1870s and had acted as an advisor to his friend in the 1893 fund episode, in the 1896 campaign, and in forming his cabinet. Discreet and controlled, the balding, slight, mustachioed lawyer provided McKinley with reliable, temperate counsel; and reporters soon recognized Day as the real power in the State Department.

To replace Day on the fact-finding mission to Cuba, William J. Calhoun, an Illinois Republican who was an associate of Charles G. Dawes, left in early May and spent almost four weeks on a tour of the devastated island. His report, submitted on June 22, 1897, led to the McKinley government's first overt statement to Spain. Calhoun found Cuba, under Weyler's reconcentration policy, "wrapped in the stillness of death and the silence of desolation." He held out little hope that Spain could reestablish its hold, that autonomy could work, or that independence for Cuba would be feasible.[10] With Calhoun's comments before him, the president informed the Spanish minister on June 26 that warfare in Cuba "shall at least be conducted according to the military codes of civilization." McKinley had articulated one of the central points of his policy toward Spain. The United States had a right to insist that the suppression of the rebellion be carried on within humane limits and that Spain not use "fire and famine to accomplish by uncertain indirection what the military arm seems powerless to directly accomplish." Spain did not accept the American position, but McKinley remained adamant that his government could monitor Spanish conduct.[11]

If dealing with the Cuban problem required clear information from the scene, it also demanded that there be an American minister in Madrid in whom the president had confidence. During the spring, McKinley approached John W. Foster, Henry White, Whitelaw Reid, Elihu Root, Jacob D. Cox, and Seth Low, who was then president of Columbia University, about the office. For personal reasons or because of the difficulty of the position, all declined.

McKinley told Low that he "was desirous to adopt every possible measure to bring about a change" in Spanish-American relations before Congress assembled in December, "when it would be necessary for him to define his 'policy.'" Opposing annexation because "the U.S. would not know what to do with the island," McKinley added that "if nothing could be done with Spain, he desired to be able to show that we had spared no effort to avert trouble." Finally, in late June, Stewart L. Woodford, an able lawyer who had been a Civil War general and lieutenant governor of New York in the 1860s, agreed to go to Madrid. The sixty-one-year-old Woodford was loyal and conscientious, but the subtleties of international diplomacy would test his abilities in 1897/1898.[12]

In the last half of 1897, relations between Spain and the United States improved as Madrid made concessions over Cuba; and Washington apparently achieved results that justified McKinley's diplomatic methods. A change in the Spanish government was the largest single cause of this temporary rapprochement. The ruling Conservative party was under heavy assault for its failure to quell the Cuban uprising. The Liberals called for autonomy and a political settlement. On August 8, 1897, the Conservative prime minister, Antonio Canovas del Castillo, was assassinated. An interim Conservative government, which held office during August and September, replied to McKinley's note of June 26. The document, delivered on August 26, rebutted McKinley's strictures on the war in Cuba. What the Spanish had done was no worse than the way the Union army had functioned in the American Civil War, Madrid said.

Two months after Canovas's death, a Liberal government, with Praxedes M. Sagasta at its head, took power. In its first cabinet meeting, the new regime decided to recall General Weyler and to offer the Cubans some form of autonomy. To Sagasta and his associates, a policy of appeasing the United States and seeking a negotiated peace with the rebels seemed to be the most promising way of resolving Spain's internal problems without doing serious damage to the nation. In a newspaper interview, however, the prime minister noted that "no Spanish party, certainly not the Liberals, could assent to foreign interference in our domestic affairs or with our colonies."[13]

While Spain passed through its political crisis, the new American minister explored official opinion in London and Paris before reaching Madrid on September 1. Three weeks after arriving in Spain, Woodford met with the foreign minister on September 18, 1897, and delivered to the Spanish the diplomatic initiatives of the

McKinley administration. McKinley had drafted the formal instructions that Woodford carried, a document that established the framework of the president's policy through the outbreak of war. Spain must, if it could, subdue the rebellion within a limited period of time. Protracted fighting brought "upon the United States a degree of injury and suffering which can not longer be ignored." The administration hoped, however, that the Spanish would accept the inevitable and consider "whether the time has not arrived when Spain . . . will put a stop to this destructive war" by offering "proposals of settlement honorable to herself and just to her Cuban colony and to mankind." If Madrid did not do this, McKinley was convinced that, "should his present effort be fruitless, his duty to his countrymen will necessitate an early decision as to the course of action which the time and the transcendent emergency may demand." Woodford repeated these remarks in September, adding the requirement that he receive an answer by November 1.[14]

McKinley did not say at the outset that Spain must relinquish Cuba, but his skepticism about a military solution reflected his lack of confidence in Spanish arms. Since the president would not make an arrangement that would be unacceptable to the rebels, the plain thrust of his policy was to induce Spain, by incremental steps and intensifying diplomatic pressure, to yield Cuba without going to war. Since Americans believed that abandonment of the island would be in Spain's best interest, it was logical to assume that, given enough time, Spain would assess the problem in the same way. The premise that Spain would eventually recognize the wisdom of peaceful submission lay at the heart of McKinley's strategy.

The Sagasta government was able to make positive gestures in apparent response to the American requests. On October 23, 1897, Woodford was told that the decrees granting autonomy to Cuba would soon be issued. During the next month the Spanish suspended the reconcentration policy, declared an amnesty for political prisoners, and released Americans who were in Cuban jails. On November 25 the autonomy plan was announced. It gave Cuba a greater degree of home rule than ever before, but it left Spanish sovereignty over military and foreign affairs intact. In late November an administration official told reporters: "Thus far Spain has surrendered everything asked of her, and the policy of the administration has been completely vindicated." McKinley knew of the shortcomings of the autonomy plan, but clearly he hoped that an affirmative answer to the Spanish actions would impel further concessions.[15]

The president's annual message on December 6, 1897, reflected the administration's desire to give the Spanish reforms a chance to work, while simultaneously maintaining the diplomatic pressure that had operated to that point. "The Government of Sagasta has entered upon a course from which recession with honor is impossible," McKinley said, adding that Spain deserved "a reasonable chance to realize her expectations and to prove the asserted efficacy of the new order of things to which she stands irrevocably committed." There was an implied time limit in other words of the message: "The near future will demonstrate whether the indispensable condition of a righteous peace, just alike to the Cubans and to Spain as well as equitable to all our interests so intimately involved in the welfare of Cuba, is likely to be attained. If not, the exigency of further and other action by the United States will remain to be taken."[16]

Because the message came out against the recognition of Cuban belligerency, the more strident champions of the rebels assailed it. The Democratic caucus in the House resolved in favor of recognizing that "a condition of war exists in the island of Cuba between the Government of Spain and the Cuban people." The Spanish government, which was more concerned with the morale of the rebels, reading the message for clues about how their enemies might react, bridled at the president's cautionary words. An American army officer in Madrid wrote: "The President's message has been received in a spirit of intense hostility by everyone except the Cabinet of Sagasta, and the unofficial expressions of some of its members are by no means friendly. They see in it a veiled threat of intervention unless war in Cuba stops. And against that all Spain is one."[17]

The first and most productive phase of McKinley's Cuban diplomacy ended in December 1897. Spain had conceded much, and public opinion in the United States seemed to be inclined to support McKinley. Additional progress, of course, depended on the effective operation of Spain's program regarding autonomy. In December the president looked for signs of success but took precautions against failure. With suffering still prevalent on the island, the White House made successive appeals on Christmas Eve, 1897, and January 8, 1898, for donations to the Red Cross. McKinley himself contributed five thousand dollars anonymously. On the military side, the navy was instructed to have the North Atlantic squadron conduct winter maneuvers in the Caribbean near Key West. The battleship *Maine* had already been ordered to that Florida port, and the Navy discussed contingency plans for sending a ship to Havana.

More ominously, on January 11, 1898, the secretary of the navy directed the commander of the European Squadron to retain sailors whose enlistments were about to run out. These orders were part of McKinley's strategy to convince Spain that the United States was not bluffing over Cuba. Behind the military decisions of these months was the directing hand of the president.

Changes in the international situation at the end of 1897 and in the early weeks of 1898 underscored the desirability of a prompt resolution of the Cuban question. In Asia the actions of European powers to gain military and economic concessions from China, which was symbolized by the German occupation of Kiaochow Bay in November 1897, troubled an administration that was interested in the expansion of trade in the Far East. Beyond involving the fate of Cuba itself, the instability in the Caribbean that grew out of strained Spanish-American relations could tempt other nations to challenge the long-term ascendancy of the United States in the area. When Germany used gunboat diplomacy against Haiti in December, the administration watched events closely. Two months later the navy sent a high-ranking officer, Arent S. Crowninshield, to visit Santo Domingo and then report on German penetration. "I do not hesitate to predict," he wrote, "that before many years have passed, Germany will succeed in acquiring one or more territorial possessions in the Western Hemisphere." Until a satisfactory end to the controversy with Spain could be achieved, however, these foreign-policy concerns would mark time.[18]

Spain's autonomy program for Cuba went into effect on January 1, 1898. Fitzhugh Lee wired the State Department eleven days later: "Mobs, led by Spanish officers, attacked to-day the offices of the four newspapers here advocating autonomy." These outbreaks, in which the pro-Spanish rioters cried, "Death to autonomy," convinced McKinley that Spain could not make its colonial reforms work. The Spanish minister told his superiors that the administration seemed to have lost all faith in Spain's success. The January 12 riots marked the beginning of the rapid deterioration in relations that exposed the irreconcilable differences between Spain and the United States over Cuba.[19]

The Havana disturbances revived congressional interest in the recognition of Cuban belligerency. For the next week, House Democrats assailed the administration as being pro-Spanish. The Republicans repulsed these challenges, but the debates revealed the shrinking limits of McKinley's options. "The President, while he does not favor the recognition of belligerency as a specific cure or as advisable, has intimated where the line of duty will take him, acting not by halves, but facing the whole question," said an administration spokesman in the House. The British ambassador, Sir Julian Pauncefote, reported "a feeling of disquietude and alarm" at what were deemed to be semiofficial comments.[20]

The attacks of the opposition, the prospect of injury to Americans in Cuba, and the need to impress Madrid also persuaded the White House that it was desirable to send an American ship to Havana. Such an act required Spain's agreement, and it appeared at first as though Dupuy de Lôme and his government, eager as they were to discredit Consul Lee, would refuse. On January 20 the Spanish minister characterized the sending of American vessels to the island as an unfriendly act. Four days later, however, in an interview with Secretary Day, Dupuy de Lôme learned that the president was inclined to give autonomy a little more time in which to work. Since Spain believed that it was already working, because "Spain and the United States were at peace," McKinley wanted to resume the navy's visits to Cuban ports.[21]

When Dupuy replied that discontinuance of the visits had not been a proper thing to do, the administration acted that same day to order the *Maine* to Havana. On January 25 the battleship "came gliding into the harbor as easily and smoothly as possible." At a diplomatic dinner the next day, McKinley sought out Dupuy publicly and said: "I see that we have only good news; I am well satisfied with what has occurred in the House, and with the discipline of the Republicans. You, who comprehend this, will understand how strong our position is and how much it has changed and bettered in the past year; you have no occasion to be other than satisfied and confident."[22]

The actual course of relations over the next two weeks belied these optimistic assertions. In Spain the prowar forces gained a temporary ascendancy. Reinforcements for Cuba were readied, and purchases of ammunition went forward. The navy began negotiations to acquire additional ships from Great Britain and several Latin American nations, repairs were rushed on Spain's larger vessels, and planners drafted operational strategies for use in North American waters. On the American side the navy stepped up its drive for greater readiness. Major commands were warned of possible trouble with Spain, and ships gathered intelligence about conditions in Cuban harbors where landings might be made.

The sterner mood in Madrid also shaped its response to American diplomatic actions at the end of 1897. On December 20

Woodford gave the Spaniards the administration's reply to the Sagasta ministry's statements and actions of October. The note said of the autonomy program: "In taking this advanced position the Government of Spain has entered upon a pathway from which no backward step is possible." The Spanish answer, given to Woodford on February 1, 1898, took a very hard line toward McKinley's assumption that the United States could monitor Spain's handling of autonomy or set implicit deadlines for its effectiveness to be established. "It is only in this formula of colonial self-government and Spanish sovereignty that peace, which is so necessary to the Peninsula and to Cuba and so advantageous to the United States, can be found." About foreign intrusion or interference, the Spanish concluded that "such interference would lead to an intervention which any nation possessing any self respect would have to repel by force, even if it were necessary to exhaust, in the defense of the integrity of its territory and of its independence, all, absolutely all, the resources at its disposal." Woodford was handed the note on February 3, but because of slowness in translating it, a cable did not go to the State Department until February 8. The wire reached the president the next day.[23]

Two incidents, successive and sensational, now lifted the Cuban problem beyond diplomacy and placed it at the center of public attention. In mid December, Dupuy de Lôme wrote a personal letter to a friend in Cuba that characterized McKinley as "weak and a bidder for the admiration of the crowd, besides being a would-be politician who tries to leave a door open behind himself while keeping on good terms with the jingoes of his party." The letter fell into the hands of the Cubans, they sent it to the junta in New York, and the *New York Journal* published it on February 9, 1898. For Dupuy it meant the end of his career, as the administration insisted on an apology from Spain in addition to his resignation. The yellow journals made the most of this "Worst Insult to the United States in Its History," and in Congress there was a renewed demand that the consular correspondence on conditions in Cuba be published. To this last request, which came to a head by February 14, the administration gave its tacit assent.

McKinley's willingness to make such a move in the direction of war, for the reports would only arouse congressional ire toward Spain, testified to the true importance of the de Lôme letter. The president brushed aside the insult to himself and instead focused on a concluding paragraph in the letter. "It would be very advantageous," Dupuy de Lôme had said, "to take up, even if only for effect, the question of commercial relations, and to have a man of some prominence sent hither in order that I may make use of him here to carry on a propaganda among the Senators and others in opposition to the junta and to try to win over the refugees." For some weeks, Madrid had been discussing a commercial treaty of reciprocity. It now seemed clear that Spain was stalling. Coupled with the note of February 1, the de Lôme letter made the chances of avoiding war slight, even before a fresh disaster overtook the two nations.[24]

About one-thirty on the morning of February 16, 1898, Secretary of the Navy Long received a dispatch from Lee that began: "*Maine* blown up and destroyed to-night at 9:40 p. m." Long sent Commander D. W. Dickens to the White House with the news. Dickens later recalled: "The President came out in his dressing gown. I handed him the despatch which he read with great gravity. He seemed to be very deeply impressed with the news, handed back the despatch to me, and took it again, two or three times, expressing great regret that the event had happened, particularly at that time." Two hundred and sixty-four enlisted men and two officers had perished. The nation instinctively asked, as McKinley did of Dickens, how the accident could have occurred, and there was an immediate disposition to blame Spain for, at best, carelessness or, at worst, conspiracy.[25]

The most modern study of the destruction of the *Maine* argues persuasively that it was caused accidentally by an internal explosion. Since it used bituminous coal as fuel, the ship was vulnerable to spontaneous combustion from its inadequately ventilated bunkers. Heat from the ensuing fire set off the gunpowder in an adjacent reserve magazine. The problems that faced William McKinley on the morning of February 16 were how to respond to this catastrophe, how to determine the cause of the explosion, and how to maintain control of the diplomatic situation. Long told the press immediately, at the president's behest, that "judgment should be suspended until a full investigation is made." Meanwhile, the administration moved toward a greater preparation for hostilities, launched a court of inquiry into the sinking, and resumed the effort to induce Spain to yield. The White House knew that the report of the naval board set an implied deadline for additional action. For the most part, McKinley remained quiet, with only an oblique public reference to the crisis. Speaking on Washington's Birthday in Philadelphia, he reviewed the career of the first president and remarked that "the exercise of a sober and dispassionate public judgment [was] the best safeguard in the calm of tranquil events, and rises superior and triumphant above the storms of woe and peril."[26]

Public opinion, of course, was much less temperate than was McKinley. The *Denver News* observed that the withdrawal of Spain from this side of the Atlantic would be a proper atonement for the *Maine*. Spaniards were hanged in effigy in numerous communities, and the French ambassador found that "a sort of bellicose fury has seized the American nation." For all the frenzy, however, the country accepted the decision that no definite action should occur until the naval board had reported.[27]

Critics of McKinley have identified the period just after the destruction of the *Maine* as a time when he should have rallied the public against war with Spain. But what could he have said? His diplomacy depended on convincing Spain to accept the loss of Cuba without making a public demand that she give up the island. Therefore, he could not make public his intentions without drawing a negative Spanish response that would bring war closer. In advance of the report, a comment that the explosion was accidental and that Spain was blameless would have risked an embarrassing repudiation. To say that the United States would not fight over Cuba was politically impossible. Peace was feasible if either Spain or the United States would modify its position; but as the next five weeks proved, this did not happen.

For the Spanish, this period revealed the limited options that confronted them. The warlike mood of the Spanish government in late January abated in the wake of the *Maine* episode, America's military preparations, and an awareness of Spain's own naval weakness. To find a solution short of war, the queen regent discussed the possibility of selling Cuba but found that the army was opposed to such a humiliation. Alternatively, the Sagasta ministry revived the idea of holding peace talks with the rebels. The need to mollify the army, however, meant that the insurgents had to request an armistice before negotiations could begin. Unsuccessful in appeasing the United States because of domestic opposition and unwilling to face war as a diversion from its internal problems, the Spanish government could only hope that support from its European allies would stave off war over Cuba.

The McKinley administration devoted this interval to renewing the pressure on Spain and to intensifying the military preparations for a possible outbreak of fighting. The president once again explored the possibility of purchasing Cuba as well as alternative governmental arrangements for the island. His most dramatic action was to call congressional leaders to the White House in early March, when he asked one of them, Joseph G. Cannon of Illinois, to introduce a bill appropriating $50 million for national defense. A Spanish naval build-up had worried American officials since the early part of the year. "Month by month the Spanish Navy has been put into a better condition to meet us," wrote Theodore Roosevelt on February 16. When the press reported on March 5 that the Spanish were discussing the purchase of two Brazilian cruisers under construction in England, McKinley acted.[28]

Within two days the president had his appropriation. Both houses passed it unanimously. The administration promptly used the money to obtain the two Brazilian ships before Spain could do so. Woodford reported that news that the defense bill had been passed had "simply stunned" the Spanish because it provided evidence of the ample material resources of the United States.[29]

While he awaited the report on the *Maine*, McKinley balanced the conflicting pressures from the parties in the Cuban imbroglio. The insurgents proposed on March 1 to pay Spain an indemnity of no more than $100 million in exchange for American and Spanish recognition of Cuba's independence and for the withdrawal of all Spanish troops. They assured the president: "We do not ask you to go to war; we only ask for your neutrality, for the recognition of Cuban belligerent rights." They did not explain how war with Spain could be averted after recognition was granted. Renewed discussions within the United States and with potential European intermediaries about possible purchase of the island found little domestic support and, in the end, resolute opposition in Spain.[30]

McKinley also looked briefly into an arrangement—drawn from the precedent of relations between Turkey and Egypt—in which Spain would keep not only a token sovereignty over the island but also some share of its customs revenues. When he examined the proposal with its author, Oscar Straus, a New York businessman, McKinley predicted: "We will have great trouble in satisfying the insurgents or in getting them to agree to anything—they are even more difficult than Spain to deal with." His forecast proved to be correct. The rebels rejected the plan quickly.[31]

Efforts to reach a settlement with Madrid in these weeks also proved fruitless. The Spanish wanted to consider America's support for Cuban autonomy, the recall of Lee from Havana, and movements of the United States Navy in the area. They made clear their lack of interest in selling Cuba, and they renewed their strategy of delay when the Cortes, the Spanish parliament, adjourned in late February until April 25. On March 19 Woodford asked Washington to set April 15 as a deadline. "They should see that the United States mean business, and mean it *now*."[32]

Events in the third week of March 1898 now surged toward an American ultimatum to Spain. As the days passed, the expectation increased that the verdict on the *Maine* would put the blame on Spain. The tense popular mood became more heated on March 17 when Senator Redfield Proctor of Vermont described to his colleagues his conclusions formed from a recent trip to Cuba. His calm, matter-of-fact analysis made a deep impression. He found "the entire native population of Cuba, struggling for freedom and deliverance from the worst misgovernment of which I ever had knowledge." The result of the Spanish campaign, he decided, was "neither peace nor war. It is concentration and desolation." Proctor's remarks captured the popular mind. To hear his speech, said Senator Francis E. Warren of Wyoming, produced "a raising of the blood and temper as well as of shame that we, a civilized people, an enlightened nation, a great republic, born in a revolt against tyranny, should permit such a state of things within less than a hundred miles of our shore as that which exists in Cuba."[33]

In the march of public opinion toward an acceptance of war, Proctor's speech marked an important milestone. Among religious newspapers the belief that intervention could be justified on moral grounds, already a pervasive conviction, became even more widespread. Of equal, or perhaps more, significance was a shift in business attitudes. From a general stance against intervention, the business community joined the rest of the nation in a greater readiness to advocate hostilities.

As the most serious national crisis since the Civil War deepened, McKinley became the object of intense and simultaneous feelings of confidence, hope, mistrust, and disgust. "The President is behaving with great dignity and apparent firmness," wrote loyal Republican Senator John Coit Spooner, while the *Nation*, not normally a friendly journal, observed that "the American people no longer fear the executive, and they no longer trust the legislative body." The dominant critical note toward the president was that he might be too reluctant or timid to act with firmness toward Spain. His enemies alleged that his closeness to business, to "the clientele of wealth who are the holders of Spanish bonds," might dispose him to accept a peaceful solution that would be favorable to the oppressors of Cuba; and theater audiences jeered at McKinley's picture in

New York.[34] The tensions surrounding the coming of war were also preparing challenges to the president's control of foreign policy and of his own government.

For the man in the White House, the approach of spring brought only mounting personal anxiety. The attempt to restrain domestic agitation for war while inducing the Spanish to submit over Cuba taxed McKinley's physical resources. George B. Cortelyou found him, in late March, looking "quite well considering the enormous strain he is under, although for the past two or three days he has looked haggard at times." Visitors throughout these days heard him say: "I pray God that we may be able to keep peace," or as he had earlier remarked to Leonard Wood: "I shall never get into a war until I am sure that God and man approve. I have been through one war; I have seen the dead piled up; and I do not want to see another." While McKinley displayed, in this period, "a good deal of weariness and nervous strain," memoir accounts that have him in tears and despair seem, aside from the factual errors that they contain, to be unreliable in substance.[35]

The climactic phase of the Cuban problem began on March 19, 1898, when four members of the *Maine* inquiry board met with McKinley. They told him that the court would conclude that an external explosion, probably a submarine mine, had caused the *Maine* to sink. The physical evidence regarding the vessel's keel and bottom plates, which had been driven upward, as an explosion from outside would do, persuaded the court to reject the hypothesis of an internal explosion. Knowing that the court's verdict would have a profound influence on the popular mind when the report officially reached him four or five days later, McKinley sent a stern message to Woodford on March 20, which conveyed the board's findings and warned: "This report must go to Congress soon." The president indicated that the *Maine* issue could be handled through a payment of reparations by Spain, but "general conditions in Cuba which can not be longer endured, and which will demand action on our part," required positive steps in Madrid. "April 15 is none too early date for accomplishment of these purposes." At home, Mc-Kinley began a round of meetings with congressional leaders of both parties to offset the impact of the *Maine* report and to retain control of events. He agreed that Congress would receive diplomatic papers on Cuba by April 20, but still, in the face of a deadline for Spain and Congress, he hoped "that something may yet happen to avert hostilities." On the day that these words appeared in the *New York Herald*, the spiral into war commenced.[36]

The *Maine* report, blaming an external cause, arrived at the White House during the evening of March 24. The next day the president, the cabinet, and some military advisors digested the lengthy document. The report, with a message from McKinley, would go to Capitol Hill on Monday, March 28. Meanwhile, McKinley prepared a message to Woodford, which went out over Day's signature shortly after midnight on March 26. This telegram briefly reviewed McKinley's policy and then stated: "The President suggests that if Spain will revoke the reconcentration order and maintain the people until they can support themselves and offer to the Cubans full self-government, with reasonable indemnity, the President will gladly assist in its consummation. If Spain should invite the United States to mediate for peace and the insurgents would make like request, the President might undertake such office of friendship." Woodford received the wire late on March 26 and immediately asked if "full self-government" meant "actual recognition of independence, or is nominal Spanish sovereignty over Cuba still permissible?" Day responded that "full self-government with indemnity would mean Cuban independence."[37]

By Sunday, March 27, the president apparently had decided that Congress would not act hastily on the *Maine* report. At the same time, Woodford was reporting that Spain had made tentative feelers toward an armistice in Cuba. With the prospect of a slight breathing space, McKinley had Day wire the American minister: "See if the following can be done: First. Armistice until October 1. Negotiations meantime looking for peace between Spain and insurgents through friendly offices of President United States." Second, the president sought the revocation of the reconcentration order. Finally, Woodford was told to add, if possible, that if peace terms between Spain and the rebels were not reached by October 1, McKinley would be the final arbiter between the parties.[38]

McKinley's second proposal offered Spain a more measured path toward Cuban independence, but both the March 26 and the March 27 messages assumed, as an end result, a Cuba that would be free of Spanish rule. There was no outright demand for independence, because the Spanish government would have peremptorily rejected it. Imprecision in diplomacy would offer a slim chance to avoid war, if Spain were to yield. Categorical ultimatums at any point in the negotiating process would have meant hostilities.

In Madrid, Woodford submitted the American proposals to Spain on March 29. Faced with intense congressional pressure after McKinley's *Maine* message, the administration wanted a prompt response. Thursday, March 31, became the deadline. The Sagasta government found that the Spanish army was opposed to an armistice, and Woodford reported that the tender of an armistice would cause a revolution. In its formal answer, Spain agreed to submit the *Maine* question to arbitration and revoked the reconcentration order. On McKinley's principal demands, however, it yielded nothing. The Cuban problem would be turned over to that island's parliament, "without whose intervention it will not be able to arrive at the final result." Spain would accept an armistice if the rebels asked for it, but its length and extent would be up to the Spanish commander in Cuba. Spain had gone to the limit of its domestic political resources, but Cuban independence, either immediately through submission or eventually through American mediation, was an impossibility. Madrid was now seeking time in order to mobilize European support against the United States.[39]

For McKinley, events in Washington were eroding his flexibility in carrying out negotiations. His message about the *Maine* was low-key and calm. He predicted that "the sense of justice of the Spanish nation" would resolve the issue that the destruction of the vessel had posed, and he promised to advise Congress of the results. "In the meantime," the president concluded, "deliberate consideration is invoked." The message, said a *New York Herald* reporter, "fell like a wet blanket on Congress"; and Cortelyou noted in his diary on March 29 that "the feeling in Congress today is not so good as it was."[40] In the Senate, members introduced resolutions demanding that Spain withdraw from Cuba and authorizing the president to use force to compel Spain to comply with American demands. While these resolutions commanded wide support, the Republican leadership would not embarrass the White House by taking them up. On the House side the Democrats offered resolutions to recognize Cuban independence, which, in the wake of McKinley's message, attracted many Republicans. Their rebellion, which grew out of an informal GOP caucus on March 29, culminated the next day in bitter procedural struggles over a resolution dealing with recognition. It took not only the exertions of Speaker Reed but also a presidential promise of a message on Cuba in order to defeat the recognition forces. The issue now hung on Spain's answer to the March 26 and March 27 messages.

The negative reply reached the White House at 10:30 P.M. on March 31. Its unsatisfactory character was clear, and it left little room for additional negotiation. Without abandoning his hope that Spain might still recognize the necessity of relinquishing Cuba,

McKinley now moved to put the nation on a war footing. On April 1 the navy stepped up its preparations, including night patrols; the administration explored taxation problems that a war would bring; and the president began to work on his message to Congress. "That the President has less confidence in a peaceable outcome," wrote a reporter in the *New York Tribune* on April 1, "was apparent from the views he expressed to several of his closest friends." Congress expected to receive the message on April 4, and influential Republicans wanted the president to "lead and not be pushed." Then, on April 3, the White House announced that the message would go in two days later, on April 6.[41]

This brief delay may have been connected to a final presidential initiative to gain concessions from Spain. Through Archbishop John Ireland of Minnesota, an informal papal envoy, McKinley was exploring the prospects of having the Vatican use persuasion with Spain. The president's remark that he would welcome help from the Holy See meant that he wanted assistance in obtaining Spain's acquiescence. Madrid interpreted these words as an invitation to use papal mediation and as evidence of a relaxation of American pressure. Woodford received proposals that, in return for an armistice that Spain would grant, the United States would withdraw its navy from Cuban waters. He cabled Washington that "when armistice is once proclaimed hostilities will never be resumed and . . . permanent peace will be secured." The White House denied the Spanish interpretation as soon as it became public, and Day wired to Woodford: "Would the peace you are so confident of securing mean the independence of Cuba?" The more the administration learned of what Spain meant in its note of March 31, the less it liked the substance of it. The manifesto regarding the autonomous government, said Day on April 4, "is not armistice" but only "an invitation to the insurgents to submit," pending further Spanish action.[42]

On April 6, the anticipated date of McKinley's message, the morning began with "an immense crowd" of "more than ten thousand people" at the Capitol. About noon, however, McKinley received a dispatch from Lee: "If message can be withheld until Monday 11th can arrange everything. If sent before will have trouble here." The president called congressional leaders in and, in response to suggestions that the message be submitted anyway, said: "I will not do it; I will not send in that message today; I will not do such a thing if it will endanger the life of an American in Cuba." The lawmakers had "nothing to do but consent" to the five-day's postponement.[43]

81

For all the drama of Lee's plea on behalf of the safety of Americans, diplomatic maneuvers made the additional time useful to McKinley. In late March, Spain had played its final card, the intervention by its European neighbors and allies. Though the American position had little support on the Continent, there was even less disposition to challenge the United States openly. Wary of European interference and concerned about maintaining a posture for peace, the president agreed to accept a statement from the ambassadors in favor of a peaceful outcome. In consultation with the British ambassador, Sir Julian Pauncefote, McKinley helped to draft a note that the envoys of the six major powers presented to him on April 6. They earnestly hoped "that further negotiations will lead to an agreement which, while securing the maintenance of peace, will afford all necessary guaranties for the reestablishment of order in Cuba." In response, McKinley spoke of the good will behind the note and expressed his desire for a settlement that would end "the chronic condition of disturbance there." McKinley may well have postponed the delivery of the message in order to avoid upstaging the Europeans and to preserve diplomatic activity related to it which was then under way in Spain.[44]

In March and early April, in response to German initiatives, Pope Leo XIII, who was sympathetic to Spain, indicated his readiness to serve as a mediator in the Spanish-American dispute. Out of these talks came, in late March, a proposal for the pope to intercede if Spain would grant Cuba its independence. The Sagasta government rejected this idea within a few days. The abortive mission of Archbishop Ireland was a part of this papal action. Finally, on April 2 the Vatican proposed to request an armistice. A week later the Spanish agreed, in an action that has been persistently misinterpreted as a capitulation to McKinley's demands. There is, the president's attackers charge, no better evidence of his fecklessness, his weakness, his lack of courage. No incident, the indictment runs, better illustrates his ranking as a mediocre president.

Spain's decision to ask for a suspension of hostilities in Cuba, not an armistice, was directed at the European powers rather than at McKinley and Washington. Knowing that capitulation to the Americans was politically impossible, the government saw the truce as a negotiating ploy in its efforts to find foreign support. Even so, there was strong opposition within the cabinet to a move that might alienate the armed forces. Proponents contended that the suspension would buy time so that Cuba could be defended against the United States. The cabinet deadlock ended on April 9, when the queen arranged for the ambassadors of the European powers to call in Madrid, as they had in Washington. The diplomats favored an armistice, in the interests of peace, and Spain could now consent, to placate potential friends. Within the cabinet, advocates of the move stressed that it would not be a prelude to surrender, and they noted that the suspension of hostilities, instead of an armistice, would not involve recognizing the rebel regime.[45]

Woodford believed, as he wired the president, that "the present Government is going, and is loyally ready to go, as fast and as far as it can." A closer reading of Spain's statement, which reached McKinley on April 10, revealed the true character of this "capitulation." The Spanish commander in Cuba could determine how long and under what conditions hostilities would stop. The insurgents were offered autonomy, with "the franchise and liberties" extended to such an extent "that no motive or pretext is left for claiming any fuller measure thereof." Whatever changes might take place in autonomy would be "within the bounds of reason and of the national sovereignty." Spain also revoked its policy of reconcentration and offered to submit the *Maine* question to arbitration. Of American mediation, a true armistice, and Cuba's independence, Spain said nothing. To Day's inquiry about whether Spain would give Cuba its independence if the United States deemed it necessary, the minister in Washington said only no.[46]

McKinley's critics place less weight on these considerations; they contend that Spain, once the fighting stopped, could not have resumed the struggle. Time would have been on the side of a peaceful solution. Such a result was, of course, possible, but now remains only a might-have-been. It is doubtful, however, that the rebels would have accepted the suspension, and it is even more unlikely that Spanish opinion would have endorsed a move toward peace. Announcement of the suspension brought public disturbances in Madrid. More important, the passage of time, after an American diplomatic concession, would have strengthened not only the Spanish will to fight but also the military power at its disposal. The minister of war told the Cuban commander, for example, that the cabinet had opted for the suspension in order to remedy "a scarcity of resources with which to defend our indisputable rights."[47] The Spanish proposal was a last-minute diplomatic gambit that, from an American perspective, revived old questions about Madrid's good faith in the negotiating process.

The belief that Spain submitted rests on a misreading of the evidence and owes much to retrospective guilt about the impact which the war had on American history. The hypothetical scenario that has McKinley risking the prestige of his office, the future of his party, and what Americans saw as the nation's honor in exchange for a settlement of the Cuban issue without war is an attractive one. Its advocates must recognize, however, the greater likelihood that after placing these elements at risk, McKinley would have been confronted with Cuban opposition, a rebellion in Congress, and mounting indications that the Spanish had abused his good will and trust. The devastating effect that such a humiliation would have had on the presidency and the government should not be weighed lightly.

After the last message from Spain came to the White House on the morning of April 10, the administration decided to take no action beyond adding the information that it contained to the president's address on the situation in Cuba. The document had been ready for a week. Hearing it in a cabinet meeting on April 4, Secretary Long noted in his diary: "I suppose it is the best he can do; yet, it seems to me, the narrative which he makes the basis of his conclusion leads to a very different result from that which he reaches."[48] Long attributed the defects in the message to the president's fatigue and overwork. It was the product, in its preliminary drafts and data, of several hands, including those of his secretary John Porter, Assistant Secretary of State Alvey Adee, Attorney General John W. Griggs, and McKinley himself. In the end, the message was something less than a ringing affirmation of an American purpose to commence war with Spain, because the president was still engaged, in these final hours, in buying more time in which Spain might yet agree to end its rule in Cuba. The ambiguity and equivocation of the message may have sacrificed something in appearances in order to serve McKinley's continuing purposes of avoiding war and of achieving his diplomatic goals.

Congress listened to the message on April 11 "with intense interest and profound silence" as the clerks droned through its seven thousand words. It was not a call to arms. McKinley began with a historical narrative of the nation's involvement with the Cuban issue. He reviewed the negotiations with Spain up to the action of the Sagasta government on March 31 in response to his note of March 27. "With this last overture in the direction of immediate peace, and its disappointing reception by Spain, the Executive is brought to the end of his effort." The absence here of any reference to Cuban independence disturbed legislators who had been assured that the administration had demanded it of Spain. Once again, categorical assertion of this goal in a presidential statement would have ensured that Spain would reject it.[49]

McKinley next turned to what the United States should do. He came out against a recognition of Cuban belligerency that would "accomplish nothing toward the one end for which we labor—the instant pacification of Cuba and the cessation of the misery that afflicts the island." American recognition of the Cuban Republic's independence was also ruled out as not being necessary "in order to enable the United States to intervene and pacify the island. To commit this country now to the recognition of any particular government in Cuba might subject us to embarrassing conditions of international obligation toward the organization so recognized." When a government appeared "capable of performing the duties and discharging the functions of a separate nation," the United States could adjust its position.

At this point in his message, McKinley weighed the alternatives of intervention as an impartial neutral or as an ally, presumably of the Cubans. He chose the former course, setting out four reasons to justify the American action. Humanitarian grounds were listed first: "It is no answer to say that this is all in another country, belonging to another nation, and is therefore none of our business. It is specially our duty, for it is right at our door." The citizens of Cuba required protection that no government currently afforded them. Therefore, "the very serious injury to the commerce, trade, and business of our people," as well as "the wanton destruction of property and devastation of the island," constituted the third ground for action. Finally, "the present condition of affairs in Cuba is a constant menace to our peace, and entails upon this Government an enormous expense." The president cited the *Maine* as "a patent and impressive proof of a state of things in Cuba that is intolerable." After quoting from Presidents Grant and Cleveland on the Cuban question and from his own annual message in 1897, McKinley asserted: "In the name of humanity, in the name of civilization, in behalf of endangered American interests which give us the right and the duty to speak and to act, the war in Cuba must stop." That sentence produced a wave of applause in the House chamber.[50]

McKinley then asked the lawmakers to "authorize and empower the President to take measures to secure a full and final termination of hostilities between the Government of Spain and the people of Cuba." He also sought authority to establish a stable government in Cuba, and "to use the military and naval forces of the United States as may be necessary for these purposes." Following two paragraphs that closed the original version of the message came two more that alluded to Spain's suspension of hostilities. "If this measure attains a successful result," the president wrote, "then our aspirations as a Christian, peace-loving people will be realized. If it fails, it will be only another justification for our contemplated action."[51]

McKinley had not submitted a war message. The possibility of further negotiations with Spain remained alive, and the language about Cuba's belligerency and independence ensured that Congress would debate the issue for several days. The executive had also requested large discretionary power to use the nation's military force short of actually going to war. Even at this moment of greatest crisis for his administration, McKinley was broadening the scope of presidential power. The debate over the message in the next week would pivot on the issue of the president's leadership in the conduct of foreign policy and implicitly on his power as commander in chief.

Reaction to the message followed the broad outlines of public opinion on Cuba. Democrats called it "a great disappointment to the American people," and a warlike Republican, Foraker of Ohio, said: "I have no patience with the message, and you can say so." These early negative responses did not reflect the predominant evaluation of what McKinley had written. Secretary Cortelyou gave the president "opinions of the message as they have come in—both sides. There are not many of the critical kind notwithstanding statements made by members of Congress and others." Comments in the press and in the White House mail did indicate a broadly based support for what McKinley had done. For a message that has often been decried as being inconsistent, insipid, contradictory, or even turgid, it had a decisive effect in reclaiming the president's prestige at the end of a painful and protracted diplomatic controversy. It also succeeded in establishing the terms of the debate by which Congress took the nation into war with Spain.[52]

After McKinley's message, the Democrats planned their strategy around two issues—whether Cuban independence should be recognized and how much power the president should have in regard to foreign policy. At a Jefferson Day dinner on April 13, William Jennings Bryan came out for a government in Cuba "of such a character that one of our ships should not be blown up while under its protection," and a Democratic newspaper complained that the president "asks Congress to delegate its war-making power and all control over the crisis to him." On April 13, House Democrats offered a resolution to recognize the Cuban republic, but the Republican majority rejected it by 150 for to 190 against. That same day, language that the president endorsed was passed by the lopsided margin of 325 to 19. The resolution authorized and directed McKinley to intervene in order to end the war, called both for a stable and independent government for the Cuban people and for putting the land and naval forces of the nation behind the resolution.[53]

McKinley had obtained all that he wanted from the House, but the Senate advocates of war and Cuban independence were hardly satisfied. The Senate Foreign Relations Committee offered a resolution that was acceptable to the president, but Foraker drafted an amendment, which was introduced by Senator David Turpie of Indiana, that would have recognized the Cuban republic "as the true and lawful government of that island." This amendment gathered the backing of the Democrats, and eleven Republicans who were suspicious of McKinley, including Foraker and William E. Chandler, voted for it. Proponents of it contended that the president was scheming to avoid war and that he was trying to protect the holders of $500 million of Spanish bonds. McKinley's defenders replied that it would be "a grave mistake" to recognize Cuba "as an independent state among the nations of the world." On April 16 the amendment passed, 51 to 37. At this time the Senate also adopted an amendment offered by Senator Henry M. Teller of Colorado, according to which the United States would disavow any intention of controlling Cuba once hostilities had ceased. The final version of the Senate resolution, which passed by 67 to 21, contained the Foreign Relations Committee's language, Teller's amendment, and the Turpie-Foraker amendment.[54]

The problem for McKinley now lay in the House, where the vote on the Senate resolution was scheduled for Monday, April 18. During the weekend, administration spokesmen told reporters that the president might veto what the Senate had done if the House adopted it. Citing "several well-informed persons in authority," the *Washington Star* reported: "The President is ready to immediately put into execution by force of arms an intervention resolution of Congress, but he would be positive against any action which would usurp his prerogatives as he sees the matter." There were also hints that, once the fighting should start, recognition might be more feasible. On the eve of the vote it seemed that the antirecognition forces were in control. When Speaker Reed counted heads on Monday morning, however, the expected majority had disappeared.

Rapid parliamentary footwork recaptured the initiative, and the administration won by 178 to 156. The recognition forces held out in the Senate during the afternoon, but then conceded defeat. Finally, on April 19, resolutions that the president approved of passed the Senate by 7 votes and by 311 to 6 in the House. Congress, said one cabinet member, had come to a reasonable conclusion. McKinley had won and, in doing so, had "asserted the primacy of the President in foreign affairs at a time when either an independent-minded Congress or an inflamed public opinion might have inspired action that he deemed unwise."[55]

The president signed the congressional resolution on April 20. Spain broke diplomatic relations at once. In Madrid, Woodford was informed of Spain's action before he could convey the resolution formally, and he asked for his passports. On April 22 a naval blockade of Cuba was imposed, and two days later, Spain declared war as American ships moved into position. The action of their government was popular with the Spanish people, a response that underlined how little room there had actually been for carrying on negotiations over Cuba. On April 25 McKinley asked Congress to declare war, and it complied by passing a resolution that said that war had existed since April 21.

Of the two dominant explanations for McKinley's Spanish-Cuban diplomacy, the view that he was a weak, indecisive executive, who yielded at last to war hysteria, has commanded more adherents than the view that he was a wily expansionist, who in the end, wanted "what only a war could provide: the disappearance of the terrible uncertainty in American political and economic life, and a solid basis from which to resume the building of the new American commercial empire."[56] The first hypothesis assumes several considerations: that the Spanish would ultimately have submitted peacefully, that they virtually gave in, in April 1898, and that McKinley lacked the courage and vision to seize the real chances for peace. The evidence from Spanish diplomatic sources does not provide much support for the first two assumptions. Madrid did not see itself as being on a road from which no backward step was possible. With resolve and purpose, it maneuvered to maintain its grip on Cuba to the end, and its celebrated concessions of April 9, 1898, were, in fact, last-minute efforts to buy more time to keep the island.

The allegation of presidential weakness remains the most damning indictment of McKinley. When seen in the light of Spanish tenacity, however, what is remarkable is how long the president was able to obtain time for the conducting of peaceful diplomacy.

At any point in the process from November 1897 onward, the two countries were likely to begin fighting. Through this morass of crisis and danger, McKinley worked his way for five months in order to allow Spain the chance to submit peacefully. Finally, in April 1898, it was obvious that diplomacy had failed, that Spain would not yield, and that war was the only alternative to the prolongation of an intolerable foreign-policy situation. His conduct up to that point reveals a subtlety of action, a fortitude of will, and a simple courage that belie the easy stereotypes of his historical reputation.

The second school of McKinley's critics presents a more sophisticated bill of particulars. They question whether the motives behind the nation's concern with Cuba were genuine or whether they sprang from less attractive premises. Behind the stated reasons for American interest in Cuba lay economic causes—the tensions within a society that was emerging from a prolonged depression, an industrial machine that was glutted with its products and was seeking foreign markets, and statesmen who, unwilling to confront internal problems, preferred to export their social difficulties. The often unstated theses of this approach seem to be that the United States had, at most, marginal interests in the Cuban crisis beyond economic ones and that McKinley took his cues from the business community. On the latter point the image of the president as the tool of capitalists has confused the situation. McKinley operated within the framework of the economic system that he knew, in pursuit of the national interest of a society whose values, he thought, were basically healthy. He sought the counsel of successful businessmen on many issues, but the ostensible connections between their advice on Cuba and his actions remains ephemeral and inferential. Though the business community and its spokesmen responded to foreign policy, they did not make it.

It is possible to visualize Americans turning away from the horrors of the Cuban conflict, rejecting anything beyond the most modest role in foreign affairs, and addressing the society's inequities through some form of democratic socialism in 1898, but this is an improbable vision. The nation's historic traditions, humanitarian impulses, and economic calculations gave the Cuban problem a strong grip on the emotions of a majority of American citizens. It would have taken a revolution in attitudes, outside the existing political consensus, to have produced any other result than intense absorption in the fate of Cuba. To that foreign-policy commitment, Americans brought motives at once cynical and elevated, crass and noble. When economic causes are omitted, the picture lacks clarity, but excessive emphasis on them reduces foreign affairs to a crude equation that misreads the national character.

But was Cuba any business of the United States? Perhaps not; but it is hard to see how the effects of the rebellion could have been escaped. Few scholars advocate that the president should have joined Spain in suppressing the uprising. Another position contends that all the United States had to do was to recognize Cuba's independence, since the rebels had won militarily. Spain would have questioned whether the verdict on the war was that clear, and recognition would have meant war in any case, as 1898 showed. An independent Cuba, free from outside influence, is a laudable goal; and a unilateral defense of the American presence there during this century is difficult. It takes a great faith in the benevolent workings of international politics in these years, however, to maintain that Cuba would not, in the absence of United States involvement, have at least been the object of attention from nations such as Germany which had a larger capacity to assert their will than did Spain.

Like most wars, the Spanish-American War occurred when two nations, both convinced that they were right, pursued their national interests to an ultimate conclusion. Spain tried to defend its territorial integrity and sense of nationhood with the limited means open to it. In order to end a bloody conflict, the United States, under the leadership of William McKinley, went to war in 1898 against a foe that had resisted all attempts at peaceful compromise. The nation's motives owed far more to the better side of American life than posterity has recognized. If the war that ensued was not splendid, it had come in a way that dishonored neither the two countries involved nor the presidency of William McKinley.

5

★★★★★

THE PRESIDENT'S WAR

The war that the United States waged against Spain for a little more than three months in 1898 lingers in the national memory as a blend of farce, drama, and unexpected world responsibility. "Was there ever before such a war with such great results, so short in duration, such wonderful successes, with no reverses?" asked Senator Redfield Proctor three days after the fighting had stopped.[1] Yet, despite the abundant information on its military and diplomatic events, the war has not received very much attention as a force for social change at the end of the nineteenth century. There has been even less examination of what the war did to the presidential office under McKinley.

Men who were close to the White House agreed that William McKinley ran the war on the American side. "In all the movements of the army and navy the President's hand is seen," wrote Cortelyou in his diary. Charles Emory Smith offered a similar opinion after McKinley's death: "From the first, President McKinley assumed a close personal direction, not only of the organization of the forces but of the general plan of operations. He was Commander-in-Chief not merely in name but in fact." This judgment is correct, as the evidence reveals, but a description of how the president waged his war requires some explanation of the technical methods through which McKinley gathered information and disseminated his decisions.[2]

As the fighting started, the White House staff took over an office on the southeast corner of the second floor, which had previously been used to house executive clerks and leftover correspondence regarding patronage, but it quickly became known as the War Room. Since it adjoined the president's working area, it emerged as the communications nerve center of the government. A switchboard with twenty telegraph wires kept McKinley in touch with French and British cable lines, which ran to Cuba and other points in the Caribbean, as well as American cable lines, which connected him with the soldiers in the field and less directly with the navy. At the height of the fighting in Cuba, messages between the president and General William R. Shafter could be exchanged within twenty minutes. A former executive clerk who was now a lieutenant colonel in the volunteers, Benjamin F. Montgomery, oversaw the cable and telephone traffic inside the War Room and recorded all messages in a running diary of the day's business.

McKinley placed Brigadier General Adolphus W. Greely of the Signal Corps in charge of the government's military communications system. At a cabinet meeting early in the war, the president instructed Greely "to assume charge of all cables, exercise such control over them as is necessary for the public welfare, and is legal."[3] Beginning with only eight hundred dollars and fifty-eight men, the Signal Corps drew on the equipment and personnel of the major telegraph companies to create a network for the army in Cuba. It monitored neutral traffic to determine ship movements, and it had an agent at the telegraph office in Havana whose daily reports revealed, among other things, that the Spanish fleet was at Santiago de Cuba. The corps also found a severed submarine cable off the Cuban coast which became the direct link between American forces and the War Department. By the end of hostilities, Greely and his force, its numbers swelled by volunteers, had become an essential source for the president in making military decisions.

The administration installed in the Executive Mansion fifteen telephone lines that ran directly to the eight executive departments and to the House and Senate. From this "cable box," which had the numbers for each of the departments, the president could now coordinate policies in a manner that previously had not seemed possible. He also employed an early version of the dictaphone, called the graphaphone, to leave messages and instructions for his aides. In the telephone, McKinley found an instrument that fit his liking for a minimum of written actions, and he conducted business over it with increasing frequency after 1898. McKinley's reliance on the telephone and telegraph during the war meant that he "used remote voice communication for the first time to project presidential presence into the battle zone on a near real time basis while he remained in Washington."[4]

To follow the progress of the fighting systematically, the War Room received a supply of up-to-date charts and maps of Cuba, the Philippines, and the ocean approaches to the combat zones. The White House staff began to collect this information in April, and the president also drew on the services of the Coast and Geodetic Survey. "It is evident that I must learn a deal of geography in this war," he said to a member of the survey who had brought him maps of the Philippines, "and I am going to turn over to you the task of furnishing me the necessary maps and charts." Soon the maps filled the walls of the War Room, and the clerks recorded the movements of American and Spanish forces. The amount of data at the president's disposal expanded daily as Montgomery, Porter, Cortelyou, and the staff tabulated the locations of enemy, neutral, and United States ships. The War Room sought, and to a large extent achieved, absolute secrecy. To this headquarters, which never closed, McKinley often went in order to monitor events. "By the President's orders, he was to be awakened at any hour of the night if important intelligence should come in." The informational pressures of modern war, because vessels and forces were thousands of miles from Washington, worked with McKinley's fondness for rapid private communication to produce an early crude version of what the twentieth-century presidency would ultimately need in order to meet the demands of world-power diplomacy and the military responsibilities connected with it.[5]

Because the full collection of McKinley's personal papers became available to historians piecemeal and because the president tended to send documents to the department or bureau concerned, an accurate picture of how he shaped strategy as commander in chief can only be assembled from scattered sources. He drafted his directives on the backs of envelopes or on Executive Mansion cards, or he sent them by graphaphone message; so the form of the resulting orders did not always reveal his influence. A mid-June order to General Nelson A. Miles regarding troop dispositions was written in McKinley's own hand, and at a key juncture in negotiations with the Spanish army about its surrender in Cuba, the president inserted tougher language in a telegram to the American commander. Day by day, and sometimes on an hour-to-hour basis, the president oversaw the war. In so doing, he laid the foundation for the modern presidency.

As hostilities began, McKinley made two additional changes in his cabinet. In late 1897 he named Attorney General Joseph McKenna to the Supreme Court. John W. Griggs of New Jersey took his place, soon becoming one of McKinley's closest advisors. Postmaster General James A. Gary stepped down because of ill health, and Charles Emory Smith, owner of the *Philadelphia Press,* succeeded him. The most important shift involved Secretary of State Sherman. For months, McKinley and Day had by-passed Sherman, but the war left no leeway for senility and ineptitude. With growing evidence of Sherman's incapacity, the president secured his resignation on April 25, 1898. Day agreed to serve as secretary of state until the end of the war, and John Bassett Moore, an expert on international law from Columbia University, became first assistant secretary. Moore had advised the state department during Cleveland's second term. Now, as he assumed a large and direct policy-making role, he became an early example of McKinley's policy of enlisting experts and academicians for his government. The Sherman mistake had now been rectified, and McKinley had a functioning team in his most vital executive department. Cabinet changes during McKinley's term worked to improve the quality of his administration. Had he dumped Secretary of War Alger at this point, his government would have been strengthened further. At the outset of the war, however, the impact that such an action would have had on public confidence precluded taking it. McKinley had not yet realized, though he was beginning to see signs, that Alger would fall short as a war leader.

Within two weeks of the start of hostilities the American people learned of Commodore George Dewey's overwhelming triumph against the Spanish at Manila Bay on May 1, 1898. This initial victory in which Dewey sank seven Spanish ships without the loss of any American vessels and with only slight casualties was, according to Senator Cushman K. Davis, "unequalled in the annals of naval warfare."[6] The battle also transformed the war against Spain into a turning point in American history. In the popular mind the immediate thought was not how the United States might avoid decisions over the fate of the Philippines but what the country should do with its prize of war.

In later years, with disillusion about American imperialism in fashion, Dewey's presence at Manila would be attributed to the fortuitous actions of Theodore Roosevelt as assistant secretary of the navy on February 25, 1898. With Secretary of the Navy Long out of the office that day, the impetuous, imperialistic Roosevelt wired Dewey: "In the event of declaration of war Spain, your duty will be to see that the Spanish squadron does not leave the Asiatic coast, and then offensive operations in Philippine Islands." A long-time advocate of a "Large Policy" in Asia, Roosevelt allegedly had seen an opportunity while the McKinley administration was asleep; and acquisition of the Philippines, with all its anguish, was the result. This popular account is dramatic and compelling. McKinley and Long recede into the background, and Roosevelt looms as almost a president three years in advance of becoming one.[7]

The actual sequence of events is more complex, and Roosevelt's message shrinks in importance. Naval planning for an attack on the Philippines dated back to 1895, when the possibility of a Spanish-American conflict over Cuba first arose. A year later the Office of Naval Intelligence proposed, if war came, to strike at Spain at a vulnerable point in its Asian colony. During the next year the Navy first discarded and then readopted this plan as its strategy against Spain. In June 1897 the naval board that was charged with war-planning recommended that an effort should be made to help the rebels against Spanish rule in the islands. A naval assault on Manila might, in aiding the insurgents, obtain for the United States "a controlling voice, as to what should become of the islands, when the final settlement was made."[8] In late October 1897 Commodore Dewey was named commander in chief of the Asiatic Squadron, and the Philippine plan, whose general outlines he already knew, was available to him in early 1898, when he took over his new assignment. As the Cuban crisis worsened, the navy relayed orders to Dewey in accordance with the plan. On January 27 he was told to retain men whose enlistments had expired. Roosevelt's wire of February 25 was part of this preparatory process. It did not change the course of events, nor did Secretary Long, when he returned the next day, rescind it.

The actual directive to attack the Spanish at Manila was based on McKinley's decision. Upon the declaration of war the navy advised Long that "we should strike at once at the Spanish fleet in the Philippines." As Long recalled, the Bureau of Navigation prepared the order, which he approved and McKinley signed. The president postponed action on the order when Long first raised the question on April 21, but three days later, on Sunday, April 24, gave the signal for the attack to begin. Dewey was told to proceed at once to the Philippine Islands. "Commence operations at once, particularly against Spanish fleet. You must capture vessels or destroy. Use utmost endeavor." A week later the battle was over, and Spanish power in the Pacific had been destroyed.[9]

Dewey's victory transformed the military and diplomatic context of the war during its opening week. To the initial aim of ousting Spain from Cuba were now added the alluring possibilities of expanding America's economic and political influence in Asia and the role of being a genuine world power. During the 1890s, interest in the potential markets of China had quickened among some members of the business community. American trade with China, though it did not constitute a large proportion of the nation's total commerce, went up from about $7 million in exports in 1892 to nearly $12 million in 1897. During the first year of McKinley's term, the advocates of a greater trade with China sent in petitions and passed resolutions calling on the administration to protect American interests in Asia. Equally vociferous were the spokesmen for the nation's Protestant churches, who saw the Far East as an arena for an evangelical effort.

The extent to which these pressures actually affected policy-making is debatable. Preoccupied with the Spanish crisis, the McKinley administration had only modest resources with which to carry on an Asian policy before the spring of 1898. It watched the European powers penetrate China in 1897/1898, as France, Russia, Germany, and Great Britain obtained trading privileges or territorial concessions. In December 1897 a cabinet officer told reporters that the government had decided "to keep a watchful eye on the situation as it developed," and the president substituted a veteran diplomat, Edwin H. Conger, for an earlier choice as minister to China. But McKinley did not wish to go beyond diplomatic probing. In March 1898 the British asked whether the United States would join "in opposing any action by foreign Powers which could tend to restrict the opening of China to the commerce of all nations." In the midst of the Cuban problem, the president did no more than assert that he was "in sympathy with the policy which shall maintain open trade" in China.[10]

After Dewey had triumphed over the Spanish, America's displeasure over Spain's rule in Cuba converged with the McKinley administration's desire to broaden the nation's economic role. Somewhere between accident and design, the United States pursued a line of policy that included an opportunistic assault on a vulnerable point for Spain, a generalized awareness that a greater naval presence in the Pacific would support economic initiatives in Asia, and a commitment to the view that foreign markets were a beneficial addition to the nation's search for prosperity. President McKinley never did set down a comprehensive statement of his position on

America's role in the Orient; but he believed, as did many of his countrymen, that good business and proper morality would fuse when western goods and Christian morality penetrated the Far East.

Few historians contend that the president had decided before May 1 to take the Philippines for the United States. Most of them date his decision well before his October 28 message to the peace commissioners in Paris, which instructed them to demand all of the islands from Spain. McKinley's conduct from May 2 onward indicates that he had never given serious consideration to relinquishing the archipelago. The question had always been whether to hold only a portion or to occupy and demand all of it. As a result, he acted in a manner that would ensure the success of any ultimate decision to take the Philippines. Therefore, in the last half of 1898, he exercised the power of his office in a manner that matched many of the assertive actions of his most noteworthy immediate successors, Theodore Roosevelt and Woodrow Wilson.

The administration did not learn officially about Dewey's triumph until May 7, but newspapers on May 2 carried the outlines of what had transpired. As Americans celebrated what seemed to be an outstanding success, the president, Secretaries Long and Alger, and the chief military commanders met at the White House to shape strategy against Spain. It was decided to send five thousand troops to the islands for, in McKinley's words, "such service as may be ordered hereafter." By May 8, as military preparations began, the State Department reported that a member of the British government had asked John Hay, the American ambassador, about terms on which the United States might make peace. As the government explored the origins of this initiative, John Bassett Moore drew up a tentative list of conditions for a settlement. On the Philippines he proposed that Spain retain them, "she ceding to us a coaling station in that group or in the Carolines." Moore noted that the United States did not yet have possession of the islands, and that they might be a bargaining chip in trying to persuade Spain to leave Cuba. The memorandum, which was discussed at a cabinet meeting on May 11, continued to be the basic formulation of the American position into early June.[11]

On the military side, however, the commitment to the Philippines was hardening. By May 11 the number of troops allocated to the expedition had risen to over ten thousand, and the War Department assigned General Wesley Merritt to lead the American forces. The president also arranged to send a geologist to the Philippines to survey their mineral resources, and he began to collect and read

97

the available information on the islands. On May 16 McKinley created the Department of the Pacific, under Merritt's command, a department that was "intended to include Philippine Islands only." His orders to Merritt, which were written on May 19, asserted a "twofold purpose of completing the reduction of the Spanish power in that quarter and of giving order and security to the islands while in the possession of the United States." The president gave the general large powers, under military authority, to set up new legal systems, to raise taxes, and to confiscate property. As to the Philippine rebels, McKinley noted that the American commander, while respecting the existing political arrangements, would be bound "to adopt measures of a different kind if, unfortunately, the course of the people should render such measures indispensable to the maintenance of law and order." On May 29 the size of Merritt's force was again increased, to twenty thousand men. It was evident, said a Washington reporter in early June, that "the United States has no idea of surrendering the newly acquired territory in the Far East."[12]

The president also threw his influence behind the renewed effort on Capitol Hill to secure the annexation of Hawaii by joint resolution. Ambassador Hay wired the State Department on May 3 that "an excellent authority in German matters" recommended "prompt action in annexation Hawaii before war closes as otherwise Germany might seek to complicate the question with Samoa or Philippine Islands." The islands would be vital if the United States had to carry on a campaign in the Philippines; there the soldiers and sailors could obtain food, water, and exercise, while their ships were refueling from Hawaiian coal supplies. On May 4 a Democratic congressman, Francis G. Newlands of Nevada, introduced a resolution in the House, and Secretary Day helped to obtain favorable action on the resolution in the House Foreign Affairs Committee on May 12. Reported to the full House on May 17, the Hawaiian measure encountered the determined opposition of Speaker Reed. For three weeks the Speaker, a bitter enemy of McKinley's who opposed expansionism on principle, blocked consideration of the resolution. The White House issued material to the press, questioning whether Reed could persist indefinitely in tactics "which may excite the active and open antagonism of a large majority of his party in the House." McKinley called congressmen to his office to emphasize the utmost importance of annexation. News leaks raised the prospect that the president would simply seize Hawaii under the war power. By early June, Reed had yielded to presidential pressure. Floor debate began on June 11, and the resolution passed four days later by 209 to 91.[13]

The resolution reached the Senate on June 17, coming up for debate on June 20; and the discussion went on until July 6. The opposition was composed primarily of Democrats, though some Republicans, wary of expansion, resisted as well. When the anti-annexation forces pressed for an early adjournment in order to forestall a vote, McKinley said, in the press and privately, that "there must be no thought of adjournment until Hawaii was acted upon."[14] Presidential lobbying succeeded when the Senate voted 42 in favor, 21 against, and 26 not voting, for the resolution on July 6. The outbreak of the Spanish-American War did not turn Hawaiian annexation from a failure into a triumph in Congress. The war did not transform the balance of voting power in the Senate. The annexationists had about 55 votes in their column in January, and allocation of the 26 nonvoters in July indicates that they were still several votes short of the required two-thirds. The basic strategy for securing annexation by joint resolution was developed before the Cuban crisis had intensified, and McKinley's pressure was a central element in the ultimate victory. The annexation of Hawaii belongs among the legislative accomplishments of his first term.

On the question of the Philippines the administration kept to the position that it had adopted in early May through the first week of June. When Ambassador Hay again reported a strong desire in London about terms of a possible peace, Secretary Day and Moore reviewed the May 9 memorandum with the president. On June 3 Hay was told that "the President, speaking for himself, would be inclined to grant terms of peace" on the basis of Spanish evacuation of Cuba, the cession of Puerto Rico to the United States, and the granting of an island, probably Guam, in the Ladrones in the Pacific. The Philippines would "be allowed to remain with Spain, except a port and necessary appurtenances, to be selected by the United States, shall be ceded to the United States." At the same time, the military commitment swelled as more ships and additional troops moved to embarkation points in San Francisco.[15]

By the middle of June, however, McKinley and his advisors were compelled to recognize an additional element in the Philippine situation. In 1896 Emilio Aguinaldo led an insurrection against Spanish rule in the islands. After a year of fighting, the rebels concluded an agreement with Spain in December 1897 that called for the voluntary exile of the leaders of the revolt, cash payments from Spain, and an amnesty. During the next three months the revolutionaries regrouped, and fighting resumed in March 1898. After the war with Spain had commenced, the American consul in Singapore, E. Spencer Pratt, met with Aguinaldo on April 24; then Pratt reported to Dewey at Hong Kong that the rebel commander would arrange for "general cooperation [with the] insurgents [in] Manila if desired." Dewey wired back that Aguinaldo should come as soon as possible; but before the Filipino could reach Hong Kong, the United States Fleet had left for Manila. Two weeks later, Dewey permitted Aguinaldo to come on an American vessel to Manila, where he "was received with great enthusiasm by the natives."[16]

Once he had returned, Aguinaldo continued to organize his revolution. He issued a proclamation on May 24, saying that the United States had come "manifesting a protection as decisive as it is undoubtedly disinterested toward our inhabitants, considering us as sufficiently civilized and capable of governing for ourselves our unfortunate country." He set up a "dictatorial government," and he also published decrees regulating the revolt against the Spanish. The administration reacted quickly to Aguinaldo's presence. A dispatch from Dewey, reporting that the Filipino leader was "organizing forces near Cavite and may render assistance that will be valuable," reached Washington on May 25. It was given to McKinley, and he replied, through Long: "It is desirable, as far as possible, and consistent for your success and safety, not to have political alliances with the insurgents or any faction in the islands that would incur our liability to maintain their cause in the future." Two weeks later the State Department received reports from the consuls in Singapore and Manila that discussed their cooperation in arranging for Aguinaldo's journey to the Philippines, cooperation that in Pratt's words had "prevented possible conflict of action and facilitated the work of occupying and administering the Philippines."[17]

Combined with other information about insurgent activity, however, these messages prompted the McKinley administration to reconsider its posture toward the islands. Hay was informed on June 14 that conditions in the June 3 peace terms would "probably have to be modified. The insurgents there have become an important factor in the situation and must have just consideration in any terms of settlement." Dewey was ordered the same day to report fully on any previous conferences with Aguinaldo and to inform Washington of any additional meetings.[18]

The State Department, conveying "the President's views on the subject of your relations with General Aguinaldo," instructed Consul Pratt, on June 16, to "avoid unauthorized negotiations with Philippine insurgents." In a fuller statement, Secretary Day warned that "this Government has known the Philippine insurgents only as discontented and rebellious subjects of Spain, and is not acquainted with their purposes." Any action taken by Pratt that involved cooperation with Aguinaldo's plans or that recognized "any political claims which he may put forward" was unauthorized and disapproved.[19]

While preventing any formal political contacts with the insurgents, McKinley told callers that though he was undecided about the eventual status of the Philippines, he favored "the general principle of holding on to what we get." As he noted in a personal memorandum at the start of the war: "While we are conducting war and until its conclusion we must keep all we get; when the war is over we must keep what we want." To Henry Cabot Lodge and others, McKinley expressed the hope that the "insurgents will develop enough strength to solve the problem by setting up a government of their own under our protection—we to keep Manila," and he worried about "the questions of race, climate, etc.," that made him "doubtful . . . about our keeping the whole group." But he added significantly, "If, however as we go on it is made to appear desirable that we should retain all, then we will certainly do it."[20]

Whatever the president had decided at this point, and his qualms are less telling than his actions, he was careful to keep his options open and his purposes obscure. By the time that American troops reached the Philippines on June 30, the direction of McKinley's policy was clear to informed observers in Washington. In carrying on negotiations over peace, said a cabinet member to the press, the United States would insist that Spain relinquish its sovereignty over Cuba, Puerto Rico, and the Philippines. Such negotiations, however, depended on the outcome of fighting in Cuba; and at the end of June, American and Spanish forces faced each other outside Santiago de Cuba.

Before the war with Spain had begun, advocates of a belligerent policy had predicted that if fighting should come, the conquest of Cuba would be easy. These optimistic forecasts had faded when United States troops went ashore near Santiago de Cuba in late June. President McKinley found that even a small war in the late nineteenth century required greater societal exertions than had been anticipated. Therefore the White House spent the first two months of the conflict raising an army, devising a strategy, and responding to the naval actions of the enemy. While these activities were occurring, the public passed from initial enthusiasm to impatience for action to a skepticism about the performance of the army and the War Department that persisted long after the hostilities had ended.

As his fostering of a modern communications capacity revealed, William McKinley expected to play the decisive part in the management of the war effort. He soon decided that the civilian and military subordinates at his disposal were not adequate to their responsibilities, and he moved to limit their influence on his policies. Secretary of War Alger, who had only recently recuperated from a heart-connected illness, displayed an inordinate sense of egotism, which impaired the efficiency of his department. His information was not always reliable, especially his optimistic predictions in April and May about how quickly the volunteer soldiers would be ready for duty. He interfered in details of mobilization, quarreled with senior army officers, and seemed to the president to make promises and then to equivocate about the War Department's performance. McKinley was already disillusioned with Alger by the late spring; the public outcry over disease in the army camps and in Cuba, as well as the state of the food that the troops received, would in the summer combine to make Alger a positive liability.

The commanding general of the army, Nelson A. Miles, who was nationally prominent, was a striking physical embodiment of the military presence. He was also vain and impractical in the high councils of the government and had presidential ambitions. McKinley wearied of his posturing, but could have forgiven that had the general not blundered over the selection of rifles for the army, erred in the choice of campsites for the volunteers, and feuded with Alger over minor points of procedure.

Looking elsewhere for reliable counsel, McKinley first turned to General James M. Schofield. The former commanding general proved to be only a modest improvement on Miles. As his advice produced disruption and rancor, Schofield gave way to the adjutant general, Henry C. Corbin. A friend of many leaders among Ohio Republicans, Corbin was smooth where Miles grated and was efficient where Alger was not. By May 1898 Corbin had McKinley's confidence and soon emerged as the most influential officer in Washington. "In all the work of organizing, planning, and operating," Charles Emory Smith remembered, "the President relied on his judgment and execution."[21] He was, in effect, the commander of the army, and he retained McKinley's trust until September 1901. With Alger's cooperation, Corbin enabled the War Department to function with greater effectiveness. In particular, he encouraged individual initiative among commanders in the Quartermaster and Medical bureaus and fostered the same spirit in line officers.

The army that McKinley and Corbin directed had changed rapidly from the 25,000 regular officers and men who were in uniform at the beginning of 1898. The War Department, when faced with the likelihood of a conflict, had originally planned to expand the army from the existing base of regular troops to a force of approximately 75,000 to 100,000 men. These soldiers, army planners thought, would be enough to meet any challenge that Spain posed, after the navy had defeated the enemy fleet. Expansion required congressional action, and a bill, sponsored by Congressman John A. T. Hull of Iowa, was introduced on March 17. During a war, the bill said, the president could raise the army's authorized strength to 104,000 men. Building upon the existing structure of regiments and companies, the bill envisioned a minimal part for volunteers and the National Guard. At the end of March the Hull bill seemed to be assured of prompt approval.

Patriotic fervor and the opposition of the National Guard soon caused the Hull measure to stall. Volunteers disapproved of the prospect of serving under regular officers, and the National Guard would have been all but excluded under the proposed legislation. When the Hull bill was debated on April 6 in the House, it encountered withering criticism from a coalition of National Guard supporters, Southern Democrats, and Populists. Even when the sponsors of the bill made substantial concessions to its opponents, the House returned it to committee on April 7 by a sizeable vote. With war only weeks away, the War Department's mobilization program was in ruins.

As the administration reshaped its thinking about the expansion of the army, it took into account the power of congressional sentiment in favor of a volunteer force. Discussions with National Guard leaders in mid April resulted in plans to have the president raise a force of volunteers who would come from the states and could serve in their National Guard units when they enlisted as a body. Once in the service, the organization of these units would have to correspond to that of the regulars. An initial call for 60,000 troops was contemplated, and the president would be responsible for appointing all volunteer officers. A bill embodying these provisions cleared Congress on April 22, but a call for 60,000 men would not have allowed all the prospective National Guard volunteers to enlist. With the Hull bill, which the army wanted, hung up in the House, the administration expanded the call for volunteers to 125,000 men.

On April 23 McKinley issued his first summons for volunteers in that amount, and the National Guard was appeased. The Hull legislation, which enlarged the regular army to 61,000 men, passed both houses easily and became law on April 26, 1898.

As a result of the popular eagerness to join the army, said Francis E. Warren, the War Department building was "filled daily so that both sides nearly bulge out with a steaming, surging and sometimes nasty crowd who are insisting for places." Secretary Alger saw an average of one hundred visitors a day about appointments, and a comparable number descended on McKinley. In May, Cortelyou attributed the strain on the president in part to "the struggle for place among the ambitious gentlemen who desire to serve their country in high salaried and high titled positions."[22]

The president devoted a large amount of time to these personnel decisions because of their obvious political implications and because of his desire to make the war an occasion to enhance national unity. The appointments of Fitzhugh Lee of Virginia and Joseph Wheeler of Alabama as major generals, along with the selection of other southerners and Democrats for lesser commissions, conciliated the South. While he gave numerous staff positions to relatives of prominent Republicans, McKinley did not neglect Democrats, nor did he put professional competence aside when he chose regular or volunteer officers.

At the outbreak of the war the American people apparently expected that the performance of the armed services would demonstrate the nation's material and military superiority. The highly professional and efficient navy lived up to these assumptions with Dewey's victory at Manila Bay and the later triumph at Santiago. By allowing his officers to execute their duties with only a minimum of direction, Secretary Long impressed McKinley as being a reliable cabinet officer whose actions contributed to the war effort and benefited the administration. The War Department was much less successful. The difficulties that it encountered and the blunders that it made soon aroused a popular distrust of Secretary Alger. The chorus of attacks on the record of the secretary and the department grew so loud in early June that Alger told reporters: "When war was declared, we were unprepared, yet obstacles almost insurmountable have been overcome." Alger would issue more defenses of his record, but cries for his resignation dotted the nation's editorial pages.[23]

In the spring of 1898 the War Department confronted conditions that would have hampered the most vigorous and effective administrator. Years of congressional penny-pinching, in response to the society's neglect of the army, had left only the nucleus of a modern armed service. In its internal organization the department lacked central authority; power was diffused among civilian officials, generals, and competing bureaus. The prospect of war with Spain had not produced much specific preparedness activity before mid April. The bulk of the money for national defense that Congress allocated in March went to the navy. With war unlikely in the 1890s, no comprehensive plan existed for equipping and training a large army of volunteers. American policy makers assumed that the navy would defeat the Spanish at sea and that an expanded regular force would prosecute a campaign in Cuba. The outcome of the Hull bill in Congress put those expectations aside, and the army turned to raising, training, and outfitting the 278,000 men who saw active service.

The first month of the war exposed all the weaknesses that neglect and parsimony had inflicted upon the army. Of the five thousand wagons needed to move men and supplies, there were only twelve hundred on hand. Delays in production were not overcome until after the war. Ammunition supplies were also inadequate. Had all the soldiers who had been mobilized seen combat, there would not have been enough bullets for them. The modern Krag-Jorgensen rifle could only be given to regular troops because there were shortages of the weapon and of the smokeless powder that it used. Uniforms, tents, cartridge belts, and mess kits were not available in the needed amounts, and supply officers improvised in order to meet the requirements of the burgeoning number of troops. The supply of food was, from the first, generally sufficient; but experiments with canned roast beef led to a postwar controversy over the army's meat supply.

Conditions in the camps where the troops assembled offered the most public evidence of the problems that the War Department faced. The army's outmoded and inefficient procedures could not deal with the masses of men to be fed, housed, clothed, and trained in the early weeks of the war. Few officers knew how to manage large numbers of troops, and conflicting responsibilities among quartermaster, ordnance, and medical officers caused frictions that multiplied the disorganization. Some camps had too much of a particular piece of equipment; others were short of everything. The most notorious camp was the one at Tampa, Florida, where a single rail line served a force of seventeen thousand men.

Some of the trouble lay with the lack of preparedness of the

National Guard. Many members were reluctant to volunteer for two years, and the units that entered the service were not as well trained as their advocates had predicted. Fewer states than anticipated were able to equip their soldiers to the standards of the army. The War Department struggled, with increasing success, to surmount these obstacles by June 1898. Alger and Corbin granted authority to officers on the scene, and as these men began to deal with immediate problems, a greater sense of order and direction emerged. By the end of July the army was in a condition of readiness and efficiency that surpassed what might have been hoped for in the near-chaos of May. Unfortunately for Alger and the McKinley administration, the first impression of bungling and confusion continued to be the fixed public memory of the army's performance. The course of the war and its consequences for American troops in Cuba only confirmed the initial verdict about Alger's ineptitude and the army's shortcomings.

Developments that had the greatest influence on the performance of the army and the War Department, causing them to make changes in strategy, were Spanish naval actions, shifts in American foreign policy, and the hazards of a land campaign in Cuba. After the fighting had ended, McKinley pondered over how the fortunes of war had affected the president's conduct as commander in chief. In Boston in February 1899 he said: "The President can direct the movement of soldiers in the field and fleets upon the sea, but he cannot foresee the close of such movements or prescribe their limits. He cannot anticipate or avoid the consequences, but he must meet them."[24] McKinley was recalling how his own priorities and war aims had adjusted to alterations in the military and diplomatic situation that confronted the United States.

In mid April the administration expected the main combat activity to be naval. Once the American fleet had defeated its Spanish counterpart, an invasion of Cuba would be considered. Because the army was unprepared and because there was a real danger of malaria and yellow fever on the island during the summer months, it seemed more prudent to rely on a naval blockade, to launch some armed raids against the Spanish forces, and to furnish arms and material to the rebels. Spanish troops in Cuba numbered about eighty thousand effective fighting men, and the capture of Havana would be a task of some difficulty. On April 20 a conference at the White House ratified these decisions. The navy blockaded Cuba on April 23, and the army prepared to send an expedition of five thousand men to the southern coast of Cuba to link up with the rebels under Máximo Gómez and to supply them with arms. A representative of the Cuban junta wrote to McKinley on April 26 to promise "the most complete co-operation of the Cuban army with the military forces of the United States." He added that "to save the lives of the unacclimated American troops," the Cubans were ready, "if arms and ammunition are promptly provided, to stand the brunt of the fighting on the Island."[25] On April 29 General William R. Shafter was directed to conduct a strike in Cuba, among other things, to help the insurgents.

The Spanish Fleet, under Admiral Pascual de Cervera, left the Cape Verde islands in the Atlantic that same day, "and for almost two weeks the Navy Department floundered in a sea of ignorance as to his whereabouts." The effective disappearance of the Spanish ships, a detachment whose fighting capacity was not underestimated, caused the Shafter expedition to be postponed on April 30. Troops continued to flow to the American base at Tampa during May. Though the port and its nearby town were adequate for the assembling of the rather small raiding force that had originally been envisioned, they were ill suited for a much larger number of troops. By the end of the month, seventeen thousand men were crowded into the camp. Two weeks later, Theodore Roosevelt, now an officer with the First Volunteer Cavalry, told his friend Henry Cabot Lodge that "no words could describe to you the confusion and lack of system and the general mismanagement of affairs here." As General Shafter explained to his superiors: "The place was overestimated and its capacities are exceeded."[26]

The expansion of the force at Tampa also reflected changes in the administration's strategy toward Cuba. The defeat of the Spanish Fleet at Manila reduced the fears about Cervera's potential effectiveness in the Caribbean; therefore the Atlantic Fleet did not appear in Cuban waters in early May, when the sailing time that had been projected for Cervera should have brought him there. Adding to the pressure for an invasion of the island were the navy's problems in sustaining a blockade of the Cuban coast and the more optimistic evaluations of the dangers from disease in Cuba. If the United States remained passive, moreover, the chances of European intervention might reappear. Finally, political control of the island's destiny at the end of the fighting could hinge on the ability of the United States to dominate the rebels with troops on the ground.

At the May 2 conference, where the Philippines expedition was arranged, McKinley decided to authorize an invasion of Cuba, with Havana as the primary target. Fifty thousand troops would compose the main force, and Alger said that they would be ready in less than three weeks. The president and the secretary of war expected that volunteers would supplement the regulars to make up the invading army. During that same week, Shafter told Washington that his troops could commence the campaign after May 12. In response he was ordered on May 9 to seize a position on Cuba's north coast from which an army could operate. A series of delays and obstacles now upset this timetable. First, the navy sought a postponement until May 16, so that it could assemble its ships to escort Shafter's soldiers. Attempts to coordinate the movement of volunteers revealed that they were less prepared than the administration had anticipated. Shortages of ammunition and deficiencies of fresh water at Key West prompted General Miles to urge McKinley to postpone the invasion in favor of an attack on Puerto Rico. Then, on May 13, Admiral Cervera's fleet was sighted off Martinique. The presence of the enemy caused the War Department to put off the attack on Havana, which nevertheless continued to be the primary target through the end of May.

A week later, on May 19, Greely's telegraph service reported that, according to a spy in Havana, Cervera's forces had escaped the American ships that were looking for him and had slipped into the harbor of Santiago de Cuba, on the southern side of the island. By May 29 the navy had confirmed that Cervera was at Santiago, and on June 1 the bulk of the American fleet, under Admiral William T. Sampson, bottled up the Spanish. Acting on the news from Greely, McKinley assembled another war council on May 26, 1898, which consisted of Alger, Long, Miles, and three navy representatives, including Captain Alfred T. Mahan. Miles argued that the assault on Havana should be shelved in favor of an expedition against Santiago and an attack on Puerto Rico. McKinley agreed. Santiago was appealing as an objective because it offered an isolated force of ten thousand Spaniards and the opportunity to destroy a substantial portion of the enemy's naval strength; its seizure would also aid in capturing Puerto Rico. Miles's idea contained some grandiose aspects, including a cavalry thrust across central Cuba. McKinley disapproved of these. On May 31 Corbin instructed Shafter to land near Santiago de Cuba and to "capture or destroy the garrison there" while aiding the navy to deal with the Spanish Fleet. Conveying McKinley's wishes, Corbin reminded the American commander of "the importance of accomplishing this object with the least possible delay." Meanwhile, Puerto Rico would be attacked, once Santiago had fallen.[27]

It required almost two weeks to load Shafter's troops for the voyage to Cuba. Tampa was by this time a tangled confusion of men, supplies, and animals. McKinley sent peremptory telegrams through Alger and Corbin, asking Shafter: "When you will get away?" The general answered that "it seems we are awfully slow in getting off, but I have been working night and day since I have been here." The president's patience with the delay in sailing wore away until, on the evening of June 7, with the loading process already begun, he ordered Shafter "to sail at once with what force you have ready." By the next day, after a disorganized scramble to get on board the ships, the American flotilla was on its way. An erroneous report that Spanish ships had been sighted then caused a postponement of the sailing until June 14. The expedition, as Theodore Roosevelt wrote, was "packed and sweltering on these troop ships in Tampa Bay under the semi-tropical June sun."[28] Finally the invasion force left Florida, arriving off Santiago on June 20. Following consultations with Admiral Sampson and General Calixto Garcia of the Cuban rebels, Shafter sent his soldiers onto the island on June 22. Four days later the landings were completed.

General William R. Shafter was a veteran of the Civil War, where he won the Medal of Honor, and he had fought Indians in the Southwest during the late 1860s and 1870s. But he lacked experience in handling large military formations, and he was not a good administrator in the field. Worst of all, he did not look like a general. At sixty-three years of age, he was fat and slovenly. But these weaknesses and his weight were balanced by his good sense, his determination, and his ability to make a decision. His appointment owed little to the Michigan background and veterans' work that he shared with Alger. Generals Corbin and Miles both recommended him to McKinley, and the president accepted the judgment of his highest military advisors.

With the war now in its land-combat phase, President McKinley followed Shafter's progress, as well as the naval engagement that accompanied it, by means of the telegraph in the War Room. On June 24, American soldiers, including the Rough Riders, had a sharp fight with the Spaniards at Las Guasimas, and Shafter sent his troops against the Spanish fortifications outside Santiago on July 1. The day-long battle for San Juan Hill ended with the Americans being in possession of the first line of the city's defenses. The cost in dead and wounded had been heavy.

Despite the direct contact with Shafter's headquarters, the

White House could only wait through the long hours of July 1 for word on the progress of the battle. The general had said that he would keep the War Department continually advised, but it was late evening before he reported that his army was in possession of the "outer works" of the Spanish. The first casualty reports were "above 400," but then Shafter's second message said that he had underestimated them. The telegraph then fell silent until July 3, when he informed Washington that he could not assault Santiago successfully, had suffered heavy losses, and was "seriously considering withdrawing about 5 miles" to new positions. He did not reveal that he had also asked the Spanish commander in Santiago to surrender. Secretary Alger replied: "Of course you can judge the situation better than we can at this end of the line"; but in words that had probably been cleared with McKinley, Alger added: "If, however, you could hold your present position, especially San Juan heights, the effect upon the country would be much better than falling back." Shafter had noted that his own health was not good, and Corbin wired him that afternoon: "The Secretary of War, no less than the President, is very desirous to know how you are feeling to-day."[29]

If the president's inquiry displayed a certain impatience, McKinley's apprehensive state of mind on July 3 is understandable. Reports reaching Washington indicated that Cervera's fleet had broken out of Santiago Harbor and escaped. A further dispatch that evening left the outcome of the naval battle in doubt, though a subsequent message from Greely's Signal Corps confirmed a complete American triumph. On the Fourth of July a telegram came from Admiral Sampson announcing that Cervera's fleet had been destroyed. The nation broke into celebrations as the full magnitude of the victory emerged. In a running fight the Americans had destroyed all the decrepit enemy vessels. General Shafter added to the pleasure in the White House late on July 3, first with the news that he had demanded the surrender of the Spanish in the city and later with the pledge that he would hold his position. Spain's position was manifestly hopeless, but the president faced more than a month of decisions and diplomacy before the fighting officially ended.

Negotiations between Shafter and the Spanish general in Santiago, José Toral, consumed the two weeks after the assault on San Juan Hill and the naval battle. McKinley closely monitored Shafter's discussions, and he kept his commander tied to the president's purposes. On July 8 Toral proposed to evacuate the city if his troops would be allowed to retreat to another location with their equipment and weapons. Shafter advised Washington to accept, because this would free Santiago Harbor, save civilian and military lives, and relieve his forces, among whom three cases of yellow fever had been found. McKinley had become dubious about the general's fighting ability. After consulting with Alger and Corbin on July 4, he authorized a message to be sent to Shafter, expressing "sorrow and anxiety" about his illness and telling him that he "must determine whether your condition is such as to require you to relinquish command." Shafter said no more about his health, and he accepted the presence of General Miles, who was sent from Washington to aid him. When Shafter's telegram about the Spanish truce proposal came in, McKinley dealt with it personally.[30]

The government's response went out over Corbin's signature in the third person. A draft containing the president's corrections survives. Shafter was reminded that he had said early in the day that his position was impregnable and that the Spanish "would yet surrender unconditionally" because the Americans could cut off their supplies. "Under these circumstances," the president continued, "your message recommending that Spanish troops be permitted to evacuate and proceed without molestation to Holguin is a great surprise and is not approved." Another presidential telegram followed: "What you went to Santiago for was the Spanish army. If you allow it to evacuate with its arms you must meet it somewhere else. This is not war."[31]

While he peremptorily rejected the idea of allowing the Spanish to evacuate, McKinley was more receptive to Alger's proposal that the United States transport the enemy troops who were in Santiago back to Spain once they had surrendered. This offer was made to Toral on July 10, but he said no. On July 10 and 11 the Americans and the Spanish fought a rifle and artillery duel at long range. When truce negotiations resumed on July 12, Toral once again asked to be allowed to leave the city under honorable conditions. The president was still adamant against any change in the instructions of July 9. At this juncture, Generals Shafter and Miles introduced a new element into the military calculations. Following an exposition of why a truce would be advisable, Miles said, in a message sent early on July 13: "There are 100 cases of yellow fever in this command and the opinion of the surgeon [is] that it will spread rapidly."[32]

The president called a cabinet meeting that day, which turned into "a long sit-down of two or three hours." Secretary Long wrote that the administration was "pained at the delays at Santiago" and that it was "inclined to think" that the American officers who were negotiating with the Spanish were being deceived "with truces and offers of terms of surrender." There was some bickering between Secretary Alger and Captain Mahan, who was a member of the naval war board and directed that service's strategy, over army-navy cooperation or lack of it in breaking the siege. Then the president decided to press Toral to surrender in accordance with the terms that had already been proposed. Miles and Shafter were told to attack, "unless in your judgment an assault would fail." As to the yellow-fever problem, troops were to be sent, once the Spanish had given up, to camps "on high ground near the coast and within easy reach of their base of supplies." Other measures were ordered for the purpose of minimizing the possible spread of the disease.[33]

While the cabinet was deliberating, Miles and Shafter conferred again with Toral, giving him twenty-four hours in which to capitulate or face another attack. Hearing of this, Alger renewed the offer to send the Spanish prisoners across the Atlantic. Faced with the prospect of a naval bombardment and an attack from Shafter's men, Toral asked for and received from his superior in Havana the permission to surrender. When the peace talks resumed, the scheduled American attacks were called off. Two days of negotiation brought about a Spanish capitulation on July 17. Toral's officers kept their sidearms, and the United States agreed to transport their enemies home. In return, Shafter obtained the surrender of Santiago and the rest of eastern Cuba.

As the surrender of Santiago neared, General Miles moved on to attack Puerto Rico. His troops, which landed on July 25, conquered most of the island, except for San Juan, with only slight losses during the two weeks that remained of the war. In contrast to the confusion in Cuba, the supply problems in the Puerto Rican campaign were minimal. Few newspapermen accompanied Miles, and the efficiency and speed of this army exercise did not receive the publicity that attended the events in Cuba.

By the last weeks in June, with American troops in Cuba, sentiment in Spain for a negotiated peace gathered strength. The main source of opposition to a peace initiative was the army. One reason for the suicidal effort of the Spanish Fleet to escape from Santiago was to demonstrate that every means of military resistance had been tried. The destruction of Cervera's vessels made the reinforcement and resupply of the army impossible. With their navy destroyed, the Spanish could not support their forces in the colonies, and the coast of the homeland lay exposed to the American navy. The foreign minister said to the French ambassador on July 9: "Our troops are ready to continue the struggle." Nine days later, after Santiago had fallen and American troops were advancing in Puerto Rico and building their numbers in the Philippines, Spain asked France to approach the United States about "negotiation of a suspension of hostilities, preliminary to definitive peace negotiations." On July 22 Jules Cambon, the French ambassador to the United States, was directed to represent Spain in peace discussions. After delays over decoding and transmitting the Spanish message to Cambon, he went to the White House on July 26, a few minutes after three o'clock in the afternoon.[34]

From the outset of the war, President McKinley had been willing to begin peace talks. He told John Bassett Moore that he wanted "not only to bring the war to a speedy conclusion, but so to conduct it as to leave no lasting animosities behind to prejudice the future friendship and commerce of the two countries." A statement of American terms, however, required that there first be an overture from Madrid. In his proclamation of thanksgiving for the naval victory at Santiago, McKinley's reference to a "just and honorable peace" seemed to diplomats in Washington to be a signal that, as Ambassador Pauncefote said, "these people want peace ardently, but they don't want a middleman." Spain would have to act. By mid July, peace talk was in the air in Europe and in Washington. These negotiations involved a continuing test of McKinley's diplomatic resolve; they also opened up the question of the Philippines to some definite statement of the intentions of the United States.[35]

During the hour that Ambassador Cambon spent with McKinley and Day, he endeavored first to limit the peace parleys to the issue of Cuba. If the fate of the island could be decided, he went on, there would cease to be any reason for continuing the war. Day immediately answered that he understood Cambon to say that "Spain, while she limits herself to asking that we seek by common agreement a solution to the Cuban question, wants to know under what conditions it would be possible to terminate hostilities in all points where they now exist." After Cambon's equivocal answer, McKinley inquired if Cambon had received any proposals from Spain, and a subsequent meeting was arranged, when the French diplomat would bring back Spain's response. The peace talks would, however, deal with Puerto Rico and the Philippines as well as Cuba. That afternoon the waiting reporters were told that Cambon had brought "a message from the Spanish Government looking

to the termination of the war and the settlement of terms of peace."
The Spanish overtures were, said James Wilson privately, "round-
about, indefinite, and all that." Nonetheless, they required that the
president and his advisors hammer out an American position on the
Philippines.[36]

Several days of cabinet meetings, at least one of which was on
a presidental boat on the Potomac, followed Cambon's July 26
interview. The administration had not only to consider the new
diplomatic and military situation that the war had produced but
also to decide the fate of the Philippines in light of the ambitions
of other world powers and the goals of the insurgents on the ground.
The overall military balance clearly favored the United States. Yet
Spain's bargaining position had certain advantages that could, in
the absence of a firm American stand, shift the scales away from
McKinley.

The emergence of the United States as a force in world affairs
had reshaped the nation's relationship to several of the European
powers. In the case of Great Britain, the war had accelerated the
improvement in the friendship between the one-time adversaries
that McKinley had begun. In Britain the American flag flew prom-
inently, the Fourth of July was celebrated, and politicians spoke
fervently of Anglo-Saxon unity. The British government, seeing the
United States as a counterweight to Germany's ambitions, interposed no objections to American expansion and even prepared to
negotiate a resolution of the questions concerning Alaska's boundary and the isthmian canal. As to the fate of the Philippines,
London not only wanted Washington to hold the islands but also
made it clear that the British would want a voice in the disposition
of the archipelago if the Americans were to withdraw.

Among the other European powers, Germany seemed to represent the greatest obstacle to American action in the Pacific. Though
Berlin had revealed from the beginning of the war that it would not
challenge the United States in the Philippines, the Germans had also
emphasized that they would not be so accommodating to an independent republic in the islands. On June 2 the German Navy
ordered Admiral Otto von Diedrichs to Manila with the Asiatic
squadron to join other European vessels that were observing American naval tactics. By the middle of July the American ambassador
in Berlin was reporting that the Germans had designs on the islands,
should the Americans leave. As Hay told Day after conversing with
the German ambassador to Great Britain, Berlin wanted a "few
coaling stations" out of "the final disposition of the Philippines."[37]

Amid the excitement of the news of the Santiago victory on July 4, a telegram from Dewey in Manila mentioned possible interference by the Germans. The admiral's relations with the German squadron had been difficult in June and July, but they were nothing like the melodrama that subsequent legends ascribed to his dealings with von Diedrichs. No British ships, for example, ever interposed themselves between the American vessels, which were attacking Manila, and the German ships, which might otherwise have been tempted to interfere. Two days after Dewey's wire, on July 6, he and the Germans disagreed sharply over whether they could identify neutral ships through the process of visit and search. By July 14 the tensions in the islands had eased. On July 13, however, Dewey informed Washington that the Germans had interfered with the Philippine insurgents. Simultaneously, Ambassador Andrew D. White was learning from the German Foreign Office that Berlin wanted "one or two positions in the Philippines group." Suggesting that Anglo-American cooperation might provoke a Continental coalition against the United States, he hoped that favorable assurances could be given with regard to what Berlin wanted. McKinley responded, through Day, that there was no need for Germany to be apprehensive about British-American relations, that the United States did not possess the Philippines, and that it could "deal with the matters suggested in your cipher telegram and with the whole situation in the end much better and upon broader terms if not pressed for assurances for which no occasion has arisen." At the time of Cambon's appearance with the Spanish proposal, the administration was alert to the prospect that abandonment of the Philippines would mean a more substantial German presence, and probably an eventual foothold, if not outright dominance.[38]

Equally troubling to those who were making calculations about the Philippines were the intentions of the insurgents. The first detachment of the army, some twenty-five hundred men, arrived on June 30 at Manila, and the second contingent, numbering thirty-five hundred, landed on July 17. At the end of the month a third group, of forty-eight hundred, reached Manila. The army officers under General Merritt did not meet or confer with the Filipino leader, who had about twelve thousand soldiers besieging Manila in a desultory campaign. The insurgents had proclaimed their independence on June 12, and Aguinaldo had asked McKinley to leave the Philippines "free and independent, even if you make peace with Spain." From Dewey the administration learned in late June that "the United States has not been bound in any way to assist insurgents by any act or promises, and he is not, to my knowledge, committed to assist us."[39]

John Bassett Moore submitted a memorandum entitled "Relations of the U.S. to Philippine Insurgents" to the president and Secretary Day on July 20. In it he reviewed the consular dispatches of April to June and then concluded that "no authorized act would therefore appear to have been done that can rightly embarrass the action of the Government." If the United States should decide against the insurgents, the memorandum contended, Aguinaldo and his allies would "accuse the United States of improper treatment of them, but without good ground." The possibility that the Filipinos would resist American domination appears to have received little attention.[40]

American public opinion, in the forms that reached President McKinley, seemed to give solid support to an expansionist policy in the Philippines. Grover Cleveland came out against "the seductive words of conquest and expansion" in June 1898, and William Jennings Bryan, shortly before he entered the army as a colonel in the Nebraska Volunteers, expressed to his Democratic brethren similar sentiments against taking the islands. Editorial opinion, however, was recorded as being strongly in favor of expansion, with about 40 percent of the papers that were surveyed being for it and 25 percent against. Political attitudes within the Republican party, which were no doubt shaped by McKinley's actions, endorsed taking the archipelago. The United States had a mission "clearly appointed by Divine Providence" in the Philippines, wrote Senator Joseph B. Foraker, and the nation would fail "to fully manifest its purposes if we allow the Philippines to remain under the yoke and in the midnight darkness to which they have been subjected." Others spoke of markets and how the new possessions could be "pickets of the Pacific, standing guard at the entrances to trade with the millions of China and Korea, French Indo-China, the Malay Peninsula, and the islands of Indonesia." Partisan reasons also entered the diplomatic equation. If the Philippines were returned to Spain, wrote Henry Cabot Lodge, "the Democrats will unite in attacking us for doing so as false to freedom & humanity & we shall have no answer."[41]

Before he called the cabinet together, on the day when he heard from Spain, McKinley jotted down, for his own use, a draft of the American position: "As a condition to entering upon negoti-

116

ations looking to peace, Spain must withdraw from Cuba and Porto Rico and such adjacent islands as are under her dominion. This requirement will admit of no negotiations." On the Philippine question the president employed open-ended language: "As to the Philippines, I am of the opinion, that with propriety and advantage they can be the subject of negotiation and whenever the Spanish gov't deems it, I will appoint Commissioners to this end." Significantly, he did not return to his mid-July remarks about an insurgent government under American protection with only a United States base at Manila. In the days of discussion that followed, McKinley steered the deliberations toward a result that he had already framed. He understood the political and diplomatic virtues of a governmental consensus on the Philippines, but he determined the precise shape that the cabinet's agreement would take.[42]

That body agreed with the president that Spain must relinquish Cuba and Puerto Rico. The Philippine question revealed that there were differences of opinion. Secretaries Bliss, Griggs, and Wilson favored taking all of the islands. Day, Gage, and Long would have settled for a naval base at Manila, or "a hitching post," as McKinley called it. Alger and Postmaster General Smith took little part in the talks. In the midst of one of the long parleys about the Philippines, the navy received a telegram from Dewey, reporting that the insurgents had become "aggressive and even threatening toward the Army." Under McKinley's guidance the cabinet voted narrowly in favor of leaving the ultimate status of the islands to the peace commission. Shortly thereafter, on August 1, 1898, General Merritt reported from Hong Kong: "It may be important [to] have my whole force before attacking if necessary to hold insurgents while we fight Spanish." The cabinet, said Secretary Wilson, read between the lines that the general might need a good many more soldiers. To ensure that the peace commission would do full justice to the insurgents and that it would take "abundant care of the spread of American powers," the administration decided that "no man will be put on that commission who is hostile to the acquisition of outside territory." McKinley was continuing the process, which he had begun in May, that led to annexation of the Philippines by the United States.[43]

Through the hours of meetings, McKinley made sure that the outcome would follow his scenario. He did not put Secretary Day's idea of a naval base at Manila to a vote, because as he said jokingly to his old friend, "I was afraid it would be carried!" When the laborious process of drafting and revision was over, Cortelyou wrote that the president's "guiding hand will be seen at every point in the negotiations." Cortelyou learned firsthand about McKinley's working methods on July 31. Closer to the center of power than ever before in his White House career, the young assistant secretary said to the president that the process of drafting a reply to Spain "was a good example of the development of a public paper under discussion—that there had been material changes by himself and the Cabinet since the first draft was made." After McKinley had shown him the July 26 memorandum, Cortelyou wrote in his diary: "These terms as thus stated by the President were exactly those which were finally transmitted to the Spanish Minister for Foreign Affairs, through the Ambassador of France."[44]

The final cabinet meeting took place on Saturday morning, July 30. As a draft of the American peace terms was being prepared, McKinley summoned Ambassador Cambon to the White House. When Cambon arrived at two o'clock, the president handed him the document, which asked Spain to relinquish all claims of sovereignty over Cuba and to cede Puerto Rico, other islands in the West Indies, and one of the Ladrone Islands in the Pacific. Finally, the paper stated that "the United States is entitled to occupy and will hold the city, bay, and harbor of Manila pending the conclusion of a treaty of peace, which shall determine the control, disposition, and government of the Philippines." Cambon attempted to explore the first two topics, but McKinley informed him: "My demands set forth in the first two articles do not admit of discussion." Only the Philippine question would be the subject of peace talks. The ambassador called them very hard terms, and he was able to achieve nothing more than a minor textual change in the article on the Philippines. McKinley remarked that Spain could have obtained easier terms in May, after the battle of Manila. If Madrid hesitated now, however, "Spain would necessarily be exposed to greater sacrifices." When Spain accepted the American offer, fighting would stop. Cambon departed at 5:30 P.M., and McKinley listened to the Marine Band that evening.[45]

Spain sent its answer to Cambon on August 1. It wondered whether other territorial indemnification might be substituted for Puerto Rico, and it said that the Philippine article was imprecise. Spain continued to assert claims to its permanent sovereignty in the islands. When Cambon returned to McKinley with this response, the president was inflexible on Puerto Rico. As to the Philippines, he said: "There is nothing determined *a priori* in my mind against Spain; likewise, I consider there is nothing decided against the United States." McKinley did agree to hold the peace conference in Paris, rather than Washington, which was his first choice. Cambon believed that he had obtained all that he could from the president and the secretary of state. "All vacillation will further aggravate the severity of the conditions," he warned Madrid.[46]

McKinley's diplomatic posture was steadfast despite revelations of the weakened condition of the army in Cuba, which undercut the American side of the negotiations in early August. During the two weeks after the surrender at Santiago the problem of the health of the troops, which was such a significant element in the parleys over the surrender, attracted less concern from the press and the War Department. Then the president was given alarming reports about conditions on two ships, the *Seneca* and the *Concho*, which were bringing troops to New York. An immediate investigation was ordered, and the War Department instructed Shafter to begin the partial evacuation of his troops. The next day, the general wired Washington that "at any time an epidemic of yellow fever is liable to occur" and advised "that the troops be moved as rapidly as possible whilst the sickness is of a mild type." The surgeon general of the army recommended that the troops move to higher ground, "where yellow fever is impossible." As Alger noted, "It is going to be a long job at best to get so many troops away." What the administration did not yet know was that sickness, malaria, and yellow fever had devastated Shafter's force.[47]

Faced with an order that he considered impossible to carry out, Shafter summoned his officers together. After opinion had been canvassed, the general told Corbin: "There is but one course to take, and that is to immediately transport the Fifth Corps and the detached regiments that came with it to the United States. If it is not done, I believe the death rate will be appalling." All he had left was an army of convalescents. With this description, Shafter sent statements from his medical officers and troop commanders which supported his decision. They did not reach Washington, but his comments were enough to impel the administration to "hurry other ships forward as rapidly as possible." Alger assured Shafter: "We are doing everything possible to relieve your gallant command."[48]

Since negotiations were in the balance, the White House hoped to sit on the news from Cuba until the evacuation of the soldiers could be begun. The press obtained a copy of the round robin from Shafter's officers, including General Joseph Wheeler, General

Leonard Wood, and Colonel Theodore Roosevelt. It stated: "The army is disabled by malarial fever to such an extent that its efficiency is destroyed and it is in a condition to be practically entirely destroyed by the epidemic of yellow fever sure to come in the near future." A separate letter from Roosevelt, written with his customary enthusiasm, said that the army was "ripe for dying like rotten sheep." On August 4 newspapers across the country carried the story in banner headlines.[49]

McKinley was furious. On August 5 he drafted a letter to Shafter that called the round robin "most unfortunate from every point of view" and said: "The publication of the letter makes the situation one of great difficulty. No soldier reading that report if ordered to Santiago but will feel that he is marching to certain death." Shafter's answer to the communications from Washington sought to smooth over the sensation that had been caused. The president was now aware that the management of the War Department had been maladroit. "Unless drastic measures are resorted to," wrote Cortelyou before the full weight of the round robin had been felt, "the Administration of that great branch of the federal service will be one of the few blots on the brilliant record made in the conduct of the war." Just how great a liability Alger had become, the president had yet to learn.[50]

That problem had to wait until the war had ended. Cambon brought the Spanish reply to McKinley's terms. Madrid could only accept the articles on Cuba and Puerto Rico. Hoping to salvage something in the Phillipines, Spain's Foreign Ministry argued that the government would have to secure the assent of the Cortes for any evacuation of Spanish territory before the treaty of peace had been concluded. This ploy irritated the president, who said: "I demanded of Spain the cession and consequently the immediate evacuation of the islands of Cuba and Porto Rico. Instead of a categorical acceptance, as was expected, the Spanish Government addresses me a note in which it invokes the necessity of obtaining the approbation of the Cortes. I can not lend myself to entering into these considerations of domestic government." With the talks in jeopardy, McKinley suggested that a protocol be drafted, setting out the American terms and specifiying when peace negotiations would start in Paris and when evacuation would commence in Cuba and Puerto Rico. At such time as Spain accepted, and if no approval of the Cortes or the Senate would be needed, the fighting would cease. Cambon warned Madrid again that McKinley would not alter these terms and that in the event of rejection, "Spain will have nothing more to expect from a conqueror resolved to procure all the profit possible from the advantages it has obtained." Spain had no option but to agree, and the government instructed Cambon to sign the protocol.[51]

The protocol was signed on Friday, August 12, on a rainy gloomy afternoon. News that the war had ended did not reach the Philippines until August 16. Three days earlier, after secret negotiations had been carried out with the Spanish commander in Manila, the American forces launched a combined land and naval assault on the city. The scenario that had been arranged between the defenders and the attackers was carried out, and after making a token resistance, Manila surrendered. Almost before it had commenced, the war with Spain was over, and the United States had prevailed on all fronts.

McKinley met the end of the war with a palpable sense of personal relief. "The days merge into each other," he remarked on July 30, and he told visitors that "the mental and physical strain of the last few months had been severe upon him." If his popularity had suffered with the coming of hostilities, the ensuing military events had restored it to the levels of 1897 or even higher. It was hardly surprising that Republican editors praised him; the remarks of foreign newspapers conveyed a judgment of greater respect. The president, said the *Spectator*, "is now by far the most influential personage in the United States."[52]

In conducting the Spanish-American War, McKinley had expanded the powers and authority of his office. Some months later, signing an order to shift American installations that lay outside the United States, he observed: "It seems odd to be directing the transfer of navy yards, naval stations &c in Cuba." He was able to accomplish these unprecedented activities because he was commander in chief, and the war power was the primary resource on which he relied in 1898. With the war behind him, McKinley approached the problems of peace with a confidence and assertiveness that would grow over the remaining years of his presidency. In bearing and manner, in action and policy, he would become something of an imperial tutor to the American people. "The true measure of duty is not what we like but what we ought to like," he wrote in August 1898. The political struggle over the Philippines during the rest of the year would reveal how much McKinley intended to shape and direct the way in which the United States would define its duty and would carry it out on the world stage.[53]

6

★★★★★

"DUTY DETERMINES DESTINY"

The most pressing political problem facing President McKinley at the close of the war was the growing clamor against Secretary Alger and the performance of the War Department. "There is a pretty general criticism here of the condition of the War Dept. in its Commissary and Medical branches," Secretary of the Navy Long was told, with the potential for "a very serious revulsion of public opinion against the administration's handling of the troops in Cuba." The partisan implications of the problem were obvious, and the Democrats intended to run in the fall on "the woeful failure of the Administration to provide proper food, sanitary conditions, clothing and hospital service from the beginning to the end of the war." From early August through the appointment of and the giving of instructions to the Commission to Investigate the Conduct of the War Department in September, the president moved to rectify the substantive difficulties within the government and simultaneously to contain the political danger.[1]

Criticism of Alger had appeared in mid May and had steadily mounted thereafter. As the revelations grew, even McKinley came under fire. "Alger is responsible for Algerism," said the *New York Evening Post*, "but McKinley is responsible for Alger." In two particular areas—the condition of the troops in Cuba and the management of the volunteer camps around the nation—the War Department and the secretary were found wanting.[2]

The army selected a site near Montauk Point, on Long Island, as the place for members of the Cuban expedition to recuperate after they returned home. When the "round robin" controversy broke, the camp was not yet ready to receive soldiers. Nonetheless, Shafter's men were ordered to be relieved as rapidly as possible and sent north. Between August 7 and August 25 the entire contingent that had fought at Santiago left Cuba. Work went forward at the rest camp, which was named Camp Wikoff after an officer killed at Santiago, but there were mix-ups and delays. The first troops, who arrived on August 14, found few tents, short rations, and inadequate hospitals. Newspapermen from New York City laid before a shocked country lurid and sometimes exaggerated accounts of suffering and neglect.

Conditions at Wikoff improved during the rest of August. The camp's commander—Joseph Wheeler—and Alger himself cut through red tape to obtain supplies and clothing. Their efforts, the hard work of the surgeon general, and an outpouring of private charity turned the installation into a more pleasant resting place for the men from Cuba. McKinley toured the camp on September 3 and told the press: "What I saw of the care of the sick in the hospitals by those in charge and by those noble women who are engaged in that work was especially gratifying to me."[3] Despite the administration's labors and the real achievements at Camp Wikoff, after its faltering start, the process of bringing the men back from Cuba was a public-relations disaster. Citizens saw soldiers on their way home, collapsing because of illness, or they read about visitors who could not find loved ones amid the confusion in the camp. Returning soldiers recounted vivid tales of the canned beef that formed part of their ration in Cuba. Never appetizing, the meat spoiled and sometimes contained foreign objects that disgusted those who ate it.

Equally damaging to Alger was the situation in the volunteer camps. Four primary bases—Chickamauga, Camp Alger near Washington, Jacksonville, and Tampa—served about 165,000 of the 200,000 men who had enlisted in the spring. Supply problems kept many of the soldiers from receiving clothing and equipment until the war was almost over. Because of poor locations, several of the camps became prime incubators of disease. Discipline broke down over the use of latrines at Chickamauga and Camp Alger. Conditions at the other camps were less onerous. With the approach of peace, however, the volunteers wanted to go home, and camp morale suffered. Simultaneously, cases of typhoid appeared, and the disease soon reached epidemic levels. Sick men crowded the hospitals, and then other cases had to be treated in the camps themselves. By the middle of August the army confronted a medical crisis.

The War Department's response to these difficulties was prompt. Hospital facilities expanded, and the quality of care rose. Troops were moved from the old camps to more healthful positions in higher places that were cooler and well watered. Better camp discipline replaced earlier laxness. These measures did not contribute directly to the abatement of the typhoid epidemic. After some weeks the disease ran its course among men who were susceptible to it. Some 2,500 officers and men died from typhoid, as compared with battle deaths of 281 officers and men. Better foresight and administration by the surgeon general, George H. Sternberg, could have reduced this grim total, as would have more careful supervision of their men by army officers. In large measure, however, typhoid fever and other diseases were inevitable, given the state of medical knowledge. In the minds of the American people, these considerations neither justified nor excused Secretary Alger's performance in office.

That Alger responded poorly to the criticism that surged around him is not surprising. His public chastisement of Roosevelt over the "round robin" only strengthened the conviction that the hero of the Rough Riders had been right. The secretary's official statements seemed to be belabored attempts to escape deserved blame. Since he had done nothing wrong, he would not step down, and he attributed the army's difficulties to circumstance rather than to errors in the conduct of the war. McKinley knew that there was a good deal of truth in Alger's defense. He told Cortelyou on August 23, after reading a letter that was critical of the secretary, that Alger "could not be responsible for many of the conditions at Santiago and other places; that if the food, medicines, etc., were not landed from the transports at Santiago it was the fault of the regular army officers who had charge of them and that Secy Alger could not know at the time what was going on." The president also realized, as did Alger, that the latter had taken the brunt of a public assault that might otherwise have struck the White House.[4]

If Alger could feel some resentment at how McKinley had treated him, the president also had grounds for a lessening of faith in his subordinate. Cortelyou did not overlook how Alger, in announcing administration decisions to newsmen, left the impression that he had originated the changes in official policy. Nor did Alger's caustic remarks about the president escape McKinley's attention. To limit the effect of Alger's troubles on the administration, then, he combined a public silence about the secretary with highly visible gestures to alleviate the army's problems. His trip to Camp Wikoff was one such act; another was the sending of a personal agent, a dietitian named Louise Hogan, to the camps in order to improve the quality of the food. When a New York newspaper editor wrote to the president in mid September about alleged starvation among American troops in Cuba, McKinley ordered an immediate probe, which revealed that there was no foundation for the charge. The most effective response, however, was the creation of a presidential commission to investigate the performance of Alger and his department.

The public outcry over the plight of the soldiers led inevitably to calls for a congressional inquiry. Such an investigation would have had a partisan dimension in an election year, and the president had little desire for an uncontrolled scrutiny of the war. Provocative statements from General Nelson A. Miles added to the inflammatory elements as McKinley vacationed during the first week of September. With characteristic adroitness, McKinley had begun to arrange for a process that he could supervise. He sent Secretary of Agriculture James Wilson to Alger to persuade Alger to ask the president "to appoint commission to report to you regarding the army and complaints concerning it." Wilson told Alger that internal reports by army officers would not satisfy the public, that the commission must have "men not in army life" who could fix "responsibility where it properly belongs." Alger agreed to Wilson's entreaties, and on September 8 he sent a letter to McKinley, asking that a board of five to seven "of the most distinguished soldiers and civilians" be named "to investigate thoroughly every bureau of the War Department." McKinley agreed to do this, and the Republican press applauded the decision to make a searching investigation.[5]

McKinley appointed his commission over the next several weeks. Some of the more prominent men whom he approached declined, but he pulled together a panel of two civilians and six soldiers who not only possessed expertise but would be fair. The chairman was General Grenville M. Dodge of Iowa, builder of the Union Pacific Railroad, who was a Civil War veteran and a Republican stalwart. The commission assembled in McKinley's office on September 26, 1898, to hear the president's instructions. "There has been in many quarters severe criticism of the conduct of the war with Spain," he told them; and he ordered a full investigation to establish "the truth or falsity of these accusations."[6] A few days later the Dodge Commission began its work. The hearings would later produce charges of scandal, in addition to a public controversy with General Miles. From its findings also came information that spurred reforms in the army. For the president, in the autumn of 1898, it deflected a formal congressional probe, and the Spanish-American War thus escaped that form of legislative scrutiny. By making the executive branch a kind of grand-jury prosecutor instead of a target, the commission extricated McKinley from a tight political corner; and this enabled him to deal with the elections and peace negotiations.

The prospects for the Republicans in the congressional elections seemed to have improved greatly since the worried predictions in early 1898. The war naturally evoked a nationalistic spirit, and as one midwesterner said in late April, "As a rule whatever arouses patriotism is good for us." Elections in Oregon in mid June appeared to signal a Republican resurgence on the Pacific Coast. At the end of the summer the organizers of the party's congressional campaign detected in the West and Midwest "a sentiment of general satisfaction" with the outcome of the war.[7]

Aware that the party in power ordinarily lost seats in an off year, Republicans looked to offset the Democratic attack on "Algerism" and the overconfidence in their own ranks. In New York, where scandals imperiled the GOP's dominance, the party machine of Senator Thomas C. Platt ran Theodore Roosevelt to supply a heroic candidate in place of the incumbent governor. The Republicans made an expansionist policy one of the keynotes of their national appeal.

McKinley took a close interest in the Republican effort. Assigning Postmaster General Charles Emory Smith to compile the campaign textbook, McKinley told him that he was "especially desirous" that the document reveal "the war situation as it existed." McKinley instinctively wanted the president to function as a party leader as well as a chief executive. Invitations also came in for the president to travel during the elections to Grand Army of the Republic meetings or to the various peace celebrations in the Midwest. To several of these inquiries, McKinley had his secretary send refusals because of the press of his duties. In late August, however, he decided to attend a peace jubilee in Omaha in October. Republicans immediately asked him to appear in closely contested districts in Iowa and other states along the route. The president said that "he would be entirely willing to do this not making political speeches, but discussing current events connected with the administration." Here was a significant departure from accepted political practice that became a precedent for the traveling White House of twentieth-century campaigns. Previously, most presidents had not campaigned for party candidates, even by implication; and the result for one who had, Andrew Johnson in 1866, was not encouraging. McKinley had been confined to Washington for a year, and he wished to renew his contacts with the public. If precedents were stretched on behalf of Republican victory, so much the better. He would also have an opportunity to mold public thinking on foreign policy. Secretary Cortelyou set in motion the arrangements for a presidential excursion.[8]

After his New Jersey vacation during the first week of September, McKinley faced a concentrated schedule of issues. In addition to the Alger controversy and the fall elections, the president had to supervise the military governments in Cuba and Puerto Rico. In the case of Puerto Rico the Spanish had departed on October 18, 1898, at which time the military occupation had commenced. The state of affairs in Cuba posed more delicate and perplexing questions.

The Cuban rebels contributed substantially to the defeat of the Spanish forces by doing reconnaisance work, by constructing trenches and supplying American troops, and, most important, by tying down large numbers of enemy reinforcements. Nonetheless, relations between the American and Cuban militaries worsened, and popular attitudes toward the erstwhile allies of the United States cooled to a near hostility. The Americans believed that the Cubans could not be trusted in combat or as co-workers. To men in Shafter's army they were a band of ill-equipped, undependable, larcenous fighters whose large contingent of black soldiers evoked the prevailing biases of North Americans. Public opinion in the United States largely agreed that McKinley had been right in not recognizing a Cuban republic.

While it readily accepted the aid that the Cuban forces provided, the administration did not accord the rebels any formal existence. They were not given an official role in the negotiations leading up to or in the surrender of Santiago de Cuba itself. In the process of notifying the Cuban junta about the adoption of the protocol with Spain, McKinley sought to make it merely a personal action. The Cubans extracted a concession that the message be transmitted to the president of their republic. At the same time, General Henry W. Lawton, who had replaced Shafter as the American military commander on the island, sought "definite instructions as to policy to be observed toward the Cuban army." The Cubans "still maintain their organization, are scattered through the country in vicinity of city, are threatening in their attitude, and keep the inhabitants stirred up and panicky by threats and acts of violence."

McKinley responded that "interference from any quarter" with the occupation by the United States would "not be permitted. The Cuban insurgents should be treated justly and liberally, but they, with all others, must recognize the military occupation and authority of the United States and the cessation of hostilities proclaimed by this Government."[9]

After the fighting had ended, Cuba was a devastated island. During the autumn of 1898 its inhabitants, with assistance from American relief agencies such as the Red Cross and the United States Army, brought some order out of the chaos and ruin that had accompanied rebellion and war. While the precise status of Cuba remained a topic for the peace talks, McKinley sent an agent to the island to gather information. Robert P. Porter, who had compiled a campaign biography of the Republican candidate in 1896, was a long-time publicist and government official with expertise in tariff matters. Named as a special commissioner to Puerto Rico and Cuba, Porter conducted hearings and interviewed residents. The recommendations that he made about trade relations between Cuba and the United States sought to raise a revenue for the islands without discriminating in favor of the occupying power. The precise form of government for the island, however, remained undecided. In November a Cuban delegation came to Washington to seek money to pay the insurgent army and other debts incurred during the rebellion. Negotiations ended inconclusively in mid December, and the emissaries reported that they had secured, at most, vague manifestations about the future policy of the United States. As McKinley said in his annual message, "Until there is complete tranquillity in the island and a stable government inaugurated military government will continue."[10]

The Philippines retained the president's primary attention in the autumn of 1898. New responsibilities overseas, in addition to the host of international issues that the war had left behind, convinced McKinley that he needed a secretary of state who had a background in diplomacy and a substantial reputation in world affairs. His old friend Judge Day, who was glad to serve on the peace commission, was equally ready to relinquish the duties at the State Department. To replace him, McKinley selected John Hay in August. After some initial hesitation because of his health, Hay accepted the diplomatic portfolio and took up his work on October 1.

John Milton Hay was sixty years old when he became secretary of state. A graduate of Brown University, he had been Abraham Lincoln's secretary and later had coauthored a multivolume biography of that president. Hay had been a diplomat, a journalist, and a successful man of letters. Financially secure, he was a reliable Republican contributor and early had supported McKinley. The new president sent him to London as ambassador, where Hay made a brilliant impression on his hosts as a promoter of Anglo-American friendship. McKinley found Hay's letters and dispatches both informative and shrewd. The ambassador's discreet flattery did not displease the president either. For McKinley's purposes, Hay was an ideal choice. The two men saw the world alike, and Hay would be an excellent instrument for the execution of McKinley's policies. The president told him at their first meeting that "he would not worry any more about the State Department." As usual, McKinley supervised and controlled the overall outlines of what Hay did.[11]

One of the most entertaining and interesting letter writers who ever ran the State Department, the witty, dapper, and bearded Hay left behind an abundance of documentary evidence on his public career. His name is indelibly linked with that verity of the nation's Asian policy, the Open Door, and he contributed much to the resolution of the longstanding problems with the British. Patient, discreet, and judicious, Hay deserves to stand in the front rank of secretaries of state. Sometimes, however, his tenure is examined as if McKinley were no more than a presidential appendix, present but superfluous, to the creative diplomat. Hay never made that error. He knew where the power resided and where the initiatives originated. Hay needed McKinley's firmness. Brilliant in statecraft, he possessed a disdain for patronage and a pathological distaste for the Senate in its constitutional role of advising and consenting to treaties. Left to himself, he would have had Congress in revolt. With McKinley to temper his failings and release his talents, Hay became the leading figure of the cabinet.

To accompany Judge Day to Paris, McKinley assembled a peace commission that symbolized his readiness to bend constitutional precedents. Whitelaw Reid received a place on it, not the ambassadorship to Great Britain that he coveted but an honor that was enough to placate him. The president also looked to the Supreme Court, but to his disappointment, Chief Justice Melville W. Fuller and Justice Edward D. White, both Democrats, declined. Ostensibly an independent branch of the government, the Supreme Court offered to McKinley the proper blend of judicial experience and political legitimacy that he sought in members of the peace commission.

Since senators would have to vote on the treaty that the commission negotiated, McKinley wanted to have several lawmakers among the peacemakers. He approached William Boyd Allison without success, and then persuaded Cushman K. Davis of Minnesota, an expansionist; William P. Frye of Maine, who shared Davis's opinions; and George Gray of Delaware, who disapproved of imperialism. Frye did not want to go, "but the President insisted that I should give a good excuse." The senator's desire "to fish and hunt" in the fall did not satisfy McKinley. As the commission's secretary, John Bassett Moore added a knowledge of international law and a firm grounding in McKinley's diplomatic objectives.[12]

McKinley was very sensitive to the role of the Senate in his plans for peace. He tried to induce George Frisbie Hoar to succeed Hay in London. Hoar's aversion for acquiring the Philippines was already public knowledge, and the appointment would have reduced the antiexpansionist bloc in the upper house. Hoar saw what the president's goal was, so he refused. Joseph Hodges Choate, a New York lawyer, filled the position. Senator William E. Chandler told McKinley that the president could not constitutionally name senators to a commission, upon whose product they would later vote. The president did not answer Chandler's protest, because he wanted the Senate to endorse what the negotiators achieved. More attuned to these legislative nuances than Woodrow Wilson two decades later, he was building a coalition in the Senate even before the peace treaty had been written.[13]

As the peace commissioners embarked for Paris, they required the president to instruct them about his intentions toward the Philippines. Since the signing of the protocol, McKinley had continued his policy of public indecision about the future of the islands while simultaneously shaping events aimed at full American control after the peace treaty was signed. His attitude emerged most clearly in relations with the Filipino insurgents.

After the assault on Manila, Aguinaldo told the American commanders that he wished to participate in the occupation of the city. General Merritt and Admiral Dewey asked Washington, "Is Government willing to use all means to make the natives submit to the authority of the United States?" Their message arrived on August 17, and the presidential response was firm: "The President directs that there must be no joint occupation with the insurgents." Since the United States was in the possession of Manila and its harbor, it had to preserve the peace and protect property in the archipelago. Therefore, McKinley ordered: "The insurgents and all others must recognize the military occupation and authority of the

United States and the cessation of hostilities proclaimed by the President. Use whatever means in your judgment are necessary to this end."[14]

With negotiations in Paris about to commence, the administration hoped to avoid a clash with the insurgents while at the same time withholding any formal recognition. The rebels themselves were divided about whether to ask for an American protectorate over an independent Philippines or to seek foreign recognition of Aguinaldo's government. Both potential adversaries wished, for the moment at least, to avoid a confrontation. The information that reached President McKinley indicated that, on the American side, the goal of establishing the army's authority in the Philippines was succeeding. Conveying information at the time that he was discussing Aguinaldo's hopes for a joint occupation of Manila, Merritt said: "Filipinos and their chief anxious to be friendly. Little confidence is to be placed in their professions. They are superior as a people than is generally represented; their leaders are mostly men of education and ability." This was the general's last policy statement. McKinley ordered him to Paris to confer with the peace commission. General Elwell S. Otis succeeded him on August 30, 1898. At the suggestion of John Bassett Moore, Otis was instructed on September 7 "to exert your influence during the suspension of hostilities between the United States and Spain to restrain insurgent hostilities against Spaniards, and, while maintaining a position of rightful supremacy as to the insurgents, to pursue, as far as possible, a conciliatory course toward all."[15]

General Otis's actions in early September seemed to comply with this presidential directive. In fact, his talks with Aguinaldo increased the tensions between the Americans and the Filipinos. He sent a formal response to the proposals that the insurgent leader made to Merritt in mid August. Should Aguinaldo not withdraw his troops from Manila by September 15, Otis warned, "I shall be obliged to resort to forcible action, and . . . my Government will hold you responsible for any unfortunate consequences that may ensue." Because of the negotiations with Aguinaldo, Otis's letter was kept private in Manila, and the withdrawal of the insurgent force was accomplished. The general could tell Corbin on September 16 that "based upon present indications," no additional American troops would be needed. The insurgent leaders were "in politics and army in excitable frame of mind, but better portion [are] amenable to reason, and desire to make approved reputation before civilized world." Otis's wire arrived in Washington on September 16, the day that McKinley met with the peace commission. He had reason to assume that his policy in the Philippines was not a source of so much intensifying friction with the insurgents that it might lead to open fighting.[16]

As he deliberated on the Philippines, the president received additional information to support his conviction that Spanish rule in the islands could not be successfully restored. The Japanese government, which conveyed this verdict, was equally cool to "a purely native Government, independent of external guarantees and guidance." Japan preferred that the United States take over the Philippines, but would, should Washington decline to accept sovereignty, help to set up "a suitable government for the territory," either by itself or with other powers. If the United States withdrew from the picture, a Philippine republic would confront, at the very least, serious threats to its existence from Japan and Germany.[17]

An American protectorate over the Philippines was an alternative possibility that McKinley weighed and then rejected. If the native government that appeared were only a façade for direct American supervision, it would be an awkward international entity. It it proved to be truly independent in its foreign policy, such a regime could easily involve the United States in commitments that the nation would not want to assume. A protectorate also involved a more complex and ambiguous obligation than did simple possession. For a president concerned about popular attitudes toward expansion and the country's willingness to support a colonial policy indefinitely, as McKinley was in September 1898, the equivocal nature of a protectorate type of obligation contributed to his dislike for the concept.

In semipublic appearances and in statements to visitors, McKinley maintained his noncommittal posture on the fate of the Philippines. To a visitor who was close to the German-American community, George Holls, he said in early September that "his mind was as yet a blank, so far as a decision upon the point of keeping or giving them back, was concerned." The president seemed to be impressed with the problem of sustaining "an army of occupation in a hot and unhealthy climate"; he talked of allowing Germany to have one of the islands or a part of the Ladrones; and he worried about whether public opinion would endorse holding the archipelago. A week later he asked a caller "whether it would not be just as well to keep only one Island in the Philippines, provided trade with the other Islands remained free and unrestricted, as for the United States to take all the Islands." As the peace commissioners prepared to meet with McKinley, the *New York Tribune* noted that the administration had not "gone beyond the determination to retain the whole of the island of Luzon." The president had decided "to establish at the outset" of the negotiations with Spain "the right of this Government to determine the fate of the islands and to make the conditions under which government shall be established there."[18]

McKinley, thus, instructed Day and his colleagues on September 16 that in the peace treaty the United States could not accept less than the island of Luzon as well as full commercial privileges in the trade of those parts of the islands that might remain with Spain. General Merritt was on his way to Paris to brief them about his own opinions and those of Admiral Dewey. The commissioners were warned that there was a need for promptness so that the Senate could consider the treaty before the Fifty-fifth Congress adjourned in March 1899.[19]

Most of the work in the White House on September 16 was devoted to conferences and ceremonies relating to the commission. Between meetings, however, another group of Americans came to see McKinley. At Saratoga, New York, on August 19 the National Civic Federation had held a conference on the direction that American foreign policy should be taking. When it met, opposition to expansionism had already emerged in Boston, where, on June 15, speakers such as Gamaliel Bradford and Moorfield Storey had criticized the prospect of an empire in Asia. Storey, Bradford, and Carl Schurz spoke at Saratoga against the acquisition of overseas possessions. The meeting adopted resolutions that were mildly critical of the administration, and it sent a delegation to see McKinley. Welcoming them in his graceful way, he expressed the hope that they had "come prepared to tell him just how much of the conquered territory should be retained, and just how much should be left within the control of Spain." The president's statement deflected the discussion into specific questions of policy such as "the expansion of our trade in the Orient" and away from a moral appraisal of imperialism. As McKinley's purposes became clearer, the opposition of Schurz and others would build.[20]

"The Peace Commission is now gone and that subject is off my mind," McKinley wrote on September 19. The Philippines did not step out of the public spotlight or leave the president's private deliberations while the peace negotiators went to Paris. At the end of the month, McKinley talked with, and received a lengthy memorandum from, Major General Francis V. Greene, who had been in the islands. Greene called Aguinaldo's form of government "a dictatorship of the familiar South American type," and he saw no reason to believe that it had any elements of stability. The insurgents did not have the hearty support of the Filipino people, whose ideal was "a Philippine republic under American protection, such as they have heard is to be granted to Cuba." The general concluded that, except for Aguinaldo, there was a consensus that "no native government can maintain itself without the active support and protection of a strong foreign government. This being admitted, it is difficult to see how any foreign government can give this protection without taking such an active part in the management of affairs as is practically equivalent to governing in its own name and for its own account."[21]

The day after Greene's memorandum had been submitted, representatives from Aguinaldo came to the White House. Felipe Agoncillo and Sixto Lopez gave the president a statement describing political conditions in their homeland. McKinley welcomed the two men "as citizens of the Philippine Islands" but specified that they had no political status. Agoncillo recounted what the Filipinos had endured from Spain, and he asserted that "they could never under any circumstances be content to be again placed in any manner or in any degree under the rule of Spain." He was going to Paris to address the peace commission, and the president invited him to present a memorandum of what he intended to say. On October 4 the document came in. It asked that the United States recognize Philippine independence and support principles of justice and human rights "in favor of the new nation which is rising logically in that part of the world in response to their well conceived and humanitarian action." The Aguinaldo regime sought to obtain the rights of a belligerent power and a part in the peace conference. The president and Assistant Secretary Adee offered no substantive comments on these claims. They not only reiterated instead that they did not recognize Lopez and Agoncillo "as agents of any governmental organization" but also denied the Filipinos' statements that Admiral Dewey, United States army officers, and diplomatic agents had engaged in de facto recognition of Aguinaldo in the campaign against Spain.[22]

Ten days later the president opened a western tour that took him through six states. During the two weeks of the trip he made fifty-seven public appearances, which included making major addresses at Omaha, St. Louis, and Chicago. The pressures of the Cuban crisis, the prosecution of the war, and the complexity of

135

making peace had tied McKinley to the White House. It was good to be out among the people again. The mechanics of presidential tours were now more efficient as well, with Secretary Cortelyou in charge. From Cortelyou the reporters on the presidential train received advance copies of McKinley's formal addresses and stenographic reports of the numerous informal speeches that he made. A steady supply of bulletins went out to the wire services as the president crossed the nation's midsection. The crowds were large and enthusiastic. McKinley's popularity had swelled after the war, and he now reaped the ample applause that accompanies a successful war leader.

In the context of his Philippine policy, this speaking tour is usually depicted as the time when a pliable chief executive heard the voice of the people on the subject of expansion and returned to Washington with his doubts removed and his commitment to the acquisition of the Asian islands crystallized. The opposite was true. "He led public sentiment quite as much as public sentiment led him," Charles Emory Smith wrote later, "and the popular manifestations on that journey were in response to the keynotes he struck." The keynotes began early. At Cedar Rapids, Iowa, on October 11, he said, to great applause: "We can accept no terms of peace which shall not be in the interest of humanity." Later that day, at Secretary Wilson's home, Tama, he added: "We do not want to shirk a single responsibility that has been put upon us by the results of the war." What could that mean but the Philippines? At the Trans-Mississippi Exposition on October 12, he drove the point home with even greater force: "Shall we deny to ourselves what the rest of the world so freely and so justly accords to us?" The audience emitted a "general cry of 'no!'" He capped off his campaign at Chariton, Iowa, on his way east, the next day. "Territory sometimes comes to us when we go to war in a holy cause, and whenever it does the banner of liberty will float over it and bring, I trust, blessings and benefits to all the people."[23]

While on his junket, McKinley also advanced themes that could assist the Republicans in the fall campaign: "Business looks hopeful and assuring everywhere, and our credit balances show the progress which the country is making." Constantly he emphasized that the war had brought the North and the South into closer union: "Never was a people so united in purpose, in heart, in sympathy, and in love as the American people to-day." But throughout he returned to the cadences of foreign policy. At the Auditorium in Chicago, he proclaimed on October 18: "My countrymen, the currents of destiny flow through the hearts of the people. Who will check them? Who will divert them? Who will stop them? And the movements of men, planned and designed by the Master of men, will never be interrupted by the American people." In his native Ohio, in Columbus, where he had been governor, he remarked: "We know what our country is now in its territory, but we do not know what it may be in the near future."[24]

McKinley's use of what Theodore Roosevelt called the bully pulpit is still one of his least recognized contributions to the emergence of the modern presidency. Outside the precise political context of October 1898, the speeches seem stuffed with generalities. When read in tandem with the epochal events of that critical year, they become masterful examples of how an adroit leader can set the terms of a public discussion in his own favor. McKinley had for the moment wrapped the Philippine decision in the folds of prosperity, patriotism, and the national interest. "Duty determines destiny," the president had said; but it was he who prescribed the nature of that duty.[25]

The trip immediately made a favorable impact upon Republican fortunes in the campaign. "We have not as yet been able to satisfy ourselves what will be the result in the next House," concluded the chairman of the party's Congressional Committee on October 15. The committee had no money, and after the excitement of the 1896 race, apathy seemed to be the most dangerous obstacle to the GOP's chances. Then McKinley went west. On his return, said one paper, he received a "continuous ovation" as he passed through Indiana and Ohio. In late October, Republican spokesmen revised downward their predictions of potential party losses so as to minimize the effect of the off-year contest. Meanwhile, the Democrats lacked decisive issues. The opposition was still divided over silver, had no consensus on imperialism, and found that McKinley had deflated the "Algerism" outcry.[26]

On the day of the election the Democrats gained fifty seats in the House. Many of the defeated were Populist incumbents whose party had waned since 1896. Republican losses totaled nineteen, but the party retained a twenty-two-vote edge in the House. Roosevelt achieved a narrow victory in New York, and the GOP added six seats to its Senate count. Expecting the customary reversal, the Republicans experienced bearable setbacks. "You have pulled us through with your own strength," John Hay informed McKinley; "this makes the work for 1900 simple and easy." Most important, the administration could look forward to controlling both houses of Congress after March 1899.[27]

While the president's trip and the political campaign progressed, the peace commissioners opened their talks with their Spanish counterparts. At an early informal meeting, the president of the Spanish delegation said that he hoped the Americans would remember that "you are the victors, and we are the vanquished; that magnanimity becomes the conqueror," and that Spain therefore might "hope for liberal terms from the American Government." The Spanish knew that they had little chance of prevailing at the peace table. Once again, they hoped that prolonged discussions would show public opinion in Spain that Cuba and the Philippines had not been easily relinquished. In the interval, the elections might produce gains for the Democrats and presumably a softer American position. More time would also make it possible for the army to return from Cuba and for the troops to be discharged peacefully.[28]

The American commissioners differed only over the Philippines. On the other points at issue they adhered closely to the terms of the August protocol and to McKinley's instructions. By means of the telegraph wire the president guided the negotiations on the side of the United States, as daily reports in cipher kept him informed of shifts in the situation. The talks began on October 1. The Spanish attempted at the outset to restore the status quo in the Philippines as it had existed before the protocol was signed. The Americans refused to accept what would have been essentially a renunciation of their sovereignty in the islands. Proceedings then turned to the protocol. Spain proposed, at the meeting of October 7, 1898, that the United States accept sovereignty over Cuba and agree as well to assume responsibility for the debts that Spain had incurred.

Both the American representatives in Paris and William McKinley rejected the ideas regarding Cuban sovereignty and debt. "We must carry out the spirit and letter of the resolution of Congress," the president cabled on October 13. The commissioners believed that their adversaries were hoping for a breakdown in the talks that might justify making an appeal to the European powers to arbitrate the question. The issue of Cuban debt dominated the ensuing two weeks of meetings, private consultations, and sessions on American strategy. Then, on October 21, Spain rejected the argument of the United States. They again proposed that the Americans not only take sovereignty over Cuba but also assume the island's debts. Day and his colleagues agreed that "unless otherwise instructed we shall reject these articles and insist upon our articles in terms of protocol and press matters on these points to a conclusion." To this communication, McKinley replied that he fully approved of the stand of the commission.[29]

At the conference session on October 24 the Americans, through Day, said: "We cannot accept *anything* which attaches the sovereignty or the debt of Cuba to the United States." Later in the deliberations he inquired whether the Spanish "would not consent to any articles relating to Cuba and Puerto Rico which did not embody or carry with them in some form an assumption of the Cuban debt, either by the United States or by Cuba or by both." The Spanish replied that they wanted the Cuban debt "somewhere" in the ultimate document. Day then repeated his question about whether Spain would reject a treaty that omitted the debt, and the commissioners from Madrid sought time for a consultation. The Americans, wrote Reid in his diary, believed "that the Spaniards would yield."[30]

To push matters to that end, Reid hinted, in a private conversation with one of the Spaniards, that concessions on the Cuban issue might stimulate American financial generosity with regard to the Philippine problem. Spain could "find something either in territory or debt which might seem to their people at home like a concession." Whether Reid's overture was decisive is unclear. It certainly impelled Spain in a direction that it would have taken in any case. On October 26 Spain agreed to the American articles, reflecting the "exact language of the protocol," that dealt with Cuba, Puerto Rico, and Guam. Only the Philippines now stood in the way of the treaty.[31]

When they were not occupied with formal meetings with the Spanish or in the inescapable round of ceremonial entertainments, the commissioners received information about, and debated the ultimate disposition of, the Philippines. They heard from John Foreman, who had written on the islands and their history; from Commander R. B. Bradford, their naval attaché, who had just visited the islands; and from General Merritt. The president also sent the Greene memorandum and a report on the talks with Agoncillo. When a message came from Admiral Dewey in mid October, that too went on to Paris. "The natives appear unable to govern," he said, and he underlined the importance of deciding what to do with the archipelago as soon as possible, so that a strong government could be established. The commissioners did not allow Agoncillo to appear before them to present the insurgents' case.[32]

After weighing the evidence and discussing the issue among themselves, the commissioners were still divided. Senator Gray wanted as little of the islands as was feasible; there was "no place for colonial administration or government of subject people in [the] American system." Day believed that the national commitment should be kept within bounds, and he recommended the taking of Luzon and other islands that would safeguard American naval interests. Davis, Frye, and Reid generally favored taking all the Philippines, because there was "no natural place for dividing" them. On October 25 the commission, as a body, asked McKinley for "early consideration and explicit instructions" about what they should now ask of Spain.[33]

The formal record of McKinley's response is now well established. In an instruction that the president drafted personally, Secretary Hay wired on October 28 that "grave as are the responsibilities and unforeseen as are the difficulties which are before us, the President can see but one plain path of duty—the acceptance of the archipelago." American public opinion agreed that "the people of the Philippines, whatever else is done, must be liberated from Spanish domination." The Spanish could not give the islands to another power, and the exercise of joint sovereignty by the United States and a third power was ruled out. "We must either hold them or turn them back to Spain." Moved "by the single consideration of duty and humanity," McKinley ordered the commissioners to demand all the Philippines from the Spanish.[34]

McKinley's instructions of October 28 were the logical culmination, indeed the inevitable result, of the policy that he had pursued since the tentative news of Dewey's victory had been learned on May 2. A subsequent presidential statement, allegedly made thirteen months afterward, in November 1899, introduced a religious element into his decision-making on the Philippines. This has provided critics of his action with powerful reasons to depict him as either a hypocrite or a bemused instrument of the Almighty. A delegation from the Methodist Episcopal Church visited the White House on November 21, 1899. As they began to leave, so one of them recalled, McKinley asked them to wait and then said "just a word about the Philippine business."

Recapitulating his predicament over what to do about these unexpected spoils of war, he confessed "I did not know what to do with them." He asked for "counsel from all sides" but obtained "little help." Then he turned to religion. "I walked the floor of the White House night after night until midnight; and I am not ashamed to tell you, gentlemen, that I went down on my knees and prayed Almighty God for light and guidance more than one night. And one night late it came to me this way—I don't know how it was, but it came." Giving the islands back to Spain "would be cowardly and dishonorable." To transfer them to France or Germany "would be bad business and discreditable." The Filipinos were "unfit for self-government—and they would soon have anarchy and misrule over there worse than Spain's was." The president concluded "that there was nothing left for us to do but to take them all, and to educate the Filipinos, and uplift and civilize and Christianize them, and by God's grace do the very best we could by them, as our fellow-men for whom Christ also died." Sleep came to McKinley, and the next day he gave instructions that the Philippines be put on his office map of the United States, "and there they will stay while I am president."[35]

McKinley's biographers have accepted the accuracy of this remarkable revelation without making much of an effort to verify its authenticity. The reporter of the interview, James F. Rusling, published it in January 1903, more than three years after the Methodists had gone to the White House. Beyond Rusling's good memory of his visit and the president's exact words, there is the coincidence in Rusling's memoir of the Civil War, published in 1899, where Abraham Lincoln said to him in 1863 after the battle of Gettysburg: "I went to my room one day and got down on my knees and prayed Almighty God for victory at Gettysburg." For Lincoln too, "after thus wrestling with the Almighty in prayer, I don't know how it was, and it is not for me to explain but, somehow or other, a sweet comfort crept into my soul" that the Union would win at Gettysburg. Rusling was very fortunate in being able to bring out the theological side of two presidents, but, in the face of two such similar accounts, there is the possibility that Rusling improved on McKinley's words with a device that had served him once before.[36]

If the religious references are left out, the rest of McKinley's remarks become a lucid outline of the considerations that confronted the president in the autumn of 1898. He was making just such outlines to other visitors in November 1899. To the editor of a German-American newspaper, McKinley read from his October 28, 1898, dispatch, and then said: "You see thus I have been carried further and further by the events." He added that "Providence had made us guardians of the group of islands." Faced with mounting criticism from anti-imperialists in the autumn of 1899, McKinley was leaking information to friends and critics in order to offset attacks on his Philippine policy. His comments to the Methodists have at best a modest value as a description of his thoughts a year before they were made; their famed religious context is very questionable. Without that rhetorical excess, his statements become only part of a presidential counterattack, directed at the impending campaign year of 1900, rather than a revealing or essential clue to McKinley's internal thought process during the Philippine crisis.[37]

McKinley's message to Paris rested the American claim to the Philippines on the right of conquest. The commissioners believed that Spain could make a strong argument on this point, since Manila was not taken until after the protocol was signed. Some concessions to the Spanish would be prudent so that they could satisfy their domestic opponents with tangible evidence of their courage. In the process, a resumption of the fighting would be avoided. Senator Frye suggested to the president on October 30 that a payment of from ten to twenty million dollars might help secure a treaty for the United States. Hay reported McKinley's reply that if the commissioners thought that the United States should pay "a reasonable sum of money to cover peace improvements which are fairly chargeable to us under established precedents, he will give cheerful concurrence." At the meeting with the Spanish on October 31 the United States demand for all the Philippines was made.[38]

The Spanish held out for several weeks, hoping still that the congressional elections, friendly powers in Europe, or some happy incident might avert their humiliation. In mid November, McKinley repeated his insistence on taking all the islands, and the American negotiators echoed his firmness. They said, on November 21, that the islands must be ceded and that a payment of $20 million would be made. Spain and her diplomats sought a way out of their predicament, but they found none. On November 28 they agreed to the American terms. There were still many details to be discussed in the remaining two weeks of negotiations. The disposition of Spanish islands in the Pacific brought the Germans into the picture briefly. In the end the treaty that was signed on December 10, 1898, largely corresponded to the terms of the protocol and to McKinley's October instructions. The United States acquired the Philippines, Puerto Rico, and the island of Guam; Spain gave up Cuba, but not its debt, and received the $20 million payment.

The signing of the Peace of Paris concluded one significant phase of McKinley's Philippine strategy. He now had to steer the document through the Senate in the lame-duck session that concluded on March 4, 1899. The Republicans would be in firmer control of the upper house when the new Congress convened in December 1899, and the president could have called a special session in early March with strong assurances that the treaty would be approved. McKinley did not want to have the lawmakers in session to confront the colonial issue. Though the fight in the short session would be a tough one, McKinley desired prompt action on the treaty, and he shaped his course in December 1898 in expectation of the battle ahead.

Celebrations to mark the end of the war drew McKinley southward in the middle of the month. Ostensibly nonpolitical, the week-long trip to Georgia, Alabama, and South Carolina enabled him to promote, among the constituents of Democratic senators, sentiment in favor of expansionism. A series of eleven speeches also allowed McKinley to arouse patriotic feelings through references to how the war had eased animosities between the North and the South. "Sectional feeling no longer holds back the love we bear each other," he told the Georgia Legislature on December 14. The president stood when "Dixie" was played, and he wore a badge of gray. To these marks of sectional accord, the southern audiences responded with enthusiastic applause.

Before a crowd at the Auditorium in Atlanta on December 15, McKinley reported that the flag had been "planted in two hemispheres, and there it remains the symbol of liberty and law, of peace and progress. Who will withdraw from the people over whom it floats its protecting folds? Who will haul it down?" Two days later, at Savannah, he returned to that theme: "If, following the clear precepts of duty, territory falls to us, and the welfare of an alien people requires our guidance and protection, who will shrink from the responsibility, grave though it may be?" Toward the end of the junket, at Augusta on December 19, he summed up his message: "There are no divisions now. We stood united before a foreign foe. We will stand united until every triumph of that war has been made permanent. [Applause]." Disgruntled critics said that the "popular clamor" was "entirely sweeping him off his feet as it has many other men." The acclaim was not swaying the president; he was evoking the applause with the same dexterity that had moved the Midwest in October.[39]

Insulated from immediate popular pressure because of the six-year terms of its members, the Senate received the treaty in early January. If all ninety senators were present, the treaty would require sixty votes for approval. There were fifty Republicans, of all persuasions, including western silver men; thirty-five Democrats; and five Populists or Independents. Complicating McKinley's task were the probable defections of Senator George Frisbie Hoar of Massachusetts and Eugene Hale of Maine. To win the treaty fight, the administration had not only to hold the rest of the Republican ranks firm but also to gain some votes from the Democrats and Populists. The president took personal charge of the protreaty drive in December and January. In the Senate the nominal leader of the ratification effort, Senator Davis, played a smaller part than did Senators Nelson Aldrich, Stephen B. Elkins, and Henry Cabot Lodge.

The McKinley administration also possessed the political initiative in this legislative battle, and it pressed this advantage. The new Congress would be more strongly Republican; therefore, delaying until after March 4, while it would be awkward for the president, would also do little for the opposition. Above all, the forces favoring the treaty argued that the peace settlement was a fact. Rejection of the document would only embarrass the chief executive and the United States abroad. Henry Cabot Lodge said to his fellow senators on January 24, 1899: "The President can not be sent back across the Atlantic in the person of his commissioners, hat in hand, to say to Spain with bated breath, 'I am here in obedience to the mandate of a minority of one-third of the Senate to tell you that we have been too victorious, and that you have yielded us too much, and that I am very sorry that I took the Philippines from you.' "[40]

The White House deployed other weapons in the contest over the treaty. It encouraged state legislatures to pass resolutions endorsing the pact. Such pressure from constituents helped to move California's senator, George C. Perkins, out of the doubtful column and into the protreaty side. Two southerners who voted as the administration desired, John L. McLaurin of South Carolina and Samuel D. McEnery of Louisiana, obtained a large voice in the allocation of patronage in their states; but Senator George Gray's federal judgeship, to which the president named him in 1899, was less a reward for his vote in the Senate than for his service in Paris. In the case of Senator Richard Kenney of Delaware, however, there were intimations that relief from his legal problems in his home state was linked with his support for the treaty.

Opponents of the treaty were less successful in pulling together the thirty-one senators that they needed in order to beat the administration. Divided counsels prevented the emergence of a clear, well-focused antitreaty strategy. William Jennings Bryan, who had just resigned from the army commission that he had held during the war, said to reporters on December 13, 1898: "It will be easier, I think, to end the war at once by ratifying the treaty, and then deal with the subject in our own way." Bryan was reluctant to turn the diplomatic task back over to McKinley; he thought that the Democrats would suffer if the treaty were not ratified and if violence were to occur in the Philippines; and he knew that sentiment for the pact was strong among western silver Democrats. His support for the treaty did not furnish the votes to approve it, but his position underlined and increased the disunity among the partisan enemies of the administration.[41]

The alternatives that the antitreaty senators presented against McKinley's clear goal of approving the peace with Spain further revealed the lack of cohesion in the opposition camp. One bloc of senators wanted to make changes in the language of the document on the Philippines by renegotiating the entire treaty. The champion of this point of view was Arthur P. Gorman of Maryland, who became the leader of the antitreaty forces in the Senate. Gorman thought that consistency on the issue of imperialism demanded that the Democrats oppose the treaty as it had come from Paris. Another group, with Augustus O. Bacon of Georgia as their spokesman, hoped to obtain a congressional resolution that would promise future independence to the Philippines.

Despite the inherent advantages that the administration possessed, the battle over the treaty in January 1899 was tense and close. Debate, which began in executive session on January 4, went on throughout the month. The Republicans asserted publicly that they had the votes for ratification and were ready to ballot at any time. In private, one of them conceded that there was "no certainty of our getting the necessary number of votes for the treaty on February 6th, although I hope that we shall do so." On January 25 the two sides agreed to take the vote on February 6. "The administration," said Senator Hoar, "is moving Heaven and earth, to say nothing of some other places, to detach individual Senators from the opposition, and we shall be very anxious until the thing is settled." As January ended, administration senators wavered over the prospects for the treaty. "Day before yesterday," wrote Senator Charles W. Fairbanks of Indiana, "it seemed there would be no doubt of ratification, but yesterday the tide seemed to be against us."[42]

Only a few days before the voting was to take place, the uncertainty continued. White House forces believed that they were within two votes of the sixty they required. They hoped to find the necessary votes among the four undecided senators. February 6 fell on a Monday, and on Saturday evening, February 4, cables came to the president reporting that fighting between American soldiers and Filipinos had begun. In his diary, Cortelyou wrote that McKinley sat well back in his chair and finally said: "It is always the unexpected that happens, at least in my case. How foolish these people are. This means the ratification of the treaty; the people will understand now, the people will insist upon its ratification."[43]

The administration knew that the military situation in the Philippines was deteriorating in early 1899. McKinley had hoped to obtain approval of the peace treaty and thereby to convince the Filipinos that American sovereignty could not be successfully resisted. Able first to control events in Paris and then in Washington from October 1898 through February 1899, the president found that developments in the Philippines were less amenable to his management during this period. Information came to him slowly and sketchily, and the reports that he gathered about relations between the Americans and the natives of the islands often conveyed an erroneous optimism. Still, the basic problem that divided the two sides was not susceptible to negotiation. McKinley intended to establish America's dominance in the Philippines; Aguinaldo and his forces wanted to limit and restrain the influence of the United States in order to preserve as much independence as they could.

The uneasy accommodation between the Filipino soldiers and their American rivals showed increasing strain during the autumn of 1898. In mid October, General Otis insisted on further withdrawals of Aguinaldo's men from positions near Manila. The insurgents complied after making some protests, and the general told Washington: "Our relations now [are] apparently friendly." That judgment was in error. Aguinaldo was consolidating the control that his men exercised in the islands; he was approaching foreign governments, especially Japan, about diplomatic recognition; and he was capitalizing on resentment against the Americans to win popular support for the revolution. The propensity of the United States soldiers for labeling Filipinos as "niggers" and for bullying their way through the towns made the insurgents' case against the invaders very plausible. By November 13 Otis recognized that his predicament was worsening. "Prudence dictates that all troops here and soon to arrive be retained," he told Washington; "Aguinaldo ambitious, acting with unscrupulous members of cabinet and advisers, cries independence, secretly assert Americans must be driven out." The general concluded: "Many important problems constantly arising here but no serious difficulty anticipated. Necessary to maintain adequate force to meet possible emergencies."[44]

As the negotiations in Paris approached an end, the administration explored the requirements for maintaining American power in the Philippines. Otis estimated that, in the event of Filipino resistance, he would need twenty-five thousand men. A week later the president asked Dewey and Otis for advice about what force and equipment would be necessary in the Philippine Islands. McKinley asserted that the government of the islands would, of necessity, "be by the Army and the Navy for some time to come," and he wanted "as kind and beneficent a government as possible given to the people." Otis responded on December 8 that the Americans should occupy the port of Iloilo, which was still under Spanish control, and he further recommended that judicial and governmental machinery be established quickly, with Filipinos in key positions. On December 14 he requested orders to seize Iloilo.[45]

McKinley's absence in the South caused his answer to be delayed until December 21: "The President directs that you send necessary troops to Iloilo to preserve the peace and protect life and property. It is most important that there should be no conflict with the insurgents. Be conciliatory but firm." Otis received this message on December 23, and troops left three days later. By the time they arrived, the Filipinos had control of the port; and as 1898 ended, the insurgents had a visible presence in extensive portions of the archipelago outside of Manila.[46]

While the military position of the United States worsened, McKinley pushed his political program to establish American ascendancy. On December 27 he sent instructions to Otis that he had prepared six days earlier. The president claimed that Dewey's victory and the surrender of Manila had "practically effected the conquest of the Philippine Islands and the suspension of Spanish sovereignty therein." The peace treaty, though it had not yet been ratified, ceded to the United States "the future control, disposition, and government of the Philippine Islands." Accordingly, McKinley maintained that "the actual occupation and administration of the entire group of the Philippine Islands becomes immediately necessary," and he wanted military government "extended with all possible dispatch to the whole of the ceded territory." If, a few weeks earlier, McKinley had felt "strange" about exercising presidential authority outside the United States, his letter to Otis seems to indicate that he had overcome such qualms.

The substance of McKinley's instructions underscored the need "to announce and proclaim in the most public manner that we come, not as invaders or conquerors, but as friends, to protect the natives in their homes, in their employments, and in their personal and religious rights." American rule would be established "with firmness if need be, but without severity so far as may be possible." The municipal laws of the Philippines would be continued, insofar as military government would allow; private property should be respected; and foreign trade would be resumed. Above all, Otis was told, the military should strive to show the Filipinos that "the mission of the United States is one of benevolent assimilation, substituting the mild sway of justice and right for arbitrary rule."[47]

Events in the Philippines now outpaced McKinley's directives. The War Department ordered Otis on December 29 "to occupy all strategic points in the island possible before the insurgents get possession of them." Otis, who replied that the Filipinos occupied most of the military posts outside Luzon, concluded: "Situation requires delicate manipulation, and our troops here can not be widely scattered at present." Washington answered that Otis should not "prosecute the occupation too rapidly, but proceed with great prudence, avoiding conflict if possible, and only resort to force as the last extremity." To avoid arousing suspicions among the inhabitants of the islands, Otis released a digest of McKinley's instructions that played down the president's claims to sovereignty and stressed the benevolent purposes of the United States. This maneuver failed when the American commander at Iloilo released the complete text of the president's letter. Aguinaldo angrily threatened to begin fighting if the Americans extended their control over the Philippines.[48]

When, on January 8, Otis reported the reaction to McKinley's orders and also the uneasy conditions between Filipinos and United States soldiers, McKinley sent him another elaboration of the administration's attitude: "Am most desirous that conflict be avoided. . . . Time given the insurgents can not hurt us and must weaken and discourage them. They will come to see our benevolent purpose and recognize that before we can give their people good government our sovereignty must be complete and unquestioned." Otis should continue the talks that he was having with Filipino leaders, and the president offered to aid in these negotiations and in the establishment of a workable civil-military government.[49]

At the end of McKinley's second year in the White House the commission device had become one of the characteristic features of his presidency. He had used commissioners on the bimetallic initiative; he had formed the Joint High Commission to negotiate with the British; and he had enlisted lawmakers to survey the political and economic needs of newly annexed Hawaii. Now he turned again to the same idea for the Philippines. On the commission that he selected on January 19, 1899, were Charles Denby, a Democrat and one-time minister to China; Dean C. Worcester, a zoologist from the University of Michigan; and Jacob Gould Schurman, president of Cornell University.

Worcester had called on the president in order to share with him the experiences gained from research trips in the Philippines. Worcester's ideas about the islands were influencing McKinley's policy by late December 1898. Schurman told the president, who asked him to head the commission, that he did not favor taking the Philippines. "Oh, . . . that need not trouble you," McKinley declared; "I didn't want the Philippine Islands, either; and in the protocol to the treaty I left myself free not to take them, but—in the end there was no alternative." Schurman acceded to the president's request, and the civilian commissioners left the United States on January 31, 1899.[50]

The commissioners could not have any immediate effect on the tense situation in the Philippines. Both sides sought to settle their differences in conference for two weeks after McKinley's message of January 8. Six meetings occurred, in which it became obvious that the Americans would insist on a recognition of United States sovereignty, while the Filipinos, at least those who represented Aguinaldo, wanted the independence of the islands to be accepted before his government would discuss the precise form of an American protectorate. Negotiations broke off on January 29, 1899. Where American and Filipino forces confronted each other, the atmosphere grew sharp and inflammable. Hostilities began on February 4, when Americans and Filipinos fired on each other. "Insurgents have inaugurated general engagement yesterday night which is continued to-day," was the form in which McKinley first received the news.[51]

The Senate voted on the treaty in midafternoon on February 6, 1899. Contrary to McKinley's forecast, news of the fighting at Manila did not make the task of the administration forces any easier. With three hours to go, the treaty was still two votes short of the necessary two-thirds. Senator McLaurin of South Carolina, induced in part by promises of patronage, then moved into the affirmative column. Senator McEnery of Louisiana followed when the Republican leadership agreed to endorse his resolution that the United States had no intention of annexing the Philippines as part of the United States. Senator John P. Jones of Nevada added an aye vote after the initial roll call. The final vote was 57 to 27, one more vote than was needed for ratification.

The effects of the battle echoed for several days. The Senate passed the McEnery resolution by four votes, but it was defeated in the House. Opponents of the treaty pushed a resolution of Senator Bacon's which promised Philippine independence. Because some administration senators were absent, there was a tie vote of 29 to 29 on the resolution. Vice-President Hobart cast the deciding vote against the proposal. The vote on this resolution provides a misleading picture of the administration's legislative strength during the winter of 1899. Had the full Senate been present, Bacon's idea would have been overwhelmingly beaten.

The greatest victory in the fight over the treaty was McKinley's. Other causes helped the treaty. Bryan's stance divided the opposition; if he had enthusiastically opposed the treaty, it would probably have been beaten. The anti-imperialist coalition in the Senate was a fragile and fractious one, and it did not offer any attractive alternative to what the administration proposed. The president made the difference. From Dewey's victory onward, he guided events so that American acquisition of the Philippines became logical and, to politicians and the people, inevitable.

Once the fighting had ended, while there was still a United States presence in the Philippines, McKinley constantly kept in mind, as he conducted affairs, that there would eventually be a Senate battle over the peace treaty. His idea of selecting senators to serve on the peace commission was an innovation that involved a merging of the legislative and executive branches for the president's own ends. Modern communications enabled McKinley, as they had in his fighting of the war, to participate directly in the peace-making process in Paris. Simultaneously, in October he exploited the publicity weapons of a strong executive during his midwestern tour to shape public opinion. He performed with equal skill in his December swing through the South. In the treaty fight itself, he returned to the techniques of close management and personal participation that he had shown in handling the Cuban and Hawaiian issues. There are few better examples, before the time of Franklin D. Roosevelt, of the exercise of presidential power in foreign affairs than McKinley's successful effort to obtain Senate approval for the Peace of Paris.

The war in the Philippines was the most unpleasant legacy of the dramatic occurrences of 1898. The future of the islands was the primary topic of McKinley's address to the Home Market Club in Boston on February 16. Almost six thousand guests and listeners heard the president deliver one of the most effective speeches of his life. Of the American commitment in the Philippines he said: "It is a trust we have not sought; it is a trust from which we will not flinch." He reviewed the options at the peace negotiations and decided that "there was but one alternative, and that was either Spain or the United States in the Philippines." As to the Filipinos, Americans had, as their sole purpose, to safeguard "the welfare and happiness and the rights of the inhabitants of the Philippine Islands." An expression of opinion from the inhabitants of the islands on the rule of the United States would, however, have to wait. "It is not a good time for the liberator to submit important questions concerning liberty and government to the liberated while they are engaged in shooting down their rescuers."

With the war behind them, McKinley went on, the American people now had the future of the Philippines before them. Until Congress acted with regard to the islands, the president would give "to the people thereof peace and order and beneficent government." McKinley underlined that "neither their aspirations nor ours can be realized until our authority is acknowledged and unquestioned." In the speech he made no specific promises about the Filipinos in the years ahead, but he sought to defuse anti-imperialist charges: "No imperial designs lurk in the American mind. They are alien to American sentiment, thought, and purpose. Our priceless principles undergo no change under a tropical sun. They go with the flag." In his peroration, McKinley invoked a picture that was not limited "by the blood-stained trenches around Manila—where every red drop, whether from the veins of an American soldier or a misguided Filipino, is anguish to my heart." He looked instead to "the broad range of future years," to the Philippines as "a land of plenty and increasing possibilities; a people redeemed from savage indolence and habits, devoted to the arts of peace, in touch with commerce and trade of all nations, enjoying the blessings of freedom, of civil and religious liberty, of education, and of homes, and whose children and children's children shall for ages hence bless the American republic because it emancipated and redeemed their fatherland, and set them in the pathway of the world's best civilization."[52]

Exactly one year before, McKinley had learned of the destruction of the *Maine*. In those twelve months the United States had struggled for peace, had won the war with Spain, and had gained an empire. At the center of the process that changed the nation's history was William McKinley. He transformed the presidential office from its late-nineteenth-century weakness into a recognizable prototype of its present-day form. The Home Market speech revealed what the developments of the Spanish-American War foreshadowed. From the seedbed of the House of Representatives, the governorship of Ohio, and the campaign of 1896 had appeared the first modern president. During his remaining years in the White House, McKinley would build upon and expand the legacy of power and authority that then passed to Theodore Roosevelt and Woodrow Wilson.

7

★★★★★

McKINLEY'S
DOMESTIC POLICIES

No administration deals with all its issues in an orderly chrono-logical way. While President McKinley was grappling with the Spanish-American War, he had an abundance of domestic concerns. On these topics his presidency compiled a mixed record, in part because of his preoccupation with the war and in part because of his own priorities and leadership. The attitudes and biases of American society also limited the options regarding such issues as race relations, trusts and regulation of them, labor relations, banking and currency, and the civil service. During the first half of 1899 the question of Secretary Alger also persisted. By the early stages of the presidential campaign of 1900, the outlines of McKinley's domestic policies had been developed.

The place of the Negro in American society confronted McKinley most directly when he made patronage decisions that involved the Republican party in the South and when he recognized the contributions of black politicians to the GOP cause generally. Confronted with a rising pressure from the white South for segregation, black Americans also looked to the man in the White House as their condition worsened. He had spoken on their behalf in Congress, had criticized lynching while in the Ohio Statehouse, and had been popular among blacks in 1896. Some offices they received; but McKinley, as his inaugural address had forecast, did very little to alienate the South, whose allegiance he hoped to win for the goals of his administration. From expectant hope when McKinley took office, Negro leaders moved to deep disillusionment as the president failed them.

It would have been rather simple for McKinley to appoint larger numbers of black men to federal jobs than earlier presidents had done. Grover Cleveland's administration was successful in seeking repeal of Reconstruction laws and gave white southerners a large role in dispensing patronage. During his first year as president, McKinley made "thirty appointments of consequence" that placed black men in his administration, and an article on "Colored Men in Office" contended, in April 1898, "that the colored man has a fair share of representatives in the Federal service." Black leaders, when writing to McKinley, said: "You have done more for this class of our fellow citizens than any of your distinguished predecessors." From the reactions that reached him, McKinley probably concluded that his patronage policies toward black Republicans had been a success.[1]

McKinley's handling of appointments for blacks fell a good distance short of what Negro Republicans had anticipated. There were some highly visible and symbolic nominations. Former senator Blanche K. Bruce was named register of the Treasury Department, a post traditionally reserved for his race in the GOP's patronage system. At Wilmington, North Carolina, and at Savannah, Georgia, blacks became customs collectors. The post of recorder of deeds in Washington, D.C., went to Henry P. Cheatham, a North Carolina Republican. For the Ohioan John P. Green, a place was found as superintendent of postage stamps. McKinley believed that there were positions in the diplomatic service and in the national government that were "proper for a colored man to hold," and he spent careful hours balancing the coalitions that constituted black Republicanism, North and South.[2]

There were limits, however, that the nation's racial mores imposed and that McKinley honored. Judson W. Lyons, a black lawyer who was the Republican national committeeman from Georgia, was designated to be postmaster at Augusta. The prospect of having a black man handle their mail evoked strong protests from the white population. McKinley yielded and asked Lyons to withdraw his name. When Bruce died unexpectedly in March 1898, Lyons succeeded him as register of the Treasury Department. Some blacks were named to postmasterships in the South, but the number of appointments never equaled what black supporters of McKinley desired.

In Ohio, Negroes who had endorsed his candidacy in 1896

complained that they, too, had been slighted in the distribution of spoils. Men such as John P. Green and George A. Myers, who had been close to Mark Hanna, resented it when they received less than their black counterparts in the South. Green had hoped to follow Bruce in the treasury post, but apparently his candidacy was ignored. As the meager dribble of offices continued, Ohio black leaders experienced greater difficulty when their constituents complained that the Republicans had lost interest in them after election day. McKinley and Hanna calculated, as would other Republican presidents, that southern blacks represented delegate votes that the administration would need again in 1900. Therefore, they warranted some modest conciliation. Northern Negroes, who were fewer in number and less significant in electoral terms, might receive even less.

The forces of racial proscription and the Spanish-American War complicated McKinley's relationship with the black community. Whites harassed and attacked Negro postmasters at Hogansville, Georgia, in 1897 and at Lake City, South Carolina, in 1898. Newspapers reported that the president was concerned about these incidents, and there were federal inquiries and a prosecution in the Lake City case; but the president did not issue any statement expressing his dismay or criticism. As the number of lynchings of black people in the South increased, Negroes looked to McKinley to reaffirm the remarks that he had made as governor and in his inaugural address. There was no comment from the White House. Apologists for the administration contended that the constitution prohibited the president from interfering in state or local affairs. Black leaders accepted this argument, but responded that McKinley could, as Benjamin Harrison had done, "at least use the influence of his great office by saying some word of condemnation against wholesale lawlessness and crime." Such an action on McKinley's part would have run counter to his zeal for sectional reconciliation and to Republican reluctance to return to the unfashionable tactics of Reconstruction.[3]

When the Spanish-American War began, members of the black community rushed eagerly to demonstrate their patriotism. Negroes asserted that there was "nothing but good in this war for the black people of America or Cuba, and of the world at large." Black politicians called on McKinley to offer the support of their people. The war would give blacks a fair chance to show their ability and would "make Uncle Sam toe the mark and show his colors." While there were some glowing spots in the record of bravery that the Negro soldiers compiled in the war, the administration and white society pursued policies that further built the resentment of blacks against their subordinate position.[4]

For the black regulars, who constituted an elite force within the army, their experiences in the South represented a depressing mixture of local bigotry, harassment, and occasional violence. To whites, wrote one Negro soldier, "it mattered not if we were soldiers of the United States, and going to fight for the honor of our country, . . . we were 'niggers' as they called us and treated us with contempt." Once in Cuba, the black regulars were outstanding fighters at El Caney and at San Juan Hill. Assessing the contribution of the black soldiers generally, a correspondent described the attitude of the army as "God bless the nigger!"[5]

Blacks who volunteered had relatively little chance to demonstrate their patriotism. National Guard units were usually segregated, and few of the existing all-black militia detachments entered the army. In state after state, Negroes were subjected to prejudice and delay that effectively barred them from service. When blacks did join the military, they found white officers in command. In response, a "no officers, no fight" campaign gained strength in the black community.

As the administration prepared in April and May 1898 for combat in the tropics, some recruitment of black volunteers came to seem prudent. Popular belief held that Negroes were immune to such tropical diseases as malaria and yellow fever. In May 1898 Congress authorized the enlistment of ten thousand men who were immune to "diseases incident to tropic climes," and four of the ten regiments were allocated to blacks. After additional pressure from black leaders, the president directed the War Department to allow the commissioning of some Negro officers above the rank of lieutenant. McKinley also made the widely publicized appointment of John R. Lynch as a major in the volunteers, sought from Congress, without success, the power to enlist twenty-five thousand colored troops, and in his second call for volunteers, urged the states to take in more blacks. The states were told that the president had "expressed particular anxiety to give colored men an opportunity to enter service."[6]

Black Republicans used these actions of McKinley's to tell their critics that "we colored Americans, from a national point of view, are being better treated now and more fully recognized under the present Administration, both in civil office and in the Army, than ever before in the history of this nation." The true state of Negro opinion emerged in the comment of an Ohio black: "This country should demonstrate its ability to protect their own citizens—within its own domain—especially when some are a part and parcel of their government (Baker at Lake City S.C.) before interfering with other Governments about the treatment of their subjects."[7]

If black Americans thought that their actions in the Spanish-American War, especially the heroics of the Negro regulars, would affect white racial attitudes, they were soon disillusioned. The last months of 1898 saw violence in the South and Midwest, with the most spectacular outbreak in Wilmington, North Carolina, where eleven Negroes were killed. The black community and some northern whites hoped that McKinley would denounce these outrages in his annual message, but that document contained no references to the race issue or the plight of the Negro.

When McKinley toured the South in December 1898, blacks criticized his wooing of Confederate sentiment. A minister called it "throwing daisies over rebel graves."[8] McKinley's visit to Tuskegee Institute and his praise of Booker T. Washington did not mollify the black Americans who were assailing the administration's inaction and its southern strategy. For McKinley, the rewards of praise in Dixie and the potential support for the Peace of Paris outweighed the reduction in Negro rights.

The blacks' grievances sharpened in 1899. Negroes watched with apprehension the evolution of the government's imperial policies. John P. Green's verdict, conveyed to the president in late June 1899, was accurate: "So far as my information goes, the war in the Philippines is *exceedingly* unpopular amongst all colored people without regard to condition." As one Ohio Republican summed up the consensus toward McKinley: "But you cannot expect much of a President who marches through the streets of a southern city decorated with a Confederate badge and feels that the nation should care for and keep green the graves and memories of men who gave their all for the overthrow of the government." T. Thomas Fortune called the president "a man of jelly, who would turn us all loose to the mob and not say a word."[9]

By the summer of 1899 the discontent among Negroes moved McKinley to take modest remedial action. One letter urged him to "be the President of the whole people, and act as he would if Indians were killing white men, as white men are killing Negroes, or if the Negroes of the south were treating the whites as the whites of the south are treating the Negroes."[10] The president did not adopt that course. He told black visitors about his appointment record, and he listened as they reminded him of violence in the South and the treatment that black soldiers had received. The War Department had indicated in early July that it would not seek the service of black volunteers in the Philippines because of the allegedly disappointing record of such troops in the war against Spain and because of the danger that black soldiers might not fight against a black enemy in the islands.

McKinley did not share this position, and he asked the new secretary of war, Elihu Root, whether some black regiments with black line officers could be recruited. Root replied, reflecting the army's judgment, that "the colored officers in the volunteer regiments raised for the Spanish war were failures," and he therefore recommended that no units be enlisted. "This subject is always one of difficulty," the president wrote back, "but I feel very much inclined to organize a colored regiment making the field officers (white) all regulars, and the line officers all colored." McKinley added that "the colored regiments fight magnificently, and I see that those in the Philippines have already shown the same splendid fighting qualities that were evidenced in Cuba." Two regiments were formed in the autumn of 1899, and they reached the Philippines in January 1900. McKinley told Negroes at the White House that the black man would now have a chance "to make a record for himself." Coupled with presidential statements praising the bravery of Negro fighting men, these actions defused some of the animosity against McKinley's racial actions.[11]

Such a symbolic gesture seemed to be all that the president would offer to black Americans. His annual message in 1899 mentioned lynching, primarily in the context of the death of Italians in Louisiana. In another section, without alluding to Negroes or the South directly, he observed: "Those who, in disregard of law and the public peace, unwilling to await the judgment of court and jury, constitute themselves judges and executioners should not escape the severest penalties for their crimes."[12] On another problem relating to race, McKinley upheld the status quo in late 1899. Henry Clay Payne, the Republican national committeeman from Wisconsin, who was a conservative member of the moneyed wing of the party in that state, advanced a proposal to change the rules of the Republican National Convention.

Payne's idea would have meant that the size of each state's delegation would be tied to the size of the Republican vote in that state; and this would have reduced the influence that southern Republican delegations would have on the proceedings at the national convention. In the short run it would have injured black power in the GOP by lessening the bargaining ability of state parties that were only shadow organizations with predominantly Negro membership. Payne contended that his alterations would produce "a live, energetic aggressive Republican party in the minority states."[13] It would also have impaired the power of Mark Hanna in the South, as Payne well knew. Neither side in the controversy saw blacks as being more than passive elements in the political equation. Negro leaders preferred that their position in the party remain as it was.

Republican leaders, including Payne, conferred with McKinley on December 15, 1899. After listening to both sides, the president observed that, in this instance, "he was simply a member of the party and must not be regarded as desiring to influence a decision one way or the other." Recent conversations with black leaders, however, had changed his initially favorable impression of Payne's idea and, according to Cortelyou, "he now doubted the expediency. Was it wise, asked the President, to introduce new questions unnecessarily at this time, when everything was running along so harmoniously? If the adoption of the resolution would lose a single state it should not be adopted." In the end the opponents of Payne's scheme, stressing that the impact on the black vote would be bad, prevailed. Payne withdrew the resolution in the face of opposition from both McKinley and Hanna.[14]

As the end of his first term approached, William McKinley had established a record regarding black Americans that did not contain either the endorsement of segregation, as would Woodrow Wilson's, or a spectacular example of injustice, such as Theodore Roosevelt's handling of the Brownsville episode. The president's kindly nature and innate courtesy prevented him from treating individual blacks with anything but dignity and politeness. Where McKinley failed to rise to the crisis of the moment was in his perception of his own duty relative to the deplorable condition of black people. Many real forces constrained him. The system of segregation in the South was entrenched and was at its most intense in the minds of its adherents. The North shared the racial attitudes that underlay the caste structure. Republicans had lost such moral fervor on this issue as they had earlier possessed, and the Democrats still found the bloody shirt a comfortable garment. With all that against him, presidential gestures from McKinley would have produced only the smallest incremental improvements for black people. The absence of even gestures, the presence of but few words of rebuke for lynching and nothing for disfranchisement, revealed that McKinley lacked the vision to transcend the biases of his day and to point toward a better future for all Americans.

As 1899 began, the growing movement for business consolidation in the form of trusts and holding companies gained new public attention. Charles G. Dawes, the comptroller of the currency, wrote in March that "the enormous capitalization of industrial concerns and combinations in apparent effort to control and raise prices is deeply stirring the people, and will force the question of further legislation on this subject into the next campaign."[15] McKinley had not referred publicly to this problem since his inaugural address, and critics now charged that the record of the Justice Department since 1897 had been meager. Scholars of the trust issue extend this negative appraisal to McKinley's entire record. Much of this criticism is justified, but it overlooks the shift of attitude in the president's mind in 1899/1900 that foreshadowed a greater vigor in this area during his second term.

Attorney General Joseph McKenna served nine months in 1897 before going on to the Supreme Court. The two antitrust suits that the government filed during his tenure continued the policies of the preceding administration. The first suit, relating to livestock dealers in Missouri, had been compiled under Grover Cleveland. The second, which derived from private complaints among users of coal in San Francisco, did not originate within the department. McKenna left the cabinet in December 1897, and John W. Griggs replaced him.

Griggs, a tall, thin man, was forty-eight years old when he became attorney general. During his early law career he not only developed a friendship with Garret A. Hobart but he also gained extensive experience with taxation and the legal problems of New Jersey's cities and counties. He rose through state politics during the 1870s and 1880s to win the governorship in 1895. From there, McKinley tapped him for the official family. Griggs rapidly gained McKinley's respect for his legal talent.

If McKinley accepted Griggs's view on the trusts, as it appears he did, he was approving a passive and minimal policy toward the burgeoning force of business expansion. The laws of that time furnished a basis for Griggs's position. After the Sherman Antitrust Act was passed in 1890, the Supreme Court decided, in the case of *United States* v. *E. C. Knight* in 1895, that in order to come under the provisions of the laws, it was necessary to show that a corporation, in this case the Sugar Trust, possessed not merely a monopoly of manufacture but a monopoly of interstate commerce. In deciding whether to proceed against corporations whose practices were alleged to violate the Sherman Act, Griggs asserted that the government could only act when "the functions of interstate commerce are interfered with." To a critic of Standard Oil who told him that it was his "imperative duty to proceed at once as the Federal antitrust law directs, to break up this unlawful combination," Griggs responded, through a subordinate, that he did not believe that "the alleged combination against which you complain is of an interstate character such as to give the courts of the United States jurisdiction under the statute mentioned." Griggs was equally cool when correspondents cited possible antitrust violations, and the department took scant action to explore the possibilities that remained for antitrust initiatives, the *Knight* decision notwithstanding.[16]

McKinley left the operation of the Justice Department to the attorney general. Given the president's greater interest in the problems of tariff and reciprocal trade than in the trust problem, he would not have altered the general outlines of what Griggs did. Indeed, McKinley was not familiar with the record of judicial and administrative action in this field. By early 1899, however, one member of his administration was discussing the subject with him; and the newspapers, which the White House closely monitored, were filled with stories about the large increase in the number of trusts. Comptroller Dawes saw him on March 28, and together they examined "the unprecedented growth of trusts." McKinley told Dawes that "he expected to call the attention of Congress to the matter in his next message and would lead in a movement for their proper restriction."[17]

By the spring of 1899 there were ample political reasons for responding to the trust question. Newspapers and popular magazines ran numerous articles about the "anti-trust agitation" that was animating the country. Adding to the public interest in trusts were the hearings of the Industrial Commission, which began in May. Congress had established the commission in 1898, though the idea of a nonpartisan commission to probe economic problems had been discussed for four years. Its membership included five congressmen, five senators, and nine individuals from private industry and labor. At its hearings on industrial consolidation, the commission heard H. O. Havemeyer, one of the organizers of the Sugar Trust, assert that "the mother of all trusts is the customs tariff bill." William Jennings Bryan had already said: "The Democratic party will continue its attack upon monopoly, whether in the standard money trust, the paper money trust, or the industrial trust." Just how much

Bryan would make of the trust question in the 1900 campaign was not clear. Still, it seemed likely that the GOP would face a stern test on the issue.[18]

Within the Republican party, of course, there was a substantial body of thought that accepted consolidation as inevitable and largely beneficial. "Jamming a stick into the machinery will only throw us back," Senator Hanna was informed; and he readily concurred. "I have as yet been unable to see any way to stop the combination of industrial interests in this country," the senator wrote to a colleague. "In the numerous discussions that I heard upon the Constitution and the Declaration of Independence during the last session I got sort of an idea that a man had a right to do what he pleased with his own."[19]

Few traces remain of what McKinley thought and did on the trust question in 1899. Dawes, who was traveling in the west, wrote him on June 4 that "there seems noticeably less rash talk about trusts, and more careful and considered comment on the situation." The public "will not be for hasty legislation so much as for *right* legislation." The president was gathering information on this issue and related matters. On June 1 he asked Justice John Marshall Harlan of the Supreme Court if that body had "ever passed upon the income tax feature of the internal revenue statute passed during the civil war." Four days later, in another conversation with Harlan, McKinley asked for "a list of cases in the Supreme Court of the United States relating to the act of Congress known as the Anti Trust Statute." What he did with the list is not known.[20]

The events of the summer of 1899 kept the trust matter alive. The resignation of Secretary of War Alger occurred when, among other things, he seemed to be identifying himself with Governor Hazen Pingree's attacks on the administration's record on trusts. Some of the problems that the GOP faced were embodied in the platform of the Maryland state convention in September. "We strongly favor laws successfully to suppress trusts and all combinations which create monopoly," the delegates resolved. They then opposed "legislation merely for popular effect in reckless disregard of business revival after prolonged depression." After Pingree had criticized Griggs for allegedly making public statements that Congress lacked the power to control trusts, the attorney general released his answer to the Michigan governor in late September. The Justice Department had brought "numerous suits," and he took credit for proceeding with actions against railroads that his predecessor had begun. "Congress," Griggs concluded, "can regulate directly that which we understood by 'interstate commerce,' but it has no power to regulate or control business or commerce carried on wholly within the limits of a State."[21]

Comptroller Dawes had been invited to address the Merchants Club of Boston in mid October, and trusts were to be his topic. On September 21, 1899, he read the speech to the president at the White House. Almost four weeks later, Dawes informed his audience that agitation over combinations had "created a just demand for the more intelligent legislative treatment of existing industrial conditions." He attributed the growth of mergers to natural causes and said that it had "proceeded in accordance with the natural laws of progress under a competitive system." Nonetheless, the problem of "the proper legislative treatment" of these industrial combinations was "one of the greatest and most practical which has ever confronted the political parties of the Nation." The American people would not accept the power of a business to control the price of the necessities of life, and they would insist that the trusts be either regulated or dissolved.

Dawes decided that the difficulties of obtaining uniform state laws warranted federal action. "Let us trust that Congress will now take up this great question," he said, "because positive action against the present and prospective evils of the trusts is one of the necessities of the hour." McKinley made no direct comment on Dawes's address, but on November 12 and again on November 18, the two men discussed what the president would say about the trusts in his annual message.[22]

The message devoted more space to the trust issue than to any other domestic question. "Combinations of capital organized into trusts to control the conditions of trade among our citizens, to stifle competition, limit production, and determine the prices of products used and consumed by the people, are justly provoking public discussion, and should early claim the attention of Congress." The president pointed to the unfinished work of the Industrial Commission and wrote of the many divergent views on the causes and extent of the problem. "There must be a remedy for the evils involved in such organizations. If the present law can be extended more certainly to control or check these monopolies or trusts, it should be done without delay. Whatever power the Congress possesses over this most important subject should be properly ascertained and asserted." McKinley concluded that legislation passed by the individual states could not provide "relief from the evils of the trusts," as Grover Cleveland had hoped, and he thought that

Congress could "supplement an effective code of State legislation as to make a complete system of laws throughout the United States adequate to compel a general observance of the salutary rules to which I have referred."[23]

What were McKinley's goals in writing these statements? With a presidential election eleven months away, it was unlikely that Congress would take action of a substantial kind. Efforts would be made on behalf of a constitutional amendment and a bill to strengthen the penalties for violation of the Sherman Act, but the president knew that Congress, in both the 1899/1900 session and the lame-duck one of 1900/1901, would hardly enact serious trust legislation. It is easy to speculate that McKinley's statement was only rhetorical and that his purpose was to deflect public concern rather than to arouse it. Yet, McKinley might have played down the subject, and the sequence of events indicates that he was preparing the ground for taking action, during his second term, on economic concentration. Like Theodore Roosevelt, McKinley made the distinction between good and bad trusts. In a conversation in January 1900 he remarked that "he didn't know but that he 'guessed' combination must necessarily control in the near future." The "great need," as he put it, "was protection to the companies as well as to consult the interests of the people at large." Just how these competing pressures would develop into tangible policy appeared during McKinley's second campaign and second term.[24]

In its relations with organized labor, the administration followed the conciliatory policies that McKinley had espoused before he became president. Appointments of union men included Terence V. Powderly, one-time head of the Knights of Labor, as commissioner general of immigration, and Frank P. Sargent, grand master of the Brotherhood of Locomotive Fireman, to the Industrial Commission. McKinley not only talked with Samuel Gompers, president of the American Federation of Labor, at the White House but also invited him to submit suggestions for the 1898 annual message. In that document the president summarized and endorsed Gompers's ideas concerning the eight-hour day for government workers and the use of convict labor, and he repeated them in 1900.

Adding to McKinley's strength with labor was his support for the Erdman Act of 1898, which created a mechanism for mediating wage disputes and other controversies on interstate railroads. Powderly's policy of pushing for the exclusion of Chinese labor also won the backing of Gompers and the AFL. A visible demonstration of McKinley's appeal to labor came in October 1899 during his tour of the Middle West. As part of the ceremony of laying the corner-stone of a new federal building in Chicago, he became an honorary member of the Brick Layers' and Stonemasons' International Union. McKinley responded by extending an invitation to them to hold their national convention in Washington in 1901. He also told the audience: "I do not want the workingmen of this country to establish hostile camps and divide into classes."[25]

In the spring of 1899, in the Coeur d'Alene mining district of Idaho, hostilities between workers and employers erupted in the most bitter labor dispute during McKinley's presidency. When state officers and mine operators asked for the army to restore order, the White House responded by sending a detachment of soldiers. The president and the War Department ordered the military to remain neutral and not to become strike breakers, instructions that the general on the scene did not always follow. A congressional probe of charges that the administration was on the side of the owners resulted in conflicting partisan verdicts regarding the troops' long stay in the state. McKinley's involvement in this matter did not disturb the good reputation that he enjoyed with organized and unorganized labor. As Sargent wrote a month before the president died: "Among the working people there is no one held in higher esteem than our present Chief Magistrate."[26]

Despite the favorable evaluation that McKinley's civil-service order of July 24, 1897, received from the reformers, students of government personnel policies knew that additional decisions lay ahead. Almost two years later, on May 29, 1899, there was another executive order which the National Civil Service Reform League immediately characterized as a backward step from the president's pledges to extend the merit system. In fact, McKinley sought a middle ground among the partisans of civil service, who wanted no changes that would reduce the classified system; members of his cabinet who desired greater freedom of executive action; and professional politicians in the GOP who were "against the prostitution of the system for the purpose of perpetuating in office Democratic partisans who have no right or claim to the protection of the law."[27]

The problem that McKinley faced stemmed from the actions of President Cleveland in broadening the coverage of the system at the end of his second term. His order of May 6, 1896, added many offices for which competitive examinations were not well suited. A more important issue was the extent to which the order, by putting division heads and chief clerks under classification, impaired the ability of the party in power to "shape the legislation of the country in consonance with the policies which it sustains." The Civil Service Commission responded that "the great bulk of the offices of the Government are purely administrative business offices" into which partisanship should not intrude. But the cabinet officers told the president, in substance, that civil-service reform had, under Cleveland, been too far-reaching.[28]

There were also strained relations between the executive branch and the Civil Service Commission itself. The president of the commission, John R. Proctor, a Democrat, "nearly drove me wild at times," said Cornelius N. Bliss, remembering his days in the Interior Department. McKinley retained Proctor in spite of such strictures against his zeal, and he also kept John B. Harlow, a Republican whom Cleveland had appointed. McKinley's choices for the other commissioners were not distinguished ones. In 1898 he picked Mark Brewer, a former Republican congressman, who often acted as a partisan. When Brewer died in 1901, William A. Rodenberg, an Illinois representative who had been defeated in 1900, succeeded him. Rodenberg had voted against civil-service appropriations, a vote that he said he "had absolutely forgotten" about. Nonetheless, McKinley seems to have given him the position while Rodenberg was waiting to resume his congressional career.[29]

The Spanish-American War kept civil service off the front pages in 1898. Republican critics in the House assaulted the system in January in a battle that Roosevelt termed "exceedingly ugly." Carl Schurz, however, said: "The anti-civil service reform force in Congress, does not seem to be nearly as strong as it looked some time ago." A Senate committee examined the operations of the merit system and then reported in March 1898. The bipartisan majority differed only over whether three thousand or ten thousand places should be excepted from Cleveland's 1896 order.[30]

The Senate report included recommendations from the heads of the executive departments for exceptions that they thought necessary. Using this information as a rough guide, the Civil Service Commission sent to the president, on June 1, 1898, a set of amendments to Cleveland's rules. Private secretaries and confidential clerks were specifically included because competitive examinations were not practical for testing whether they were qualified to carry out their duties. McKinley held these proposals for the rest of the year. Late in 1898 he told the National Civil Service Reform League that he would be altering the Cleveland ruling. The league made a public protest about the proposed action and sent McKinley some opposing arguments. Until the end of the short congressional session in 1899 the president did not begin to work on the order.

In April 1899 the White House asked each cabinet officer for a statement about proposed modifications in the civil-service rules. Using the recommendations of the Civil Service Commission and working with Secretary of the Treasury Gage and two of his subordinates, McKinley compiled his order. As he did so, an Ohio colleague who was an arch foe of civil service told him that "the complications in Ohio growing out of the civil service condition are of the most formidable character." Loyal Republicans were irritated because Democrats still held positions on pension boards and in other places. Their complaints may have affected the timing of the order, but they had no apparent impact on its substance.[31]

The order, which was released on May 29, 1899, largely drew critical comment. McKinley had placed a number of positions on the list of those that would be exempt from competitive examinations, a total that a White House release from Secretary Gage set at between three and four thousand. The National Civil Service Reform League, using an expansive definition of who was covered, contended that the correct figure was more than ten thousand. Gage became the administration's spokesman as public reaction against the order intensified. Cleveland's actions had been too broad, and the need for confidential relations in the executive branch justified the exceptions for clerks and private secretaries. Changes in the War, Treasury, and Interior departments, moreover, were justified because special requirements for such positions as people who packed mules, surgeons who examined people for pensions, and storekeepers and gaugers could not be measured by competitive tests.

The administration's arguments did not convince the public. Republican newspapers seconded the attacks of the Democrats and the advocates of civil service. Carl Schurz, who was already opposed to McKinley on foreign policy, decided that the president's prestige had "suffered immensely by that characteristic demonstration of mental and moral weakness." McKinley did not remain passive under these charges. Through Gage he counterattacked, using the evidence that had, in his opinion, justified his action. Gage sent him a draft of an article that ultimately appeared in *Forum*, for which the president wrote the concluding paragraph. "Indeed, the conduct of the public business by President McKinley and his counsellors and associates has been always characterized by freedom from partisanship and by devotion to the public interests."

Writing about himself, McKinley said: "With deliberation and high purpose to benefit the Service, he has issued an order which men familiar with public administration approve, and which those who condemn will, with greater knowledge easily acquired, commend."[32]

McKinley's direct role in shaping the policy statements of the administration was typical. In this case, some of his irritation was warranted. The civil-service reformers had overreacted, allowing their anger at the government's foreign policy to influence their response to the president's order. The ruling represented, not a wholesale capitulation to the spoils system, but a retreat from the extreme position that Cleveland had adopted. President McKinley was a partisan, and he believed that, to fill certain positions at least, the president should be able to name men who would support his policies. As he saw it, his order would result in a deserved loosening up in a too-rigid system. Whether such a stance would bring consequent corruption was problematical. The vigilant civil-service reformers found a number of apparent cases of malfeasance, but the evidence does not sustain the charge that the McKinley administration was less upright than the one that succeeded it.

Modern critics admit that McKinley's record in staffing the colonial administrations in Cuba, Puerto Rico, and the Philippines was very creditable. As he said to William Dudley Foulke, when they were discussing the selection of an attorney general for Puerto Rico, "If this were in our own country I would have no difficulty, there are many men who would do, but we must take a great deal better care of the people of Porto Rico than of ourselves." The merit system was used for the operation of civil affairs in the Philippines from the outset. McKinley supported, indeed laid down, the large principles that Elihu Root, Leonard Wood, and William Howard Taft followed. He would have endorsed Root's remark, which applied to Cuba when scandals emerged in the postal service, "The first essential of administration in this island is that we shall be perfectly honest with ourselves."[33]

The civil-service issue did not bulk large in the 1900 election. William Jennings Bryan believed in using the spoils system on a scale that would have been worthy of the most greedy Republican; but with the reformist Theodore Roosevelt as his running mate, McKinley had the better of the case. The GOP platform was disappointing, for it reflected the pervasive distrust that professionals felt toward reform. McKinley compiled a record on civil service that disappointed both the champions of reform and the advocates of partisanship. The president was probably satisfied with that outcome on a matter that offered no simple answers.

In the field of financial policy, which had so occupied the administration in 1897, the changes that the war produced, coupled with the rapidly improving economic climate, led McKinley and the Republicans toward the Gold Standard Act of 1900. As Europe purchased more farm products and other raw materials from the United States, gold flowed into the country. The economy had rebounded from the depression of mid decade, and industry and commerce were expanding rapidly. Gold production inside the nation rose, as it did in South Africa and Canada. The gold reserve increased from $170 million as the war began to $250 million at the close of the year. As the price of silver fell, the bimetallic movement lost most of its political force. The congressional elections of 1898 left the Republicans with a House majority for gold; in the Senate the silver men had less power to forestall legislation regarding the gold standard.

That the GOP should affirm the gold standard was something on which party members agreed in 1899/1900, but the precise means for accomplishing the goal remained in dispute. In the financial community, banking reformers, represented by the Indianapolis Monetary Convention of January 1897, wanted to limit the role of the treasury in banking and to expand the functions of the national banks. These ideas, more favored in the East than in the Midwest, would have divided the sound-money camp. The president took a cautious stance, as did congressional leaders; he wanted to improve the financial system within its existing structure. His purposes were to establish the government's responsibility to redeem all its money in gold, to provide for some expansion of the currency, but to leave intact the existing blend of national bank notes, paper money, and treasury notes that could be redeemed in gold.

In 1898 and early 1899 the more advanced wing of the banking-reform movement pushed for a measure, sponsored by Congressman James T. McCleary, that would have decreased the power of the treasury and would have allowed national banks to issue notes based on commercial assets rather than government bonds as security. The administration was split on the bill, with Secretary Gage in favor and Comptroller of the Currency Dawes opposed. In his annual report for 1898, Dawes leveled a number of charges at the assets-currency scheme, and he recommended that Congress shun it. Friends of the idea responded angrily, but Dawes drew praise from bankers in the South and the West. National bankers did not support the assets-currency bill as its backers had hoped. By early 1899 McCleary's bill was in trouble in both the House and the Senate, and on January 17, 1899, it was removed from the House calendar.

With an election year ahead, McKinley and the Republican congressional leadership wanted to resolve the monetary issue while the economic signs favored the GOP. Two weeks after McCleary's bill was withdrawn, the Republican caucus in the House voted to name an eleven-member committee to draw up a banking bill for presentation at the next session of Congress. Among its members were David B. Henderson of Iowa, who became Speaker when Reed resigned in the summer of 1899; the chairman of the Ways and Means Committee; and other congressmen who were close to the party's mainstream. The Committee on Currency gathered in Atlantic City in mid April for two weeks of deliberations. There had been talk of having the meeting in the fall, but "the President suggested that it would be well to formulate a plan as early as possible." To move the lawmakers along, McKinley also raised the prospect of a special session in the fall.[34]

The committee agreed at the outset that all its members must concur in the final product. The bill that emerged was put before McKinley, who was not "thoroughly satisfied" with the outcome. He wanted "a provision that will make the so-called endless chain caused by the redemption of greenbacks with gold and consequent runs upon the Treasury reserve impossible." He also sought the permission for national banks to issue notes up to the full value of the bonds that were "deposited to secure that circulation"; a reduction of the tax on national bank notes; and a provision to make it easier to charter national banks in small towns. The eventual measure, as the newspapers leaked it in late May 1899, conformed to the president's desires, as did the caucus legislation when Speaker Henderson outlined it on the eve of the congressional session.[35]

The House Republican caucus met on December 6, 1899, and after making minor amendments, it unanimously endorsed House Bill 1. The bill was formally introduced on December 11. A week later, eleven Democrats joined all the Republicans in approving the measure, 190 to 150. In the Senate the issue of financial legislation posed delicate problems. There were still enough silverites so that they could produce protracted debate in an election year. The Senate Finance Committee, which was dominated by Nelson Aldrich, William Boyd Allison, and Orville H. Platt, kept the House committee at a distance during the spring and summer of 1899. And

Allison said, in early June, "I do not anticipate any very radical measures." Members of the Finance Committee met shortly before Congress opened, and they decided to frame their own bill in place of what the House had done. Senator Aldrich outlined the changes to his colleagues on January 4, 1900.[36]

The early sections of the Senate version paralleled those resulting from House action. The dollar was defined in gold, and the treasury was pledged to redeem greenbacks and other of its notes in gold alone. The senators set up a gold reserve of $150 million to redeem notes. The Senate's major deviation from the House measure lay in the language about refunding the national debt. Aldrich argued that this action would improve the nation's credit situation and would expand the amount of national banknotes in circulation. At the same time, the refunding idea offered national banks a greater chance to make profits by circulating bank notes. With enactment of the bill, Aldrich contended, an increase in the circulation of national bank notes could be expected. Refunding had the approval of Secretary Gage and the administration.

During debate on the bill, Senate leaders agreed to pass an amendment that would endorse, or at least not preclude, international bimetallism. This placated western silver Republicans, such as Edward O. Wolcott. Another amendment made it possible for national banks that had a capital of $25,000 to be set up in small towns of fewer than four thousand residents. On February 15, 1900, with only three Republicans in the negative column, the bill passed by a vote of 46 to 29. It then went to a conference committee.

The Senate members of the committee, Aldrich and Allison, dominated their House counterparts. The refunding idea, which the House members did not like, was kept, and the language on the gold standard reflected the looser wording of the Senate bill. The conference report went through the Senate easily on March 6, 1900, by a partisan vote of 44 to 26. The House acted on March 13 with a tally of 166 to 120. McKinley signed the Gold Standard Act into law with a gold pen the next day. Though the difficulties with the nation's banking system remained to be solved, the Gold Standard Act wrote an end to the monetary controversy of the 1890s.

The most persistent domestic issue that McKinley faced in the first half of 1899 was the problem of what to do with Secretary of War Alger. "You have got a great load in the management of the War Department," an old friend told the president in March.[37] The work of the commission to investigate the handling of the war had, in October and November 1898, at first lessened some of the political damage. The commission conducted wide-ranging hearings which did not produce sensational revelations. Testimony from Generals Leonard Wood, Henry W. Lawton, and Joseph Wheeler, the latter a Democrat, provided little on which the opposition could capitalize.

While the commission was sitting, the administration drafted legislation for sustaining an expanded army after the war with Spain had officially ended. The White House wanted an enlarged regular army that would have a permanent authorization for one hundred thousand men. Complicating the legislative agenda were controversial issues about reorganization of the army's structure and about where the commanding general, the secretary of war, and the president would stand in the chain of command and responsibility. Out of the internal debates of the military came a bill that Congressman John A. T. Hull of Iowa introduced on December 7, 1898. It specified a force of one hundred thousand regulars, retained the command structure, and provided for a corps of artillery to replace the existing regiments in that branch of the army. Other bills, several from Democrats and one from General Nelson A. Miles, proposed other changes. As chairman of the Military Affairs Committee, Hull supervised the hearings that led to the reporting of his bill on December 20, 1898, by a vote that mirrored the partisan division of his panel. The Democrats said that the one-hundred-thousand-man force was unnecessary and would be a potential threat to personal liberties.

On December 21, 1898, General Miles gave the Dodge Commission his criticism of the war. He did not testify under oath, responded only to direct questions, and spent only a brief time in the witness chair. The next day a newspaper that was unfavorable to McKinley carried an interview with Miles in which he elaborated on his remarks. He was conducting his own probe of the meat scandal, and he spoke about chemicals in the beef that had been given to the army, which had caused the meat to spoil. Miles was making new and grave charges about the food that had been given to soldiers in the field, a point that enemies of the administration quickly emphasized. However, his evidence on the refrigerated beef was less reliable than he thought it was; and Miles had ambitions for the White House that helped to shape the charges.

The officer who was responsible for the canned roast beef was the commissary general, Charles P. Eagan. A product of the major meat-packing houses, the meat was, for the most part, an adequate ration when cooked. When eaten raw in the field, it had a bland, unappetizing flavor, and it spoiled quickly. Some of the cans contained foreign elements and dead insects; so the meat was highly unpopular with the soldiers. Unsuitable for the tropics, the canned roast beef was a mistake, but it was an error of judgment, not an example of corruption or conspiracy. The commissary general demanded the right to reply to Miles's charges. On January 12, 1899, he termed the allegations "a scandalous libel," adding: "I wish to force the lie back into his throat, covered with the contents of a camp latrine."[38]

For using insubordinate and extreme language, Eagan was court-martialed and convicted in February 1899. McKinley moderated the sentence to suspension of the officer from his duties and rank but with full pay for the six years before his retirement. Meanwhile, the Dodge Commission issued its report. "There was lacking in the general administration of the War Department . . . that complete grasp of the situation which was essential to the highest efficiency and discipline of the army." On the other points, the commission cleared Alger of any corruption, attributed the War Department's difficulties to longstanding organizational weaknesses, and rejected Miles's charges about the beef in its refrigerated and canned varieties. Newspaper reaction tended to follow partisan lines.[39]

General Miles returned to the offensive even before the commission's conclusions had been aired. He said on January 31 that he now had abundant and overwhelming evidence to support his charges about the "embalmed beef." The beef that the soldiers received had been "loaded and saturated with chemicals—various acids which made them sick, filled the men's systems with poison, unfitting them for fighting or campaign work." Miles disavowed the interview, but asked the president for a court of inquiry. The board, which met from late February through April, concluded that Eagan had erred in using the canned beef. Miles's charges were groundless. He had been wrong in not reporting them to the secretary of war at once, and he should not have given out interviews. With that verdict, the beef "scandal" disappeared from the front pages. For the American people and subsequent historians, however, embalmed beef and the war with Spain remained permanently linked.[40]

While the Miles-Eagan controversy proceeded, Congress debated the Hull bill and army reform. The House took up the legislation on January 24, 1899, and passed it, with some amendments, on January 31, by a partisan vote of 168 to 126. By the time the Senate addressed the bill, the war in the Philippines had begun, adding to the need for legislative action. In the Military Affairs

Committee, Republicans and Democrats became stalemated and finally sent two bills to the full Senate. The House measure won the support of the GOP with its continuation of the sixty-five-thousand-man army of the Spanish-American War, plus the authority to raise thirty-five thousand native troops for duty in the new possessions. The Democrats wanted to limit McKinley to using them for subduing the insurrection in the Philippines.

The administration and the opposition took hard, conflicting positions between February 19 and February 23. The War Department refused to endorse the Democratic proposal, and the president raised the possibility of calling a special session if Congress failed to act. Democrats threatened to filibuster the legislation. In the end, the Republicans struck a compromise, basing a bill on what the Democrats offered. The army would get the sixty-five thousand regulars plus thirty-five thousand two-year recruits, who could be Americans rather than Filipinos or Cubans. The bill, though far less than what the army wanted, represented a real advance toward greater federal control of the armed services. The president also received more flexibility in regard to the allocation of officers and men within the army. Despite last-minute resistance from a group of Populists and Democrats, the bill cleared the Senate on February 27 and the House on March 1. McKinley signed it on March 2.

The report of the Dodge Commission, the passage of the army bill, and a general improvement in the army's performance in the waging of the war against the Philippine insurrection combined to alleviate some of the problems regarding military policy. They did not remove the Alger issue as a liability. McKinley defended the secretary, although he had decided in December 1898 that Alger had to go. Returning from Boston and the Home Market Club speech in February 1899, Alger bridled at the suggestion from someone in the president's party that the negative reaction of the crowds to his presence had marred their reception of McKinley. The chief executive smoothed over the incident quickly.

Republicans who were unfriendly to McKinley doubted that the president would have the nerve to ask Alger to resign.[41] The dilemma was more subtle than that. To sack Alger would be to admit tacitly that there was some substance to the charges against the War Department. McKinley thought that Alger, for the good of the administration, should spare him the embarrassment of asking for a letter of resignation. A graceful exit for the secretary would relieve McKinley of any sense that he had failed to sustain Alger against his enemies or that the president had not acknowledged his

174

own responsibility for the record of the department. Preferring in personal relations to use finesse rather than to confront, McKinley attempted to outwait his cabinet officer. If an excess of scruples immobilized the president, Alger, who now disliked McKinley, allowed no such restraints to hamper his actions. He acted as if his position were impregnable. After a tour of Cuba and Puerto Rico, he announced that he would not resign until he had completed his full term.[42]

Having said that, Alger then embarked in June 1899 on a political campaign that cost him his post. The governor of Michigan, Hazen Pingree, was trying to impair the power of Senator James S. McMillan, an influential member of the upper house who was close to Aldrich, Allison, and the Republican leadership. Pingree had been engaged in a prolonged contest for party supremacy over state tax policy, and he now viewed Alger as a potential ally. Since the governor was a bitter critic of the McKinley administration with regard to expansionism and trust policy, a union with him would place Alger in an awkward position relative to the White House. In late June the secretary's senatorial ambitions became public knowledge. Seeing no need to resign until his election had occurred, he stated that Pingree was "for President McKinley first, last and all the time." Pingree told reporters, "If Gen. Alger knows that President McKinley is opposed to territorial expansion, and is not an advocate of the murders and the destruction being visited upon the innocent Filipinos, he has a right to say that I am for McKinley." Similar statements about McKinley and the trusts followed. The president, wrote Charles G. Dawes, "is annoyed at the Alger situation."[43]

Alger kept up a brave public façade, but in private he was negotiating with the president over a graceful departure. He submitted a letter of resignation in early July that would have taken effect in January 1900. McKinley prepared a draft reply to this letter, which he apparently did not send, in which he said to Alger: "It is not for me to ask you to resign. Our relations should require you to spare me that painful course as well as save you from any humiliation which such action would cause." Presumably the president said something to the same effect in his private conversations. Alger seemed unresponsive. He said to reporters on July 12, "I have never yet retired under fire, and I do not propose to do so now." When McKinley heard that statement, he acted to secure Alger's exit.[44]

McKinley's instrument was Vice-President Garret A. Hobart.

During a weekend visit at the Hobart home on the New Jersey shore, Alger learned that the president wanted him to retire. The secretary came to the White House on the morning of July 19 and, after an awkward conversation, left a brief letter of resignation. Alger recalled later that he was told that his alliance with Pingree, "who was opposed to the Administration," had caused McKinley embarrassment. After stating his own case, Alger wrote out his resignation. Then, the president and Cortelyou walked through the grounds, and McKinley said: "Well, he was over and left it with me." The *New York Sun* credited the outcome to Hobart's "crystal insight" and "velvet tact." The vice-president, who was desperately ill, wired the White House a message, which Mrs. Hobart composed: "My 'crystal insight' is still clear but the nap is slightly worn off my velvet tact vide New York Sun."[45]

The reaction to Alger's leaving was highly positive. Alger wrote his memoirs of the war, defending his own record, and later spent a term in the Senate. In time his private bitterness toward McKinley grew, and he concluded that the president was "more of a follower than a leader." From the beginning, Alger's membership in McKinley's cabinet had been a mistake. The secretary of war had done his best during the conflict, and many of his problems were not of his making or were beyond his control. But he stayed too long, once the war had ended, and the president moved too slowly in obtaining Alger's resignation.[46]

To succeed Alger, McKinley wanted a man who could deal with the administrative and colonial side of the War Department's work in 1899. "The rest of the fighting to put down Aguinaldo" concerned him less than "the subsequent task of civil government to be exercised for a year or two under the direction of the War Department." As the "good legal and governmental man" he needed, the president chose Elihu Root of New York. Root offered a strong blend of personal talent and political advantage. He filled New York's seat in the cabinet, he was a Republican but not a blatant partisan, and his experience as a corporate lawyer had revealed his shrewd and determined mind. Root had impressed McKinley when he declined the Spanish mission in 1897, and his name was kept in the president's well-stocked memory.[47]

Former Secretary of the Interior Cornelius N. Bliss, who was well disposed toward Root, had earlier suggested him for other cabinet slots. Senator Thomas C. Platt was aloof in public about it but was pleased in private. Soon after Alger resigned, one of Platt's friends telephoned Root on Long Island from the White House to tell him: "The President directs me to say to you that he wishes you to take the position of Secretary of War." When Root answered, "I know nothing about war, I know nothing about the army," the word came back: "President McKinley directs me to say that he is not looking for any one who knows anything about war or for any one who knows anything about the army; he has got to have a lawyer to direct the government of these Spanish islands, and you are the lawyer he wants."[48]

Root was one of McKinley's best appointments. "I was compelled to choose between money-making and comparative ease on the one side and a distinct call to render a public service on the other," the new secretary wrote Theodore Roosevelt, but after consideration, "I had not the slightest doubt as to what I ought to do."[49] The president's cabinet selections became stronger as his administration progressed. In Root he found the man whom he needed for grappling with the complex and interrelated issues in colonial affairs that the war had left. With Hay in the State Department and with his new secretary of war in place, McKinley was ready to deal with the questions of foreign policy and imperialism that overshadowed domestic matters in 1899 and 1900.

8

★★★★★

"WE HAVE EXPANDED"

The war left a cluster of foreign-policy issues for McKinley to deal with in 1899 and early 1900, and the government's responses reflected the broadened international obligations of the country. In the Philippines the insurrection required that the president balance military needs, the transition to civil government, and the continuing controversy with the anti-imperialist opposition. Cuba did not pose a military challenge to the American occupation, but a coherent program for that damaged island emerged slowly. To attain the larger goal of American dominance in the Caribbean and North America, there were negotiations with Great Britain and Canada that had as their ultimate prize the building of a canal across Central America. In Asia, 1899 was the year of the Open Door notes, which laid the foundations for an involvement with the fate of China. Other items on the presidential agenda included the Boer War and international arbitration at The Hague Conference. The range of problems before the president was reaching proportions that modern chief executives would find familiar.

The conflict in the Philippines was the most potentially dangerous subject for McKinley. If the fighting lasted only a short time, the administration would escape domestic political repercussions, but prolonged hostilities would be far more troublesome. During the early months of fighting, the army could only hold onto the position that it already had. Of the twenty thousand American soldiers in the islands, fifteen thousand were volunteers who would be discharged as soon as the peace treaty had been ratified. Some of these men agreed to stay on until replacements could arrive; others were ordered to do so. Because Congress passed helpful army legislation and because of recruiting at home, the military built up its forces throughout 1899.

The American commander, General Elwell S. Otis, moved cautiously with the available resources. His men probed outside of Manila to prevent the Filipinos from massing around the city. Elsewhere, Americans controlled ports and cities, but the insurgents dominated the interior. Otis was a bewhiskered, bald man in his early sixties, a glutton for work and detail, who tried to supervise all aspects of the American presence. In many ways he performed capably. The general did the best with what he had, and he avoided any disastrous reverses. His dispatches to the War Department were crisp and optimistic. "Present indications denote insurgent government in perilous condition," he cabled on April 3, adding that the rebel army was "defeated, discouraged, and shattered." McKinley had confidence in his general, a conviction that never really wavered; Otis was the commander in the field, to be sustained and supported.[1]

McKinley had spoken of "benevolent assimilation" in late 1898. Both the army and the Philippine Commission tried that approach to the Filipinos in the first half of 1899. If as most Americans incorrectly believed, the rebels represented only a minority of the native population, the war could end when the majority became convinced of the good intentions of the United States. For the soldiers this meant the establishment of a fair judicial and legal system, the building of sanitation projects, the opening of schools, and the setting up of municipal and local governments for the Filipinos. Such tactics were not, sadly, always followed, and they did not, because of the nationalism, propaganda, and terrorism of the insurgents, prove effective in and of themselves. Nonetheless, in the conduct of official army policy during the first year of the war, there was a strong strain of benevolence that remained during the American presence.

Benevolence occurred, however, within a framework of paternalism toward the Filipinos. The policy makers in the United States imperfectly understood the nature of the society that they were seeking to govern and transform. Believing the reports of the army and his civilian commissioners, McKinley did not think that Aguinaldo's insurrection was a genuine manifestation of popular sentiment in the islands. To have done so would have called into question the American presence in the Pacific. It was simpler to conclude, as McKinley did, that if the United States ruled equitably and firmly, the conservative element in Filipino society would be won over, and the base of the rebellion would be exposed as fragile. On the one side, in McKinley's words, was "the peaceable and loyal majority, who ask nothing better than to accept our authority." On the other, there was "the minority of armed insurgents." To some extent the American analysis was valid. A substantial portion of the Philippine upper class viewed the rebellion with skepticism. But the position of the United States underestimated the genuine support that Aguinaldo, his government and the independence movement enjoyed.[2]

The rainy season in May 1899 put an end to large-scale military efforts until October. While the army consolidated its position, the administration, through the Philippine Commission, attempted to establish a framework of government for the islands. The commission, with Jacob Gould Schurman as its president, reached Manila in March, and within a month it issued a proclamation. This document, which was released on April 4, 1899, offered the prospect of "an enlightened system of government" that would give the people of the Philippines "the largest measure of home rule and the amplest liberty consonant with the supreme ends of government and compatible with those obligations which the United States has assumed toward the civilized nations of the world." The proclamation provoked dissent among the rebels, and Aguinaldo, needing a respite so that he could resupply his forces, sent an emissary to see Otis and the commission about a suspension of hostilities and about the American proposal.[3]

Otis did not grant a truce, but Aguinaldo's agent did secure from the commission an expression of its willingness to ask Washington about the kind of government the islands would have under American rule. McKinley replied through Hay on May 5, 1899: there would be an American governor general, a cabinet that he would select, and an elected "advisory council." Native Filipinos would be included, and McKinley again said that he earnestly desired "the cessation of bloodshed, and that the people of the Philippines at an early day shall have the largest measure of local self-government consistent with peace and good order." American sovereignty would be preserved. The president's plan also produced divisions within the Filipino leadership; the Malolos Congress of the rebels tried to dispatch negotiators to talk about the McKinley governmental framework. The more militant elements among the insurgent army intervened, sending emissaries who were committed to independence. Armistice talks broke down in May 1899 over General's Otis's insistence that the Filipinos surrender their weapons and break up their army as conditions for an end to the fighting.[4]

Within the Philippine Commission as well, there was disagreement over the merits of a conciliatory policy. President Schurman decided, after his discussions with the rebel spokesmen, to urge McKinley "to adjust United States sovereignty and responsibility with reasonable aspiration of Filipinos governing and garrisoning mainly through themselves." He warned of the possibility of guerilla warfare and concluded his lengthy cable: "Believe magnanimity our safest, cheapest and best policy with Filipinos, it would seem negotiations can do no harm, for conciliation failing, force remains." The president wired back, rejecting Schurman's ideas: "Those of the leaders who have willfully and for their own purposes placed us in a false position before their deluded followers cannot be relied upon to set us right." McKinley, said Schurman, had decided to fight it out. Faced with opposition from the other commissioners, who agreed with McKinley, and disliked by General Otis, Schurman decided to return to the United States in time for the fall term at Cornell. The other two commissioners stayed on, collecting information for the administration. In late 1899 they rejoined Schurman in Washington to prepare a report on this mission.[5]

In the United States the Philippines question presented a succession of potential embarrassments. The anti-imperialists stepped up their criticism after the treaty had been ratified. Through public meetings and an extensive distribution of literature, the opponents of the administration tried to rally public opinion against what George S. Boutwell of Massachusetts called an aggressive, unjustifiable, cruel war. Their main vehicle was the Anti-Imperialist League, which claimed a national membership of thirty thousand and included on its roster or among its allies such figures as Carl Schurz, Moorfield Storey, Andrew Carnegie, Gamaliel Bradford, and Edward Atkinson. "It looks as if the imperialists were getting into a desperate state of mind," Schurz wrote in May 1899, "feeling that they are fast losing their hold upon the people. It is therefore good policy to press on without ceasing."[6]

Edward Atkinson decided to transmit the antiwar literature that he had composed directly to the soldiers in the Philippines. Atkinson, who was a somewhat erratic champion of a variety of reforms in the late nineteenth century, asked the government for the addresses of five hundred or so officers to whom he could send his pamphlets "The Hell of War and Its Penalties," "The Cost of a

National Crime," and "Criminal Aggression: By Whom Committed?" The administration told General Otis to take the pamphlets from the mail and then destroy them. When Otis responded that the pamphlets should be stopped before they left the United States, Postmaster General Charles Emory Smith ordered that they be removed from the mail at San Francisco. Predictably enough, this decision publicized Atkinson's cause and raised questions about the government's belief in freedom of speech. Despite subsequent attempts to elicit a similar censorship from him, the postmaster general did not repeat his actions in the Atkinson case.

The censorship issue arose in another form in the summer of 1899, when the correspondents in the Philippines issued a round robin that charged General Otis with suppressing unfavorable news. "We believe," the newsmen said, "the dispatches err in the declaration that 'the situation is well in hand,' and in the assumption that the insurrection can be speedily ended without a greatly increased force." McKinley informed Otis that the question of censorship would be left to his discretion and judgment. The president suggested, however, "that all consideration within limits of good of the service be shown." Otis maintained that much of the problem arose from distortions in the reporting that came out of Manila; for he did not enjoy good relations with the press corps. If there was something less than a cover-up of military disaster, the censorship and the round robin fed the impression in Washington, if not in the president's mind, "as confirming fears which have long existed in regard to the situation in the Philippines."[7]

The perceived need for a stronger Philippine policy helped to produce Alger's resignation in July 1899 and the selection of Elihu Root for the War Department. "There is a feeling," an influential congressman told the new secretary, "that Otis has underestimated the magnitude of the work to be accomplished by the American soldiers." The criticism of Otis that came from Theodore Roosevelt and others did not move McKinley. The administration acted in mid August 1899 to increase the number of troops at Otis's disposal above the forty thousand or so who were already in the islands or on their way across the Pacific. The general wanted his authorized strength to be increased to sixty thousand men. Root responded by requesting McKinley to double the call for volunteer regiments from five to ten. "The impression is growing strongly upon me that they are quite likely to be required, and evidence accumulates upon all sides that the country will fully sustain the action." Through Root's efforts the original Philippine volunteers were brought home in 1899, replacements of regulars and volunteers were sent over to Otis, and an effective force of sixty-three thousand men had been furnished to the general by early 1900.[8]

The anti-imperialists hammered away in the spring and summer of 1899 at the matter of retaining the volunteer detachments in the Philippines after ratification of the treaty. Senator Richard F. Pettigrew of South Dakota wrote McKinley: "The blood of the South Dakota boys sacrificed in that contest must be laid at the door of your administration, and that impartial history must place you among the most dishonored of rulers in all time." Parents of Nebraska soldiers insisted that "the government send back home those who have not contributed their precious fever-stricken or bullet-torn bodies to enrich the soil of Luzon." It seemed likely that the state of mind of the volunteers would become a political issue in the off-year elections, which would provide hints about 1900.[9]

By the end of August the volunteer regiments of the Spanish-American War were on their way home. While on vacation from the heat of Washington, McKinley decided to attend the Pittsburgh reception for the Tenth Pennsylvania Volunteers. He had already told Catholic school children that the flag of the United States was "the hope of the oppressed; and wherever it is assailed, at any sacrifice, it will be carried to a triumphant peace." Then at Ocean Grove, New Jersey, on August 25 he restated American policy in the Philippines: "Peace first; then, with charity for all, the establishment of a government of law and order, protecting life and property and occupation for well-being of the people, in which they will participate under the Stars and Stripes." To the returning Pennsylvanians he said, on August 28, of the volunteers generally: "They did not stack arms. They did not run away. They were not serving the insurgents in the Philippines or their sympathizers at home." One by one he read the names of regiments that had "resisted the suggestion of the unpatriotic" that they should come back early. As each regiment was called, the Pennsylvania veterans shouted approval. The insurgents, he said, had struck the first blow, repaying "our mercy with a Mauser." With American sovereignty under attack, there would "be no useless parley, no pause, until the insurrection is suppressed, and American authority acknowledged and established."[10]

These speeches irritated the administration's enemies. "How can a president of the great republic be blind to the truth that freedom is the same, that liberty is as dear and that self-government is as much a right in the Philippines as in the United States?"

184

complained the *New York World*. Carl Schurz said: "The honor of our flag sorely needs protection. We have to protect it against desecration by those who are making it an emblem of that hypocrisy which seeks to cover a war of conquest and subjugation with a cloak of humanity and religion." The president did not cease making public remarks on foreign affairs. He returned to the hustings in the fall, once again using the power of his office by articulating administration policy. "Our flag stands for liberty wherever it floats," he told a Fargo, North Dakota, audience on October 13, "and we propose to put sixty-five thousand men behind that flag in Luzon, to maintain the authority of the United States and uphold the sovereignty of the republic in the interest of civilization and humanity. We accept the responsibility of duty at whatever cost it imposes." At Iowa Falls on October 16, he added: "It is no longer a question of expansion with us. We have expanded. (Laughter and great applause.) If there is any question at all it is a question of contraction; and who is going to contract?" Through these speeches and through information leaked to reporters and White House visitors, McKinley sought successfully to reassert the terms of the debate over the Philippines.[11]

Military success was the surest guarantee that there would be continued popular support. In mid October, Otis launched his offensive across Luzon as the dry season began. The Americans were able to destroy the Filipino army as an effective combat instrument for regular warfare. Otis cabled home on November 24: "Claim to government by insurgents can be made no longer under any fiction." On the military side, he added: "Its generals and troops in small bands scattered through these provinces, acting as banditti, or dispersed, playing the rôle of amigos with arms concealed." The army, the president said in his annual message, "now look forward confidently to a speedy completion of their task." What McKinley did not know, and what General Otis failed to recognize, was that Aguinaldo and his advisors had decided to shift from conventional warfare to guerilla tactics. When this change in strategy became effective in 1900, the predicament of the United States was transformed.[12]

Members of the Philippine Commission submitted its preliminary report in early November and a larger, more elaborate statement in January 1900. "There is no course open to us now," they said in the first report, "except the prosecution of the war until the insurgents are reduced to submission." Their final document added that no time "for the withdrawal of American sovereignty over the archipelago" could be set, "as no one can forsee when the diverse peoples of the Philippine Islands may be molded together into a nationality capable of exercising all the functions of independent self-government." McKinley, drawing upon the conclusions of Schurman and his colleagues, intended, as the insurrection appeared to wind down, to push ahead with establishing a civil government for the Philippines.[13]

In his annual message he said that as long as the rebellion continued, "the military arm must necessarily be supreme. But there is no reason why steps should not be taken from time to time to inaugurate governments essentially popular in their form as fast as territory is held and controlled by our troops." McKinley decided to send a second commission across the Pacific to perform this task. As its members he named Dean C. Worcester, a holdover from Schurman's panel; Professor Bernard Moses of the University of California, whose works on Spanish government McKinley had read; Henry C. Ide of Vermont; and Luke Wright of Tennessee. For the commission's chairman, the choice was William Howard Taft of Ohio.[14]

Taft and McKinley had corresponded, and perhaps had known each other slightly, before 1899. They met for the first extended time when the president went home to Ohio to vote in November. Returning to Washington, McKinley said to Secretary Root that Taft was "just the man for the Philippines." When it came time to select the second commission in January 1900, the president sent a telegram summoning Taft to Washington. When McKinley said that he wanted a man to go to the Philippines to establish a civil government, Taft protested that since he opposed the acquisition of the islands, he thought that the administration should look elsewhere. McKinley replied: "We've got them. What I want you to do now is to go there and establish civil government." Elihu Root added his persuasive power: "We need you to do pioneer work. We want you to pull your weight in the boat." While Taft thought the offer over, the president wrote to William R. Day, who was now a federal judge, to ask him to "get the consent of Judge Taft to go." He argued that "a commission made up of men of the character of Judge Taft will give respose and confidence to the country and will be an earnest of my high purpose to bring to those peoples the blessings of peace and liberty. It will be an assurance that my instructions to the Peace Commission were sincere and my purpose to abide by them."[15]

Taft took the assignment, and Root drafted the instructions that accompanied the new commissioners. They were to set up "municipal governments, in which the natives of the islands, both in the cities and in the rural communities, shall be offered the opportunity to manage their own local affairs to the fullest extent of which they are capable, and subject to the least degree of supervision and control which a careful study of their capacities and observations of the workings of native control show to be consistent with the maintenance of law, order and loyalty." Provincial governments would then follow. The commission was given broad legislative powers, to begin on September 1, 1900, which included creating a system of taxation, an educational system, a judiciary, and a civil service. Close cooperation with the army would be necessary in order to make the commission work. Taft and his colleagues left San Francisco on April 17, 1900, with the "large powers and a wide jurisdiction" that McKinley had promised.[16]

The anti-imperialists argued throughout 1899, as they would until the insurrection ended, that American military policy in the Philippines was cruel and barbarous. "We are laying waste the country with fire and sword, burning villages and slaughtering the inhabitants, because they will not submit to our rule."[17] The question of atrocities being committed in the war aroused a large public controversy during the McKinley and Theodore Roosevelt administrations and later during other disputes about war and foreign policy. Sixty-five years after these events, the Vietnam War revived the issue, as participants in the quarrel over American actions in Southeast Asia looked back to the Philippines as a prelude to the atrocities of the 1960s or accused the McKinley administration of genocide on a scale that was unmatched until the Nazi horrors of the Second World War.

Some problems relating to this sensitive subject can be disposed of with little difficulty. The charges that the United States had a conscious policy of killing Filipinos indiscriminately between 1898 and 1902 and that it, in fact, slaughtered several million people are untrue. Estimates of the population of the archipelago in 1898 fell somewhere between six and eight million people. The census of 1903 arrived at a total of more than 6.9 million inhabitants. One American general estimated in 1901 that one-sixth of Luzon's population "have either been killed or have died of the dengue fever in the last few years." From this statement, critics of McKinley calculated that some six hundred thousand people had died on this island alone. More sweeping totals for the whole group of islands grew from this total. The general who made the statement, James M. Bell, was not heavily involved in the fighting, and his figure is very unreliable. The American presence did not produce—through combat, atrocities, or other causes—any disastrous effects on the Filipino population as a whole. Actual Filipino deaths in combat ranged somewhere between the army's low total of around fourteen thousand to the more recent guesses of approximately fifty-seven thousand.[18]

But what of combat atrocities and war crimes? Such actions were never the stated policy of the United States government nor were they ever officially condoned. The army court-martialed far more cases than it covered up. There was no killing of prisoners on an organized basis, nor were the wounded mistreated as a rule. In the day-to-day rigors of combat, American soldiers committed acts that violated the rules of war and the regulations of their own army. Defenders of the troops and the government pointed to the terrorism carried out by the Filipinos, directed against both the Americans and residents of the islands, as part of the ugly environment in which the war was fought. Such arguments might explain how the water cure, other tortures, and destruction of secular and religious property marred the record of the army in the Philippines; but they could not excuse the acts themselves. The United States, which had condemned "Weylerism" in Cuba, found itself employing similar tactics in a colonial war of its own. The unhappy outcome of the Philippine imbroglio was a potent warning against engaging in similar ventures in the future.

William McKinley knew about general charges that his administration was practicing and countenancing "wanton and deliberate cruelty" in the Philippines. He agreed with Secretary Long, who styled such attacks in the spring of 1899 as "an unutterably mean, unwarranted and contemptible assertion." The president repeatedly pledged not to let the American government in the islands become a tyranny. "If any orders of mine," he told Congress in 1899, "were required to insure the merciful conduct of military and naval operations, they would not be lacking; but every step of the progress of our troops has been marked by a humanity which has surprised even the misguided insurgents."[19] That the policy of the United States was not dictatorial, purposely oppressive, or genocidal under William McKinley is clear. That the conduct of the United States Army fell below the highest standards of the rules of war is also evident. Of course, it would not have mattered if the Americans in the Philippines had somehow managed to be truly benevolent and effectively imperial. The rule of one national group by another contradicted the nation's traditions, but it was an idea whose philosophical foundations were already crumbling. The Philippine episode in United States history was flawed and doomed, not because bad men carried out harsh and callous policies, but because good men, such as William McKinley, were trying to do the impossible.

The war in the Philippines gave the administration its greatest concern in 1899, but the fate of Cuba aroused nearly as much worry. Elihu Root later recalled his fears that fighting might occur between Cubans and Americans. In shaping Cuban policy so as to avoid such a calamity and to further the interest of the United States, McKinley had to reckon with the previous decisions of Congress about the island, the international situation, and the state of American public opinion. Most important in this process was the Teller Amendment of April 1898, which had renounced any intention of controlling Cuba after the island had been pacified. Though the government found the amendment an irksome restraint on its freedom of action, McKinley made it clear that he would honor the congressional pledge.

Within the Republican party there were several schools of thought about how Cuba could best become part of the United States. One group, of whom Senator Joseph B. Foraker, Senator William E. Chandler, and General James H. Wilson were representative spokesmen, sought a rapid American exit, in the belief that Cuba would, in a few years, naturally seek annexation, as Hawaii had done. On the other side were Leonard Wood, Theodore Roosevelt, and their allies, who believed that the experience of military occupation, with its efficiency and fairness, would persuade the Cubans to favor annexation. McKinley leaned toward the second position, and he might well have been more determined to lean toward annexation in the absence of the Teller Amendment. With it, however, the president felt morally bound to move toward Cuba's independence.

At the same time, McKinley was anxious that Cuba not once again become a source of diplomatic difficulty. The government that emerged must be strong enough to maintain its existence while remaining friendly with and in the orbit of the United States. Still sensitive to the possible incursions of European countries such as Germany, McKinley wished to see Cuba obtain a stable form of government that would not be susceptible to outside interference. As he said in his annual message of 1899, the American mission in Cuba was "not to be fulfilled by turning adrift any loosely framed commonwealth to face the vicissitudes which too often attend weaker States whose natural wealth and abundant resources are offset by the incongruities of their political organization and the recurring occasions for internal rivalries to sap their strength and dissipate their energies." If the Cubans would not accept this verdict, McKinley believed, the United States would have to create political constraints on a newly independent island when the American army relinquished control.[20]

Whether Cuba's ultimate condition proved to be independence, independence under American protection, or annexation, the military government that began its work on January 1, 1899, had to be a success if the United States were to achieve any of its policy objectives. The president placed Major General John R. Brooke in command of the Division of Cuba on December 13, 1898, as military governor, and then sent him instructions for the conduct of his assignment nine days later. Since April 1898 McKinley had insisted that the United States have a free hand in Cuba. He now asserted that the authority of the United States in Cuba rested on "the law of belligerent right over conquered territory." Only the president, exercising on behalf of Cuba "his constitutional function of Commander-in-Chief of the military forces of this nation," had the necessary power to govern the island until Congress acted or the Cubans should "have established a firm and stable government of their own, capable of performing its international obligations." The military government, the president continued, was "not to be exerted for military purposes." Rather it was "intended to take the place, for the time being, of the former civil administration, and should be so conducted as to foster and encourage all classes in peaceful pursuits by throwing around them the powerful arm of our military protection in order to secure a wise, just, and equal administration of law."[21]

During the first seven months of 1899, until Elihu Root became secretary of war, the military government in Cuba had been able to repair the ravages of the war but had been much less successful with the political revival of the island. Under General Brooke and military commanders in the seven departments, such as Leonard Wood in Santiago and Puerto Principe, Cubans were fed, their medical needs were attended to, sanitation projects went forward, and a system of schools was created. Between January and November, Americans distributed free 5,493,000 daily rations to the Cubans. In Havana, garbage collection, disease control, and food allocation proceeded at an accelerated pace. All this occurred while the size of the United States occupying force rose from twenty-four thousand in early 1899 to a high figure of nearly forty-five thousand in March, and then dropped off to around eleven thousand by the end of the year.

The administration avoided a number of potentially dangerous problems during these months. The Cuban army posed obvious difficulties, if only as a rallying point for unhappiness with the occupiers. It took five months for the Cuban military commander, Máximo Gómez, the Cuban Assembly, and the American army to agree on $3 million as the total amount that the rebel soldiers would receive. The Cubans wanted a larger payment, but the administration was adamant. Finally, at the end of May, the disbursement of funds—$75 to each man—got under way. The dispersal of the Cuban soldiers was a substantial victory for the president's occupation policy. On a less visible level, of course, the Cubans bridled at a regime that did not know their language, that labeled some of them as dagoes, and that imposed upon them laws to prohibit the ringing of church bells, gambling, or opening of taverns on Sunday.

In Congress, too, McKinley encountered challenges to his authority in regard to Cuba. With the American victories in the war came entrepreneurs, seeking profits. As this process of economic penetration gathered momentum in late 1898, the president instructed General Brooke not to allocate concessions or franchises for railroads, utilities, and other projects without first obtaining permission from the secretary of war. Early in February 1899 newspapers announced that a board had been created within the department, with an Ohio associate of McKinley's as chairman, to review applications for such concessions. Senator Foraker regarded the board, not as a means of regulating franchises, but as a method of encouraging them. On February 28, 1899, the senator offered an amendment to the army appropriations bill that barred the granting of franchises or concessions for the duration of the American occupation. A second clause in the amendment authorized McKinley to withdraw the army from Cuba. After debate that reviewed McKinley's power to govern Cuba without congressional directives and despite assurances that the administration would not use franchises as a means for staying in Cuba, the Senate passed the amendment, 47 to 11. The House concurred. Like the Teller Amendment, Foraker's amendment was a self-imposed restraint on American action that owed a good deal to political considerations. It reduced economic activity, which might have encouraged annexation, but it also retarded projects that could have benefited the Cubans.

By mid 1899 there was a good deal of confusion about Cuban policy. Some of the responsibility for this lay with the slowness in settling the question of the Cuban army, and the deteriorating position of Secretary Alger made the War Department ineffective until Root took over. The treaty of peace also imposed a barrier, because residents of Cuba had until April 1900 to decide between Spanish and Cuban citizenship. McKinley contended that governmental organization of the inhabitants could not occur before that date. General Brooke also had not proved to be anything more than adequate as a military governor. Constant sniping from ambitious rivals such as Leonard Wood and James H. Wilson undercut his position, and he seemed passive and ineffective to Washington as the months passed. Instead of moving ahead with the creation of political institutions in Cuba, the general appeared to be reluctant to intrude in areas of civilian responsibility. Ultimately the authority lay with President McKinley. There had not been clear directives from the White House, and the man whom McKinley had selected to command had not grasped the nuances of McKinley's position between outright annexation and complete Cuban independence.

The selection of Elihu Root as secretary of war provided the president with the proper instrument for administering his Cuban policy. Root carried forward an initiative, begun under Alger, for a census of the island's population. The proclamation of August 1899 said that the tabulation would be the first in "the successive steps by which" the Cubans "will proceed to the establishment of an effective system of self-government." The senior military officers in Cuba were also asked to furnish reports about the status of the occupation. Using these documents, which ranged from recommendations for virtually immediate self-government to ones for a prolonged occupation, Root and McKinley were left to make fundamental decisions. They decided to replace Brooke with Leonard Wood, to set in motion the political process that would lead to Cuban self-government, but finally, to indicate that the independence of the island would have to serve American interests in the Caribbean.[22]

As the session of Congress neared and McKinley's message loomed, newspapers and Washington sources indicated that the military government in Cuba would soon yield to a civil authority. Since a civil government could lead to annexation, there was a flurry of apprehension in Cuba and the United States. On the island, rallies and demonstrations showed that popular opinion there stood strongly for independence and that annexation commanded little support. If there had been any illusions about the Cubans' favoring annexation, the outpouring of discontent probably dispelled them.

The policy statements of late 1899 outlined what the McKinley administration planned. Root's first annual report, released on December 1, 1899, said that American control in Cuba "should not be, and of course will not be, continued any longer than is necessary to enable that people to establish a suitable government to which the control shall be transferred, which shall really represent the people of Cuba and be able to maintain order and discharge its international obligations." Once the census had been taken, and the April 11, 1900, deadline for deciding between Cuban and Spanish citizenship had passed, municipal elections could select local governments. A constitutional convention would then "frame a constitution and provide for a general government of the island, to which the United States will surrender the reins of government. When that government is established the relations which exist between it and the United States will be matter for free and uncontrolled agreement between the two parties."[23]

McKinley's annual message, read on December 5, 1899, said, in regard to the Teller Amendment, that "the pledge contained in this resolution is of the highest honorable obligation and must be sacredly kept." Yet, while reviewing the achievements of the military government, the president warned: "The new Cuba yet to arise from the ashes of the past must needs be bound to us by ties of singular intimacy and strength if its enduring welfare is to be assured. Whether those ties shall be organic or conventional, the destinies of Cuba are in some rightful form and manner irrevocably linked with our own, but how and how far is for the future to determine in the ripeness of events." The administration already had received suggestions that foreshadowed the principles of the Platt Amendment of 1901, and McKinley intended that whatever government resulted from the tutelage process would act in the interests of the United States.[24]

On December 13, 1899, General Leonard Wood was placed in command of the Division in Cuba, replacing Brooke, in the last of McKinley's decisions on Cuban policy. Wood was just thirty-nine at the time of his promotion. After receiving a medical education, Doctor Wood had helped to capture the Indian chief Geronimo, had become the White House doctor in 1892, and had gained the confidence of the ailing Mrs. McKinley when her husband took office. In 1898 Wood had commanded the Rough Riders at Santiago, and he had stayed on to direct the military government in the province. Ambitious and hard-working, he undercut General Brooke through his friends Theodore Roosevelt and Henry Cabot Lodge. Wood's ability to subordinate his own views to those of the administration persuaded Root that he was the proper choice, and McKinley agreed. "I want you to go down there to get the people ready for a republican form of government," the president informed Wood. "I leave the details of procedure to you. Give them a good school system, try to straighten out their courts, and put them on their feet as best you can. We want to do all we can for them and to get out of the island as soon as we safely can."[25]

Wood moved rapidly to implement McKinley's directive. "By the instructions of my government, we are marching toward independence," he announced to Cuban leaders at a meeting on January 1, 1900. The census was completed in the spring, and an electoral law went into effect in mid April. When municipal elections took place on June 16, the Cubans elected candidates who were favorable to independence. By late July the election of delegates for a constitutional convention had been set for September 3, 1900. Once again the nationalists on the island prevailed, controlling the largest bloc of votes at the convention, which was to begin on November 5, 1900.[26]

The McKinley administration had been free of scandals involving corruption in the federal service until the spring of 1900. Then Washington learned that the director of the Cuban postal system, Estes G. Rathbone, and some of his subordinates, including Charles F. Neely, had been involved in a plot to embezzle at least one hundred thousand dollars from their official accounts. What made the case particularly sensitive were Rathbone's long friendship with Mark Hanna and the eagerness of the Democrats to exploit an opening during a presidential election year.

To probe postal corruption in Cuba, McKinley appointed the fourth assistant postmaster general, Joseph L. Bristow. Before his agent left the United States, the president told him that "I have been more pained by this scandal than by anything that has occurred during my administration." Bristow was instructed: "Be thorough; do no one an injustice but shield nobody who has committed a wrong. I want every offender properly punished." If politicians complained, "do your duty and leave that to me." Root sent similar directives to Leonard Wood. "I want you to scrape to the bone, no matter whose nerves are hurt by it." The administration's response helped to forestall criticism from the opposition. Hanna did try to influence the case against Rathbone, but McKinley kept him at a distance. Legal proceedings, which resulted in convictions, went forward.[27]

Running parallel in 1899 with the new issues of colonial governance, which called forth innovative exercises of presidential power, were the continuing diplomatic controversies with Great Britain. The consequences of the war gave one issue—alteration of the Clayton-Bulwer Treaty regulating the status of an isthmian canal—special urgency, because of the United States' ambition to establish its dominance in the Caribbean. Less momentous in themselves, but significant because of being linked with the canal problem, were the problems with Canada over the Alaskan Boundary and, at the end of 1899, with Britain over its involvement in the Boer War in South Africa.

The preferred forum for the resolution of disputes with Canada was the Joint High Commission. The delegations of British, Canadian, and United States representatives gathered at intervals in Ottawa and Washington between August 1898 and February 1899. Despite pressures from economic interests in the United States and Canada, progress was made regarding fur seals, fisheries, and trade relations. The negotiations broke down over the Alaska Boundary. A complex controversy, the boundary question turned on conflicting interpretations of an Anglo-Russian Treaty of 1825, which established claims to the panhandle of Alaska that lay southwest of the Yukon and British Columbia. With the weaker legal case, the Canadians disliked United States control; they wanted London to give them diplomatic assistance in securing easier access to the Yukon and its gold. The United States, believing its claims to be solid, stood firm against any arbitration of their differences. To compromise and thereby grant Canada something to which it was not entitled, the Americans contended, was not acceptable. On this basic disagreement the Joint High Commission suspended its talks in late February 1899. A few weeks later the death of the chief British negotiator, Lord Herschell, left deliberations in such disarray that the commission never did resume its work.

Much of the rest of the year, until late October, was devoted, first, to efforts to settle the boundary differences through diplomatic channels. When that failed because of Canadian resistance and because of British unwillingness to coerce Ottawa, Hay and the ambassador in Washington, Julian Pauncefote, agreed on a modus vivendi. Facing the greater crisis of the Boer War at the same time, London realized that it could not afford to continue arguing with the United States over Canadian territory.

The most important Anglo-American issues, as Washington saw it, were the isthmian canal and the need to revise or dispense with the Clayton-Bulwer Treaty of 1850. That document bound Britain and the United States not to establish colonies in Central America. Neither could have exclusive power over a canal in the area, and such a canal could not be fortified. The treaty also provided mutual guarantees of the neutrality of a canal. Unless this treaty were renegotiated, the United States could not construct an American canal. The British, and especially the Canadians, hoped that the desire for the canal might induce Washington to make concessions on Alaska. Secretary Hay found this blending of the two issues deplorable, and he told a British journalist that he was disappointed that "this important matter, in which the two countries are absolutely agreed, has to be held up until the exigencies of American and Canadian politics can be sufficiently reconciled to let it pass."[28]

Further complicating these matters were the proponents of different routes across the Central American isthmus. After the financial debacle of the French Panama Canal Company in the 1880s, the Nicaraguan route gained an ascendancy throughout the 1890s, a position that it still enjoyed when McKinley took office. The leading champion of Nicaragua in Congress was Senator John T. Morgan of Alabama, and it seemed likely that his irrepressible exertions would bring him success in the early part of McKinley's term. Though Morgan had not obtained the financial support that he wanted from Congress, McKinley had spoken favorably of Nicaragua in his inaugural address. The president had also named the Nicaraguan Canal Commission in the spring of 1897. It appeared unlikely that the competition, the New Panama Canal Company, an offshoot of the earlier, bankrupt French company, and its lobbyist, William Nelson Cromwell, could thwart Morgan's lifelong ambition.

During the war the battleship *Oregon* had steamed ten thousand miles around Cape Horn from the Pacific to join the Atlantic Fleet. Arriving too late to join the battle of Cuba, the *Oregon* had dramatized the need for a canal and for revision of the Clayton-Bulwer Treaty. McKinley spoke for American business interests, the navy, and citizens generally in his annual message of 1898. A canal was "now more than ever indispensable to that intimate and ready intercommunication between our eastern and western seaboards demanded by the annexation of the Hawaiian Islands and the prospective expansion of our influence and commerce in the Pacific." The president asserted that "our national policy now more imperatively than ever calls for its control by this Government," and he was sure that Congress would "duly appreciate and wisely act upon" his recommendation.[29]

Some months earlier, McKinley had informally indicated to the British government how the administration intended to proceed with its canal policy. Through a private emissary the president had told Arthur Balfour, the prime minister's nephew, that in his annual message he would announce the American desire to proceed unilaterally. In the fall, once John Hay was in the State Department, the secretary asked Pauncefote to prepare a draft treaty that would meet Washington's reservations about the Clayton-Bulwer Treaty. In late December and early January the diplomats had generally agreed on language that would give the United States the right to build a canal across Central America.

While these negotiations proceeded, Congress was considering legislation to guarantee the financing of a canal in Nicaragua. Sponsored by Senator Morgan, the bill received Senate approval on January 21, 1899, by a vote of 48 to 6. It called for a canal that the United States would construct and control, but it was silent on the obvious conflict with the Clayton-Bulwer Treaty. Though the Morgan bill represented a prod to the British, London did not respond favorably to America's eagerness. Within the Salisbury government, there was a strong sentiment to secure appropriate concessions in exchange for approval of what the McKinley administration wanted. Moreover Lord Salisbury insisted that Canada, too, must be consulted, and that nation resisted agreeing to a canal until there had been a settlement of the Alaskan Boundary. In the end the British decided not to go ahead with the draft treaty. Negotiations apparently reached a dead end in the general deterioration of the Joint High Commission in February 1899.

In the House the Morgan bill ran into difficulty from proponents of Panama and from Republicans who did not want a Democrat to be associated with the success of canal legislation. The advocate of a GOP measure, William P. Hepburn of Iowa, devised a substitute for the Morgan draft, but he was unable to bring his own bill to a vote during the short session. With adjournment imminent, Senator William P. Frye attached a rider regarding a Nicaraguan canal to the rivers and harbors bill. Clearing the Senate on February 24, it seemed likely to prevail in the House as well, in the general sentiment to endorse a pork-barrel law.

At that point the friends of Panama, with William Nelson Cromwell in the lead, told a House committee and the president that their proposed route, which would include the unfinished

French construction, was superior to one in Nicaragua. Out of the climactic debate and amid intense lobbying, the House decided to name a commission to survey all isthmian routes. Panama's chances had revived, and they blossomed further later in June 1899, when McKinley named the Isthmian Canal Commission. Later events proved this to be a turning point in the process of selecting a Panamanian route. But the administration still had to get the British to accept a new treaty.

When the lawmakers convened for the first session of the Fifty-sixth Congress in December 1899, the legislative branch's desire to goad the British government was transparent. Congressman Hepburn sent in his canal bill again on December 7, 1899, and he now had the backing of Morgan in the Senate. With Hepburn's bill likely to pass, London confronted a grim international situation. British armies in South Africa were not achieving the anticipated victories over the rebellious Boers. Instead, in the "Black Week" of December 9 to 16, 1899, the British suffered a series of defeats. Great Britain could not afford to alienate the United States when Congress could proceed to authorize a canal anyway.

The British government received a report from its ambassador and a similar analysis from John Hay in late January 1900. Canada was informed that refusal to sign the treaty "would tend to shake position of President whose friendly attitude is in the present condition of public affairs of great importance." The Canadians did not like their predicament, but there was no alternative. On February 5 the Hay-Pauncefote Treaty was signed. The British agreed that the United States could build its canal. The waterway would be "free and open, in time of war as in time of peace, to the vessels of commerce and of war of all nations on terms of entire equality," and the canal would not be fortified. In the euphoria of what he had achieved, Secretary Hay expected unanimous ratification of the treaty. Instead, the administration would encounter a rancorous controversy.[30]

The outbreak of the Boer War facilitated the concluding of the canal treaty with the British. It also added to the domestic political burdens of the administration. As the British found themselves in a widening conflict, the Democrats saw an opportunity to gain votes among the Irish and the Germans. Irish-Americans hated Great Britain and relished its embarrassment in Africa. German-Americans shared their Anglophobia and applauded the rebellion of a people to whom they felt ethnically related. When the president sent Adelbert Hay, the secretary's son, to Pretoria as the United

States consul, enemies of the administration labeled the appointment as further evidence of an anti-Boer posture. "We do not want an Englishman for Secretary of State just yet but we might as well as to have the Hon. John Hay," the president was told.[31]

President McKinley and Secretary Hay knew that any overt expression of support for the Boer cause would anger London. Ambassador Pauncefote wrote home that "the warmth & friendliness of manner shown towards me by the President & all his cabinet is very marked, . . . & evidently intended to show their desire to maintain & promote the entente cordiale & the 'unwritten Treaty' which undoubtedly exists in spite of the outcry about the word 'alliance.'" In his annual message of December 5, 1899, McKinley said that the United States government had "maintained an attitude of neutrality in the unfortunate contest between Great Britain and the Boer States of Africa." The president added that if the parties to the quarrel had suggested that an expression of American interest might have helped to stave off the war, "good offices would have been gladly tendered."[32]

As the Boer War progressed, sentiment in the United States grew for some favorable response to be given to the appeals for international assistance that whites in Africa were making. In March 1900 the Boer government asked Washington for a document indicating the latter's willingness to mediate the conflict. Hay sent such a document to London without directly requesting the British to accept it but with assurances of the president's "earnest hope that a way to bring about peace may be found." This action defused domestic opposition. The British also used the American initiative to their own advantage. The United States had acted alone, thus preempting a joint approach by powers that were less favorable to London, and the coolly negative response from Britain forestalled any other kind of international campaign for mediation.[33]

With public opinion still running in favor of the Boers, but with the British gaining the military superiority, the Boers tried a more direct appeal to the American government two months later. Three emissaries found Hay prepared with a reply before they had even stated their case. "It was a bit discouraging," one of them told a reporter, "to see our answer lying on the table as we entered and before we had had opportunity to open our mouths." Their conversation with McKinley was more polite but equally barren of actual result. He diverted the discussion into a rumination on the view from his office window, and the envoys went away persuaded "that the American government is in league with Great Britain." With that inconclusive outcome the Boer issued faded. The Democrats criticized administration policy in their platform in 1900, but an anti-British theme did not draw many votes to William Jennings Bryan in his second battle for the White House.[34]

The record of American foreign policy under McKinley in 1899/1900 also included the nation's participation in The Hague conference on disarmament, international arbitration, and the codification of the rules of war. The czar of Russia had proposed the conference in 1898, and McKinley said approvingly in his annual message that "it behooves us as a nation to lend countenance and aid to the beneficent project." The president noted simultaneously that American armed forces were "in time of peace so conspicuously less than that of the armed powers to whom the Czar's appeal is especially addressed" that disarmament talks had only a general and not a specific relevance to the United States. Early in 1899 a delegation composed of Andrew D. White, the ambassador to Germany; Captain Alfred T. Mahan; Seth Low, the president of Columbia University; Captain William R. Crozier; and the minister to the Netherlands, Stanford Newel, was appointed. George Frederick William Holls, who was a prominent German-American lawyer, a friend of the president's, and a nuisance to Secretary Hay, went along as secretary. The conference, which opened in mid May, ran for a little more than two months.[35]

On disarmament the gathering made little progress, because the American delegates, especially Crozier and Mahan, were opposed to restrictions on the invention or the development of new weapons. The delegation's part in the discussion on rules of war was modest. The Americans were more influential in the establishment of the Permanent Court of Arbitration. Collaborating with the British, they helped to convince the Germans that the court, restricted as it was, would not be a threat to that nation's interests. In his annual message of 1899 President McKinley included paragraphs that favored the convention to create the arbitration tribunal. Noting that the American delegates had reaffirmed the nation's "traditional policy of not intruding upon, interfering with, or entangling itself in the political questions or policy or internal administration of any foreign state," the chief executive called the convention a noble achievement and urged the Senate to ratify the treaty. The pact went to the Senate on December 20, 1899, and after some delay, it and a convention relating to aerial warfare were ratified. Two other conventions went to the Senate later in the spring, and in time they were also approved. McKinley named his predecessor

Benjamin Harrison, George Gray, Chief Justice Melville W. Fuller, and Attorney General John W. Griggs to The Hague Court in 1900.[36]

The most enduring diplomatic initiative that the McKinley presidency produced after the war was the Open Door policy, which was launched in September 1899. Few episodes in the history of American foreign policy have been more intensely examined than the notes that Secretary Hay sent to the powers on September 6, 1899, regarding China. To the process of formulation came businessmen interested in Chinese markets, British advocates of the integrity of China, an American expert on Asian issues, and John Hay. The extent to which President McKinley involved himself is still unclear. The sequence of events suggested that he approved Hay's actions, but given the evidence that is now available, it is impossible to do more than infer plausibly the president's supervisory presence.

The acquisition of the Philippines and the expanded role of the United States in Asia intensified the existing concern, both in the government and in the private sector, about the fate of China in 1898. In June 1898 the administration asked Congress for $20,000 to set up a commission to examine the prospects of trade with China. The next month, in response to a query from then Ambassador Hay in London about joint moves with the British on China, the president replied through Secretary Day that it was not the time to act on China with another power. McKinley did not, however, rule out the possibility of the expansion of American interests in Asia. Addressing the peace commissioners on September 16, 1898, about the Philippines, he also said: "Incidental to our tenure in the Philippines is the commercial opportunity to which American statesmanship can not be indifferent. It is just to use every legitimate means for the enlargement of American trade; but we seek no advantages in the Orient which are not common to all. Asking only the open door for ourselves, we are ready to accord the open door to others." After this first reference to the Open Door policy, the president added that "the commercial opportunity" that went with the Philippines "depends less on large territorial possession than upon an adequate commercial basis and upon broad and equal privileges."[37]

Extensive public support existed for a more forceful policy in China in January 1899. The problem lay in determining the best means to use in accomplishing the desired ends, and the administration spent the twelve months after September 1898 waiting for the right moment to shape a China policy. The options that were open were relatively limited. The Philippine insurrection tied down the available military resources that might have sustained direct American action in China, and the domestic controversy over imperialism, as well as the national tradition of noninvolvement in the affairs of other countries, made overt intervention in China politically dubious. The power with whom the country might logically cooperate was Great Britain, but such an alliance, even if informal and tacit, also posed risks for the Republicans from Democratic critics of the president. In addition, London entered into an agreement with Russia in April 1899 that divided up railroad spheres in China, a decision that indicated that Britain was committed to achieving areas of influence that would be comparable to those of its European rivals.

Events in midsummer 1899 persuaded the president and the secretary of state that the United States should set forth its own attitude toward the future of China, as the European powers continued to establish spheres of influence and leases on the mainland. An interview with Jacob Gould Schurman, upon his arrival at San Francisco from the Philippines, carried his statement that in the Orient "the great question there is not Formosa nor the Philippines, but China." Probably more decisive in the administration's calculations was the ukase that Czar Nicholas II issued on August 11, declaring that the port of Talienwan in Manchurian territory, which was under Russian control, would be open to the merchant ships of all nations. The Russian action indicated that that nation and Great Britain would both be receptive to an assertion of American policy about the Open Door.[38]

To prepare the case for the United States, Hay turned to an old friend and long-time student of Asian affairs, William W. Rockhill. In the 1880s Rockhill had served in the American legations in China and Korea; during the Cleveland administration he had been an assistant secretary of state. When the Republicans came to power, supporters of Rockhill tried to have him named minister to China. The best position that could be found for a sometime Democratic officeholder was that of minister to Greece. After two dreary years the diplomat came home to be director of the Bureau of American Republics. In the summer of 1899 Rockhill was corresponding with a British friend, Alfred Hippisley, about China's problems. As an official of the Chinese Maritime Customs Service, Hippisley was concerned about convincing the United States to preserve the Open Door in China.

Rockhill and Hippisley exchanged ideas and data throughout

July and August, and they kept Hay informed of their thoughts. The secretary told Rockhill on August 7 that he was "more than ready to act. But the senseless prejudices in certain sections of the 'Senate and people' compel us to move with great caution." By August 18, with the czar's ukase known and Schurman's interview released, Rockhill had "pretty clear assurances from the State Department" that action might come sooner than expected. Less than a week later, on August 24, Hay asked his American colleague to draft instructions to ambassadors in Great Britain, Germany, Russia, and France. Rockhill's memorandum was ready on August 28, and Hay and the president discussed it on September 2. McKinley approved the transmission of what became the Open Door notes. After Rockhill and Assistant Secretary Alvey Adee prepared them formally on September 5, they were sent to the American diplomats in the four major countries on September 6. The rationale for McKinley's timing remains vague. Presumably, the influence of the business community and Jacob Gould Schurman, the Russian ukase, the arguments of Rockhill and Hippisley, and the president's own interest in China converged to produce a decision.[39]

The Open Door notes sought to have the powers that were involved, which also came to include Italy and Japan, accept three American assumptions. In China the nations that were already there would "in no wise interfere with any treaty port or any vested interest within any so-called 'sphere of interest.'" The Chinese would continue to have their tariff duties apply inside the areas of foreign influence, and they would collect the customs duties. Finally, there would be no discriminatory harbor dues or railroad rates within the respective spheres of influence.[40] If these proposals were agreed to, the United States would retain many commercial advantages which might otherwise disappear under the economic system that the powers were imposing on China. The Open Door notes also attempted to preserve for the Chinese some part of their government's power and their nation's integrity. At the same time the administration was responding to and restraining the imperialistic surge in China through an independent policy that cooperated with the British in substance, answered the felt needs of the business community, and yet circumvented any need for consultation with the Senate.

The powers reacted to the initiative in ways that fell far short of acceptance of the American position. Great Britain most nearly approached agreement with the proposal. The Russians were essentially negative, and the Germans, French, Italians, and Japanese said, as the British and Russians had, that they would only agree if all the other nations did. In March 1900 Hay proceeded to announce that the replies from the six nations satisfied him and the American government. The secretary had put the best possible face on the diplomatic situation, and his public posture enjoyed wide domestic support.

The merits of the Open Door policy in its initial stage have received elaborate attention and have evoked considerable historical debate. As a foreign-policy response to the specific conditions that faced the United States in 1899, the notes made the most of the modest resources at the disposal of McKinley and Hay. There was no way to force the powers to grant Americans equality inside their spheres of influence. It might be possible to bluff them and thus "realize the benefits of the 'imperialism of free trade' while the other powers paid the costs of colonial administration in their spheres." Whatever it later became as a guiding precedent of American foreign affairs, the Open Door policy is a further indication of the tactical skill of McKinley and Hay as diplomats. That there were deeper problems with manipulating China in this way would become obvious when the Boxer Rebellion exploded in 1900.[41]

At the end of McKinley's third year in office, the president's opponents spoke less often of his weakness as a leader or of his alleged indecision. A theme of executive supremacy and excessive presidential power emerged in critical reviews of the administration. "Has Congress abdicated?" asked Joseph Pulitzer in December 1899. Through partisanship and patronage, McKinley had established his ascendancy over the legislative branch. Pulitzer complained particularly about the naming of senators to the peace commission and the use of White House influence to sway votes in ratifying the treaty. "Congress has failed as a check upon the Executive and is no longer the guardian of popular liberty." Another Democrat, Perry Belmont, argued that "since the inauguration of President Mc-Kinley there has been an enormous extension of Executive power."[42]

Allowing for partisan exaggeration, these judgments were essentially correct. McKinley was, as Root put it, "wielding an enormous and arbitrary power over Spanish islands."[43] Military government in Cuba, Puerto Rico, and the Philippines rested on the war powers of the president, and the role of Congress in colonial policy had become a subordinate one. In the conduct of diplomacy the president kept the initiatives in his own hands and again offered little more to the lawmakers than the chance to react to what he had already done. The executive machinery of the White House had not diminished after the war; it had continued at its expanded dimensions. McKinley's capacity to mold public attitudes increased as George B. Cortelyou's role in the White House grew.

Not all the policies of the administration had prospered in 1899. The Philippines persisted as a nasty dilemma. In Cuba, the policy of annexation was bankrupt, and the president would have to move carefully to achieve an American presence after Cuba attained its independence. Relations with Great Britain had succeeded in resolving or postponing major points of irritation, but these agreements were still subject to congressional approval. In none of these cases, however, had President McKinley been reluctant to employ the authority of his office in order to achieve his goals. Both on domestic and foreign matters the emergence of the strong presidency went on in the year before McKinley was to face the voters.

9

★★★★★

THE CAMPAIGN OF 1900

Aware of the custom against a president's campaigning for reelection, William McKinley used the off-year contests in 1899 to take his case to the nation once again. The most elaborate excursion consumed two weeks in October, across nine states of the Middle West. In Minnesota the presidential party received a noisy welcome from tugboats and grain ships at Duluth; a crowd of almost ten thousand people greeted the chief executive at Battle Creek, Michigan. An opposition newspaper labeled the tour "an electioneering enterprise" that raised questions about "the good taste, if not the propriety, of the action taken." Republican leaders were eager to have McKinley in their states to capitalize on his popularity, and the president made eighty speeches and brief addresses during the trip.[1]

In his remarks, McKinley spoke again of duty overseas and prosperity at home. "The hum of industry has drowned the voice of calamity, and the voice of despair is no longer heard in the United States, and the orators without occupation here are now looking to the Philippines for comfort," he said at Kewanee, Illinois, on October 7. In the Philippines, he admitted, "we have yet some trouble . . . but the gallantry of the brave boys who have gone there will, I trust, soon put down that rebellion against the sovereignty of the United States."[2]

The state elections a month later represented a series of victories for the GOP and the administration. In Ohio the Democrats were beaten in the gubernatorial race, with the Republican winner running well ahead of the party's total in 1897. Iowa, Massachusetts, New York, New Jersey, Kansas, and South Dakota were solid for the Republicans. The Democrats did well in Maryland but had setbacks in most of the rest of the nation outside of the South. Bryan did carry his home state of Nebraska for a fusion ticket of Democrats and Populists after a hard struggle, thereby strengthening his hold on the nomination for 1900. "The elections mean a victory for imperialism in a majority of the states voting," conceded the *New York World*. One Republican wrote McKinley that the campaign "has settled the issues and the candidates for the presidential election in 1900." The president would be unanimously renominated, while Bryan was certain of a second nomination. The death of Vice-President Hobart in November raised the issue of who would be McKinley's running mate. No other problems clouded the Republicans' prospects.[3]

When the first session of the Fifty-sixth Congress began in December, the Republicans had a majority of twenty-two votes in the House over the Democrats and a margin of nineteen seats against the Democrats and Populists in the Senate. "The President goes before Congress today," said Secretary of State John Hay, "in an attitude which I think is impregnable." Hay's judgment was correct if one evaluated the president's chances for reelection. On Capitol Hill, however, several controversies, most notably the Hay-Pauncefote Treaty and the question of the Puerto Rican tariff, shook the GOP in Congress and subjected McKinley's leadership to exacting tests.[4]

The first difficulty emerged over the tariff policy toward Puerto Rico. In September a hurricane had killed nearly three thousand people and had devastated the coffee crop that furnished the bulk of the revenues for the island. Secretary of War Elihu Root concluded that the complete removal of tariff barriers between Puerto Rico and the United States would best promote rapid economic recovery and "avoid trouble in the island." The secretary did not take into account any larger considerations of overall colonial policy. He particularly did not reach a judgment regarding Congress's power to legislate for the possessions that Spain had relinquished in 1898. As the president wrote in his annual message, Puerto Rico had "lost her free intercourse with Spain and Cuba without any compensating benefits in this market." Therefore the solution was simple: "Our plain duty is to abolish all customs tariffs between the United States and Puerto Rico and give her products free access to our markets."[5]

McKinley and Root had blundered. Their stance on the Puerto

Rican tariff had undercut the protective system of the Republicans and had called into question whether Congress had the authority to make rules for the new possessions. Senator Orville H. Platt of Connecticut supported the proposition that "we must not admit that any of our new possessions are a part of the United States in the sense that the Constitution extends itself over them, or that we must have free trade with them." The president seemed to be adopting the position of the Democrats that the Philippines, Hawaii, and Puerto Rico had now been brought within the United States and that tariff regulations therefore did not apply to goods imported from them to the mainland. Platt recognized the political dangers of a course that offended American beet sugar growers, "the sugar industry, the tobacco growers and cigar manufacturers." If the Republicans "let goods from Porto Rico in free, we put our home laborers into competition with the cheapest of cheap labor. I already hear the mutterings of the coming storm."[6]

McKinley did not grasp the partisan implications of his policy on the Puerto Rican tariff until after a bill providing free trade for the island was introduced on January 19, 1900. Eight days later, however, Republican senators close to the White House said that the president was "willing that a small or nominal rate of duty shall be imposed on imports from the island." This change of attitude came because McKinley realized that the Democrats were arguing, as one of them later wrote, that "we have never held and can not hold territory as a political dependency and subject to unequal taxation." McKinley regarded the constitutional question as "paramount—for upon the proposition that Congress had the right to govern the Islands by legislation with a 'free hand,' depends the success of our colonial policy—especially in the Philippines."[7]

There was, in McKinley's mind, also the issue of effective party leadership. "I could ride a white horse in this situation and pass the original bill," he said privately to a reporter; "the vital thing is to keep as many votes as possible in Congress back of the whole programme of the Administration." As he noted to his friend H. H. Kohlsaat, in a letter that was drafted but apparently not sent: "The President must to a large extent rely upon his own party in the administration of public affairs. He might have a personal triumph, but that would weigh little against the demoralization and disorganization of his own party in the legislative branch of the Government upon which he must depend."[8]

These arguments made a plausible case for McKinley on the issue of the Puerto Rican tariff. The way in which he presented his new policy to the public and the methods he used in handling Congress, however, lacked his usual skill. The House Ways and Means Committee reported out a new Puerto Rican bill on February 2, 1900. It specified that Congress not only could legislate for a territory such as Puerto Rico but also could set a tariff. The rates in the revised measure were 25 percent of the Dingley Tariff. During the two weeks after the report came out, the Republicans in the House found that they could not assemble a majority to support the bill as written. Ten to twenty-four Republican defectors stood ready to defeat the legislation.

The position that McKinley stated publicly at this juncture was ambiguous. Two congressmen who saw him on February 13 said that he would sign the substitute bill but that he "still adhered to his original idea that the island ought to have free trade with this country." To provide a clearer statement of his views, the president gave an interview to a reporter, Henry Loomis Nelson, which was published on February 18. Unfortunately, the comments on the tariff issue did not make his changed position apparent. The House bill was "the result of his measure urging free trade," and he reportedly thought that "Republican congressmen will yet come to his views, although he will probably do nothing more to impress that view upon them." In another part of the interview the president's overall ideas about foreign policy were attributed to anti-Catholic influences within the Methodist Church, and that language had to be repudiated. The public-relations initiative had been a failure.[9]

During the week before the vote the Republican leaders tried to pull together some form of compromise. In a party caucus on February 26 the rates in this bill were reduced to 15 percent, and a two-year limit was placed on the operation of them. All revenues that were collected would be "expended in the island for the benefit of its people." This language, noted a cabinet member, "is the prominent feature which reconciles the President to its passage." For his part, McKinley authorized a statement on the day that the caucus met: "The President earnestly hopes that all the republicans will unite and stand together on this measure, and not allow the Democrats to take control of the House."[10]

The vote on the Republicans' substitute measure came on February 28. With their majority still in doubt, the leadership brought in eight votes from members who were home sick or in the hospital. McKinley had his staff telephone three or four of the waverers and called them to the White House. The final vote was 172 to 161, but the Republicans survived the vote to recommit by a margin of only six ballots. The president's personal intervention had made the difference, and he tried to ease the political damage even further on March 2. In a message to the House he asked that the duties already collected from Puerto Rico—amounting to more than $2 million—be returned to the island. As one reporter said, he was "particularly anxious to secure prompt action in order that the indignation all over the country over the passage of the tariff bill might be allayed as soon as possible by an evidence of good faith and generosity toward the Porto Ricans."[11]

McKinley had gotten the bill through Congress, and the Republicans had not divided. Nonetheless, the episode revived stories about his indecisiveness. The White House never directly contradicted the president's endorsement of free trade in his annual message. Many Republican congressmen were being attacked at home for abandoning the president, and they had no precise word from McKinley to counter these assaults. Speaker Thomas B. Reed, an old enemy, observed: "I have always told them that when it came to the point of any difficulty, this administration would, with Andrew Jackson firmness, yield." After the reaction of the GOP congressional leadership to his initial sponsorship of free trade with Puerto Rico, McKinley altered his posture too quickly and too covertly. He had left politicians and the Republican press exposed, without the face-saving grace that a direct presidential statement of a changed opinion would have provided. "All together," wrote Senator John Coit Spooner, "it is a bad mess."[12]

In the Senate, which took up the issue on March 1, the tariff question became involved with the problem of civil government for the island. The sponsor of the legislation was Joseph B. Foraker, who believed that a civil government should be created immediately. So confused were the alignments in the Senate that the administration had a cabinet member remind the public that "there is the world-wide difference between reserving full discretionary power to deal with the new possessions as their varying interests and ours may require, and leaving no discretionary power in Congress whatever. And this is the real issue which has been forced by the attitude of the minority in Congress." Once again, the president had acted through an agent, and senatorial opposition continued.[13]

By the last week of March, after long conferences between senators and the president, a compromise emerged. The 15 percent duty remained, in general, and concessions were made to remove duties on food and some other products in order to conciliate lawmakers who supported free trade. The leadership also included a provision that when the civil government's system of taxation had begun to operate, all tariff duties would cease. The Senate passed the bill on April 2 by a vote of 42 to 31 that split along party lines. The House considered the Senate's version on April 4, and the line-up of late February repeated itself. On April 11, again by a party-line vote, the bill passed, 161 to 153. McKinley signed it the next day. Despite the strong popular feelings that the controversy aroused among midwestern Republicans, the issue of the Puerto Rican tariff did not last into the campaign of 1900. The administration had escaped with relatively light political damage from the president's initial misstep.

As the Puerto Rican problem emerged, unexpected opposition over the Hay-Pauncefote Treaty also developed. Secretary Hay and the president had not kept key senators informed about the status of the talks with Great Britain. More important, the provisions of the pact that forbade the United States from fortifying the canal and required that the waterway be open to all nations in time of war drew fire in and out of the Senate. Theodore Roosevelt issued a statement to the press, urging that the treaty be rejected unless it was changed to ensure that "the canal, when built, shall be wholly under the control of the United States, alike in peace and war." He disliked the provisions that would have involved other powers in maintaining the neutrality of the canal.[14]

John Hay was disturbed enough to write angrily to Roosevelt: "Cannot you leave a few things to the President and the Senate, who are charged with them by the Constitution?"[15] The secretary of state found his treaty under attack from the Foreign Relations Committee, from Henry Cabot Lodge, and from influential newspapers. By mid March the opposition appeared to be substantial enough to block ratification. Cushman K. Davis added an amendment, which said that the language relating to nonfortification of the canal did not apply to steps that the United States might need to adopt for it own defense or for maintaining order near the canal.

So dismayed was Hay at the Davis amendment that he resigned after a cabinet meeting on March 13, 1900. "The action of the Senate indicates views so widely divergent from mine in matters affecting, as I think, the national welfare and honor, that I fear my power to serve you in business requiring the concurrence of that body is at an end." The secretary also referred to newspaper attacks on the department that could also injure the president. McKinley responded: "Your administration of the State Department has had my warm approval. As in all matters you have taken my counsel, I will cheerfully bear whatever criticism or condemnation may come. Your record constitutes one of the most important and interesting pages of our diplomatic history. We must bear the atmosphere of the hour. It will pass away. We must continue working on the lines of duty and honor. Conscious of high purpose and honorable effort, we cannot yield our posts however the storm may rage." Hay did not resign.[16]

McKinley's warm words to Hay did not have a public counterpart in a strong endorsement of the treaty or in any apparent willingness to face down the senatorial opposition. The administration did attempt, by means of public statements from John Bassett Moore, William R. Day, and Richard Olney, to build support for the treaty. There was not, however, explicit word from the White House in favor of the document. This silence did not occur because of McKinley's passivity; there simply were not enough votes in the Senate for the treaty in its original form. Senator Davis placed the total as low as twenty; even the amended version lacked a majority.

The interaction of other issues was also important. Faced with an uphill battle on the Puerto Rican tariff question, the president would have risked the loss of both the canal treaty and the revenue legislation. Moreover, the administration also had several treaties regarding tariff reciprocity before the Senate. These pacts were encountering opposition as well. A stern presidential attack on the upper house in an election year would not have advanced the prospects of any of these items and might well have caused all three proposals to be defeated. It seemed more prudent to acquiesce when the senators suspended debate on the Hay-Pauncefote Treaty until after the elections. The White House and the State Department also recognized that the critics of the treaty were making analytical points of some substance. McKinley could have gained public applause if he had denounced the Senate's inaction and resistance. He could not have single-handedly compelled ratification, and self-inflicted wounds to a president's prestige lack appeal when an election is near.

After debating colonial policy, the canal issue, trusts, the tariff, and the nation's position in the Philippines, Congress adjourned in early June 1900. Both parties were now concerned with the state of the upcoming presidential contest, in what was clearly going to be a rematch of the 1896 election.

There had been no question, since the end of 1899, that McKinley would be renominated. In September he told old friends that he was not eager to have a second term. "I have had all the honor there is in the place, and have had responsibilities enough to kill any man." Despite this disclaimer of enthusiasm, McKinley sounded and acted like a candidate. He followed closely the results of the off-year elections; his speaking tour was nonpolitical only in name; and he shaped policy with a view to another term. In a conversation with Jacob Gould Schurman in May, McKinley said that "the Philippines would be the paramount and dominating issue in the campaign" against Bryan.[17]

In one of his last appearances before the traditions of the campaign took him out of the public's gaze, McKinley used an address before the Ohio Society of New York on March 3, 1900, to repeat his position on the Philippines. "We must choose between manly doing and base desertion," he said, and then he spoke about the sectional harmony that the war had evoked. To those who were worrying about the nation's course overseas, he asserted: "There can be no imperialism. Those who fear it are against it. Those who have faith in the republic are against it." He then assured his audience: "The liberators will never become the oppressors. A self-governed people will never permit despotism in any government which they foster and defend."[18] Such comments indicated how the apparent differences over foreign policy would be narrowed in the campaign to deflect much of the effectiveness of the Democratic attack.

Of the political problems that McKinley had before the Republican National Convention, three involved the management of men. After the victory at Manila Bay, Admiral George Dewey experienced a tempest of popular enthusiasm that was comparable to what the next century would lavish on athletes and entertainers. When he reached the United States in October 1899, there were parades, rallies, and endless dinners. On John Hay's advice, McKinley carefully allowed the admiral to call upon him, rather than greeting Dewey in New York. As the lure of the presidency invaded the hero's mind at the end of the year, he undid his own slim chances with naïve mistakes. His marriage to a wealthy widow, a recent convert to Catholicism, irked his Protestant admirers, and he compounded the situation when he gave her the home that a grateful people had built for him. In the spring, Dewey threw his bemedaled candidacy before the public. The presidency was not a taxing job, he told reporters; he would merely execute the laws that Congress passed. The public derision that followed these statements ended Dewey's political ambitions.

In the case of Senator Hanna, McKinley wanted his friend to

serve once again as chairman of the Republican National Committee. At the same time, the president resented newspaper attacks that produced, as William R. Day put it, "in the minds of many people unjust ideas of [Hanna's] character and his relations to the Executive." The senator, who himself enjoyed his public position as a presidential confidant, readily gave out statements that were taken as evidence of McKinley's thinking. When he became enthusiastic about an invention or a project, Hanna lobbied strongly in the departments, without, perhaps, as keen a sense of propriety as the president now deemed appropriate. The senator's behavior introduced what one of Hanna's biographers called "a faint coolness" between the two men.[19]

Exercising a kind of quiet discipline, McKinley took his time in expressing a specific preference to Hanna about the campaign chairmanship. Finally, in April 1900 the president informed a reporter, in response to a story that Hanna might resign, "that Mr. Hanna would not resign if he [the President] could help it—that he wanted him to stay and run things." By the end of May he was saying the same things to Charles G. Dawes, and the matter was resolved. The campaign, however, would reveal how intense the strains on the Hanna-McKinley relationship had become.[20]

The death of Vice-President Hobart after a long illness left the president with the task of selecting a running mate for 1900. McKinley had used Hobart effectively as a liaison with Congress, and the working partnership between the two men had revitalized the office of vice-president. McKinley's first choice for the place was Elihu Root, whose ability and New York residence complemented the president's assets. But Root and McKinley decided in late December that problems in the Philippines and Cuba made it imperative that Root not leave the cabinet. John Hay wrote at the New Year that "the Vice Presidency now lies *in grevio majoram.*"[21]

Of the many candidates mentioned for the vice-presidential slot, only one aroused Republican enthusiasm. The president would have been glad to see Cornelius N. Bliss on the ticket, and he listened favorably to suggestions about Seth Low, Andrew D. White, and William Boyd Allison. He did not encourage, but neither did he reject, the ambitions of Secretary of the Navy Long. Less credible was the candidacy of Timothy Woodruff, lieutenant governor of New York. In the spring, Jonathan P. Dolliver of Iowa, then a conservative congressman with a reputation as a speaker, appealed to Hanna and to a lesser extent to the president. None of these men, however, was able to arouse the dynamic excitement that the Republican governor of New York stirred in the early months of 1900.

Theodore Roosevelt wanted to be president, and he was weighing his options and the probabilities all through 1899. To challenge McKinley would be futile and fatal; so he came out publicly for the incumbent at the end of June. His second term in the Statehouse would expire in 1902, two dangerous years before the 1904 convention. A cabinet post seemed a pleasing alternative. Roosevelt wanted to be secretary of war; and after Root was chosen for that post, he hoped to become governor general of the Philippines. As his governorship went on and as he pursued the mild reformism that he then was practicing, Roosevelt worried that any disagreement with Senator Thomas C. Platt might undermine his political base. The senator thought that Roosevelt, the man whom he believed he had made governor, had demonstrated, during his first year in office, enough independence to make the vice-presidency a proper landing spot after a kick upstairs.

The party faithful viewed Roosevelt as an excellent counterweight to McKinley. He was an easterner with western connections, he was young, and he was a symbol of Republican success in foreign policy. They maintained a persistent enthusiasm for "Teddy" that the administration could not overlook. Close friends such as Henry Cabot Lodge, along with such political allies as Senator William E. Chandler, told Roosevelt that the vice-presidency offered the best chance for him to become McKinley's successor. Senator Platt, meanwhile, came under mounting pressure from his business supporters, who disliked not only the governor's having sponsored a franchise tax on corporations but also his antitrust program, to move Roosevelt out of New York State.

It is not easy to determine Roosevelt's own feelings about the vice-presidency, probably because he was not sure himself. The duties of the office, such as they were, held little attraction for him. He did not want to leave the governor's mansion because of Platt's nudging, and he wished to preserve his option to run for the White House in 1904. With all that on one side, Roosevelt did not intend to rule himself out entirely from the most available national post that the Republicans had in 1900. He made all the right moves to take himself out of the race without going the extra step that would have placed him beyond the reach of a draft.

In early February, Roosevelt told the press that "*under no circumstances* could I or would I . . . accept the nomination for the Vice-presidency." Lodge believed that he had "withdrawn absolutely and finally from the Vice Presidency." But had he? The newspapers and the party refused, as the spring went on, to take his renunciation as final. To put a stop to the boom, Roosevelt would virtually have had to withdraw from politics and issue a Sherman-like statement of disavowal. Such a course he would not follow. If he went to the national convention as a delegate, he might set off a stampede in his favor. "I believe that I would be looked upon as rather a coward if I didn't go." By the late spring he had backed away some distance from his February declaration. "I did *not* say," he wrote Lodge, "that I would not under any circumstances accept the vice-presidency." His repeated disclaimers of interest only aroused additional enthusiasm as the convention neared.[22]

The president's position on Roosevelt did not emerge with much clarity either. In January, Lodge found the president ready to have Roosevelt run with him. Two months later, Nicholas Murray Butler reported that McKinley was uncommitted and that Mark Hanna was strongly negative. After another conversation at the White House in mid April, Lodge wrote to Roosevelt that McKinley said "that he had talked with you in New York and much as he should like to have you on the ticket he had been convinced by what you had said and that he was inclined to think that your running for Governor might help the ticket more than in any other way." McKinley told Roosevelt the same thing on the brink of the convention; and when Roosevelt said he shouldn't run, Root added the wry comment: "Of course not—you are not fit for it." At that moment, McKinley also offered at least tacit encouragement to Senator Charles W. Fairbanks. Though no doubt the president would have preferred a less flamboyant spirit than Roosevelt, he did not intend to interpose the White House in the way of the general wishes of the party.[23]

The forces behind Roosevelt's candidacy converged at the national convention in Philadelphia in mid June. No other candidate had found a broad range of support, and the average delegate, especially those from the West, wanted him. Senator Platt, frightened by the threats of large corporations that they would withhold campaign funds, wished to bend the enthusiasm to his own purposes. Roosevelt came to the conclave and was "circulating actively through the hotel lobbies and frequently appeared in the headquarters of different state delegations, wearing an army hat and awakening enthusiasm wherever he went." He still denied that he was interested in the nomination. More skeptical Republicans called his headgear "an acceptance hat."[24]

Senator Hanna's worst fears were now realized. Over the long-distance phone on June 17 he asked McKinley for a statement to stem the Roosevelt wave. Shrewdly, the president answered in generalities, which Cortelyou relayed: "The choice of the convention will be his choice; he has no advice to give." Hanna had already extracted a promise from Roosevelt to withdraw. On June 18 the governor issued a release stating that he felt "most deeply that the field of my best usefulness to the public and to the party is in New York State." The wording, speaking as it did of the vice-presidency as "an office so high and so honorable that it is well worthy the ambition of any man in the United States," did not preclude accepting a draft; and his popularity was growing. Unless McKinley directly intervened, Roosevelt would be chosen. Hanna wanted McKinley to go that far, but men such as Charles G. Dawes and the insurance executive George W. Perkins advised caution.[25]

In another long-distance phone conversation on the evening of June 19, McKinley ended the "stop Roosevelt" effort: "The President's friends must not undertake to commit the Administration to any candidate. It has no candidate." The president disavowed any attempt to dictate to the delegates and said: "The Administration wants the choice of the convention." With Hanna disciplined, the anti-Roosevelt men had no weapons with which to combat the parliamentary maneuvers of Senators Platt and Matthew S. Quay of Pennsylvania on June 20 that signaled their willingness to force the New Yorker onto the Ohio senator. On June 21 McKinley was renominated unanimously, and the selection of Roosevelt followed. The president did not bring about the choice of the Rough Rider, nor did he welcome it. He was not about to dampen the genuine fervor of the rank and file, however; and he may have thought that Roosevelt's strengths would benefit from the constraints that the vice-presidency would impose. Whether by accident or by prearrangement, McKinley had allowed talent to enter his government in a way that improved the party he led.[26]

The Republican National Convention exuded the confidence, even the smugness, that GOP leaders felt about the approaching campaign. In the keynote address Senator Edward O. Wolcott of Colorado said of the president: "Never in the memory of this generation has there stood at the head of the Government a truer patriot, a wiser or more courageous leader, or a better example of the highest type of American manhood." As to the Republicans, Henry Cabot Lodge told the delegates that "so far as government and legislation can secure the prosperity and well being of the

American people our administration and our policies will do it." For some friends of the party, it was all a little too much. Albert Shaw told a friend in Great Britain that the GOP "is a little too fat and sleek and prosperous, and its moral tone is not quite what it ought to be. It looks back with pride, rather than forward with aspiration."[27]

The political worries that the Republicans had on the eve of the campaign were not imposing ones, though they gave the leadership appropriate concern. Many Civil War veterans, particularly the active members of the Grand Army of the Republic, disliked the efficiency and rigor of Henry Clay Evans, commissioner of pensions. Throughout 1899 and into 1900, lobbyists for the soldier vote urged the president to dismiss Evans. McKinley refused to fire an appointee on the basis of dubious reasons of the kind that the veterans and their spokesmen advanced.

Republicans devoted much attention in 1900 to overcoming potential and actual disaffection among German-American voters in the Middle West. The administration's apprehension about German activity in the Caribbean, a general suspicion about imperialism within this key voting bloc, and several well-publicized episodes of tension between the two nations had cooled the German-Americans' enthusiasm for the Republican ticket. Dewey had an overdramatized run-in with the commander of the German squadron at Manila in 1898; and one of Dewey's subordinates made an anti-German speech in April 1899, for which he received an official reprimand. The kaiser wanted more than that, but McKinley deftly deflected the protest. The perception that McKinley and Hay were pro-British with regard both to the Boer War and to other foreign-policy questions intensified this feeling of alienation among the German-Americans. The voters in Nebraska and Ohio were reported to be "still sullen and angry" in October 1899, with the Democrats benefiting from German newspapers "that are opposing expansion and criticizing the administration."[28] The White House countered by making references to the success of American insurance companies in gaining readmittance to Prussia, by giving greater visibility to Germans in the campaign organization, and by repeating earlier strictures about what the Democratic commitment to free silver would mean to the gold standard.

With the Republican National Convention concluded, the Democrats assembled in Kansas City on July 4, 1900, to do the expected and to nominate Bryan a second time. To run with him, the delegates chose Adlai E. Stevenson of Illinois, who had been vice-president during Cleveland's second term. The central issue of debate at the convention was whether the platform ought to give more weight to an attack on expansionism or to a restatement of the 1896 pledge to the free coinage of silver. The Democrats decided that imperialism, "growing out of the Spanish war, involves the very existence of the Republic, and the destruction of our free institutions. We regard it as the paramount issue of this campaign." As for the Philippines, the opposition offered "first, a stable form of government; second, independence; and third, protection from outside interference." At Bryan's explicit insistence, the platform contained a reaffirmation of the free coinage of silver at a ratio of sixteen to one with gold.[29]

By the time the Democrats had acted, Republican newspapers were discussing the party platform that had been adopted at Philadelphia. The final draft had omitted several planks that McKinley had specifically wanted to include. Senator Hanna's pet project of subsidies for the merchant marine had been dropped because of middle-western opposition. More important, a statement affirming that Congress would have full power over territory that belonged to the United States had been left out. A civil-service plank had also disappeared, as the shapers of the platform removed controversial issues that might, in their minds, have injured Republican chances.

McKinley made his speech accepting the nomination at Canton on July 12, 1900, from his front porch. He reviewed the party's achievements during his three years in office: "We have prosperity at home and prestige abroad." About the Philippines, he said: "American authority must be supreme throughout the Archipelago"; and he rejected a "scuttle policy." He then asserted, in the language of the missing plank, that Congress had full legislative power over the newly acquired territories but that "the doctrine, first proclaimed in the cause of freedom, will never be used as a weapon for oppression." Dawes called the address "a keynote—one of the most timely he has delivered." The president had remedied the most important lapse in the platform; his letter of acceptance in early September would attend to the other points of omission.[30]

Toward the end of his remarks McKinley alluded to the "sudden and terrible crisis in China." His listeners knew that he meant the Boxer Rebellion, which had trapped Americans and other westerners in the Chinese capital of Peking and had put their lives at risk. Throughout the summer of 1900, as preparations for the presidential campaign went ahead, McKinley dealt with the crisis by using the long-distance telephone from his summer residence in

Canton. Since he did not have to campaign personally, McKinley had ample time to devote to events in Asia.

At the root of the Boxer Rebellion lay antiforeign sentiments. The secret associations that called themselves "Righteous and Harmonious Fists" drew upon the support of farmers, who were confronted with drought, and upon the backing of some elements of the court of the Chinese Empress. The rebels moved out from their base in North China to menace the foreigners in the legations at Peking in May 1900. In early June, several hundred foreign troops arrived in Peking, but a relief force of fifteen hundred was repulsed. By June 13 the Chinese capital was isolated as the Boxers cut the telegraph lines. Western opinion feared the worst. "It looks now," wrote Senator William Boyd Allison on July 8, "as though all foreign legations have been destroyed and those connected with the legations murdered."[31]

The administration's first responsibility was for the safety of the Americans under siege. Initially the president hoped that E. H. Conger, the American minister, would "act independently in protection of American interests where practicable, and concurrently with representatives of other Powers, if necessity arise." A few days later, Hay reiterated that the United States sought only "to protect with energy American interests, and especially American citizens and the legation." The secretary stressed: "There must be no alliances." At the port of Taku an American naval detachment under Rear Admiral Louis Kempff remained apart when ships of the other powers captured forts there on June 17. By this time, however, the United States had no alternative but, as the Navy Department ordered Kempff to do on June 18, to "act in concurrence with other powers so as to protect all American interests." Despite the demands connected with subduing the Philippine insurrection, the army moved some twenty-five hundred men into the China Relief Expedition. This process commenced in late June 1900, and the exact size of the contingent became a subject of debate. The commander in the Philippines, General Arthur MacArthur, wanted the number of troops taken to be as small as possible; the administration recognized that "the sentiment of the country and the conditions seem to warrant" moving troops to China until the situation could be clarified.[32]

Even in the anxiety of the moment, the constitutional basis for McKinley's decision to send soldiers into a country with which the United States was not at war received criticism. The *Philadelphia Times* called the action "an absolute declaration of war by the executive without the authority or knowledge of Congress, and it is without excuse because it is not a necessity." To head off Democratic charges of imperialism, men such as J. A. T. Hull of Iowa advised the president to summon a special session of Congress. Assembling the lawmakers on the eve of a presidential campaign would only have furnished the Democrats with a forum; furthermore, the president believed that he had enough authority under the war power to dispatch troops to China.[33]

Events seemed to justify his decisions when the siege of Peking was lifted on August 14. The army and navy, in tandem with the other powers, had helped to liberate the foreigners in the capital. Indeed, through Secretary Hay, the world learned in late July that the legations were holding out. As relief seemed imminent, McKinley told Root over the phone on August 13: "It seems to me that we have been most fortunate in all our dealings with this most delicate question."[34]

As the United States helped to accomplish the freeing of the western diplomats, the administration moved to prevent the crisis from ending in the breakup of China. During late June and early July, Hay was more committed to preserving the territorial integrity of China than was the president. McKinley, said Hay to John Bassett Moore on July 1, "seems to take the other view and to want a slice." Two days later, however, the vacationing McKinley approved the wording of a circular that Hay sent to American diplomats. This document became the second Open Door note, a significant elaboration of American policy on the subject. The purpose of McKinley's policy, it contended, was to rescue the besieged Americans, to protect "American life and property" and "all legitimate American interests," and to check the spread of other rioting. The aim of the United States, then, was to "preserve Chinese territorial and administrative entity, protect all rights guaranteed to friendly powers by treaty and international law, and safeguard for the world the principle of equal and impartial trade with all parts of the Chinese Empire."[35]

The circular announced to the American people and to the world that the nation wanted Chinese independence and territorial integrity to be part of the Open Door. The government had no plans for taking additional action if the principles it espoused were flouted. Hay knew that the circular would stave off Democratic criticism and that the other nations involved could hardly demur from what the Americans had advocated. The political results were gratifying. Republican senators were "greatly pleased with the conservative position which the administration is taking on the Chinese matter. It will keep us out of infinite trouble in the future."[36]

In the aftermath of the lifting of the Boxer siege and the enunciation of the expanded Open Door policy, the president had to contend with the consequences of the broadened American commitment in Asia. At some point, McKinley may have wanted a "slice" of China, but during the summer of 1900 he did not find much attraction in an American military presence of even a semipermanent kind. The United States sought to recognize as much of Chinese authority and diplomatic influence as possible in mid August so as to facilitate the prompt withdrawal of the American contingent.

The difficulties of such a course, however, were manifold. On August 28 the Russians proposed that the powers leave Peking. The next day the cabinet met to shape a reply. Root and McKinley drafted versions, with the secretary of war moving less quickly and voluminously than the president in the process of dictation. The answer to the Russians was ambiguous and convoluted. The United States wished, while adhering to its previous statements, to extricate itself from its military commitments in China as soon as it could. McKinley pushed Hay, who was then ill, about withdrawal. Root was advising the president against keeping the army there "for a very long period of diplomatic bargaining in which we will be but a chip floating on the surface of the currents of intrigue and aggression of other Powers." McKinley wrote to Hay on September 14: "I know of no way to get out but to come out."[37]

Immediate withdrawal of the American forces did not occur. Both the army commander in Peking and the minister advised Washington to leave the troops where they were. Secretary Hay also believed that if the United States were to pull out, "we shall be left out in the cold." The British and Germans would be resentful, and Russia and Japan were undependable. "There is, therefore, not a single power we can rely on, for our policy of abstention from plunder and the Open Door."[38] The administration decided to retain a modest contingent of soldiers in Peking, at the same time accepting the members of the Chinese court as official representatives of the government for the purposes of negotiating an end to the diplomatic controversy. A German initiative to have the powers inflict punishment on those who had been responsible for the uprising was turned down. Washington also put the best face on the Anglo-German agreement of October 16, 1900, which appeared to, but did not in fact, buttress the Open Door and Chinese independence. Since the presidential election was only days away, no other posture was feasible. Still, because of the reduction in the American military presence in China in late 1900 and because of the emphasis on a diplomatic settlement, the Chinese question became less of an immediate crisis for the White House in the middle of the election campaign.

As the Chinese issue occupied the time of the cabinet, which was sweltering in Washington, and of the president, who was vacationing in Canton, the friendship of McKinley and Hanna encountered fresh tension. In the Cuban postal-fraud case, the senator sent to the president a letter from Estes G. Rathbone, giving "his side of the situation." McKinley returned the materials to Hanna, with the suggestion that copies be sent to the postmaster general and to the secretary of war. Two weeks later, Hanna wrote again about layoffs in the Brooklyn Navy Yard and about the hiring of Democrats at another installation in New York. "The matter," Hanna's informant said, "should be viewed from the standpoint of practical result [more] than Mr. Long seems inclined to do."[39]

McKinley prepared a formal and official answer on Executive Mansion stationery, saying, "I am sure when you know the facts you will have no reason for criticism or complaint." The president reminded his old friend about the government procedures regarding each of the questions raised, and then he added: "This is a time when every effort will be made to have the administration do questionable things. It is a period of great temptation, just the sort that will require the highest courage to meet and resist. If elected I have to live with the Administration for four years, and I do not want to feel that any improper or questionable methods have been employed to reach the place." When Hanna received the letter, he threw it down angrily. The president, or so the senator believed, had written for his biographer and had made Hanna appear as if he needed to be reminded about campaign ethics. The letter was overbearing, as Hanna's answer itself implied. Still, McKinley could remember when Hanna had lobbied him about munitions contracts during the war and the Rathbone episode. Even as he was writing to the president, Hanna, on behalf of steel companies, was calling Cortelyou about naval contracts for armor plate during the first phase of an involvement that lasted for several months. In view of the senator's habits, a reminder from the president about morality in office seemed to be in order.[40]

The two men had one more encounter. Hanna had become a public figure as his senatorial career blossomed, and he found platform appearances increasingly to his liking. In mid September he made speeches in the Middle West, and the Republican National Committee announced that he would also go to Nebraska and South Dakota. Hanna especially wanted to speak in South Dakota, where the incumbent senator, Richard F. Pettigrew, was running for re-election. A silverite who had bolted the GOP in 1896, Pettigrew was a bitter foe of McKinley and had quarreled with Hanna on the floor of the Senate. Hanna hoped to end the political career of his maverick enemy.

The White House had reservations both about the wisdom of Hanna's trip and about what he might say on the stump. In Chicago on September 18 he had announced: "There is not a trust in the United States. There is a national law, and in every state there is a law against trusts. They cannot exist, and every law against trusts, national or state, has been the product of Republican lawmakers." With Bryan making the policy of the GOP toward trusts one of his central domestic issues, Hanna's statement gave the opposition an opening. It simultaneously undercut McKinley's comment, in his letter of acceptance, that trusts were "obnoxious to the common law and the public welfare." Through Postmaster General Smith, the president suggested that perhaps Hanna might not want to make the trip. Learning where these ideas had originated, the senator said: "Return to Washington and tell the President that God hates a coward."[41] In fact, McKinley and Hanna had lunch together on September 22, and the next day the senator modified his remarks to agree with the president's position on the trusts. Hanna's midwestern tour was a great success as audiences responded to his rough-hewn style of speaking.

The main campaign task that McKinley had was to write his letter of acceptance to keynote the Republican canvass. Released on September 8, the lengthy document served as a surrogate platform for the GOP. After first examining Bryan's continued fidelity to free silver, the president concluded about the Democratic candidate and his Populist allies: "It is, therefore, the imperative business of those opposed to this financial heresy to prevent the triumph of the parties whose union is only assured by adherence to the silver issue." He then reviewed the nation's economic situation, which he found excellent, and endorsed an expanded merchant marine, an isthmian canal, and lower taxes.

On the trust issue he was more explicit than the party platform had been. Written by Hanna and edited by McKinley, the plank had approved "honest co-operation of capital to meet new business conditions and especially to extend our rapidly increasing foreign trade." It condemned "all conspiracies and combinations intended to restrict business, to create monopolies, to limit production, or to control prices" and favored legislation that would "effectively restrain and prevent all such abuses." McKinley now went further. Trusts were "dangerous conspiracies against the public good and should be made the subject of prohibitory or penal legislation." In common with those in the mainstream of Republican opinion, including Theodore Roosevelt, he thought that "publicity will be a helpful influence to check this evil."[42]

After recounting his foreign-policy accomplishments, McKinley devoted the bulk of his letter to the Philippines. As the letter was being prepared, Senator George Frisbie Hoar lobbied for inclusion of a promise of eventual independence for the islands. There would have to be a government that would be capable of maintaining the islands' existence. When that should occur, Hoar thought, the United States should not then reject a Filipino expression of a wish for independence. McKinley considered the idea, but in the end he rejected it. He thought that "the insurrection was kept alive by the anti-imperialist agitation" and that a modification of the American position would further hearten the rebels. He was equally unyielding to Bryan's idea of a protectorate, as he had been to the notion since 1898. "We must be supreme and our supremacy must be acknowledged." A visitor, John Bassett Moore, who heard the president on these topics two weeks after the letter came out, thought that "the tone in which he spoke of the 'consent of the governed,' as applied to the Filipinos, and the necessity of our being 'supreme' in the islands, would hardly have quieted the misgivings of the imperialists, if they had heard it."[43]

McKinley spent most of his prose in this section explaining how the United States had acquired the archipelago, rebutting charges that there had been an alliance with Aguinaldo and discussing what the two Philippine commissions had done. He noted that the Taft Commission had taken up legislative power in the islands on September 1, 1900, and he used a report from that body to claim, as it did, that "large numbers of people long for peace, and [are] willing to accept government under the United States." To the Democrats he posed questions about whether they would not have sent Dewey to Manila and whether they would have abandoned the islands before or after the peace treaty. "It is our purpose," he continued, "to establish in the Philippines a government suitable to the wants and conditions of the inhabitants and to prepare them for self-government, and to give them self-government when they are ready for it and as rapidly as they are ready for it." Any other policy, in his mind, simply would prolong the insurrection.

As to the protectorate concept held by the opposition, Mc-Kinley claimed that the primary issue was "whether we shall be responsible for the government of the Philippines with the sovereignty and authority which enable us to guide them to regulated liberty, law, safety, and progress, or whether we shall be responsible for the forcible and arbitrary government of a minority without sovereignty and authority on our part, and with only the embarrassment of a protectorate which draws us into their troubles without the power of preventing them." The choice, he concluded, was "between duty and desertion—the American verdict will be for duty and against desertion, for the republic against both anarchy and imperialism."[44]

The acceptance letter was a masterful political document. Bryan, at his acceptance ceremonies on August 8 in Indianapolis, had announced that, if he were elected, he would call Congress into special session to give the Philippines a stable government, then independence, and then to establish an American protectorate over the islands. McKinley's letter skillfully narrowed the foreign-policy differences between himself and Bryan, while undermining the idea of a protectorate. The letter also drew attention again to the role of the Democracy in bringing on the war with Spain and to Bryan's own part in securing the ratification of the peace treaty. By mid September, Bryan was ready to shift his campaign to other, more promising issues.

Bryan's campaign suffered from all the infirmities of his party during these years. The Democrats lacked available cash, had to rely primarily on their standard-bearer, and encountered wounding factionalism in such key states as New York. In September, Bryan took up the trusts, charging that "the Republican party to-day stands sponsor at the cradle of more trusts than ever sprang into existence before." Republicans responded that Cleveland had done no better in enforcing antitrust laws, and prominent Democrats were involved with the ice trust in New York. The shift in campaign emphasis did not help Bryan to overcome the advantages that prosperity, superior organization and finance, and a secure electoral base gave to the GOP. "Bryan is doing more for you than any twenty republican speakers," James Wilson told McKinley. "His threat of free trade is alarming the industries. Men of patriotism and some education are disgusted at his efforts to set the masses against the classes." The trust issue would be more effective for the Democrats in future elections. In 1900 the circumstances of good times lessened its impact, and Bryan was unable to make it hurt McKinley.[45]

In contrast to the Democrats, the Republicans saw "General Apathy" as their most dangerous foe. The GOP duplicated the campaign organization of 1896. They raised and spent about $2.5 million. That amount, drawn largely from wealthy and corporate donors, was all that Hanna believed would be necessary. With McKinley's victory apparently a sure thing, it also represented about what the party could raise. Hanna had systematized the process of campaign finance. He also solidified the actual and political identification of his party with the nation's consolidated wealth. As a friendly journalist said, "The Republican party may suffer innocently from a bad name, but I do not believe that one voter in ten in the United States honestly thinks that, if continued in power, it will wage successful warfare upon the trusts."[46]

The Republican National Committee used its funds to underwrite an elaborate publicity drive. A total of 125 million documents were issued, and over 21 million postcards were sent out. The president's letter of acceptance was published in German, Swedish, and Polish. Two million copies of newspaper material went out each week to over five thousand papers. The campaign textbook provided political ammunition to the more than six hundred speakers that the national committee employed. McKinley himself supervised the distribution of at least some of this data, and he contributed personal letters to campaign workers and party rallies. There were polls of the undecided and a constant watch on the movement of events. To Catholics, black Americans, organized and unorganized labor, and almost all potential voting blocs, the Republicans made their case.

The campaign itself, though often dull and predictable, produced one modest Republican crisis and completed Theodore Roosevelt's emergence as a national figure. In Pennsylvania a coal strike among the workers in the anthracite fields threatened to slow the GOP bandwagon in September. Senator Hanna, who knew the coal business, decided that the United Mine Workers were correct in their grievances, and he threw himself into an arbitration effort. With the aid of J. P. Morgan, he arrived at a negotiated conclusion that both sides could accept. The troubles in the industry lingered, to flare again in 1902, but for the moment a possible injury to the Republican cause had been averted.

Theodore Roosevelt, with Hanna, carried the main load of Republican oratory. From early September until the end of the race, Roosevelt visited the Middle West, the Far West, the border states, and then finished up in New York. As the audiences changed, Roosevelt emphasized sound money in the Middle West and expansionism in the West, and always he assailed Bryan: "If the farmer, the business man, and the wage-worker want prosperity to continue, they must make up their minds that the incoming of Mr. Bryan would mean terrible and wide-spread disaster." After a month of canvassing, Lodge wrote overseas that "Theodore has had a very successful trip, has addressed great crowds, has spoken extremely well and has helped the party enormously."[47]

McKinley never felt any real doubt about the outcome of the election. Toward the end of October, Cortelyou found the outlook "very favorable, and we continue to receive encouraging reports from all parts of the country." After early discouragement, the campaign to maintain Republican control of Congress gained momentum.[48] All observers commented on the relative lack of the enthusiasm and excitement that had marked elections during the preceding twenty years. The calm arose in part from the certainty regarding the election results. It also stemmed from the general decline, now in its earliest stages, of interest in and concern for partisan politics that has characterized the twentieth century.

Tuesday, November 6, 1900, was election day. The issue was speedily resolved as the counting of the returns commenced. McKinley received 7,218,491 popular votes to Bryan's 6,356,734. The margin in the electoral college was 292 to 155. As compared with 1896, the Republicans gained about 114,000 votes, while Bryan's total dropped some 146,000. McKinley's percentage of the popular vote was 51.7; Bryan garnered 45.5 percent. Six states, including Nebraska, that had gone for the Democrats four years earlier moved into the Republican column. Bryan carried the South, Colorado, Nevada, Montana, and Idaho. McKinley took all the rest. The turnout of voters in the northern states slipped almost seven percentage points from the 1896 peak of 78.3—to 71.6 in 1900. In the Senate the Republicans held 55 seats to 31 for the Democrats and 4 for the minor parties. The GOP won 197 seats in the House, as compared with 151 for the Democrats. The outcome in 1900 confirmed the position of the Republicans as the majority party.

Compared to the true landslides of the next century, McKinley's victory was not that decisive. In light of the election results since the Civil War, however, it was an impressive mandate. Prob-

229

ably the Republican dominance best explained their triumph, with economic prosperity a powerful contributing cause. Imperialism as an issue was less significant. The campaign had moved the nation toward a consensus. Few voters wished to undo the consequences of the war. There was even less disposition to go beyond what the McKinley administration had done.

The president did not exult publicly in his reelection. "You are here to celebrate a victory won, not by a single party," he said at Salem, Ohio, on November 7, "but by the people of all parties." He told members of his cabinet that much of the credit for the party's success was theirs, and he asked them to continue for another term. Only Attorney General Griggs indicated that he planned to retire. As he envisioned his second term, McKinley construed his reelection as placing him in a uniquely nonpartisan position with the nation. "I can no longer be called the President of a party; I am now the President of the whole people."[49] During the ten months that remained of his presidency, William McKinley showed the outlines of how he planned to use the powers of his office to start the United States into the new century with energy and accomplishment.

10

★★★★★

THE FIRST MODERN PRESIDENT

Three weeks after his reelection, McKinley spoke in Philadelphia to the Union League Club. The election recorded "the unquestioned indorsement of the gold standard, industrial independence, broader markets, commercial expansion, reciprocal trade, the open door in China, the inviolability of public faith, the independence and authority of the judiciary, and peace and beneficent government under American sovereignty in the Philippines." On foreign policy, he said once again: "Be not disturbed; there is no danger from empire; there is no fear for the Republic." As for himself, the election was "not the triumph of an individual, nor altogether of a party," and the nation's problems would require the energies of "the whole American people."[1]

McKinley's annual message to Congress, which was longer by some two thousand words than any previous "State of the Union" document, cited the nation's prosperity as proof of the strength of American institutions. His message ranged over foreign and domestic concerns, many of its early pages discussing Chinese developments in 1900, with subsequent paragraphs on particular countries. The president asked the Senate to take up the Hay-Pauncefote Treaty, and he endorsed the reciprocity treaties that were then before the upper house. He spoke for merchant-marine legislation, and he repeated his comments of 1899 about the trusts. On the Philippines and Cuba he reviewed the policy decisions of 1900, but gave no indication that lawmakers would soon have these subjects to consider.

Some issues were omitted. Midwestern shippers and commercial associations had urged that he support congressional measures, introduced by Shelby M. Cullom of Illinois, to strengthen the Interstate Commerce Commission's power over the railroads. The president had done some reading on the railroad question several years before, but he made no comments on the Cullom bill in his message. Neither did he accept Cullom's earlier suggestions that the administration back his bill. In Congress the Republican leadership kept the measure bottled up in committee. The flurry of telegrams, however, revealed that the Republicans would soon confront questions of governmental regulation rather than simply the promotional policies that had brought the GOP to power.

The attempt to subsidize the construction of American merchant vessels encountered other sectional tensions that existed below the surface of Republican unity. The sponsors of the bill were William P. Frye of Maine, in the Senate, and Sereno E. Payne of New York, in the House; but Mark Hanna was its most vocal advocate. "It is one of those measures," he said in December 1900, "whose influence will permeate every industry and every class in the length and breadth of the United States." Building up the merchant fleet would facilitate the capture of world markets that other nations controlled through a policy of granting subsidies to their own shipping. In the Middle West the ship-subsidy idea was unpopular because it represented, according to one politician, "a tendency to court the favor of corporate wealth, to the end that liberal contributions may be secured for campaign purposes." The Republicans could not bring the bill to a vote in the short session. In the next Congress, after McKinley's death, it passed the Senate but never came to a vote in the House.[2]

The most controversial foreign-policy question in December 1900 was the Hay-Pauncefote Treaty. In the spring the House passed the Hepburn bill for an American canal in Nicaragua by 224 to 36; the Senate committee on interoceanic canals acted favorably on it within two weeks. As the lawmakers reconvened, the Senate prepared to take it up. To forestall the outright repudiation of the Clayton-Bulwer Treaty, Republicans in the Senate adopted the Davis amendment, and then abrogated the Clayton-Bulwer Treaty and removed the clause in the Hay-Pauncefote draft that invited other powers to take part. Senators Lodge, Foraker, and Aldrich discussed these changes with McKinley, who advised them that the British would not approve the treaty as amended. Nonetheless, if no action were taken on the treaty, the Hepburn bill would pass; so, McKinley allowed the Senate to go ahead. The treaty, as amended, was ratified on December 20, 1900; debate on the canal bill was postponed.

McKinley could have resubmitted the treaty to the Senate, but that course would have been extremely dangerous. There was not a two-thirds majority for the original treaty, and additional consideration was probably not possible during the short session. Moreover, resubmission would only have caused the Hepburn bill to be revived. The president sent the treaty to London for the British response. After Congress had departed, on March 11, 1901, Pauncefote informed Hay that his government could not accept the pact. Repressing his distaste for his senatorial opponents and borrowing some of McKinley's techniques, Hay now reshaped a new treaty. He consulted with leading senators and then tailored his work so as to secure a two-thirds majority. For the British he offered wording that formally abrogated the Clayton-Bulwer Treaty, that applied the neutrality provisions only to the United States, and that dropped the Davis amendment without limiting the right of the nation to defend the canal in wartime. On April 25, 1901, the new draft went to the British. Much negotiation lay ahead, but Hay had made possible the eventual signing and ratification of the second Hay-Pauncefote Treaty in November and December 1901.

Constituting not a matter for congressional action but a continuing diplomatic worry as 1900 ended were the discussions about what the Chinese would have to do in the aftermath of the Boxer Rebellion. On one level, American action belied its stated concern for the territorial integrity of China. Since the summer of 1900 the navy had been seeking support for the establishment of a base on the Chinese coast. In mid November, Hay requested Conger to see what could be done about this and to ask the Japanese for their views. Conger reported that Japan would not approve the American presence; he also expressed his own opposition. The navy returned later to this scheme, but for the moment the matter was closed.

In the shaping of a protocol for presentation to the Chinese, the McKinley administration acted as a moderating influence. The terms that were given to China in late December 1900 included less stringent provisions than the Germans, Russians, French, and British had originally envisioned. During the negotiations that followed, the United States reduced its military commitment in China, pressed for low payments from Peking as indemnities, and accepted its share of the financial settlement, with the understanding that eventually some of the money would go back to China. William W. Rockhill conducted the parleys, which resulted in a protocol signed on

September 7, 1901, one day after McKinley was assassinated. The president died, having established the principles of the Open Door and China's territorial integrity as two major precepts of the nation's foreign policy in Asia.

In the short session of 1900/1901, it seemed unlikely that Congress could act on a bill to grant, in explicit terms, the power to the president to govern the Philippines after the insurrection had been suppressed. Senator Spooner had introduced this bill in January 1900, and the Senate Committee on the Philippines reported it the following March. The Republicans decided not to bring the bill to a vote before the election; so it was carried over to the next session. In late November, McKinley told Henry Cabot Lodge "that the bill ought to be passed and that he wanted it passed." The president, however, made no such recommendation in his message. Judging from his later comments, McKinley believed that other subjects had to take precedence over the Philippines.[3]

The Taft Commission had been in the islands for seven months as 1900 ended, and it had exercised legislative power since September 1. The commission assumed that the rebels had virtually been defeated and that resistance would end once McKinley had been reelected. For the majority of Filipinos who wanted peace under American sovereignty, Taft argued that there should be an effort made to train them in self-government, while real power should be kept in American hands. The commission promulgated laws for municipal government, for provincial governments, and one for the creation of a system of public schools. Other policies were established for implementing judicial reform, restructuring the tax system, and pursuing economic development. After Bryan had been defeated, Taft also encouraged the formation of a political party, the Federal party, which advocated ultimate annexation and statehood as being preferable to perpetual colonial status.

In carrying out its mandate, the commission met far greater difficulty with the American military commander, General Arthur MacArthur. When the Taft panel was appointed in 1900, General Otis asked to be relieved, and MacArthur replaced him. Differences between the civil and military agents of the United States rested on divergent conceptions of how suppression of the insurrection was proceeding and what power each side had in the shaping of policy. Initial cordiality gave way to rancorous hostility in the latter months of 1900. MacArthur contended that the army held supreme power in the archipelago; the commission responded that McKinley, under the war power, had "chosen to exercise this power partly through a military commander and partly through civilian legislators and administrators."[4]

On the strictly military aspect of Philippine affairs, the insurgent strategy of guerilla resistance was in full operation throughout 1900. MacArthur attempted to counteract it with a proclamation of amnesty in June, but after three months, only a relatively small number of Filipinos had turned themselves in. After the presidential elections, when the insurrection had not subsided, the army adopted harsher tactics, which were embodied in a declaration of martial law for what were called unpacified areas of the islands. Captured insurgent leaders were deported to Guam, and stringent penalties were exacted for cooperation with the guerillas. As the more rigorous military policy proceeded, McKinley decided that civil government, under the publicly benign and smiling guidance of William Howard Taft, would best serve the goal of bringing the fighting to a close.

In the context of these developments, especially the deadlock between the civil and the military branches, Taft informed Root on January 2 that enactment of the Spooner bill was "greatly needed to secure best results from improving conditions." McKinley's first response was negative, according to Lodge: "There are so many things of importance to be done that he [McKinley] thought it could go out." During the next several weeks, however, the president decided, in consultation with Spooner, to attach the latter's bill as an amendment to the army appropriation bill. With a deep knowledge of how timing could affect congressional action, McKinley believed that the bill would, as an amendment, have support that it might not otherwise attract, since few legislators wanted to defeat the whole measure and thus force a special session. On January 25, 1901, McKinley transmitted the reports of the Taft Commission to Congress, and Spooner moved his amendment on February 8. The White House also said, on February 12, that Taft would become governor general of the islands once Spooner's amendment had passed.[5]

The amendment was debated on February 27. That day, Senator Fairbanks called the president to express apprehension about the language "which vests the judicial, executive and legislative power similar to the Louisiana Purchase. This has raised a good deal of difference of opinion, and there is much antagonism on the part of Republicans." Was the White House really anxious about it, Fairbanks inquired, or would a simple resolution satisfy McKinley? Cortelyou replied: "The President most emphatically desires it in its present shape. He thinks it would be the gravest of blunders, having gone so far, to now recede." McKinley did not intend to let his colleagues on Capitol Hill dodge the task that he had presented to them.[6]

To his original proposal, Spooner had added wording that would have authorized the Philippine civil government to grant franchises for mining claims and internal improvements. The section came under Democratic attack and could have blocked action on the amendment. Senator Hoar offered an amendment restricting the franchise power. With that deal struck, the Democrats agreed to let the bill pass. The Senate acted on February 28 by a party-line vote. When the House took up the appropriation bill the next day, Congressman Joseph G. Cannon called to confirm that the president wanted the measure to be passed with Hoar's amendment. McKinley responded that the House should concur in what the Senate had done. Again, by a strictly partisan division, the House approved the bill with the Spooner amendment. McKinley had used publicity, private pressure on the Senate and the House, and close consultation with GOP leaders in order to secure his goals. To gain so sweeping a legislative victory through the amending process in a short session was a testament to McKinley's effective exercise of power in the latter years of his presidency.

Once Congress had confirmed his authority to move forward with civil government for the Philippines, McKinley directed that Taft assume full executive powers there. The explicit transfer of power from soldiers to civilians occurred on July 4, 1901. Meanwhile, the insurrection had received a heavy setback when Emilio Aguinaldo was captured on March 23. Taken to Manila, he said: "The country has declared unmistakably for peace. So be it." In fact the insurgents fought on for another year before the United States declared that the islands had been pacified. Other resistance sputtered on for several years. By the time that McKinley died, in September 1901, American supremacy in the archipelago seemed to be an accomplished fact. In his second inaugural address the president repeated his earlier pledges to the Philippines: "The settled purpose, long ago proclaimed, to afford the inhabitants of the islands self-government as fast as they are ready for it will be pursued with earnestness and fidelity." Avowals of a purpose to build a nation in this way would not impress Americans in the twentieth century, sensitive as they had become to the postponement of Filipino independence and the failures of and excesses in the performance of the United States that accompanied these presidential statements. Misguided by present-day standards and certainly paternalistic, McKinley was, in his way, a sincere friend of the people of the Philippines, and he was not the worst ruler who might have followed the end of Spain's domination.[7]

Through the middle of January 1901 the president was in bed with influenza. The illness, the first during his presidency, was serious, and it took him almost a week to resume his full schedule. As he did so, the administration was adding Cuba to the already crowded congressional agenda. The Cuban constitutional convention had been meeting since November 1900 to draft the fundamental law for an independent republic. At the same time, the Americans expected the Cuban delegates to recognize Washington's right to intervene in the new country's affairs in order to protect it from internal chaos or foreign domination. This power, the McKinley government contended, was necessary to fulfill the international obligations of the Paris Peace Treaty and to preserve the "people of that Island from the domination and control of any foreign power whatever." The administration also expected the Cubans to grant naval stations to the United States. Worried about foreign influences in the Caribbean, especially a German presence, and dubious regarding the Cubans' ability to manage their own affairs, McKinley and his advisors believed that the United States had to possess the formal, recognized ability to prevent domestic disruption or outside intrusion.[8]

Throughout December 1900 and into January 1901, the delegates were reluctant to do what the McKinley administration desired. They wanted a prompt end to the military government, and Leonard Wood thought that tariff concessions would be required to appease Cuban opinion. Exploratory feelers to Republican senators revealed that a reciprocity treaty was the only way of securing reductions in the island's products; but such a pact would have to wait until Cuba was independent. As February began, the White House was sending out strong signals that an extra session would be required. The president believed that "the Philippine question will have become acute in the next year and . . . he does not want both that and the Cuban situation on hand at the same time."[9]

The formulation of the Platt Amendment began on January 11, 1901. Root asked Hay to consider whether the United States should compel Cuba to recognize that America had a right to intervene in order to preserve Cuba's independence and stability. Further, the administration might bar a Cuban government from concluding with a foreign power a treaty that would infringe the island's sovereignty; it might also insist that the United States had a right to have naval bases on Cuba and to validate all the acts of the military governor. Matters then apparently lay dormant until the end of January. McKinley at that time discussed with Republican senators the possibility of calling an extra session, and the cabinet thrashed over the problem on January 29. The next day there was a statement, "made on high authority," that unless Congress took action on both Cuba and the Philippines, an extra session would almost be inevitable.[10]

Senator Orville H. Platt chaired the Committee on Cuban Relations. On January 30 he summoned its Republican members to a meeting on Sunday, February 3. The committee agreed to act along the lines of Root's ideas, and Platt set about putting these proposals on paper. He not only wrote to Root on February 5 that a resolution was being formulated but also asked to see the secretary and the president about the subject. On February 7 Platt and John Coit Spooner hammered out a memorandum "of what we should ask of Cuba by way of definition of the relations which should exist between Cuba and the United States after the government has been turned over to the people of Cuba." Spooner dictated most of the final text to his secretary. The next morning the two men took their draft to the White House, where McKinley said: "That is exactly what I want."[11]

Root sent Leonard Wood a letter on February 9, transmitting five points on which the senators and the administration had agreed: Cuba could not impair its independence through a treaty with a foreign power; its government could not assume public debts beyond its capacity to repay; the United States would be able to intervene "for the preservation of Cuban independence and the maintenance of a stable government"; all the acts of the military government were to be approved; and the Americans would be allowed to have naval bases on the island. Platt's committee met again on February 10 to draft the precise language of an amendment, the wording of which McKinley approved on February 11. In later years there would be some public discussion over who was the author of the Platt Amendment. Elihu Root, John Coit Spooner, William E. Chandler, and Orville H. Platt, in addition to others who were outside the government, shared a common store of ideas, all of which found some expression in the final wording of the amendment. The role of President McKinley has earned less attention. He had, as far as the shapers of the amendment were concerned, "guided them in large part in their deliberations."[12]

Senate debate on the Platt Amendment, which opened on February 25, continued for several days. The Democrats were relatively passive about the proposal, in part because of financial inducements in the pending rivers-and-harbors bill and in legislation for expositions in Missouri and South Carolina. Probably more influential was the sense of the opposition that the legislation was, as one Democrat said, "not to be so drastic and so savage as I had supposed."[13] On February 27 the Senate voted 43 to 20 in favor of the amendment, and the House followed suit, 161 to 137, on March 1, 1901. Congressional action in this way, under McKinley's guidance, mirrored a general agreement in the legislative and executive branches that the Platt Amendment was an appropriate means of safeguarding the nation's stake in Cuba. Secretary Root, and presumably McKinley, envisioned the third clause, which dealt with potential interventions to protect Cuban independence, not as a blank check for America to interfere but rather as a grant of authority to forestall a repetition of the events of 1898. To that end they were willing to abridge Cuba's sovereignty. If it had relevance in the international situation of 1899 to 1903, during which time the fears of German intrusion were probably overdrawn, the amendment lost its rationale thereafter and became only a source of Cuban-American discord.

The Cubans reacted to the Platt Amendment with immediate unhappiness. The delegates to the constitutional convention had learned of the substance of the American position in mid February, but they declined to accept the concept of intervention, to offer naval stations, or to restrict their government's power to go into debt. When they received news of the congressional action, one of them commented: "Should we concede this, there will be born a government resting upon a supposition of incapacity." The people of Cuba demonstrated against the amendment, and petitions were circulated in opposition to it.

The McKinley administration was willing, in the face of Cuban unrest, to offer assurances that the third article of the amendment did not mean "intermeddling or interference with the affairs of a Cuban Government." In mid April a delegation of Cubans came to Washington and talked with Root and McKinley. The two men privately repeated earlier interpretations of the intervention article and indicated that a tariff-reciprocity treaty would go forward once Cuba had become independent.[14]

By the middle of May the Cubans were proposing further textual changes. Root and the president replied, in McKinley's words,

"I shall regret if the Platt Amendment is not accepted without change." The convention then offered to accept the amendment if it would also include the Teller Amendment, the Peace of Paris, and many of Root's private interpretive comments. In this form it passed by 15 to 14 on May 28. The secretary of war responded that the new version was "in many respects very objectionable." Faced with no alternative but to accept the Platt Amendment, the Cuban convention voted 16 to 11 on June 12 to adopt it. The president had only three months to live when the convention acted. Cuba became independent on May 20, 1902. McKinley believed that the United States had gone a great distance toward the goal for which the American people were "accountable to the Cubans": namely, to achieve "the reconstruction of Cuba as a free commonwealth on abiding foundations of right, justice, liberty and assured order."[15]

Before Congress adjourned on March 4 it also passed an army reorganization bill, which increased the size of the army and began Secretary Root's quest for military reform. The rivers and harbors bill, which McKinley threatened to veto "if they send me a whopper of a bill with a lot of bad things in it," died when western advocates of irrigation filibustered against it in the closing hours of the session. Surveying what the president had accomplished in the short session with regard to enacting the Spooner and Platt amendments, a Republican newspaper, the *Philadelphia Press*, said: "No executive in the history of the country . . . has given a greater exhibition of his influence over Congress than President McKinley."[16]

Although McKinley's second inauguration took place in a driving rainstorm, the crowds stayed out to see the president, and he delivered his address with crisp assurance. Four years before, the nation had been in economic trouble, but "now every avenue of production is crowded with activity, labor is well employed, and American products find good markets at home and abroad." This very prosperity, he added, and the burgeoning productive capacity that fed it "admonish us of the necessity of still further enlarging our foreign markets by broader commercial relations. For this purpose reciprocal trade arrangements with other nations should in liberal spirit be carefully cultivated and promoted."

The remaining paragraphs treated in broad terms the war with Spain and the implications of it. He spoke of sectional harmony and asserted again that Americans would not become imperialistic because of their new foreign commitments. "Our institutions will not deteriorate by extension, and our sense of justice will not abate under tropic suns in distant seas." Before turning to Cuba and the

Philippines, his concluding subjects, he told the world that "we adhere to the principle of equality among ourselves, and by no act of ours will we assign to ourselves a subordinate rank in the family of nations." As the rain subsided, the president returned to the White House in an open carriage amid large and friendly crowds.[17]

A second term meant few changes for a staff that, under Cortelyou's supervision, had grown in response to the changes of McKinley's presidency. The staff of one private secretary and six clerks of March 1897 had swelled to nearly thirty stenographers, telegraphers, clerks, and doorkeepers. The daily rate of mail approached a thousand letters even in quiet periods as Americans looked more and more to the White House as the center of the government. Having handled four hundred thousand items during the first term, the men in the Executive Mansion routinely routed the relevant materials to the executive departments and expertly culled out the one percent of the flow that McKinley regularly saw. Each letter was filed, or a record of the disposition of it was made; and items that were sent to the president were digested and briefed for his action. The presidency was becoming more institutionalized as it assumed the tasks of its modern role.

Relations with the press were also systematized and were generally harmonious. The staff clipped data and editorial opinion from newspapers, and a file went to the president daily. Cortelyou had developed procedures for coordinating the release of major presidential messages and speeches so that all newspapers and press services would receive equal treatment. Under McKinley the emergence of the presidency as a major news center hinged on Cortelyou's capacity as an embryonic press secretary and chief of staff.

McKinley would still not allow the newsmen who saw him to make direct quotations on policy matters, but he gave the journalists more time and attention during the spring of 1901. The president had always been a more adept student of press relations than the public realized, and reporters conceded that he was a master of the timely leak or the trial balloon. "While apparently not courting publicity," Francis E. Leupp wrote twelve years after McKinley's death, he "contrived to put out, by various shrewd processes of indirection, whatever news would best serve the ends of the administration."[18]

The presidential schedule was now well defined and comfortable. McKinley rose and breakfasted at eight. For the next hour or so he looked over the clippings file and read the daily newspapers. Then he entered the Cabinet Room, except on days when the cabinet met, for appointments that went on until 1:30 in the afternoon. After lunch he worked until four. A drive or walk followed, with a regular half-hour nap before dinner at seven. A single bodyguard accompanied him on his outings. McKinley's attitude toward his personal safety was fatalistic, and he often slipped away from his protection to take a walk by himself. His evenings were spent with Mrs. McKinley and friends, often reading the Bible aloud, until ten. An hour of work completed his day, though he frequently read late into the night. Novels, works of history, and the endless reports were his reading materials. McKinley was far more bookish and better informed than his reputation as a nonreading president would seem to indicate. When an army officer in 1899 remarked, after the president had interrogated him closely about Cuban finances, "You do a great deal of work over here." McKinley replied, with heavy irony: "Oh no! We don't work any over here. We just sit around."[19]

At the center of McKinley's emotional life in the White House was his wife, Ida Saxton McKinley. He bore with her determination to carry on as his hostess despite her frequent fits and fainting spells. When one occurred, the president would pass a handkerchief or napkin over her face until the seizure ended. Her physical resources were too limited to meet the demands of being an active First Lady, and during the years of the first term there was a round of near embarrassments, periodic relapses, and incessant demands on McKinley's time. Thanks to Mrs. Garret Hobart, some of the social burdens were eased in 1898 and 1899. Through it all, McKinley remembered his wife as he first knew her. "Ida was the most beautiful girl you ever saw," he said. "She is beautiful to me now." Nothing gave him more pleasure in 1899 than acquiring their old house in Canton and discussing with his wife how they would renovate and restore it. McKinley loved her as he did no one else, and he never chafed under the weight of her invalidism and selfishness. To her he was, until he died, "Your faithful husband and always your lover."[20]

Reporters who saw the president in that spring found him confident and robust. "His face," wrote Julian Ralph, "was plump and glowing with health, with that bloom that belongs to hard, healthy flesh." A visiting journalist from the French paper *Matin* came to the president's office. "You are going to see the Emperor in a dress suit," a diplomat warned him. "His face is as serious and distant as that of a Roman Emperor," the Frenchman decided, and he described McKinley as having "an air of goodness, contentment, and humanity. He is a happy man." Happiness manifested itself in a palpable aura of authority that friends and visitors noticed and remarked upon when they talked with McKinley in 1901.[21]

The end of four years in the presidency occasioned some appraisals of McKinley's performance. A writer in the *Chicago Tribune*, recalling the forecasts that McKinley would be sadly lacking in backbone, concluded that the president now stood with "every pledge redeemed, every awkward situation bravely met and wisely mastered, cool, well poised, popular, honest, suave, but masterful, a man who yields only to have his every way in the end. If this man, the first President of the new century, has no backbone, then we are invertebrate animals." Henry Litchfield West, writing about "The Growing Powers of the President," argued that "in the legislative branch of the Government, it is the executive which influences, if it does not control, the action of Congress; while the power originally vested in the executive alone has increased to an extent of which the framers of the Constitution had no prophetic vision." One Republican author, Henry B. F. Macfarland, looked over McKinley's record, and wrote flatly: "It is simple truth to say that he has met all the extraordinary requirements of an extraordinary period, and met them easily and well, and this is to say that he is a great President."[22]

Now that Congress had adjourned and there were no crises, McKinley wanted to travel once more. These journeys were for him both therapeutic and politically useful. He told a British diplomat in June 1899 that "each trip he made from Washington enabled him to carry out what he considered an important function of his office, viz: that the President and the people should be brought closely together." Even during his first term McKinley had considered leaving the continental United States for a trip to Hawaii, but the communications problems involved in the sea voyage and the absence of a cable to the islands made the trip unworkable. During his second term, as he informed the French ambassador in July 1901, he intended to go to Hawaii, Puerto Rico, and Cuba. The "slightly mixed character" of the Cuban government "would be a step made on the path which would allow the President to leave the soil of the United States." Had he lived, McKinley would have made his travels the occasion, before Roosevelt or Wilson, for breaking the precedent that confined presidents to the nation's continental boundaries.[23]

In the spring of 1901, however, McKinley contented himself with a six-weeks' swing through the South and the Southwest, then on to the West Coast, and back east for the Pan-American Exposition in Buffalo, New York. Five cabinet members accompanied him at various stages of the trip, as did three press photographers and seven reporters. Forty-three people made up the presidential party that departed on April 29. Cortelyou and the staff were there to provide the stenographic reports of McKinley's remarks, the daily itineraries, and the transmission facilities that so pleased the newsmen and converted a "railroad train into an executive office."[24]

The presidential excursion in 1901 also had important policy implications. He intended to make a series of speeches on behalf of the tariff-reciprocity treaties, which the administration had negotiated with several foreign countries but on which the Senate as yet had failed to act. Reciprocity had been emerging as a significant initiative during his first term, though the war and the demands of other issues had delayed its full impact. Now McKinley was ready to throw the weight of his office behind a program of gradual, controlled reductions in the protective system, which would open foreign markets to the United States.

The effort to make the broader reciprocity provisions of section 4 of the Dingley Tariff Act the means to achieve tariff concessions from other nations gathered momentum in 1898 and 1899. Reciprocity commissioner John A. Kasson, once his duties on the Anglo-American Joint High Commission had ceased, commenced talks with France, with Great Britain about its Caribbean colonies, with European nations such as Portugal, and with Latin American countries, the most important of which was Argentina. The French, especially, found Kasson, who was in his late seventies, a difficult bargainer. McKinley closely supervised the discussions, and the dynamic of the evolving negotiations deepened the president's commitment to reciprocity.

Reciprocity with France was a cornerstone in the administration's program. After the signing of the May 1898 agreement under section 3 of the Dingley Tariff Act, both nations moved rapidly to take up the options of section 4, which allowed the United States to offer reductions of up to 20 percent in its tariff rates in exchange for reciprocal concessions from the other party. Then the war and Kasson's obligations with regard to Canadian problems put off further exchanges until November 1898. The United States wanted to obtain the minimum tariff that France offered to its trading partners instead of the maximum rates that were a reaction to the Dingley Tariff Act. France wanted the United States to lower its duties on woolens, silks, cotton products, ready-made clothing, leather products, eyeglasses, and an extensive list of other items.

244

Negotiations went on for eight months. Since the law specified a two-year deadline after July 24, 1897, the White House needed some tangible results from its reciprocity efforts. Attempts in the French Parliament to raise duties on American cottonseed oil in retaliation for higher American rates on olive oil slowed the treaty process. At several critical stages in the bargaining, McKinley intervened to keep the momentum alive. In early June 1899 the talks quickened, when the French sent a special envoy to assist their ambassador. During the next seven weeks the two countries worked out a reciprocity convention, which was signed on July 24, 1899, and in which France applied its minimum tariff duties to some American products and the United States responded not only by reducing duties on hosiery, shoes, eyeglasses, wines, machinery for making clothing, and other commodities but also by giving most-favored-nation treatment to these products. Concessions that France had gained in the last weeks were the result, its diplomats reported, "of a real personal pressure of President McKinley," whose "secret desire and ambition" it was to launch the reciprocity policy.[25]

Kasson concluded other conventions along similar lines with Jamaica and Argentina. The Jamaican document involved lower rates on the island's citrus products. For Argentina the Americans offered reductions on wool, a product that had a powerful constituency in Congress. The president wanted "very much to assure the success" of the reciprocity conventions, and one French writer believed that McKinley sought to break down the European system of maximum and minimum tariffs that excluded American farm and industrial goods.[26]

Reciprocity claimed some political support within the Republican party in the year 1899/1900. Manufacturers of heavy machinery and farm equipment in the Middle West applauded the conventions as providing a way of penetrating European and Latin American markets which had hitherto been closed to their wares. Reductions would also reduce the cost of their raw materials. "The duties are higher on iron and steel than there is any necessity for whatever." Opponents of the policy were more vocal; they pressured protectionist senators to defeat the president. "Is it possible," asked Congressman Charles Grosvenor, "that we are entering upon a system of repudiation and repeal of the Dingley Tariff law?"[27]

McKinley mentioned the state of the reciprocity negotiations in his 1899 annual message. Because the two-year time limit of the Dingley Tariff Act had expired, the president sent them to the Senate as regular treaties, though they had been framed under the provisions of sections 3 and 4 of that act. The early session of 1900 was not a propitious one for favorable action in the upper house. By February the issues of the Puerto Rican tariff and the Hay-Pauncefote Treaty had aroused so much trouble that the pact with Argentina, which had a time limit for consideration of February 10, 1900, was soon faltering. Senator Warren of Wyoming, the leader of the wool men, proclaimed happily that the pact was "deader than a mackrel."[28]

The French convention went to the Senate Committee on Foreign Relations, where Kasson testified for it. To assist the reciprocity commissioner, McKinley enlisted Robert P. Porter, who had previously been an advisor on Cuban policy, to collect support in the Senate. "I think the outlook for the French Treaty is materially improving," Porter said, but the administration in early February could only count forty-seven out of a needed sixty-two votes for the document. The desire to win approval for the Hay-Pauncefote Treaty in these weeks overshadowed the reciprocity convention. In the middle of February the president decided that if the Senate had not ratified the convention by March 24, 1900, he would seek, "as a way of wearing down Senate resistance," an extension of several months in the time allowed for approving it.[29]

Prospects for the treaty darkened in the first half of March. On the positive side, the Committee on Foreign Relations reported it favorably, and Porter thought that a combination of Republican, Democratic, and Populist votes might be assembled. The Senate Finance Committee, however, asked for an opportunity to consider the agreement; and its powerful chairman, Nelson Aldrich, claimed that he needed to study its provisions. The Hay-Pauncefote Treaty was in trouble; and the problem of the Puerto Rican tariff was still unresolved. In an election year, a third quarrel with the Senate, it seemed to the president, would be one too many. McKinley asked the French for a twelve-months' extension of the deadline for ratification. The necessary documents were exchanged in late March 1900. The ratification period for the Argentine treaty was also renewed.

After the election, McKinley endorsed the French and other treaties in his annual message of December 1900. The death of Senator Cushman K. Davis and the defeat of Senator William E. Chandler reduced the number of reciprocity supporters, especially since Davis had chaired the Foreign Relations Committee. The chances for action during the short session were modest. By February 1901 the administration had decided that there was no hope that the Senate would vote on reciprocity before it adjourned. The French were again asked for a further extension of another year, and this was accomplished on March 8, 1901. Other extensions were also secured from Great Britain and Argentina.[30]

Weary from his labors regarding reciprocity, Kasson stepped down in April 1901, "unwilling to proceed with a work which promised to be without result." McKinley was less pessimistic and discouraged. He knew about the forces that were gathering both internally and abroad for tariff changes. When the United States imposed an export bounty on Russian sugar, that nation responded with retaliatory tariffs on American goods. It was a signal of the international reaction against protection. Among the Republicans, Congressman Joseph W. Babcock of Wisconsin had introduced a bill to reduce tariff rates on competing products of the newly formed United States Steel Company. Following up on the remarks in his inaugural address, McKinley told Kasson and a French visitor in late April that he would, on his forthcoming tour, "seize all occasions that would present themselves to defend the policy of commercial reciprocity and change opinion on it."[31]

The major speeches of the trip were to be delivered on the West Coast and throughout the nation's heartland as the president returned home. In the South, where he was warmly received, he began to develop his theme. "We can now supply our own markets," he said in Corinth, Mississippi. "We have reached that point in our industrial development, and in order to secure sale for our surplus products we must open up new avenues for our surplus." A leading protectionist told a senator privately "that our cause is most endangered by the persistent utterances of men in high position, in favor of broadening our policy and relaxing our defenses."[32]

The tour itself was a triumphal procession. In the South, in Texas, in New Mexico, and finally in Los Angeles, large crowds appeared. The president's popularity was impressive, even to the reporters who accompanied him. Then the trip took a somber turn. Mrs. McKinley's inflamed finger became infected, and her health faltered. Death seemed imminent. The First Lady did not give in to her malady, and she gradually rallied as the president attended to a limited schedule of ceremonial duties in San Francisco. Finally, she was well enough for their train journey to Washington. There were no speeches for reciprocity in the spring of 1901, and McKinley postponed the trip to the Pan American Exposition. A month of work in Washington remained. He then planned to spend several quiet months of vacation in Canton before making his speech in Buffalo in early September.

While he had been gone and during the first half of 1901, old problems were solved, and the early hints of new troubles appeared. The Supreme Court on May 27, 1901, in the Insular Cases, resolved the issue of whether the constitution covered the Philippines and Puerto Rico. The justices decided that the new possessions belonged to the United States and were therefore under the authority of Congress but that their inhabitants were not United States citizens. The ruling upheld the position that the administration had taken regarding the Puerto Rican legislation of 1900.

In the cabinet the president first sought to have Joseph Hodges Choate replace Attorney General Griggs, who was retiring. When Choate declined, McKinley turned to Philander C. Knox of Pennsylvania. Also from Pennsylvania came a request from the United Mine Workers that before taking his trip, the president mediate between workers and owners in the impending anthracite-coal strike. A similar appeal was made to Senator Hanna, which resulted in an agreement that ran until April 1902, when the coal strike began that Theodore Roosevelt eventually settled later in the year. In the political arena, McKinley appears, by using direct patronage support, to have encouraged Senator John L. McLaurin of South Carolina in a campaign to create a "Commercial Democracy" in the South. To what extent the president thought that McLaurin might become a Republican or that this initiative represented an effort to build up a Lily White GOP in Dixie is not certain. One of the president's agents told Cortelyou: "If McLaurin is properly backed there will be a revolution in the 'Solid South.'" McKinley's death and the senator's own mistakes ended the campaign before it could have any impact on southern politics.[33]

During McKinley's travels there was a brief panic on the New York stock market, when J. P. Morgan, James J. Hill, and E. H. Harriman were battling for control of the Northern Pacific Railroad. Following closely on the creation of the United States Steel Company, this additional demonstration of consolidation added to popular fears about the trusts. When the truce among the railroad leaders produced the Northern Securities Company in late 1901, Theodore Roosevelt instructed the Justice Department to prosecute it under the antitrust law. At that time Senator Hanna said: "I warned Hill that McKinley might have to act against his damn company last year. Mr. Roosevelt's done it." Cortelyou remembered McKinley's saying to him as they spent the summer in

Canton, "This trust question has got to be taken up in earnest, and soon." Cortelyou believed that there was a direct line of continuity between McKinley's desire to address the "evils inseparable from the new conditions" and the trust policies of Roosevelt's early years.[34]

In this connection, tariff reciprocity could play a significant part. Reductions of tariff duties, if they did not attack the entire protective system, could defuse discontent about rising consumer prices and about the selling of protected products at a lower cost overseas. McKinley used his time at Canton to prepare material "for a series of speeches in which he proposed to develop progressively his ideas on the extension of our foreign trade through the means of reciprocity treaties." He also asked for "the collection of data on the subject of trusts." Cortelyou told an interviewer in 1908: "I never saw him more determined on anything than on this."[35]

Throughout the spring and summer of 1901, evidence of the president's intentions accumulated in the manner that was so characteristic of McKinley. The administration supported the Chicago-based National Business League in its lobbying for the French treaty. Senator Hanna, though he was opposed to the pact, described McKinley in June 1901 as "a strong advocate of reciprocity" who would "consider treaties along the line of mutual interest between this country and another." In that same month, Senator Lodge wrote to Nelson Aldrich about reciprocity: "I suppose you know that that policy is going to be pressed upon us next winter." Lodge also expected a proreciprocity majority to emerge on the Foreign Relations Committee unless the protectionists convinced their colleagues to oppose the White House.[36]

When the president talked about the tariff in late June with Cortelyou, "he said that it would be intensely amusing to have the tariff revived as an issue, that the only party that could revise the tariff was the Republican," since the Democrats had so often mishandled it. "The President doubts," Cortelyou wrote, "whether the tariff will be an issue of the next campaign." In June, McKinley also quelled third-term talk that might have cast doubt on the sincerity of his forthcoming speeches. When several Republicans came out for his renomination in 1904, an irritated president released a crisp statement. "I will say now, once for all, expressing a long settled conviction, that I not only am not and will not be a candidate for a third term, but would not accept a nomination for it if it were tendered me."[37]

The announcement allowed the Republican hopefuls for 1904,

particularly Vice-President Theodore Roosevelt, to resume their early drives to round up backers. From his Canton retreat, McKinley pressed on with the shaping of his Buffalo remarks and signaled his intentions to the party and to the nation. In early August, Senator Shelby Cullom, likely the next chairman of the Foreign Relations Committee, told newsmen, after a visit to McKinley, that "it would be wise" to ratify some of the treaties. A British diplomat informed London that Cullom's words "have been taken as an indication that there will be a renewal on the part of the Executive to recommend Congress to take action" on the reciprocity issue.[38]

Amid the calm rhythms of the Ohio summer, McKinley pulled his speech together. Cortelyou assembled literature on reciprocity from the State Department, and he clipped items from the press regarding campaigns in Europe to conduct tariff reprisals against the United States. As the speech neared completion in August, the president received an indication of the domestic impact of his policy. Iowa Republicans included a plank in their state platform seeking "any modification of the tariff schedules that may be required to prevent their affording a shelter to monopoly." To a visiting Iowan, Congressman Jonathan P. Dolliver, he spoke of the need to press for reciprocity.[39]

August ended, and the president's party prepared to leave for Buffalo on September 4. The speech was ready, typed out on the small papers that he used. Other copies went to the newspapers, with the usual restrictions on formal release only after the speech had been delivered. On the President's Day at the Exposition, to a crowd estimated at nearly fifty thousand, McKinley gave the speech that was to keynote the policy goals of his second term. "Expositions are the timekeepers of progress," he said. He spoke of how modern inventions had changed American life and explained that, because of greater ease of communication, "isolation is no longer possible or desirable." As examples, he cited how the government had directed the war over the telegraph and how accustomed citizens had become to having information readily accessible. International disputes, he concluded, would now not arise from misunderstandings, and could be settled through international arbitration.

The nation's "unexampled prosperity" in 1901 next drew his attention. "We have a vast and intricate business built up through years of toil and struggle, in which every part of the country has its stake, which will not permit of either neglect or undue selfishness. No narrow, sordid policy will subserve it." Looking to the country's trade needs, McKinley reached the heart of his speech. "By sensible trade arrangements which will not interrupt our home production, we shall extend the outlets for our increasing surplus," the president said, adding that "we must not respose in fancied security that we can forever sell everything and buy little or nothing." Therefore, "reciprocity is the natural outgrowth of our wonderful industrial development under the domestic policy now firmly established." Then he summed up his policy: "The period of exclusiveness is past. The expansion of our trade and commerce is the pressing problem. Commercial wars are unprofitable. A policy of goodwill and friendly trade relations will prevent reprisals. Reciprocity treaties are in harmony with the spirit of the times; measures of retaliation are not."

In the rest of the address he discussed the merchant marine and ended with a warm invocation of the name of James G. Blaine, "whose mind was ever alert and thought ever constant for a larger commerce and a truer fraternity of the republics of the New World." The crowd applauded enthusiastically the reference to the man who had brought the Republicans to protectionism in the 1880s and who had converted McKinley to reciprocity in 1890.[40] The speech summed up an era of Republican policy and forecast the GOP's movement into another age of its history under McKinley's adroit direction. He had never been averse to using the presidency as a bully pulpit. In the Buffalo appearance he sounded a loftily, enlightened theme that revealed how much he had brought to the office, how much he had grown in it, and how he was shaping it for the challenges of a new century.

As part of his visit, McKinley scheduled a public reception at the Temple of Music on the afternoon of September 6. Even though three secret-service men were now guarding the president, along with four special guards and a number of soldiers, Cortelyou worried about the security arrangements that afternoon. McKinley, who waved aside his secretary's apprehensions, was in the hall at four o'clock. Seven or eight minutes later, Leon Czolgosz, an anarchist, fired two shots at the president as the two men stood in the receiving line. One bullet bounced off a button; the other entered McKinley's stomach and was never located. When the crowd fell upon Czolgosz, McKinley said to Cortelyou: "Don't hurt him." The assassin was, McKinley added, "some poor misguided fellow." Wounded and in shock, the president thought first of Mrs. McKinley. "My wife," he told Cortelyou, "be careful how you tell her—oh, be careful." In these moments the presidency of William McKinley was ended. He had a little more than a week to live as gangrene and infection eroded his strength and eventually killed him. He died in the early morning of September 14, 1901, whispering the words of "Nearer My God to Thee." McKinley, John Hay said in his eulogy in 1902, "showed in his life how a citizen should live, and in his last hour taught us how a gentleman could die."[41]

The nation experienced a wave of genuine grief at the news of McKinley's passing. The state funeral in Washington and the formal services at Canton echoed to the music of the last hymn that he had sung. On the day of his burial, September 19, 1901, Americans paused for five minutes of silence at 3:30 in the afternoon. A month of mourning followed, and with it the plans for memorials, the eulogies, and the hastily written biographies. In Canton arose the McKinley Memorial, dedicated in 1907, where the bodies of the president, his wife, and their children lie. Cortelyou took custody of the presidential papers, and using this source, Charles S. Olcott published the authorized two-volume *Life of William McKinley* in 1916.

Despite the warmth and love that McKinley had evoked in the people of the United States, the memory of him faded rapidly. Roosevelt let the broad campaign for reciprocity slide away, and he pursued the trusts with lawsuits and legislation. The new president's youth, his enthusiasm, and the controversies that crackled around him directed the public's thoughts into fresh avenues. There was the Square Deal, then William Howard Taft, then Woodrow Wilson. By the time of World War I the picture of McKinley as president, which had been so vivid in 1901, had grown fuzzy and vague.

Historical scholarship after 1920 created the McKinley that textbooks and general accounts have made so familiar. His handling of the Cuban crisis came in for particular criticism, but the whole record of his administration was deemed to have been no more than a mediocre prelude to the vigor and energy of Theodore Roosevelt's. In the 1950s and 1960s McKinley's reputation received a more favorable evaluation from specialists in the late nineteenth century, and that process of reappraisal is continuing. Within the general profession of history, however, his standing improved slightly for a time and then fell back. Placed eighteenth in a 1948 survey on "presidential greatness," he rose three notches by 1962 to stand fifteenth, trailing behind Rutherford B. Hayes. Six years later, in another survey, his "accomplishments" were evaluated at seventeenth among chief executives, behind Taft and Cleveland. The most recent such poll places him twenty-second, with Cleveland rated eleventh.[42]

William McKinley did not often speculate on his place in history. A man, he once said, might aspire "to be an inspiration for history,"[43] but he probably would not have been surprised that historians have ranked his presidency in the middle range and lower. Greatness is appropriately reserved for only a few presidents, a group in which McKinley does not belong. Yet, if the standards of judgment include strength as president and impact on the history of the office, then McKinley's tenure gains in importance. On these grounds, for instance, he easily merits a higher place than Hayes or Cleveland. He was a political leader who confirmed the Republicans as the nation's majority party; he was the architect of important departures in foreign policy; and he was a significant contributor to the evolution of the modern presidency. On these achievements rest his substantial claims as an important figure in the history of the United States.

Notes

CHAPTER 1

1. William H. Crook to John Addison Porter, March 19, 1897, William McKinley Papers, Manuscript Division, Library of Congress; C. C. Buel, "Our Fellow-Citizen of the White House: The Official Cares of a President of the United States," *Century Magazine* 53 (1897): 653.
2. John Addison Porter to Charles W. Fairbanks, March 20, 1897, McKinley Papers.
3. John Sherman, *John Sherman's Recollections of Forty Years in the House, Senate and Cabinet*, 2 vols. (Chicago: Werner Co., 1895), 1:375.
4. "Cleveland, the 'Strong Man,'" *Literary Digest* 14 (1897): 290; Henry Loomis Nelson, "The Weakness of the Executive Power in Democracy," *Harper's Monthly* 98 (1899): 213.
5. Henry L. Stoddard, *As I Knew Them: Presidents and Politics from Grant to Coolidge* (New York: Harper & Bros., 1927), p. 208.
6. Champ Clark, *My Quarter Century of American Politics*, 2 vols. (New York: Harper & Bros., 1920), 1:239, on Thurber; *Review of Reviews* 15 (1897): 387; David S. Barry, "News-Getting at the Capital," *Chautauquan* 26 (1897): 283.
7. Julia B. Foraker, *I Would Live It Again* (New York and London: Harper & Bros., 1932), p. 263.
8. *Speeches and Addresses of William McKinley* (New York: D. Appleton & Co., 1893), p. 430; Charles S. Olcott, *The Life of William McKinley*, 2 vols. (Boston and New York: Houghton Mifflin Co., 1916), 1:186.
9. *Speeches and Addresses of William McKinley*, pp. 190, 194.
10. "Reminiscences," Charles Warren Fairbanks Papers, Lilly Library, Indiana University, Bloomington.
11. Thomas C. Platt, *The Autobiography of Thomas Collier Platt*, comp. and ed. Louis J. Lang (New York: B. W. Dodge & Co., 1910), p. 313.
12. Olcott, *Life of William McKinley*, 2:346, italics in original.
13. Statement of Sen. Charles Dick, February 10, 1906, Hanna-McCormick Family Papers, Manuscript Division, Library of Congress.
14. George W. Steevens, *The Land of the Dollar*, 2d ed. (Edinburgh and London: William Blackwood & Sons, 1897), p. 129.
15. Olcott, *Life of William McKinley*, 1:313.
16. Richard J. Jensen, *The Winning of the Midwest: Social and Political Conflict, 1888–1896* (Chicago: University of Chicago Press, 1971), p. 288.
17. McKinley to Hermann H. Kohlsaat, August 5, 1896, McKinley Papers; *McKinley's Speeches in August*, comp. Joseph P. Smith (n.p.: Republican National Committee, 1896), p. 32.
18. Thomas Beer, *Hanna* (New York: Alfred A. Knopf, 1929), p. 163.
19. Edward Nelson Dingley, *The Life and Times of Nelson Dingley, Jr.* (Kalamazoo, Mich.: Ihling Bros. & Everard, 1902), pp. 411–412.
20. Lyman J. Gage to F. O. Willey, August 10, 1898, author's collection, quotes him on labor; Moses

P. Handy, "Lyman J. Gage: A Character Sketch," *Review of Reviews* 15 (1897): 300, quotes McKinley.

21. *Public Opinion* 22 (1897): 135.
22. Sherman to Hanna, November 13, 1896, in Herbert Croly, *Marcus Alonzo Hanna: His Life and Work* (New York: Macmillan Co., 1912), p. 234; Sherman to Hanna, December 15, 1896, McKinley Papers.
23. McKinley to Sherman, January 4, 1897, and William M. Osborne to Charles Grosvenor, January 6, 1897, McKinley Papers.
24. Sherman to "My Dear Sir," November 8, 1898, in Joseph Benson Foraker, *Notes of a Busy Life*, 2 vols. (Cincinnati, Ohio: Stewart & Kidd Co., 1916), 1:508–509.
25. Osborne to McKinley, December 11, 1896, and McKinley to Joseph Medill, February 8, 1897, McKinley Papers.
26. Sherman to McKinley, February 15, 1897, McKinley Papers.

27. Hanna to McKinley, February 1, 1897, and McKinley to Asa S. Bushnell, February 22, 1897, McKinley Papers.
28. *Washington Post*, March 5, 1897; D. Nicholson to Francis B. Loomis, February 23, 1897, Francis B. Loomis Papers, Stanford University Library.
29. Henry Cabot Lodge to Theodore Roosevelt, December 2, 1896, in *Selections from the Correspondence of Theodore Roosevelt and Henry Cabot Lodge, 1884–1918*, ed. Henry Cabot Lodge, 2 vols. (New York and London: Charles Scribner's Sons, 1925), 1:241.
30. Charles G. Dawes, *A Journal of the McKinley Years*, ed. Bascom N. Timmons (Chicago: Lakeside Press, 1950), p. 115; George F. Parker, *Recollections of Grover Cleveland* (New York: Century Co., 1909), pp. 249–250.
31. *Washington Post*, March 5, 1897; *San Francisco Examiner*, March 4, 1897.

CHAPTER 2

1. *New York Tribune*, March 5, 1897.
2. The statistics in this paragraph and in the pages that follow appear in United States, Bureau of the Census, *Historical Statistics of the United States: Colonial Times to 1970* 2 vols. (Washington, D.C.: Government Printing Office, 1975).
3. *Speeches and Addresses of William McKinley from March 1, 1897, to May 30, 1900* (New York: Doubleday & McClure, 1900), p. 2.
4. *London Economist*, March 20, 1897, p. 420, and March 27, 1897, p. 453.
5. *Speeches and Addresses of William McKinley from March 1, 1897*, pp. 2–3.
6. Paolo E. Coletta, *William Jennings Bryan*, vol. 1: *Political Evangelist, 1860–1908* (Lincoln:

University of Nebraska Press, 1964), p. 213.
7. "The Courting of Prosperity," *Literary Digest* 15 (1897): 181–182.
8. *Speeches and Addresses of William McKinley from March 1, 1897*, p. 4.
9. Ibid., p. 6.
10. George Frisbie Hoar to Moorfield Storey, March 6, 1900, George Frisbie Hoar Papers, Massachusetts Historical Society, Boston.
11. *McKinley's Speeches in August*, comp. Joseph P. Smith (n.p.: Republican National Committee, 1896), p. 12; *Speeches and Addresses of William McKinley from March 1, 1897*, p. 14.
12. *Speeches and Addresses of William McKinley from March 1, 1897*, p. 7; Lord Herschell to Lord Salisbury, November 25, 1898, Papers of the Third Mar-

quess of Salisbury, 3M/A 140/6, Hatfield House, Hertfordshire, England.

13. *Speeches and Addresses of William McKinley from March 1, 1897*, pp. 8, 9.

14. George Sinkler, *The Racial Attitudes of American Presidents, from Abraham Lincoln to Theodore Roosevelt* (Garden City, N.Y.: Doubleday & Co., 1971), pp. 295-296; Edmund L. Drago, "The Black Press and Populism, 1890-1896," *San Jose Studies* 1 (1975): 102.

15. Sinkler, *Racial Attitudes*, p. 297; *Speeches and Addresses of William McKinley from March 1, 1897*, p. 168.

16. *McKinley's Speeches in August*, p. 47; *Speeches and Addresses of William McKinley from March 1, 1897*, p. 15.

17. *Speeches and Addresses of William McKinley from March 1, 1897*, pp. 9-10; *Public Opinion* 22 (March 11, 1897): 295, quoting the *Terre Haute Gazette*; George T. Oliver, "Industrial Combinations," *Forum* 23 (1897): 298.

18. *Republican Campaign Text Book, 1896* (Washington, D.C.: Hartman & Cadick, 1896), pp. 247, 252.

19. *Speeches and Addresses of William McKinley, from His Election to Congress to the Present Time* (New York: D. Appleton & Co., 1893), pp. 327, 465-466.

20. *A Compilation of the Messages and Papers of the Presidents, 1789-1897*, comp. James D. Richardson, 10 vols. (Washington, D.C.: Government Printing Office, 1898), 9:761; *Speeches and Addresses of William McKinley from March 1, 1897*, p. 10.

21. *Republican Campaign Text Book*,

p. 256; *McKinley's Speeches in August*, p. 45; *Speeches and Addresses of William McKinley from May 1, 1897*, p. 10.

22. *Speeches and Addresses of William McKinley from May 1, 1897*, p. 10; *Speeches and Addresses of William McKinley from His Election*, p. 396; *McKinley's Speeches in August*, p. 46; George Frederick William Holls to H. W. Diederich, February 19, 1897, George Frederick William Holls Papers, Columbia University Library.

23. *Speeches and Addresses of William McKinley from May 1, 1897*, pp. 10-11.

24. *New York Times*, December 18, 1895; Henry Cabot Lodge to Theodore Roosevelt, December 2, 1896, in *Selections from the Correspondence of Theodore Roosevelt and Henry Cabot Lodge, 1884-1918*, ed. Henry Cabot Lodge, 2 vols. (New York and London: Charles Scribner's Sons, 1925), 1:241; Mayo W. Hazeltine, "The Foreign Policy of the New Administration," *North American Review* 164 (1897): 486.

25. Robert M. La Follette, *La Follette's Autobiography* (Madison, Wis.: Robert M. La Follette Co., 1913), p. 115; "La Prorogation de la convention americaine," *L'Exportation française* 25 (1900): 100.

26. Carl Schurz, *Speeches, Correspondence and Political Papers of Carl Schurz*, ed. Frederic Bancroft, 6 vols. (New York: G. P. Putnam's Sons, 1913), 6:270-271.

27. *Speeches and Addresses of William McKinley from May 1, 1897*, p. 24.

28. Ibid., p. 11.

29. Ibid., p. 12.

30. Ibid.

31. Ibid., pp. 13, 14.

32. Ibid., p. 15.

CHAPTER 3

1. *Pittsburg Times*, March 22, 1897.

2. *Baltimore American*, April 4,

1897, made the comparison with Grant; Henry L. Stoddard, *As I*

Knew Them: Presidents and Politics from Grant to Coolidge (New York: Harper & Bros., 1927), p. 231.

3. *New York Tribune*, March 24, 1897.

4. *New York Tribune*, June 15, 1897, described the Vanderbilt incident; *Ohio State Journal*, October 30, 1897, discussed the journalistic ceremony.

5. Charles Emory Smith, "McKinley in the Cabinet Room," *Saturday Evening Post*, August 30, 1902, p. 1; John Sherman to W. S. Ward, April 28, 1898, John Sherman Papers, Manuscript Division, Library of Congress; Diary, April 16, 1898, box 52, George B. Cortelyou Papers, Manuscript Division, Library of Congress.

6. *New York Tribune*, March 14, 1897.

7. *Washington Post*, April 9, 1897; Edward O. Wolcott to Henry White, May 4, 1897, Henry White Papers, Manuscript Division, Library of Congress.

8. Jules Patenôtre to Gabriel Hanotaux, May 13, 1897, Correspondance consulaire et commerciale, Washington, vol. 33, Archives du Ministère des Affairs étrangères, Paris, hereafter cited as MAE.

9. *Chicago Tribune*, May 9, 1897.

10. U.S., Congress, *Congressional Record*, 55th Cong., 1st sess. (May 25, 1897), p. 1227.

11. Edmond Bruwaert to Maurice Bompard, July 2, 1897, Correspondance consulaire et commerciale, Washington, vol. 33, MAE.

12. Bruwaert to Bompard, July 23, 1897, Correspondance consulaire et commerciale, Washington, vol. 33, MAE.

13. *New York Tribune*, October 15, 1897; John A. Kasson to William E. Chandler, October 22, 1897, William E. Chandler Papers, Manuscript Division, Library of Congress.

14. Jules Cambon to Gabriel Hanotaux, June 2, 1898, Correspondance consulaire et commerciale, Washington, vol. 34, MAE.

15. Draft Agreement on Bimetallism, June 1897, Edward O. Wolcott Papers, Colorado Historical Society, Denver.

16. Henry White to Henry Cabot Lodge, October 29, 1897, Henry Cabot Lodge Papers, Massachusetts Historical Society, Boston; Sir Michael Hicks-Beach to Wolcott, August 5, 1897, Wolcott Papers.

17. Lord Elgin et al. to Lord George Hamilton, September 16, 1897, Wolcott Papers.

18. McKinley to John Hay, July 27, 1897, McKinley Papers; Charles J. Paine to Chandler, September 16, 1897, Chandler Papers.

19. *A Supplement to A Compilation of the Messages and Papers of the Presidents, 1789–1902*, by James D. Richardson, comp. George Raywood Devitt (Washington, D.C.: Bureau of National Literature and Art, 1903), pp. 23, 24; *Speeches and Addresses of William McKinley from March 1, 1897, to May 30, 1900* (New York: Doubleday & McClure, 1900), pp. 55, 64.

20. William Adam Russ, *The Hawaiian Republic, 1894–98, and Its Struggle to Win Annexation* (Selinsgrove, Pa.: Susquehanna University Press, 1961), p. 127.

21. U.S., Senate, *Report*, no. 681, 55th Cong., 2d sess. (Washington, D.C.: Government Printing Office, 1898), p. 66.

22. Merze Tate, *The United States and the Hawaiian Kingdom: A Political History* (New Haven, Conn.: Yale University Press, 1965), p. 282; George Frisbie Hoar, *Autobiography of Seventy Years*, 2 vols. (New York: Charles Scribner's Sons, 1903), 2:308.

23. Lodge to Stephen P. O'Meara, January 3, 1898, Lodge Papers.

24. Diary, June 8, 1898, box 52, Cortelyou Papers; *Nation* 66 (1898): 80; *New York Times*, March 14, 1898.

25. Herbert Croly, *Marcus Alonzo Hanna: His Life and Work* (New York: Macmillan Co., 1912), p. 297.

26. Joseph L. Bristow, *Fraud and Politics at the Turn of the Century* (New York: Exposition Press, 1952), p. 95.

27. Ibid., p. 70.

28. Max Seckendorff to Whitelaw Reid, May 7, 1897, Whitelaw Reid Papers, Manuscript Division, Library of Congress.

29. Shelby Cullom to James H. Wilson, June 25, 1897, James H. Wilson Papers, Manuscript Division, Library of Congress; Cullom to McKinley, July 30, 1897, McKinley Papers.

30. *American Monthly Review of Reviews* 20 (1899): 261.

31. *Washington Post*, November 30, 1897; William Dudley Foulke, *Fighting the Spoilsmen: Reminiscences of the Civil Service Reform Movement* (New York and London: G. P. Putnam's Sons, 1919), p. 129.

32. *Philadelphia Public Ledger*, July 30, 1897; Carl Schurz to McKinley, October 17 and December 24, 1897, in Carl Schurz, *Speeches, Correspondence and Political Papers of Carl Schurz*, ed. Frederic Bancroft, 6 vols. (New York: G. P.

Putnam's Sons, 1913), 5:430, 450.

33. McKinley to James Ford Rhodes, September 18, 1897, McKinley Papers; Theodore Roosevelt to Seth Low, October 15, 1897, in *The Letters of Theodore Roosevelt*, ed. Elting E. Morison et al., 8 vols. (Cambridge, Mass.: Harvard University Press, 1951-1954), 1:697; Seckendorff to Reid, October 22, 1897, Reid Papers.

34. *Chicago Tribune*, November 4, 1897; *New York Tribune*, November 4, 1897.

35. McKinley to Schurz, October 13, 1897, McKinley Papers; McKinley to Hanna, November 4, 1897, Hanna-McCormick Family Papers.

36. James H. Wilson to John J. McCook, November 9, 1897, Wilson Papers; *Washington Post*, November 12, 1897; McKinley to J. P. Jones, January 10, 1898, and McKinley to Hanna, January 10, 1898, box 66, Cortelyou Papers.

37. Thomas C. Platt to Lucien L. Bonheur, January 26, 1898, author's collection; *New York World*, March 4, 1898.

38. George F. W. Holls to Andrew D. White, September 3, 1897, Albert Shaw Papers, in Astor, Lenox and Tilden Foundations, New York Public Library.

CHAPTER 4

1. Philip S. Foner, *The Spanish-Cuban-American War and the Birth of American Imperialism, 1895-1902*, 2 vols. (New York and London: Monthly Review Press, 1972), 1:2.

2. Ibid., 1:128, 129.

3. Thomas Hart Baker, Jr., "Imperial Finale: Crisis, Decolonization, and War in Spain, 1890-1898" (Ph.D. diss., Princeton University, 1977), pp. 186-187.

4. Ibid., p. 205, quotes the song; Enrique Dupuy de Lôme to Richard Olney, June 4, 1896, U.S., Department of State, *Papers Relating to the Foreign Relations of*

the United States, 1897 (Washington, D.C.: Government Printing Office, 1898), p. 546 (hereafter cited as *For. Rel.*, with year).

5. *Public Opinion* 23 (1897): 35.

6. Richard Olney to Enrique Dupuy de Lôme, April 4, 1896, *For Rel.*, 1897, p. 543.

7. Dupuy de Lôme to Olney, June 4, 1896, *For. Rel.*, 1897, p. 547.

8. *A Compilation of the Messages and Papers of the Presidents, 1789-1897*, comp. James D. Richardson, 10 vols. (Washington, D.C.: Government Printing Office, 1898-1899), 10:719, 721.

9. *New York Tribune*, April 15, 1897.
10. Foner, *Spanish-Cuban-American War*, 1:117.
11. John Sherman to Dupuy de Lôme, June 26, 1897, *For. Rel.*, 1897, pp. 507–508.
12. "Offer of Spanish Mission to Mr. Low, May 1897," John Bassett Moore Papers, box 1, Manuscript Division, Library of Congress.
13. *Washington Post*, October 4, 1897.
14. Sherman to Stewart Woodford, July 16, 1897, *For. Rel.*, 1898, pp. 559–561.
15. *Chicago Tribune*, November 20, 1897.
16. *For. Rel.*, 1897, p. XX, for McKinley's message.
17. *New York Tribune*, December 15, 1897; Tasker H. Bliss to Major Wagner, memorandum dated January 3, 1898, Russell A. Alger Papers, William L. Clements Library, University of Michigan, Ann Arbor.
18. Arent S. Crowninshield to John D. Long, February 28, 1898, box 9, William R. Day Papers, Manuscript Division, Library of Congress.
19. Lee to Day, January 12, 1898, *For. Rel.*, 1898, p. 1024; Dupuy de Lôme to Pio Gullon, January 16, 1898, *Spanish Diplomatic Correspondence and Documents, 1896–1900: Presented to the Cortes by the Minister of State* (Washington, D.C.: Government Printing Office, 1905), pp. 64–65; Baker, "Imperial Finale," p. 310.
20. Julian Pauncefote to Lord Salisbury, January 20, 1898, FO5/2361, Public Record Office, London; U.S., House of Representatives, *Congressional Record*, 55th Cong., 2d sess. (January 19, 1898), p. 769.
21. Memorandum of Day's interview with Dupuy de Lôme, January 24, 1898, box 35, Day Papers.
22. Memorandum, January 24, 1898, box 35, Day Papers; Lee to Day, January 26, 1898, box 124, Moore Papers; Dupuy de Lôme to Pio Gullon, January 28, 1898, *Spanish Diplomatic Correspondence*, p. 71.
23. Woodford to Gullon, December 20, 1897, and Gullon to Woodford, February 1, 1898, *For. Rel.*, 1898, pp. 649, 664, 660.
24. Dupuy de Lôme to Don José Canalejas, n.d., *For. Rel.*, 1898, pp. 1007–1008.
25. Lee to Day, February 16, 1898, *For. Rel.*, 1898, p. 1029; D. W. Dickens, "Memorandum for the Secretary," December 8, 1898, Ohio State Historical Society, Columbus.
26. John L. Offner, "President McKinley and the Origins of the Spanish-American War" (Ph.D. diss., Pennsylvania State University, 1957), p. 213; *Speeches and Addresses of William McKinley from March 1, 1897, to May 30, 1900* (New York: Doubleday & McClure, 1900), p. 77.
27. Offner, "President McKinley," p. 221; Ernest R. May, *Imperial Democracy: The Emergence of America as a Great Power* (New York: Harcourt, Brace & World, 1961), pp. 142, 143.
28. *New York Tribune*, March 8, 1898; Theodore Roosevelt to John D. Long, February 16, 1898, in *The Letters of Theodore Roosevelt*, ed. Elting E. Morison et al., 8 vols. (Cambridge, Mass.: Harvard University Press, 1951–1954), 1:773.
29. Woodford to McKinley, March 8, 1898, *For. Rel.*, 1898, p. 684.
30. "Memoranda prepared by H[oratio]. S. R[ubens]. and delivered to Assistant Secretary Day, March 1, 1898," box 56, Cortelyou Papers; Foner, *Spanish-Cuban-American War*, 1:248.
31. Diary, March 19, 1898, Oscar S. Straus Papers, Manuscript Division, Library of Congress.
32. Woodford to McKinley, March 19, 1898, *For. Rel.*, 1898, p. 693, italics in original.
33. *Congressional Record*, 55th Cong., 2d sess. (March 17, 1898), pp.

2919, 2917; Francis E. Warren to Gibson Clark, Francis E. Warren Papers, University of Wyoming Library, Laramie.

34. John Coit Spooner to N. L. James, March 14, 1898, John Coit Spooner Papers, Manuscript Division, Library of Congress; *Nation* 66 (1898): 195; Paul S. Holbo, "The Convergence of Moods and the Cuban-Bond 'Conspiracy' of 1898," *Journal of American History* 55 (1968): 59.

35. Diary, March 26, 1898, box 52, Cortelyou Papers; *New York Tribune*, April 1, 1898; Hermann Hagedorn, *Leonard Wood*, 2 vols. (New York: Harper & Bros., 1931), 1:141; John Davis Long, *America of Yesterday, as Reflected in the Journal of John Davis Long*, ed. Lawrence Shaw Mayo (Boston: Atlantic Monthly Press, 1923), p. 175.

36. Day to Woodford, March 20, 1898, *For. Rel.*, 1898, pp. 692–693; *New York Herald*, March 25, 1898.

37. Day to Woodford, March 26 and 28, 1898, and Woodford to Day, March 27, 1898, *For. Rel.*, 1898, pp. 704, 712–713.

38. Day to Woodford, March 27, 1898, *For. Rel.*, 1898, pp. 711–712.

39. Woodford to Day, March 31, 1898, *For. Rel.*, 1898, pp. 726–727.

40. *New York Herald*, March 29, 1898; Diary, March 29, 1898, box 52, Cortelyou Papers; *Congressional Record*, 55th Cong., 2d sess. (March 28, 1898), pp. 3278–3279.

41. *New York Tribune*, April 2, 1898; Diary, March 31, 1898, box 52, Cortelyou Papers; Elihu Root to Cornelius N. Bliss, April 2, 1898, Elihu Root Papers, Manuscript Division, Library of Congress.

42. Woodford to McKinley, April 3, 1898, and Day to Woodford, April 3 and 4, 1898, *For. Rel.*, 1898, pp. 732–733.

43. Lee to Day, April 6, 1898, quoted in Offner, "President McKinley," p. 328; Diary, April 6, 1898, box 52, Cortelyou Papers; Journal, April 6, 1898, Lodge Papers.

44. *For. Rel.*, 1898, pp. 740–741.

45. Baker, "Imperial Finale," p. 392.

46. Woodford to McKinley, April 10, 1898, Luis Polo de Bernabé to John Sherman, April 10, 1898, *For. Rel.*, 1898, pp. 747–748; May, *Imperial Democracy*, p. 157.

47. Baker, "Imperial Finale," p. 394.

48. Journal, April 4, 1898, John D. Long Papers, Massachusetts Historical Society, Boston.

49. *For. Rel.*, 1898, pp. 754–755; Henry Cabot Lodge, *The War with Spain* (New York and London: Harper & Bros., 1899), p. 35.

50. *For. Rel.*, 1898, pp. 757–759; Lodge, *War with Spain*, p. 35.

51. *For. Rel.*, 1898, pp. 759, 760.

52. *Washington Star*, April 11, 1898; Diary, April 12, 1898, box 52, Cortelyou Papers.

53. *Washington Star*, April 14, 1898; *Washington Evening Times*, April 11, 1898, quoted in Paul S. Holbo, "Presidential Leadership in Foreign Affairs: William McKinley and the Turpie-Foraker Amendment," *American Historical Review* 72 (1967): 1325; *Congressional Record*, 55th Cong., 2d sess. (April 13, 1898), pp. 3819–3820.

54. Holbo, "Presidential Leadership," p. 1328; William Boyd Allison to M. M. Ham, April 18, 1898, William Boyd Allison Papers, box 323, Iowa State Department of History and Archives, Des Moines.

55. *Washington Star*, April 16, 1898; Cornelius N. Bliss to Root, April 19, 1898, Root Papers; Holbo, "Presidential Leadership," p. 1333.

56. Walter LaFeber, *The New Empire: An Interpretation of American Expansion, 1860–1898* (Ithaca, N.Y.: Cornell University Press, 1963), p. 400.

CHAPTER 5

1. Redfield Proctor to Russell A. Alger, August 15, 1898, Alger Papers.

2. Diary, June 8, 1898, box 52, Cortelyou Papers; Charles Emory Smith to Elihu Root, August 12, 1903, Henry C. Corbin Papers, Manuscript Division, Library of Congress.

3. Adolphus W. Greely, *Reminiscences of Adventure and Service: A Record of Sixty-five Years* (New York and London: Charles Scribner's Sons, 1927), p. 179.

4. Richard T. Loomis, "The White House Telephone and Crisis Management," *United States Naval Institute Proceedings* 45 (1969): 64–65.

5. Henry S. Pritchett, "Some Recollections of President McKinley and the Cuban Intervention," *North American Review* 189 (1909): 399; De B. Randolph Keim, "The President's War," *Frank Leslie's Popular Monthly* 50 (1900): 120, 121.

6. Cushman K. Davis to C. A. Severance, May 5, 1898, Cushman K. Davis Papers, Minnesota Historical Society, St. Paul.

7. Theodore Roosevelt to George Dewey, February 25, 1898, in *The Letters of Theodore Roosevelt*, ed. Elting E. Morison et al., 8 vols. (Cambridge, Mass.: Harvard University Press, 1951–1954), 1:784–785.

8. John A. S. Grenville, "American Naval Preparations for War with Spain, 1896–1898," *Journal of American Studies* 2 (1968): 43.

9. Long to Agnes Long, October 9, 1898, Long Papers; Long to Dewey, April 24, 1898, in John Davis Long, *The New American Navy*, 2 vols. (New York: Outlook Co., 1903), 1:181-182.

10. Memorandum read by William R. Day to Sir Julian Pauncefote, March 16, 1898, box 8, Day Papers; Thomas J. McCormick, *China Market: America's Quest for Informal Empire, 1893–1901* (Chicago: Quadrangle Books, 1967), pp. 96, 97, 99–100.

11. McKinley to Alger, May 4, 1898, U.S., Army, *Correspondence Relating to the War with Spain and Conditions Growing out of the Same, Including the Insurrection in the Philippine Islands and the China Relief Expedition, between the Adjutant-General of the Army and Military Commanders in the United States, Cuba, Porto Rico, China, and the Philippine Islands, from April 15, 1898, to July 30, 1902*, 2 vols. (Washington, D.C.: Government Printing Office, 1902), 2:635 (hereafter cited as *Correspondence*); Memorandum, May 9, 1898, box 186, and undated memorandum, box 192, Moore Papers.

12. Theodore Schwan to Wesley Merritt, May 16, 1898, and McKinley to Alger, May 19, 1898, *Correspondence*, 2:649, 676, 677; *New York Tribune*, June 2, 1898.

13. Hay to Day, May 3, 1898, John Hay Papers, Manuscript Division, Library of Congress; *New York Tribune*, May 6 and 27 and June 4, 1898; William P. Frye to James H. Wilson, June 6, 1898, Wilson Papers.

14. Henry Cabot Lodge to William Laffan, June 16, 1898, Lodge Papers.

15. Undated memorandum, box 192, Moore Papers; Day to Hay, June 3, 1898, Hay Papers.

16. E. Spencer Pratt to Day, April 28, 1898, and *Singapore Free Press*, June 1, 1898, enclosed with Pratt to Day, June 2, 1898, in *A Treaty of Peace between the United States and Spain: Message from the President of the United States, Transmitting a Treaty of Peace between the United States and Spain, Signed at the City of Paris, on December 10, 1898*, Senate document no. 62, 55th Cong., 3d sess. (Washington, D.C.: Govern-

ment Printing Office, 1899), pp.
321, 342, 347 (hereafter cited as
Treaty of Peace).
17. United States, Senate, *Communications between the Executive Departments of the Government and Aguinaldo*, Senate document no. 208, 56th Cong., 1st sess., pp. 88, 89; Long to Dewey, May 26, 1898, in Long, *New American Navy* 2:109; Pratt to Day, April 28, 1898, *Treaty of Peace*, p. 342; Long to Alger, May 27, 1898, *Correspondence*, 2:674.
18. Day to Hay, June 14, 1898, Hay Papers; Long to Dewey, June 14, 1898, box 186, Moore Papers.
19. Day to Pratt, June 16, 1898 (wire and letter), and July 20, 1898, *Treaty of Peace*, pp. 353–354, 357.
20. Charles S. Olcott, *The Life of William McKinley*, 2 vols. (Boston and New York: Houghton Mifflin Co., 1916), 2:165; Journal, July 7, 1898, William Laffan to Lodge, July 14, 1898, Lodge Papers.
21. Charles Emory Smith to Root, August 12, 1903, Corbin Papers.
22. Diary, May 15, 1898, box 52, Cortelyou Papers; Francis E. Warren to F. E. Wolcott, May 28, 1898, Warren Papers.
23. "Charges of Incompetence in the Army," *Literary Digest* 16 (1898): 722.
24. *Speeches and Addresses of William McKinley from March 1, 1897, to May 30, 1900* (New York: Doubleday & McClure, 1900), p. 187.
25. Tomas Estrada Palma to McKinley, April 26, 1898, box 68, Cortelyou Papers.
26. Long, *New American Navy*, 1: 238; Roosevelt to Lodge, June 10, 1898, in *Letters of Theodore Roosevelt*, 2:837; Shafter to Corbin, June 7, 1898, Corbin Papers.
27. Corbin to Shafter, May 30, 1898 (sent on May 31), *Correspondence*, 1:18–19.
28. Corbin to Shafter, June 1, 1898, and Alger to Shafter, June 7,

1898, *Correspondence*, 1:21, 30; Shafter to Corbin, June 7, 1898, Corbin Papers; Roosevelt to Lodge, June 12, 1898, in *Letters of Theodore Roosevelt*, 2:841.
29. Shafter to Alger, July 1, 1898, Shafter to Corbin, July 1 and 2, 1898, Shafter to Alger, July 3, 1898, Alger to Shafter, July 3, 1898, and Corbin to Shafter, July 3, 1898, *Correspondence*, 1:70, 72, 74–75, 76.
30. Corbin to Shafter, July 4, 1898, *Correspondence*, 1:82.
31. Draft of Corbin to Shafter, July 9, 1898, with McKinley's changes, box 68, Cortelyou Papers; Corbin to Shafter, July 9, 1898, *Correspondence*, 1:119; Olcott, *Life of William McKinley*, 2:50.
32. Miles to Alger, July 13, 1898, *Correspondence*, 1:134.
33. John Davis Long, *America of Yesterday, as Reflected in the Journal of John Davis Long*, ed. Lawrence Shaw Mayo (Boston: Atlantic Monthly Press, 1923), pp. 203–204; Alger to Miles, July 13, 1898, and Corbin to Shafter, July 13, 1898, *Correspondence*, 1:135–136.
34. Jules Patenôtre to Théophile Delcassé, July 9, 1898, and Delcassé to Jules Cambon, July 19, 1898, Ministere des Affaires étrangères, *Documents diplomatiques français, 1871–1914*, vol. 14: *4 janvier–30 décembre 1898* (Paris: Costes, 1957), pp. 376, 393.
35. "Autobiography," box 213, Moore Papers; Cambon to Delcassé, July 8, 1898, *Documents diplomatiques français*, p. 372.
36. Cambon to Delcassé, July 27, 1898, *Documents diplomatiques français*, p. 403; Diary, July 26, 1898, box 52, Cortelyou Papers; James Wilson to William Boyd Allison, August 3, 1898, box 329, Allison Papers.
37. Hay to Day, July 14, 1898, in Alfred L. P. Dennis, *Adventures in American Diplomacy, 1896–1906* (New York: E. P. Dutton & Co., 1928), p. 93.
38. Dewey to Long, July 4, 1898,

quoted in Ronald Spector, *Admiral of the New Empire: The Life and Career of George Dewey* (Baton Rouge: Louisiana State University Press, 1974), p. 81; Andrew D. White to Day, July 12 and 13, 1898, and Day to White, July 14, 1898, Dispatches from Germany, State Department, record group 59, National Archives.

39. Aguinaldo to McKinley, June 10, 1898, *Treaty of Peace*, pp. 360–361; Dewey to Long, June 27, 1898, in *Annual Reports of the Navy Department for the Year 1898, Appendix to the Report of the Chief of the Bureau of Navigation*, House document no. 3, vol. 12, 55th Cong., 3d sess. (Washington, D.C.: Government Printing Office, 1898), p. 103.

40. "Relations of U.S. to Philippine Insurgents," July 20, 1898, box 187, Moore Papers.

41. Cambon to Hanotaux, June 24, 1898, *Documents diplomatiques français*, p. 357, quotes Cleveland; Joseph B. Foraker to W. S. Cappeller, July 29, 1898, Joseph B. Foraker Papers, Cincinnati Historical Society; Lodge to Day, July 29, 1898, box 10, Day Papers; McCormick, *China Market*, p. 115.

42. McKinley Memorandum, July 26, 1898, McKinley Papers.

43. Wilson to Allison, August 3, 1898, box 329, Allison Papers; Merritt to Corbin, August 1, 1898, *Correspondence*, 2:743; Dewey to Long, July 26, 1898, *Annual Reports of the Navy Department for the Year 1898, Appendix*, p. 118.

44. Olcott, *Life of William McKinley*, 2:63; Diary, July 30 and 31, 1898, box 52, Cortelyou Papers.

45. Cambon to Delcassé, July 31,

1898, *Documents diplomatiques français*, pp. 409–413; Diary, July 30, 1898, box 52, Cortelyou Papers.

46. Almodóvar del Rio to León y Castillo, August 1, 1898, and León y Castillo to Almodóvar del Rio, August 4, 1898, *Spanish Diplomatic Correspondence and Documents, 1896–1900: Presented to the Cortes by the Minister of State* (Washington, D.C.: Government Printing Office, 1905), pp. 214–217.

47. Shafter to Corbin, August 2, 1898, and Alger to Shafter, August 2, 1898, *Correspondence*, 1:194, 196.

48. Shafter to Corbin, August 3, 1898, and Alger to Shafter, August 4, 1898, *Correspondence*, 1:200, 204.

49. Shafter to Corbin, August 3, 1898, *Correspondence*, 1:202; Roosevelt to Shafter, August 3, 1898, in *Letters of Theodore Roosevelt*, 2:864–865.

50. McKinley to Shafter, August 5, 1898, draft in box 56, Diary, August 4, 1898, box 52, Cortelyou Papers.

51. León y Castillo to Almodóvar del Rio, August 11, 1898, *Spanish Diplomatic Correspondence*, pp. 219–220; Cambon to Delcassé, August 10, 1898, *Documents diplomatiques français*, pp. 444–445.

52. *Spectator*, July 30, 1898, clipping enclosed with Hay to McKinley, August 2, 1898, box 56, and Diary, July 30, 1898, box 52, Cortelyou Papers.

53. Draft of letter, McKinley to Commission for the Evacuation of Cuba, December 6, 1898, with Cortelyou's note of McKinley's remark, box 70, "Suggestions, Protocol, August 12, 1898," box 56, Cortelyou Papers.

CHAPTER 6

1. F. H. Gillette to John D. Long, August 5, 1898, Long Papers; George Fred Williams to Moreton Frewen, September 21, 1898,

Moreton Frewen Papers, Manuscript Division, Library of Congress.

2. "The Bombardment of the War

Department," *Literary Digest* 17 (1898): 303.

3. *New York Tribune*, September 4, 1898.

4. Diary, August 23, 1898, box 52, Cortelyou Papers.

5. James Wilson to McKinley, September 7, 1898, box 69, Cortelyou Papers; Alger to McKinley, September 8, 1898, in Russell A. Alger, *The Spanish-American War* (New York and London: Harper & Bros., 1901), p. 376.

6. *Speeches and Addresses of William McKinley from March 1, 1897, to May 30, 1900* (New York: Doubleday & McClure, 1900), p. 82.

7. Frank L. Brown to Joseph L. Bristow, April 27, 1898, Joseph L. Bristow Papers, Kansas State Historical Society, Topeka; *New York Tribune*, August 25, 1898.

8. Joseph W. Babcock to Jacob H. Gallinger, August 27, 1898, Jacob H. Gallinger Papers, New Hampshire Historical Society, Concord; *New York Tribune*, August 31, 1898; William P. Hepburn to John F. Lacey, September 12, 1898, John F. Lacey Papers, Iowa State Department of History and Archives, Des Moines.

9. Henry W. Lawton to Henry C. Corbin, August 16, 1898, and Corbin to Lawton, August 16, 1898, U.S., Army, *Correspondence Relating to the War with Spain* . . . , 2 vols. (Washington, D.C.: Government Printing Office, 1902), 1:230, 231 (hereafter cited as *Correspondence*).

10. David F. Healy, *The United States in Cuba, 1898–1902: Generals, Politicians, and the Search for Policy* (Madison: University of Wisconsin Press, 1963), pp. 50, 51.

11. Tyler Dennett, *John Hay: From Poetry to Politics* (New York: Dodd, Mead, & Co., 1933), p. 197.

12. William P. Frye to William E. Chandler, September 6, 1898, William E. Chandler Papers, New Hampshire Historical Society, Concord.

13. Chandler to McKinley, August 17, 1898, McKinley Papers.

14. Wesley Merritt and George Dewey to Corbin, August 13, 1898, and Corbin to Merritt, August 17, 1898, *Correspondence*, 2:754.

15. Merritt to Corbin, received August 27, 1898, and Corbin to E. S. Otis, September 7, 1898, *Correspondence*, 2:765, 788.

16. Otis to Emilio Aguinaldo, September 8, 1898, and Otis to Corbin, September 16, 1898, *Correspondence*, 2:826, 791.

17. Memorandums, August 4, 1898, and September 8, 1898, box 187, Moore Papers.

18. Pierre J. Smith to McKinley, September 15, 1898, box 68, Cortelyou Papers; George F. W. Holls to Andrew D. White, September 10, 1898, Albert Shaw Papers; *New York Tribune*, September 15, 1898.

19. U.S., Department of State, *Papers Relating to the Foreign Relations of the United States*, 1898 (Washington, D.C.: Government Printing Office, 1901), pp. 904–908, for McKinley's instructions (hereafter cited as *For. Rel.*, with year).

20. George McAneny to Carl Schurz, September 17, 1898, Carl Schurz Papers, Manuscript Division, Library of Congress.

21. McKinley to Garret A. Hobart, September 19, 1898, McKinley Papers; "Memoranda Concerning the Situation in the Philippines on August 30, 1898, by F. V. Greene, Major General, Volunteers, and Accompanying Papers," *Treaty of Peace*, pp. 422, 424, 425.

22. Memorandum, October 1, 1898, Felipe Agoncillo, "Memorandum," October 4, 1898, and Hay to Day, October 4, 1898, McKinley Papers.

23. Charles Emory Smith, "McKinley in the Cabinet Room," *Saturday Evening Post*, October 11, 1902, p. 7; *Speeches and Addresses of*

William McKinley from March 1, 1897, pp. 87, 90–91, 105, 114.

24. *Speeches and Addresses of William McKinley from May 1, 1897*, pp. 98, 117, 131, 153.

25. Ibid., p. 137.

26. Joseph W. Babcock to John Coit Spooner, October 15, 1898, Spooner Papers; *New York Tribune*, October 22, 1898.

27. Hay to McKinley, November 9, 1898, box 57, Cortelyou Papers.

28. Day to McKinley, September 30, 1898, McKinley Papers; Whitelaw Reid, *Making Peace with Spain: The Diary of Whitelaw Reid, September–December 1898*, ed. H. Wayne Morgan (Austin: University of Texas Press, 1965), p. 53.

29. Hay to Day, October 13, 1898, Day to Hay, October 22, 1898, and Hay to Day, October 23, 1898, *For. Rel.*, 1898, pp. 927–930.

30. Reid, *Making Peace with Spain*, pp. 104, 112, 113; Day to Hay, October 25, 1898, *For. Rel.*, 1898, p. 931.

31. Reid, *Making Peace with Spain*, pp. 114–117; Day to Alvey Adee, October 27, 1898, *For. Rel.*, 1898, pp. 936–937.

32. Reid, *Making Peace with Spain*, p. 82; Hay to Day, October 14, 1898, *For. Rel.*, 1898, p. 928.

33. Peace Commissioners to Hay, October 25, 1898, *For. Rel.*, 1898, pp. 932–935.

34. Hay to Day, October 28, 1898, *For. Rel.*, 1898, pp. 937–938. There is a draft of this message in McKinley's handwriting, box 69, Cortelyou Papers.

35. Charles S. Olcott, *The Life of William McKinley*, 2 vols. (Boston and New York: Houghton Mifflin Co., 1916), 2:109–111.

36. James F. Rusling, *Men and Things I Saw in Civil War Days* (New York: Eaton & Mains, 1899), p. 15; McKinley used a variant of this Lincoln story himself in 1892. *Speeches and Addresses of William McKinley from*

His Election to Congress to the Present Time (New York: D. Appleton & Co., 1893), p. 607.

37. *Washington Post*, November 24, 1899.

38. Frye to Adee, October 30, 1898, and Hay to Frye, November 1, 1898, *For. Rel.*, 1898, pp. 939–940.

39. *Speeches and Addresses of William McKinley from May 1, 1897*, pp. 158, 161, 174, 182; *New York Tribune*, December 16, 1898; Asher Hinds Diary, December 19, 1898, Manuscript Division, Library of Congress.

40. U.S., Senate, *Congressional Record*, 55th Cong., 3d sess. (January 24, 1899), p. 959.

41. *New York Tribune*, December 14, 1898.

42. Lodge to Paul Dana, January 26, 1899, Lodge Papers; Hoar to Schurz, January 28, 1899, Schurz Papers; Charles W. Fairbanks to W. T. Durbin, February 1, 1899, Fairbanks Papers.

43. Diary, February 4, 1899, box 52, Cortelyou Papers.

44. Otis to Alger, received October 30, 1898, and Otis to Corbin, November 13, 1898, *Correspondence*, 2:831, 836.

45. Corbin to Otis, December 4, 1898, *Correspondence*, 2:850.

46. Corbin to Otis, December 21, 1898, *Correspondence*, 2:857.

47. McKinley to Alger, December 21, 1898, *Correspondence*, 2:858–859.

48. Alger to Otis, December 29 and 30, 1898, and Otis to Alger, December 30, 1898, *Correspondence*, 2:863, 864.

49. Corbin to Otis, January 8, 1899, *Correspondence*, 2:872–873.

50. Jacob Gould Schurman, *Philippine Affairs* (New York: Charles Scribner's Sons, 1902), pp. 1–2.

51. Dewey to Long, received February 5, 1899, *Correspondence*, 2:893.

52. *Speeches and Addresses of William McKinley from May 1, 1897*, pp. 187, 188, 189, 191, 192, 193.

CHAPTER 7

1. Blanche K. Bruce to McKinley, February 10, 1898, McKinley Papers; *New York Tribune*, April 3, 1898.
2. John Addison Porter to John Sherman, June 28, 1897, stating the president's view, McKinley Papers.
3. R. C. Ransom to John P. Green, June 27, 1899, McKinley Papers.
4. Willard B. Gatewood, Jr., *Black Americans and the White Man's Burden, 1898–1903* (Urbana: University of Illinois Press, 1975), pp. 38, 40.
5. Ibid., p. 107.
6. Ibid., pp. 87, 92.
7. John P. Green to John M. Clark, June 20, 1898, and George A. Myers to Green, May 3, 1898, John P. Green Papers, Western Reserve Historical Society, Cleveland.
8. Emma Lou Thornbrough, *T. Thomas Fortune: Militant Journalist* (Chicago: University of Chicago Press, 1972), p. 182.
9. John P. Green to McKinley, June 29, 1899, McKinley Papers, italics in original; William Parham to George Myers, June 30, 1899, quoted in David A. Gerber, *Black Ohio and the Color Line, 1860–1915* (Urbana: University of Illinois Press, 1976), pp. 362–363; *New York Tribune*, May 11, 1899.
10. R. C. Ransom to Green, June 27, 1899, McKinley Papers.
11. Root to McKinley, August 17, 1899, and McKinley to Root, August 18, 1899, McKinley Papers; Gatewood, *Black Americans*, pp. 215–216.
12. *A Supplement to A Compilation of the Messages and Papers of the Presidents, 1789–1902, by James D. Richardson*, comp. George Raywood Devitt (Washington, D.C.: Bureau of National Literature and Art, 1903), pp. 68–70, 101.
13. Diary, December 15, 1899, box 53, Cortelyou Papers.
14. Ibid.
15. Charles G. Dawes, *A Journal of the McKinley Years*, ed. Bascom N. Timmons (Chicago: Lakeside Press, 1950), p. 185.
16. "Attorney General Griggs on the Trust Law," *Public Opinion* 26 (1899): 391; George Rice to John W. Griggs, November 5, 1898, and John K. Richards to Rice, November 15, 1898, U.S., House, *Appendix to the Congressional Record*, 56th Cong., 1st sess. (June 1, 1900), p. 642.
17. Dawes, *Journal of the McKinley Years*, pp. 185–186.
18. *New York Tribune*, June 15, 1899, for Havemeyer; for Bryan, "Mr. Havemeyer, the Tariff, and the Trusts," *Literary Digest* 18 (1899): 720.
19. Andrew Van Bibber to Hanna, April 6, 1899, McKinley Papers; Hanna to William E. Chandler, March 25, 1899, Chandler Papers.
20. Dawes to McKinley, June 4, 1899, box 58, Cortelyou Papers, italics in original; John Marshall Harlan to McKinley, June 2 and 6, 1899, McKinley Papers.
21. *Public Opinion* 27 (1899): 327, for the Maryland platform; *New York Tribune*, September 27, 1899, for Griggs.
22. Dawes, *Journal of the McKinley Years*, pp. 199, 205; *Speech of Charles G. Dawes on Trusts and Trade Combinations, Delivered at Annual Meeting of Merchants' Club of Boston, October 17, 1899* (Washington, D.C.: Judd & Detweiler, 1899), pp. 1, 3, 4, 6, 7, 8.
23. *Supplement to A Compilation of the Messages and Papers*, pp. 57, 58, 59, 60.
24. Diary, January 5, 1900, box 53, Cortelyou Papers.
25. *New York Tribune*, October 11, 1899; *Speeches and Addresses of William McKinley from March 1, 1897, to May 30, 1900* (New York: Doubleday & McClure, 1900), p. 249.
26. F. P. Sargent to Charles G.

Dawes, August 14, 1901, Charles G. Dawes Papers, Northwestern University Library, Evanston, Illinois.

27. "President's Changes in Civil Service," *Literary Digest* 18 (1899): 657; *New York Tribune*, June 2, 1899, quotes Congressman W. S. Kerr.

28. Leonard D. White, *The Republican Era: 1869–1901: A Study in Administrative History* (New York: Macmillan Co., 1958), pp. 319–321.

29. Cornelius N. Bliss to W. E. Curtis, June 16, 1899, author's collection; William A. Rodenberg to Dawes, March 29, 1901, Dawes Papers.

30. Carl Schurz to Moorfield Storey, January 1, 1898, and Roosevelt to Schurz, January 11, 1898, Schurz Papers.

31. Charles Grosvenor to McKinley, May 22, 1899, McKinley Papers.

32. Schurz to Edwin B. Smith, July 12, 1899, Schurz Papers; Gage to McKinley, July 6, 1899, with statement in McKinley's handwriting, box 58, Cortelyou Papers; Lyman J. Gage, "The Civil Service and the Merit System," *Forum* 27 (1899): 705–712. McKinley's words appear on p. 712.

33. William Dudley Foulke, *Fighting the Spoilsmen: Reminiscences of the Civil Service Reform Movement* (New York and London: G. P. Putnam's Sons, 1919), p. 128; Philip C. Jessup, *Elihu Root*, 2 vols. (New York: Dodd, Mead & Co., 1938), 1:291.

34. *New York Tribune*, May 5, 1899.

35. Ibid., May 10, 1899.

36. Ibid., June 6, 1899.

37. W. M. Osborne to McKinley, March 3, 1899, McKinley Papers.

38. Eagan is quoted by Graham A. Cosmas in *An Army for Empire: The United States Army in the Spanish-American War* (Columbia: University of Missouri Press, 1971), p. 290.

39. Ibid., pp. 295–296.

40. U.S., Senate, *Food Furnished by Subsistence Department to Troops in the Field*, Senate document no. 270, 56th Cong., 1st sess., 3 vols. (Washington, D.C.: Government Printing Office, 1900), 3:1924–1926.

41. James H. Wilson to Anthony Higgins, March 3, 1899, Wilson Papers.

42. *Literary Digest* 18 (1899): 475.

43. *New York Tribune*, June 26, 1899; *New York Times*, June 27, 1899; Dawes, *Journal of the McKinley Years*, p. 194.

44. Memorandum in McKinley's handwriting, July 19, 1899, and draft letter of McKinley to Alger; also see John Hay memorandum, with clipping from *New York Tribune*, July 13, 1899, McKinley Papers.

45. Memorandum, November 26, 1900, Alger Papers; Garret A. Hobart to McKinley, July 21, 1899, McKinley Papers; Charles S. Olcott, *The Life of William McKinley*, 2 vols. (Boston and New York: Houghton Mifflin Co., 1916), 2:90–91; Jennie Hobart, *Memories* (Paterson, N.J.: privately printed, 1930), pp. 68–69.

46. Alger to Beriah Wilkins, December 8, 1899, Alger Papers.

47. Albert Shaw to George F. W. Holls, July 21, 1899, Shaw Papers.

48. Jessup, *Elihu Root*, 1:215–216.

49. Ibid., p. 218.

CHAPTER 8

1. Elwell S. Otis to Henry C. Corbin, April 3, 1899, U.S., Army, *Correspondence Relating to the War with Spain . . .* , 2 vols. (Washington, D.C.: Government Printing Office, 1902), 2:957 (hereafter cited as *Correspondence*).

2. *A Supplement to A Compilation of the Messages and Papers of the Presidents, 1789–1902*, by James D. Richardson, comp. George Ray-

wood Devitt (Washington, D.C.: Bureau of National Literature and Art, 1903), p. 95.

3. Dean C. Worcester, *The Philippines, Past and Present* (New York: Macmillan Co., 1930), p. 790.

4. Hay to Schurman, May 5, 1899, U.S., Senate, *Communications between the Executive Departments of the Government and Aguinaldo, Etc.*, Senate document no. 208, 56th Cong., 1st sess., p. 156.

5. Schurman to Hay, June 3, 1899, McKinley Papers; Hay to Schurman, June 5, 1899, quoted in Phil Lyman Snyder, "Mission, Empire, or Force of Circumstance? A Study of the American Decision to Annex the Philippine Islands" (Ph.D. diss., Stanford University, 1972), pp. 232–233; Virginia Frances Mulrooney, "No Victor, No Vanquished: United States Military Government in the Philippine Islands, 1898–1901" (Ph.D. diss., University of California at Los Angeles, 1975), p. 139, quotes Schurman.

6. Carl Schurz to Edwin B. Smith, May 4, 1899, Schurz Papers; E. Berkeley Tompkins, *Anti-imperialism in the United States: The Great Debate, 1890–1920* (Philadelphia: University of Pennsylvania Press, 1970), p. 203.

7. *New York Tribune*, July 18, 1899; Corbin to Otis, July 27, 1899, *Correspondence*, 2:1041, gives McKinley's directions.

8. J. A. T. Hull to Root, August 12, 1899, Root Papers; Root to McKinley, August 15, 1899, quoted in Philip C. Jessup, *Elihu Root*, 2 vols. (New York: Dodd, Mead & Co., 1938), 1:334.

9. Richard F. Pettigrew to McKinley, April 17, 1899, McKinley Papers; Daniel B. Schirmer, *Republic or Empire: American Resistance to the Philippine War* (Cambridge, Mass.: Schenkman Publishing Co., 1972), p. 151.

10. *Speeches and Addresses of William McKinley from March 1, 1897, to May 30, 1900* (New York: Doubleday & McClure, 1900), pp. 209, 211, 213, 214–215, 216.

11. "The President's Recent Speeches," *Public Opinion* 27 (1899): 293; Carl Schurz, *Speeches, Correspondence and Political Papers of Carl Schurz*, ed. Frederic Bancroft, 6 vols. (New York and London: G. P. Putnam's Sons, 1913), 6:115; *Speeches and Addresses of William McKinley from March 1, 1897*, pp. 282, 302.

12. Otis to Corbin, November 24, 1899, *Correspondence*, 2:1107; *Supplement to A Compilation of the Messages and Papers*, p. 91.

13. *Report of the (Schurman) Philippine Commission to the President*, Senate document no. 138, 56th Cong., 1st sess., 4 vols. (Washington, D.C.: Government Printing Office, 1900–1901), 1:175, 103.

14. *Supplement to A Compilation of the Messages and Papers*, p. 95.

15. Charles S. Olcott, *The Life of William McKinley*, 2 vols. (Boston and New York: Houghton Mifflin Co., 1916), 2:174–177.

16. McKinley to Day, January 30, 1900, McKinley Papers; Worcester, *Philippines, Past and Present*, p. 982, for the commission's instructions.

17. Tompkins, *Anti-imperialism*, p. 203.

18. *New York Times*, May 2, 1901.

19. *New York Tribune*, May 2, 1899, for Long's speech; *Supplement to A Compilation of the Messages and Papers*, p. 96.

20. *Supplement to A Compilation of the Messages and Papers*, pp. 74–75; Charles Emory Smith to James H. Wilson, August 28, 1899, Wilson Papers.

21. McKinley to John R. Brooke, December 22, 1898, in Olcott, *Life of William McKinley*, 2:196–197, 198.

22. David F. Healy, *The United States in Cuba, 1898–1902: Gen-*

erals, Politicians, and the Search for Policy (Madison: University of Wisconsin Press, 1963), p. 110.

23. Annual Report of the War Department for the Fiscal Year Ended June 30, 1899. Report of the Secretary of War, House document no. 2, 56th Cong., 1st sess. (Washington, D.C.: Government Printing Office, 1899), pp. 31–32.

24. Supplement to A Compilation of the Messages and Papers, pp. 74–75.

25. Hermann Hagedorn, Leonard Wood: A Biography, 2 vols. (New York and London: Harper & Bros., 1931), 1:259, 261.

26. Ibid., 1:266.

27. Joseph L. Bristow, Fraud and Politics at the Turn of the Century (New York: Exposition Press, 1952), p. 100; Hagedorn, Leonard Wood, 1:295.

28. John Hay to Henry White, February 14, 1899, and Hay to John St. Loe Strachey, June 13, 1899, Hay Papers.

29. A Compilation of the Messages and Papers of the Presidents, 1789–1897, comp. James D. Richardson, 10 vols. (Washington, D.C.: Government Printing Office, 1898), 10:180.

30. Charles S. Campbell, Jr. Anglo-American Understanding, 1898–1903 (Baltimore, Md.: Johns Hopkins Press, 1957), pp. 191–193.

31. Theodore Wiese to McKinley, February 15, 1900, McKinley Papers.

32. Campbell, Anglo-American Understanding, pp. 171–172; Supplement to A Compilation of the Messages and Papers, p. 68.

33. Hay to Henry White, March 10, 1900, Hay Papers.

34. Alfred L. P. Dennis, Adventures in American Diplomacy, 1896–1906 (New York: E. P. Dutton & Co., 1928), pp. 132–133.

35. Compilation of the Messages and Papers, 10:189.

36. Supplement to A Compilation of the Messages and Papers, pp. 81–82.

37. Day to Hay, July 14, 1898, Hay Papers; U.S., Department of State, Papers Relating to the Foreign Relations of the United States, 1898, House document no. 1, 55th Cong., 3d sess. (Washington, D.C.: Government Printing Office, 1901), p. 907.

38. New York Times, August 16, 1899, for Schurman; New York Tribune, August 16, 1899.

39. Alfred Whitney Griswold, The Far Eastern Policy of the United States (New York: Harcourt, Brace & Co., 1938), pp. 67–68, 73.

40. Ibid., pp. 497–498.

41. Peter W. Stanley, "The Making of an American Sinologist: William W. Rockhill and the Open Door," in Donald Fleming, ed., Perspectives in American History, vol. 11 (Cambridge, Mass.: Charles Warren Center for Studies in American History, 1978), pp. 442, 443.

42. Joseph Pulitzer, "Has Congress Abdicated?" North American Review 169 (1899): 893; Perry Belmont, "The President's War Power and an Imperial Tariff," North American Review 170 (1900): 434.

43. Root to George W. Davis, September 11, 1899, Root Papers.

CHAPTER 9

1. New York Tribune, October 14, 1899; "The Importance of the Ohio Election," Public Opinion 27 (1899): 519.

2. Speeches and Addresses of William McKinley from March 1, 1897, to May 30, 1900 (New York: Doubleday & McClure, 1900), pp. 237, 256, 331.

3. Public Opinion 27 (1899): 615, 616; Day to McKinley, November 18, 1899, McKinley Papers.

4. Hay to Joseph Hodges Choate, December 4, 1899, Hay Papers.
5. *Annual Report of the War Department for the Fiscal Year Ended June 30, 1899. Report of the Secretary of War*, House document no. 2, 56th Cong., 1st sess. (Washington, D.C.: Government Printing Office, 1899), pp. 32–33; *A Supplement to A Compilation of the Messages and Papers of the Presidents, 1789–1902, by James D. Richardson*, comp. George Raywood Devitt (Washington, D.C.: Bureau of National Literature and Art, 1903), p. 100.
6. Louis A. Coolidge, *An Old-Fashioned Senator: Orville H. Platt of Connecticut* (New York and London: G. P. Putnam's Sons, 1910), pp. 360, 362.
7. *New York Tribune*, January 29, 1900; U.S., House, "To Regulate the Trade of Puerto Rico, and for Other Purposes," House report no. 249, 56th Cong., 1st sess. (Washington, D.C.: Government Printing Office, 1900), p. 18; Charles G. Dawes, *A Journal of the McKinley Years*, ed. Bascom N. Timmons (Chicago: Lakeside Press, 1950), p. 217.
8. Henry L. Stoddard, *As I Knew Them: Presidents and Politics from Grant to Coolidge* (New York: Harper & Bros., 1927), p. 257; McKinley to H. H. Kohlsaat, March 5, 1900, box 59, Cortelyou Papers.
9. *Washington Post*, February 15, 18, 1900; Memorandums, February 24, 1900, McKinley Papers.
10. Statement, February 26, 1900, and Memorandum, February 27, 1900, McKinley Papers; Diary, February 27, 1900, box 54, Cortelyou Papers; *Washington Post*, February 28, 1900.
11. Diary, February 28, 1900, box 54, Cortelyou Papers; *Washington Post*, February 29 and March 3, 1900.
12. *Washington Post*, March 7, 1900; Asher Hinds Diary, March 8, 1900, quotes Reed; John C.

Spooner to Henry Fink, March 19, 1900, Spooner Papers.
13. *Washington Post*, March 9, 1900.
14. Roosevelt's statement, February 12, 1900, in *The Letters of Theodore Roosevelt*, ed. Elting E. Morison et al., 8 vols. (Cambridge, Mass.: Harvard University Press, 1951–1954), 2:1187.
15. Hay to Roosevelt, February 12, 1900, Hay Papers.
16. Hay to McKinley, March 13, 1900, and McKinley to Hay, March 13, 1900, in William Roscoe Thayer, *The Life and Letters of John Hay*, 2 vols. (Boston and New York: Houghton Mifflin Co., 1915), 2:226–228; Diary, March 13, 1900, box 54, Cortelyou Papers.
17. Olcott, *Life of William McKinley*, 2:307; Schurman to McKinley, June 1, 1900, McKinley Papers.
18. *Speeches and Addresses of William McKinley from March 1, 1897*, pp. 364, 365.
19. Day to William J. Spear, March 28, 1900, Day Papers; Thomas Beer, *Hanna* (New York: Alfred A. Knopf, 1929), p. 234.
20. Memorandum, April 8, 1900, box 59, Cortelyou Papers.
21. Hay to Choate, January 3, 1900, Hay Papers.
22. Henry F. Pringle, *Theodore Roosevelt: A Biography* (New York: Harcourt, Brace & Co., 1931), p. 218, quotes Roosevelt; Lodge to George H. Lyman, February 8, 1900, Lodge Papers; Roosevelt to Lodge, April 17 and 23, 1900, *Letters of Theodore Roosevelt*, 2:1264, 1269.
23. Lodge to Roosevelt, April 16, 1900, in *Selections from the Correspondence of Theodore Roosevelt and Henry Cabot Lodge, 1884–1918*, ed. Henry Cabot Lodge, 2 vols. (New York and London: Charles Scribner's Sons, 1925), 1:458–459; Hay to Henry Adams, June 15, 1900, in Tyler Dennett, *John Hay: From Poetry to Politics* (New York: Dodd, Mead & Co., 1933), p. 340.

24. "Reminiscences—the Vice Presidency," Charles W. Fairbanks Papers.
25. Olcott, *Life of William McKinley*, 2:274; *Letters of Theodore Roosevelt*, 2:1337.
26. Olcott, *Life of William McKinley*, 2:279.
27. *Official Proceedings of the Twelfth Republican National Convention, . . . 1900*, reported by Milton W. Blumenberg (Philadelphia: Press of Dunlap Printing Co., 1900), pp. 34, 90; Albert Shaw to W. T. Stead, June 25, 1900, Shaw Papers.
28. Charles M. Pepper to McKinley, October 3, 1899, McKinley Papers.
29. *Life and Speeches of Hon. Wm. Jennings Bryan* (Baltimore, Md.: R. H. Woodward Co., 1900), pp. 374, 375.
30. *Official Proceedings*, pp. 148, 149, 150; Dawes, *Journal of the McKinley Years*, p. 236.
31. Allison to James H. Wilson, July 8, 1900, Wilson Papers.
32. Hay to E. H. Conger, June 8, 1900, McKinley Papers; Hay to Conger, June 10, 1900, U.S., Department of State, *Papers Relating to the Foreign Relations of the United States*, 1900, House document no. 1, 57th Cong., 1st sess. (Washington, D.C.: Government Printing Office, 1901), p. 143 (hereafter cited as *For. Rel.*, with year); Memorandums of phone conversations, July 3, 1900, box 64, Cortelyou Papers; Frank W. Hackett to Louis Kempff, June 18, 1900, U.S., Army, *Correspondence Relating to the War with Spain . . .* , 2 vols. (Washington, D.C.: Government Printing Office, 1902), 1:414.
33. "Developments in China," *Literary Digest* 21 (1900): 3.
34. Memorandum of phone conversation, August 13, 1900, box 64, Cortelyou Papers.
35. "Talk with John Hay," July 1, 1900, box 214, Moore Papers; *For. Rel.*, 1901, *Appendix: Affairs in China*, p. 12.
36. Eugene Hale to McKinley, July 19, 1900, John D. Long Papers.
37. Root to McKinley, September 11, 1900, McKinley Papers; McKinley to Hay, September 14, 1900, Hay Papers.
38. Hay to Adee, September 14, 1900, Hay Papers.
39. Hanna to McKinley, July 23 and August 3, 1900, box 69, Cortelyou Papers.
40. McKinley to Hanna, August 7, 1900, box 69, and Hanna to McKinley, August 10, 1900, box 64, Cortelyou Papers.
41. *Des Moines Leader*, September 19, 1900; *Official Proceedings*, p. 161; Herbert Croly, *Marcus Alonzo Hanna: His Life and Work* (New York: Macmillan Co., 1912), p. 333.
42. *Official Proceedings*, pp. 158, 105, 161.
43. "Conversation with Pres. McKinley," September 20, 1900, box 214, Moore Papers.
44. *Official Proceedings*, pp. 171–172, 174, 175, 178, 179.
45. James Wilson to McKinley, October 25, 1900, McKinley Papers; *Washington Post*, September 19, 1900.
46. Henry Litchfield West, "The Republican and Democratic Platforms Compared," *Forum* 30 (1900): 93.
47. *The Works of Theodore Roosevelt*, vol. 14: *Campaigns and Controversies* (New York: Charles Scribner's Sons, 1926), p. 348; Lodge to Henry White, October 8, 1900, Lodge Papers.
48. Cortelyou to Ethan Allen Hitchcock, October 29, 1900, Ethan Allen Hitchcock Papers, National Archives, record group 316.
49. *Des Moines Leader*, November 8, 1900; Olcott, *Life of William McKinley*, 2:296.

CHAPTER 10

1. *New York Tribune,* November 25, 1900.
2. Herbert Croly, *Marcus Alonzo Hanna: His Life and Work* (New York: Macmillan Co., 1912), p. 351; James A. Mount to Charles W. Fairbanks, February 26, 1900, Fairbanks Papers.
3. Lodge to William Howard Taft, November 22, 1900, Lodge Papers.
4. Taft to Arthur MacArthur, September 18, 1900, copy in Bernard Moses Papers, Bancroft Library, Berkeley, California.
5. Taft to Root, January 2, 1901, McKinley Papers; Lodge to Taft, January 9, 1901, Lodge Papers, quotes McKinley.
6. Diary, February 27, 1901, box 54, Cortelyou Papers.
7. MacArthur to Corbin, April 10, 1901, *Correspondence Relating to the War with Spain and Conditions Growing out of the Same . . . from April 15, 1898 to July 30, 1902,* 2 vols. (Washington, D.C.: Government Printing Office, 1902), 2:1268; *A Supplement to A Compilation of the Messages and Papers of the Presidents, 1789–1902, by James D. Richardson,* comp. George Raywood Devitt (Washington, D.C.: Bureau of National Literature and Art, 1903), p. 166.
8. Root to Leonard Wood, February 9, 1901, McKinley Papers.
9. Diary, January 20, 1901, box 54, Cortelyou Papers, reported McKinley's remarks; *New York Tribune,* February 2, 1901.
10. *Washington Post,* January 30, 1901.
11. Memorandum, March 15, 1916, box 76, Cortelyou Papers, reports on a conversation with John Coit Spooner and quotes McKinley.
12. Root to Wood, February 9, 1901, McKinley Papers; "Provisions which should be incorporated in the Cuban constitution," dated in McKinley's handwriting, February 12, 1901, box 76, Cortelyou Pa-

pers; Charles G. Dawes, *A Journal of the McKinley Years,* ed. Bascom N. Timmons (Chicago: Lakeside Press, 1950), p. 263.
13. Henry M. Teller, the Democrat, is quoted in Cornelius Wendell Vahle, Jr., "Congress, the President, and Overseas Expansion, 1897–1901" (Ph.D. diss., Georgetown University, 1967), p. 202.
14. Philip S. Foner, *The Spanish-Cuban-American War and the Birth of American Imperialism, 1895–1902,* 2 vols. (New York: Monthly Review Press, 1972), 2: 593; Root to Wood, April 2, 1901, McKinley Papers.
15. McKinley memorandum, May 19, 1901, and Root to Wood, May 28, 1901, McKinley Papers; *Supplement to A Compilation of the Messages and Papers,* p. 165.
16. Diary, February 3, 1901, box 54, Cortelyou Papers; "Reflections on the Fifty-sixth Congress," *Literary Digest* 22 (1901): 278.
17. *Supplement to A Compilation of the Messages and Papers,* pp. 162, 164.
18. Francis E. Leupp, "The President —And Mr. Wilson," *Independent* 76 (1913): 394.
19. Diary, June 8, 1899, box 53, Cortelyou Papers.
20. Margaret Leech, *In the Days of McKinley* (New York: Harper & Bros., 1959), pp. 29, 30, 433–461.
21. Translation of article in *Matin,* March 19, 1901, enclosed with Joseph I. Brittain to David J. Hill, March 20, 1901, McKinley Papers; Julian Ralph, "McKinley as I Saw Him," *Washington Post,* April 7, 1901.
22. *Chicago Tribune,* March 4, 1901, enclosed with Raymond Chandler to Charles G. Dawes, March 19, 1901, McKinley Papers; Henry Litchfield West, "The Growing Powers of the President," *Forum* 31 (1901): 25; Henry B. F. Macfarland, "Mr. McKinley as Presi-

dent," *Atlantic Monthly* 87 (1901): 302.

23. Reginald Tower to Lord Salisbury, June 29, 1899, FO5/2391, PRO; Jules Cambon to Theophile Delcassé, July 13, 1901, Etats-Unis, vol. 8, MAE.
24. David S. Barry, "George Bruce Cortelyou," *World's Work* 5 (1903): 3340.
25. Jules Cambon to Delcassé, July 28, 1899, Correspondance consulaire et commerciale, Washington, vol. 36, MAE.
26. Edmond Bruwaert to Delcassé, October 31, 1899, Correspondance consulaire et commerciale, New York, vol. 50, MAE.
27. Charles H. Grosvenor to John A. Kasson, December 14, 1899, Papers of the Reciprocity Commissioner, Records of the Department of State, record group 59, National Archives: J. A. Johnson to John Coit Spooner, January 14, 1900, Spooner Papers.
28. Francis E. Warren to C. W. Burdick, February 10, 1900, Warren Papers.
29. Cambon to Delcassé, February 9 and 21, 1900, Correspondance consulaire et commerciale, Washington, vol. 37, MAE.
30. Pauncefote to Lord Lansdowne, February 15, 1901, FO5/2463, PRO.
31. Kasson to Edward S. Ready, April 29, 1901, Reciprocity Commissioner Papers; Cambon to Delcassé, May 6, 1901, Correspondance consulaire et commerciale, Washington, vol. 38, MAE.
32. *New York Tribune*, May 1, 1901; Albert Clarke to George Frisbie Hoar, May 4, 1901, Hoar Papers.
33. R. D. Redfern to Cortelyou, June 17, 1901, box 7, Cortelyou Papers.
34. Thomas Beer, *Hanna* (New York: Alfred A. Knopf, 1929), pp. 245–246; James Creelman, "Mr. Cortelyou Explains President Mc-

Kinley," *Pearson's Magazine* 19 (1908): 570, 572.
35. Memorandum in McKinley's handwriting, May 1901, McKinley Papers; Creelman, "Mr. Cortelyou," p. 572.
36. *American Economist* 27 (1901): 281, quotes Hanna; Lodge to Nelson Aldrich, June 20, 1901, Nelson Aldrich Papers, Manuscript Division, Library of Congress.
37. Diary, June 22, 1901, box 54, Cortelyou Papers; *New York Tribune*, June 12, 1901.
38. *New York Tribune*, August 6, 1901; Gerard Lowther to Lord Lansdowne, August 9, 1901, FO5/2463, PRO.
39. *Iowa State Register*, August 8, 1901.
40. For copies of the Buffalo speech, see McKinley Papers; Charles S. Olcott, *The Life of William McKinley*, 2 vols. (Boston and New York: Houghton Mifflin Co., 1916), 2:377, 379, 381, 382, 383 for the quotations.
41. A. Wesley Johns, *The Man Who Shot McKinley* (South Brunswick, N.J.: A. S. Barnes & Co., 1970), pp. 89–100, details the events of the shooting. The quotations are from James Creelman, *On the Great Highway: The Wanderings and Adventures of a Special Correspondent* (Boston: Lothrop, Lee & Shepard Co., 1901), p. 406; John Hay, *Addresses of John Hay* (New York: Century Co., 1906), p. 175.
42. Gary M. Maranell, "The Evaluation of Presidents: An Extension of the Schlesinger Polls," *Journal of American History* 57 (1970): 105, 108, 109, 110, 111; Ronald A. Wells, "American Presidents as Political and Moral Leaders: A Report on Four Surveys," *Fides et Historia* 11 (1978): 39–53.
43. Leech, *In the Days of McKinley*, p. vi.

Bibliographical Essay

MANUSCRIPTS

The basic manuscript source for William McKinley's presidency is the microfilm edition of his papers that are housed in the Manuscripts Division of the Library of Congress (hereafter LC). The ninety-eight reels contain the incoming correspondence, the president's letter books, the outgoing letters of his secretaries, and clippings, speeches, and other data. The *Index to the William McKinley Papers* (Washington: Library of Congress, 1963) makes the collection easy to use. The *Index*, p. v, says that "no other large group of McKinley manuscripts is known to exist."

George B. Cortelyou took custody of the McKinley Papers after the president died, and he gave them to the Library of Congress in 1935. Apparently some portion of the collection remained with the Cortelyou family, because an addition to the Cortelyou Papers (LC) in 1966 contributed the secretary's diaries and some twenty boxes of McKinley materials. Many of the gaps, particularly for the war months, were filled. Taken together, the McKinley Papers and the Cortelyou Papers permit almost a day-by-day reconstruction of White House decision-making under McKinley.

The Stark County Historical Society, Canton, Ohio, has a miscellaneous assortment of McKinley items, some of which are of interest for the presidential years. The Benjamin F. Montgomery Papers, Rutherford B. Hayes Memorial Library, Fremont, Ohio, consist of seven volumes of typed transcripts of information that came to the White House over the telegraph. They duplicate material that is available elsewhere.

The papers of the cabinet officers are relatively well preserved. The Russell A. Alger Papers, William L. Clements Library, University of Michigan, detail the secretary of war's stormy career. The John D. Long Papers, Massachusetts Historical Society, Boston, are most useful for Long's journal. The Ethan Allen Hitchcock Papers are at the National Archives, record group 316. At the Manuscripts Division, LC, the John Hay Papers, which have been microfilmed, are vital for studying diplomacy between 1899 and 1901. The William R. Day Papers (LC) are central for the coming of the Spanish war and the peace-making process. The Elihu Root Papers (LC) have much on military affairs and foreign policy from mid 1899 onward. The John Sherman (LC), Lyman J. Gage (LC), and Philander Knox (LC) collections are less significant. The papers of Joseph McKenna, John W. Griggs, Cornelius N. Bliss, and James Wilson are either dispersed or are still in private hands.

For subcabinet officials, the most valuable source is the John Bassett Moore Papers (LC), which contain voluminous amounts about the Spanish-American War and the peace negotiations. The Joseph L. Bristow Papers, Kansas State Historical Society, Topeka, form a microfilmed collection which contains revealing items about Bristow's service in the Post Office Department. The Charles G. Dawes Papers, Northwestern University, Evanston Illinois, are ample, but somewhat disappointing.

Materials in the National Archives were examined on a selective basis. In the State Department files, record group 59, Dispatches from United States Ministers to Spain, 1897/1898, were crucial for evaluating Stewart Woodford's part in the coming of the war. Useful for particular topics were Dispatches from United States Minister to Germany, 1898, Communications from Special Agents, and the Papers of the Reciprocity Commissioner, 1899–1901. The Miscellaneous Letters of the Department of State were interesting but not directly helpful. The Records of the Department of State Relating to the Paris Peace Commission, 1898, RG 43, had little that was not in the 1898 volume of *Foreign Relations*.

For foreign archival material, the correspondence and records relating to the United States, 1897–1901, in the files of the Foreign Office, Public Record Office, London, were most enlightening; and the Archives of the Ministry of Foreign Affairs, Paris, provided a fresh perspective on the issue of bimetallism and on the diplomacy of the tariff.

The footnotes indicate the manuscript collections in the United States that were used in connection with this study. The most helpful for McKinley were the William Boyd Allison Papers, Iowa State Department of History and Archives, Des Moines; the William Jennings Bryan Papers (LC); the William E. Chandler Papers (LC); the Charles Warren Fairbanks Papers, Lilly Library, Indiana University, Bloomington, Indiana; the Hanna-McCormick Family Papers (LC); the Henry Cabot Lodge Papers, Massachusetts Historical Society, Boston; the Whitelaw Reid Papers (LC); the Carl Schurz Papers (LC); and the James H. Wilson Papers (LC).

DOCUMENTS, PERIODICALS, AND SECONDARY WORKS

In part because so much of what the McKinley administration did was later to become controversial, the official documents of his presidency offer rich source material on his policies and decisions. *Speeches and Addresses of William McKinley from March 1, 1897, to May 30, 1900* (New York: Doubleday & McClure, 1900), is a volume that, when examined in connection with other evidence on the president's activities, reveals much about McKinley. Volume 10 of *A Compilation of the Messages and Papers of the Presidents, 1789–1897*, comp. James D. Richardson, 10 vols. (Washington, D.C.: Government Printing Office, 1899), contains data on McKinley. Most pertinent for this study was *A Supplement to A Compilation of the Messages and Papers of the President, 1789–1902, by James D. Richardson*, comp. George Raywood Devitt (Washington, D.C.: Bureau of National Literature and Art, 1903).

For McKinley's foreign policies, *Papers Relating to the Foreign Relations of the United States, 1897–1901* (Washington, D.C.: Government Printing Office, 1897–1902), were indispensable. The 1898 volume contains important information on the advent of the Spanish-American War and the peace negotiations. United States Congress, Senate, *A Treaty of Peace between the United States and Spain*, 55th Cong., 3d sess., Senate document no. 2 (Washington, D.C.: Government Printing Office, 1898), has an abundance of data on the administration's actions toward the Philippines in 1898.

On the war with Spain, the fighting in the Philippines, and the Boxer Rebellion, many significant documents can be found in *Correspondence Relating to the War with Spain and Conditions Growing out of the Same, Including Insurrection in the Philippine Islands and the China Relief Expedition, between the Adjutant-General of the Army and Military Commanders in the United States, Cuba, Porto Rico, China, and the Philippine Islands from April 15, 1898 to July 30, 1902*, 2 vols. (Washington, D.C.: Government Printing Office, 1902). The two investigations of the War Department and the army in 1898–1899 have relevant data. See, United States Congress, Senate, *Report of the Commission Appointed by the President to Investigate the Conduct of the War Department in the War with Spain*, 56th Cong., 1st sess., Senate document no. 221, 8 vols. (Washington, D.C.: Government Printing Office, 1900), and United States Congress, Senate, *Food Furnished by the Subsistence Department to Troops in the Field*, 56th Cong., 1st sess., Senate document no. 270, 3 vols. (Washington, D.C.: Government Printing Office, 1900).

Other documents that were consulted include the annual reports of the War Department, the Treasury Department, the Civil Service Commission, the Comptroller of the Currency, and the reports of the Philippine Commissions. The *Congressional Record* and documents and reports of the House and the Senate were used where appropriate.

For the diplomacy of the Spanish war, the volume of *Spanish Diplomatic Correspondence and Documents, 1896–1900: Presented to the Cortes by the Minister of State* (Washington, D.C.: Government Printing Office, 1905), was central. Ministere des Affaires étrangères, *Documents diplomatiques français, 1871–1914*, vol. 14: *4 janvier–30 decembre 1898* (Paris: Costes, 1957), prints the important documents of the French intermediaries in the summer of 1898.

There is a wealth of information in the newspapers of the era. The *New York Tribune* covered the White House from a Republican perspective. Also enlightening were the *New York Times*, the *Washington Post*, the *Washington Star*, and the *Chicago Tribune*. The *Literary Digest* and *Public Opinion* covered press views and opinion well. The journals of the day were indispensable, with *Forum, Nation, North American Review*, and *American Monthly Review of Reviews* being the most rewarding.

Aside from campaign biographies and books written soon after the president's death, the first serious biography of McKinley was Charles S. Olcott's *Life of William McKinley*, 2 vols. (Boston and New York: Houghton Mifflin Co., 1916). The McKinley Papers and the Cortelyou Papers were Olcott's major sources, and his insights have now largely been superseded. Margaret Leech's *In the Days of McKinley* (New York: Harper & Bros., 1959) covers the presidency in great detail. Leech had the Cortelyou diary at her disposal, as well as McKinley's papers, and her portrait of her subject is detailed and in many places persuasive. Howard Wayne Morgan's *William McKinley and His America* (Syracuse, N.Y.: Syracuse University Press, 1963) is a full life that reflects Morgan's mastery of the politics of the Gilded Age. His conclusions about McKinley are more cautious than is the evidence of presidential strength that he offers. Briefer assessments of McKinley's career are H. Wayne Morgan's "William McKinley as a Political Leader," *Review of Politics* 28 (1966): 417–432; Lewis L. Gould's "William McKinley and the Expansion of Presidential Power," Ohio *History* 87 (1978):

5–20; and Richard H. Bradford's unpublished essay "Mask in the Pageant: William McKinley and American Historians."

The memoirs and letters of the men around McKinley are of some use. Russell A. Alger, in *The Spanish-American War* (New York and London: Harper & Bros., 1901), defends his cabinet service. Joseph L. Bristow's *Fraud and Politics at the Turn of the Century* (New York: Exposition Press, 1952) is an affectionate and perceptive reminiscence of its author's governmental service. James Creelman's "Mr. Cortelyou Explains President McKinley," *Pearson's Magazine* 19 (1908): 569–585, is important for McKinley's last months in office. Charles G. Dawes's *Journal of the McKinley Years*, ed. Bascom N. Timmons (Chicago: Lakeside Press, 1950), gives informative, private glimpses of the president. The *Memoirs of Lyman J. Gage* (New York: House of Field, 1937) is thin. Adolphus W. Greely's *Reminiscences of Adventure and Service: A Record of Sixty-five Years* (New York and London: Charles Scribner's Sons, 1927) has a chapter on wartime communications of the White House. John A. Kasson's "Impressions of President McKinley, with Especial Reference to His Opinions on Reciprocity," *Century Magazine* 63 (1901): 269–275, has interesting remarks by McKinley on several subjects. For John D. Long, see his article "Some Personal Characteristics of President McKinley," *Century Magazine* 63 (1901): 144–146, and his book *The New American Navy*, 2 vols. (New York: Outlook Co., 1903). *America of Yesterday, as Reflected in the Journal of John Davis Long*, ed. Lawrence Shaw Mayo (Boston: Atlantic Monthly Press, 1923), offers the best parts of Long's contemporary record of his tenure. *Papers of John Davis Long, 1897–1904*, ed. Gardner Weld Allen (Boston: Massachusetts Historical Society, 1939), contains the cream of Long's incoming mail. Henry S. Pritchett, "Some Recollections of President McKinley and the Cuban Intervention," *North American Review* 189 (1909): 397–403, is revealing. The first two volumes of *The Letters of Theodore Roosevelt*, ed. Elting E. Morison et al., 8 vols. (Cambridge, Mass.: Harvard University Press, 1951–1954), have the significant sources for Roosevelt's relations with McKinley. *Selections from the Correspondence of Theodore Roosevelt and Henry Cabot Lodge, 1884–1918*, ed. Henry Cabot Lodge, 2 vols. (New York: Charles Scribner's Sons, 1925), discloses enough to suggest that a complete edition of their correspondence would be a major contribution. Charles Emory Smith, in "McKinley in the Cabinet Room," *Saturday Evening Post*, August 30, 1902, pp. 1–2, September 13, 1902, pp. 6–7, and October 11, 1902, pp. 6–7, recalled how the president made key decisions.

Among the numerous biographical studies of the men with whom McKinley worked, the following were the most relevant. Benjamin Temple Ford's "A Duty to Serve: The Governmental Career of George Bruce Cortelyou" (Ph.D. dissertation, Columbia University, 1963) does not meet the need for a sound biography of this key figure. George William Duncan's "The Diplomatic Career of William Rufus Day, 1897–1898" (Ph.D. dissertation, Case Western Reserve University, 1976) is thorough. Ronald Spector's *Admiral of the New Empire: The Life and Career of George Dewey* (Baton Rouge: Louisiana State University Press, 1974) is definitive. Herbert Croly's *Marcus Alonzo Hanna: His Life and Work* (New York: Macmillan Co., 1912) and Thomas Beer's *Hanna* (New York: Alfred A. Knopf, 1929) are both valuable books, but it is time for a modern biography of Hanna. Tyler Dennett's *John Hay: From Poetry to Politics* (New York: Dodd, Mead & Co., 1933) has stood well the passage of four decades. Kenton J. Clymer's *John Hay: The Gentleman as Diplomat* (Ann Arbor: University of Michigan Press, 1975) does not do justice to Hay's diplomatic career. Philip C. Jessup's *Elihu Root*, 2 vols. (New York: Dodd, Mead & Co., 1938), has many strengths, but Root, too, needs a fresh full-scale treatment. Hermann Hagedorn's *Leonard Wood*, 2 vols. (New York and London: Harper & Bros., 1931), is a sound study, and Jack C. Lane's *Armed Progressive: General Leonard Wood* (San Rafael, Calif., and London: Presidio Press, 1978) is a new biography. For McKinley and the ratification struggle in 1898, Richard E. Welch, Jr.'s *George Frisbie Hoar and the Half-Breed Republicans* (Cambridge, Mass.: Harvard University Press, 1971) is a biography that has large analytical consequences.

The changes in the institution of the presidency and the domestic policies of the McKinley years have received relatively sparse coverage. For the shifts in how White House business was conducted, Ida M. Tarbell's "President McKinley in War Times," *McClure's Magazine* 11 (1898): 209–224; De B. Randolph Keim's "The President's War," *Frank Leslie's Popular Monthly* 50 (1900): 107–122; Albert Halstead's "The President at Work—A Character Sketch," *Independent* 53 (1901): 2080–2086; and W. W. Price's "President McKinley's Tours," *Cosmopolitan* 34 (1903): 383–392, are significant contemporary accounts. A modern view is that of Robert C. Hilderbrand, "Power and the People: Executive Management of Public Opinion in Foreign Affairs, 1869–1921" (Ph.D. dissertation, University of Iowa, 1977).

On McKinley and the race issue, George Sinkler's *The Racial Attitudes of American Presidents, from Abraham Lincoln to Theodore Roosevelt* (Garden City, N.Y.: Doubleday & Co., 1971) is balanced. Richard B. Sherman's *The Republican Party and Black America from McKinley to Hoover, 1896–1933* (Charlottesville: University Press of Virginia, 1973) is thorough. Also very informative were Willard B. Gatewood, Jr.'s *Black Americans and the White Man's Burden, 1898–1903* (Urbana: University of Illinois Press, 1975) and David A. Gerber's *Black Ohio and the Color Line, 1860–1915* (Urbana: University of Illinois Press, 1976).

The standard works on the trust issue are Hans B. Thorelli's *The Federal Antitrust Policy* (Baltimore, Md.: Johns Hopkins Press, 1955) and William Letwin's *Law and Economic Policy in America: The Evolution of the Sherman Antitrust Act* (New York: Random House, 1965). John Waksmundski's "McKinley Politics and the Changing Attitudes toward American Labor, 1870–1900" (Ph.D. dissertation, Ohio State University, 1972) is the best starting point for the administration's labor policies. On banking and currency up to the Gold Standard Act, see Richard McCulley's "Origins of the Federal Reserve Act, 1897–1913" (Ph.D. dissertation, University of Texas at Austin, 1980).

There is an ample literature on the civil-service problem. A thorough memoir is William Dudley Foulke's *Fighting the Spoilsmen: Reminiscences of the Civil Service Reform Movement* (New York and London: G. P. Putnam's Sons, 1919). Adelbert Bower Sageser, in his *First Two Decades of the Pendleton Act: A Study of Civil Service Reform* (Lincoln: University Studies of the University of Nebraska, 1935), is critical of McKinley, as is Paul P. Van Riper in his *History of the United States Civil Service* (Evanston, Ill.: Row, Peterson & Co., 1958). Leonard D. White's *Republican Era: 1869–1901: A Study in Administrative History* (New York: Macmillan Co., 1958) is more balanced.

Treatments of domestic politics tend to stop with 1896 or begin with 1901. A notable exception is R. Hal Williams's *Years of Decision: American Politics in the 1890s* (New York: John Wiley, 1978). David W. Brady's *Congressional Voting in a Partisan Era: A Study of the McKinley Houses and a Comparison to the Modern House of Representatives* (Lawrence: University Press of Kansas, 1973) fulfills the promises contained in its title but has little to contribute to a study of McKinley's presidency. Göran Rystad, in

Ambiguous Imperialism: American Foreign Policy and Domestic Politics at the Turn of the Century (Stockholm: Esselte Studium, 1975), explores the 1900 campaign thoroughly.

For the foreign-policy context in which McKinley functioned, David F. Healy's *US Expansionism: The Imperialist Urge in the 1890s* (Madison: University of Wisconsin Press, 1970) and Robert L. Beisner's *From the Old Diplomacy to the New, 1865–1900* (New York: Thomas Y. Crowell, 1975) are good introductions to an immense field.

There are few overviews of McKinley's record in foreign affairs. *Threshold to American Internationalism: Essays on the Foreign Policies of William McKinley*, ed. Paolo E. Coletta (New York: Exposition Press, 1970), summarizes well, but does not reinterpret. Cornelius W. Vahle, Jr.'s "Congress, the President, and Overseas Expansion, 1897–1901" (Ph.D. dissertation, Georgetown University, 1967) is an interesting treatment of key episodes.

On Hawaiian annexation, the following books were helpful. Julius W. Pratt's *Expansionists of 1898: The Acquisition of Hawaii and the Spanish Islands* (Baltimore, Md.: Johns Hopkins Press, 1936), William A. Russ, Jr.'s *The Hawaiian Republic, 1894–98 and Its Struggle to Win Annexation* (Selinsgrove, Pa.: Susquehanna University Press, 1961), and Merze Tate's *The United States and the Hawaiian Kingdom: A Political History* (New Haven, Conn.: Yale University Press, 1965). The problems and sources of economic diplomacy are examined by Paul S. Holbo in "Economics, Emotion, and Expansion: An Emerging Foreign Policy," in *The Gilded Age*, ed. H. Wayne Morgan (rev. and enl. ed., Syracuse, N.Y.: Syracuse University Press, 1970), pp. 199–221; by Tom E. Terrill, in *The Tariff, Politics, and American Foreign Policy, 1874–1901* (Westport, Conn.: Greenwood Press, 1973), and by Lewis L. Gould, in "Diplomats in the Lobby: Franco-American Relations and the Dingley Tariff of 1897," *Historian* 39 (1977): 659–680.

The improvement in Anglo-American relations during the McKinley years has received much attention. The basic analysis is Charles S. Campbell, Jr.'s *Anglo-American Understanding, 1898–1903* (Baltimore, Md.: Johns Hopkins Press, 1957) and, for a broad overview, Bradford Perkins's *Great Rapprochement: England and the United States, 1895–1914* (New York: Atheneum, 1968). On the Panama Canal, David G. McCullough's *Path between the Seas: The Creation of the Panama Canal, 1870–1914* (New York: Simon & Schuster, 1977) presents an effective synthesis.

The publication of Joseph A. Fry's "William McKinley and the

Coming of the Spanish-American War: A Study of the Besmirching and Redemption of an Historical Image," *Diplomatic History* 3 (1979): 77–97, makes superfluous an elaborate examination of the literature on the origins of the war. The most important single source was John Layser Offner's "President McKinley and the Origins of the Spanish-American War" (Ph.D. dissertation, Pennsylvania State University, 1957). Ernest R. May, in *Imperial Democracy: The Emergence of America as a Great Power* (New York: Harcourt, Brace & World, 1961), uses foreign sources effectively but is weak on the domestic context and reaches a critical judgment on McKinley that his own evidence refutes. Walter LaFeber's *The New Empire: An Interpretation of American Expansion, 1860–1898* (Ithaca, N.Y.: Cornell University Press, 1963) stresses economic reasons but should be used cautiously. Howard Wayne Morgan's *America's Road to Empire: The War with Spain and Overseas Expansion* (New York: John Wiley, 1965) is more forceful and convincing about McKinley than is his biography of him.

John A. S. Grenville and George Berkeley Young's *Politics, Strategy, and American Diplomacy: Studies in Foreign Policy, 1873–1917* (New Haven, Conn.: Yale University Press, 1966) has a perceptive chapter on McKinley. Paul S. Holbo's "Presidential Leadership in Foreign Affairs: William McKinley and the Turpie-Foraker Amendment," *American Historical Review* 72 (1967): 1321–1335, is an important essay. Philip S. Foner, in *The Spanish-Cuban-American War and the Birth of American Imperialism, 1895–1902*, 2 vols. (New York and London: Monthly Review Press, 1972), contends that the rebels did not need American help. Charles S. Campbell's *Transformation of American Foreign Relations, 1865–1900* (New York: Harper & Row, 1976) is an uneasy blend of contradictory conclusions about the war and about McKinley. Thomas Hart Baker, Jr.'s "Imperial Finale: Crisis, Decolonization, and War in Spain, 1890–1898" (Ph.D. dissertation, Princeton University, 1977) is most revealing about Spanish policy. Hyman G. Rickover, in *How the Battleship Maine Was Destroyed* (Washington: Department of the Navy, 1976), argues convincingly for an internal explosion as the cause of the sinking.

On the war itself, Gerald F. Linderman's *The Mirror of War: American Society and the Spanish-American War* (Ann Arbor: University of Michigan Press, 1974) is interpretive. Graham A. Cosmas's *An Army for Empire: The United States Army in the Spanish-American War* (Columbia: University of Missouri Press, 1971) is now considered standard. See also Edward Ranson's "The

Investigation of the War Department, 1898–99," *Historian* 34 (1971): 78–99, and Edward F. Keuchel's "Chemicals and Meat: The Embalmed Beef Scandal of the Spanish-American War," *Bulletin of the History of Medicine* 48 (1974): 249–264.

American postwar policy in Cuba is discussed by David F. Healy in *The United States in Cuba, 1898–1902: Generals, Politicians, and the Search for Policy* (Madison: University of Wisconsin Press, 1963) and by James H. Hitchman in *Leonard Wood and Cuban Independence, 1898–1902* (The Hague: Martinus Nijhoff, 1971).

The scholarship on the Philippines is mushrooming. John A. S. Grenville's "American Naval Preparations for War with Spain, 1896–1898," *Journal of American Studies* 2 (1968): 33–47, is a central article, and Phil Lyman Snyder's "Mission, Empire, or Force of Circumstances? A Study of the American Decision to Annex the Philippine Islands" (Ph.D. dissertation, Stanford University, 1972) is critical of McKinley but recognizes his key role. Older, but still worth reading, are Paolo E. Coletta's two articles "Bryan, McKinley, and the Treaty of Paris," *Pacific Historical Review* 26 (1957): 131–146, and "McKinley, the Peace Negotiations, and the Acquisition of the Philippines," *Pacific Historical Review* 30 (1961): 341–350. On the Paris talks, *Making Peace with Spain: The Diary of Whitelaw Reid, September-December 1898*, cd. H. Wayne Morgan (Austin: University of Texas Press, 1965), is valuable. Brian Paul Damiani, in "Advocates of Empire: William McKinley, the Senate and American Expansion, 1898–1899" (Ph.D. dissertation, University of Delaware, 1978), sees McKinley as cautious and tentative.

John Morgan Gates's *Schoolbooks and Krags: The United States Army in the Philippines, 1898–1902* (Westport, Conn.: Greenwood Press, 1973) is a balanced review of the military record. Richard E. Welch's *Response to Imperialism: The United States and the Philippine-American War, 1899–1902* (Chapel Hill: University of North Carolina Press, 1979) appeared after this book had been completed. Anti-imperialism is examined by Robert L. Beisner in *Twelve against Empire: The Anti-Imperialists, 1898–1900* (New York: McGraw-Hill, 1968), by E. Berkeley Tompkins in *Anti-Imperialism in the United States: The Great Debate, 1890–1920* (Philadelphia: University of Pennsylvania Press, 1970), and by Daniel B. Schirmer in *Republic or Empire: American Resistance to the Philippine War* (Cambridge, Mass.: Schenkman Publishing Co., 1972).

On American governance of the Philippines under McKinley,

the following works were informative: Peter W. Stanley, *A Nation in the Making: The Philippines and the United States, 1899–1921* (Cambridge, Mass.: Harvard University Press, 1974); Glenn Anthony May, "America in the Philippines: The Shaping of Colonial Policy, 1898–1913" (Ph.D. dissertation, Yale University, 1975); and Virginia Frances Mulrooney, "No Victor, No Vanquished: United States Military Government in the Philippine Islands, 1898–1901" (Ph.D. dissertation, University of California at Los Angeles, 1975).

The most important studies of the administration's Far Eastern policy are Thomas J. McCormick's *China Market: America's Quest for Informal Empire, 1893–1901* (Chicago: Quadrangle Books, 1967) and Marilyn Blatt Young's *Rhetoric of Empire: American China Policy, 1895–1901* (Cambridge, Mass.: Harvard University Press, 1968). Peter W. Stanley's "The Making of an American Sinologist: William W. Rockhill and the Open Door," in Donald Fleming, ed., *Perspectives in American History*, vol. 11 (Cambridge, Mass.: Charles Warren Center for Studies in American History, 1978), pp. 419–460, is the most recent contribution to the literature on the Open Door.

Index

287